The Moral Foundation of Economic Behavior

BY DAVID C. ROSE

OXFORD
UNIVERSITY PRESS

OXFORD
UNIVERSITY PRESS

Oxford University Press is a department of the University of Oxford.
It furthers the University's objective of excellence in research, scholarship,
and education by publishing worldwide.

Oxford   New York
Auckland   Cape Town   Dar es Salaam   Hong Kong   Karachi
Kuala Lumpur   Madrid   Melbourne   Mexico City   Nairobi
New Delhi   Shanghai   Taipei   Toronto

With offices in
Argentina   Austria   Brazil   Chile   Czech Republic   France   Greece
Guatemala   Hungary   Italy   Japan   Poland   Portugal   Singapore
South Korea   Switzerland   Thailand   Turkey   Ukraine   Vietnam

Oxford is a registered trade mark of Oxford University Press
in the UK and certain other countries.

Published in the United States of America by
Oxford University Press
198 Madison Avenue, New York, NY 10016

Library of Congress Cataloging-in-Publication Data
Rose, David C.
The moral foundation of economic behavior / by David C. Rose.
    p.   cm.
Includes bibliographical references and index.
ISBN 978-0-19-978174-4 (cloth : alk. paper); 978-0-19-936059-8 (paperback)
1. Economics—Moral and ethical aspects.
2. Cooperation. I. Title.
HB72.R656   2011
174—dc22   2010051996

Additional Praise for *The Moral Foundation of Economic Behavior*

"Following in the tradition of Adam Smith, David Rose provides a modern economic perspective on how 'the wealth of nations' depends on 'a theory of moral sentiments.' This book provides such a theory and explains why all societies attempt to inculcate moral restraints on homo economicus. After reading it you have new insights into how and why morality is so important to economic prosperity."
—Terry L. Anderson, Senior Fellow, Hoover Institution, Stanford University and Executive Director, Property and Environment Research Center

"As members of the American body politic, we are failing to transmit intergenerational elements of our cultural heritage without which a free and prosperous society cannot exist. This book brings attention to the moral bases for the civic order that we too often take for granted. Only if we first understand what is happening can the erosion of our moral capital be turned around."
—James M. Buchanan, Nobel Laureate in Economics, 1986

"How did we move from the hunter-gatherer societies of our forbearers to the complex globally-interconnected world of today? How does one maintain prosperity when localized knowledge and large numbers of market participants make 'golden opportunities' for undetected opportunistic behavior ever more possible? What sets of moral beliefs are most conducive to maximizing general prosperity, and how are they inculcated? Drawing on, but also going beyond, the ideas of such thinkers as the Smiths (both Adam and Vernon), Douglass North, F. A. Hayek, and others, as well as his own fertile mind, David Rose provides the answers to these and other questions in a book that explores the interstices of economics, cultural studies, and applied moral theory. It is a compelling account."
—Bruce Caldwell, Duke University

"Modern economics is returning to its moral philosophy roots; David Rose's *The Moral Foundation of Economic Behavior* moves that process along by reconsidering the role of trust and culture in the economy. His approach is unique, insightful, and definitely worth reading."
—David Colander, Christian A. Johnson Distinguished Professor of Economics, Middlebury College

"David Rose has usefully taken economics—and, one hopes, many economists—back to the origins of our discipline in moral philosophy. Adam Smith was, first and foremost, a moral philosopher, and a very insightful one at that. *The Moral Foundation of Economic Behavior* explores what underlies the attitudes and impulses that today's economics simply takes as given; and as Smith suggested, the moral force behind this behavior stands at the heart of the matter."
—Benjamin M. Friedman, William Joseph Maier Professor of Political Economy, *The Moral Consequences of Economic Growth*

"A Solid and Insightful Contribution to the Theory of Economic Morality...David Rose's fine analysis of the morality of economic behavior is inspired by the economist Friedrich Hayek... as well as the philosopher Immanuel Kant, who stressed that moral behavior is based on adhering to moral rules, not acting benevolently on behalf of others. For Kant and Rose, and I think this is the correct view, is that one is not honest because one cares about one's exchange partner, but because being honest is the right thing to do."

—Herbert Gintis, Central European University and the Santa Fe Institute.

"It is commonly argued that markets promote moral behavior by rewarding it. David Rose considers market morality from a different and more intellectually ambitious perspective. He examines how the prevailing morality affects the performance of a market economy to ascertain the features of that morality that are most conducive to market coordination. At all times Rose is careful to limit his analysis to moral behavior that is consistent with the constraints imposed by our evolution of a small-group species. And beyond the particulars of his analysis, Rose makes clear that economists sell their discipline short when they dismiss, as some do, the relevance of moral concerns to understanding what is necessary for a free and prosperous social order."

—Dwight R. Lee, William J. O'Neil Chair of Global Markets and Freedom,
Cox School of Business, Southern Methodist University

"The book is an extended thought experiment launched by this question: '*If a society's sole objective is to maximize general prosperity and it can choose its own moral beliefs, what kinds of moral beliefs would it choose?*' (p. 4, emphasis in original). The author proposes a sophisticated, novel, and compelling answer to this question. It therefore deserves to be read by anyone with an interest in how to promote human prosperity."   —James R. Otteson, Yeshiva University, *The Independent Review*

"Economists and scholars in other fields working on culture, trust, and economic development should consider this book. Experimental economists working on trust and trustworthiness who want more insight into these behaviors should, too. Each chapter builds on the previous ones, taking the reader through organized and pointed discussions in building a case for the primacy of duty-based moral restraint to trust to economic prosperity."   —*The Journal of Economic Literature*

For Angela, Matthew, and Christopher

CONTENTS

PREFACE

Most people believe that being moral is an important part of a life well-lived and a healthy moral climate is a hallmark of a flourishing society. Today there is even a cottage industry for the character and morals education of children. There has always been religious moral instruction, of course, but this is different—it is not about God or any particular religious narrative. It is instead an attempt to improve society by inculcating specific moral values and by improving moral decision making.

But how much do we really know about the connection between morality and the functioning of human societies? Before we begin imparting moral values and coaching moral decision making in an effort to produce a better society, shouldn't we first think carefully about how morality might actually affect the functioning of societies? And since a society's economic system has so much to do with how it functions and to what ends, doesn't this require an examination of the connection between economics and morality?

A natural place to start in addressing these questions is to think carefully about the connection between morality and economic behavior. That is the purpose of this book. In this book it is the concept of trust that connects morality to economic behavior. Of course conjecturing that trust is related to morality is hardly surprising since nearly everyone believes that behaving in an untrustworthy way is immoral. But conjecturing that trust is related to economics is not so obvious.

Although many social scientists now believe that trust is an important element of economic behavior, there are thoughtful detractors to this position. They deserve and will get a full response to their concerns, so I ask those of you who count yourselves among them to keep reading. Indeed, the first task I undertake in this book is to show precisely how trust can positively affect the operation of a market economy. In addition to reviewing the familiar arguments, I introduce a new one based on the ideas of Friedrich A. Hayek and Ronald Coase. It involves combating a particular form of opportunism that has not received attention from economists but that I will argue impedes directing economic activity in large groups in an entrepreneurial rather than bureaucratic way.

Even among those who are prepared to believe that trust is important, some are still uncomfortable with the notion that trust behavior is *necessarily* rooted in morality. Therefore being able to connect economics to trust is only a necessary condition for connecting economics to morality through trust. One must also connect trust to morality. To most people this would seem an odd concern. But even if most people believe that behaving in an untrustworthy way is immoral, it does not necessarily follow that morality is a necessary condition for trustworthiness. There may be reasons why people who are unconcerned with morality might nevertheless behave in a trustworthy manner.

This is not a distinction without a difference. Many social scientists are eager to explain as much behavior as possible as a mere rational response to incentives. For them, the natural approach to exploring why people are trustworthy is to explore when, where, and why trustworthy behavior is simply an exercise in the rational promotion of one's own welfare. This approach has served the social sciences quite well.

Let me stress before going any further that it is not the purpose of this book to identify any particular religious or ideological narrative that best supports the operation of a market economy. The purpose of this book is to identify characteristics that moral beliefs must possess in order to do so. While the natural approach to identifying these characteristics would be to compare existing moral beliefs across societies to their levels of economic performance, this would constrain the search to the characteristics of moral beliefs that already exist. My search for the required characteristics was instead intentionally open ended, proceeding vis-à-vis a thought experiment launched by the following question:

If a society's sole objective is to maximize general prosperity, and it can choose its own moral beliefs, what kind of moral beliefs would it choose?

Because this was not a story told to fit existing facts, the characteristics I identify are not constrained by human history. This means it is possible that more than one religious or ideological narrative produces moral beliefs that possess the required characteristics. It also means that it is possible that none do, none ever have, and none ever will. A more likely outcome of this exercise is that some existing moral beliefs possess some but not all of the required characteristics. For this reason, while this book is ultimately a conceptual rather than empirical exercise, it might nevertheless have important implications for future empirical work. Specifically, evidence should show that societies whose moral beliefs come closest to the ideal—what I call the moral foundation of economic behavior—will have the highest levels of general prosperity in the long-run.

If the moral beliefs of a given society possesses some or all of the required characteristics, it would seem prudent that it learn of the role played by these foundations of success so it can preserve them. If, instead, a society is still struggling to develop, it would seem prudent that it undertake a frank assessment of which of the required characteristics that its moral beliefs appear to lack. Even if it is unwilling to change its moral beliefs, the exercise might point the way toward modifications to institutions that can circumvent development obstacles that it would have otherwise not known it had.

Here are some of the new ideas introduced in the book:

1. Opportunism is *the* fundamental impediment to development and maximizing general prosperity. Institutions can limit opportunism, but one important form of opportunism is beyond their reach and can therefore only be combated by internalized restraint.
2. Moral values can be divided between those that pertain to negative moral actions and those that pertain to positive moral actions. The former supports economic behavior by combating opportunism while the latter are either superfluous or inefficient.
3. Our natural reluctance to behave opportunistically is derived from our reluctance to harm others and generally weakens with increasing group size. Yet it is organizing economic activity in large groups that makes general prosperity possible.
4. Trustworthiness is antithetical to opportunism, but when it is derived from our natural reluctance to harm others, repeat play effects, or institutions, it is insufficient to overcome the important form of opportunistic behavior noted in (1) above.
5. We are willing to genuinely trust others who don't particularly care about us in large group settings only if we conclude that they are unconditionally trustworthy. But to reach this conclusion what really matters is not how moral they are but how the content of their moral beliefs affects how they think about morality.
6. There is no getting around the need for trustworthiness to be based on moral tastes and the need for moral tastes to be instantiated by moral beliefs. If a high trust society matters for economic performance, then the content of moral beliefs matters.
7. Because culture solves a time consistency problem associated with unconditional trustworthiness, culture provides a particularly plausible mechanism for instantiating the kind of moral beliefs that are necessary to maximize prosperity. Culture matters.

Regarding point 6, the idea that the kind of trustworthiness that best supports the operation of a market economy must be derived from moral tastes did not originate with me. Robert Frank made this point over 20 years ago, when doing so was even more heretical than it is now.

This book is aimed at a wide academic audience, so its technical content is presented in footnotes and appendices. This allows me to include formal material for those who want it without becoming a distraction to those who don't. There are a few equations in the main presentation, but don't be put off by them. They involve very simple math and really do make it easier to understand the arguments involved. Indeed, I took great pains to insure that one can skip *all* of the equations and still follow the argument without missing a beat.

ACKNOWLEDGMENTS

This book was written over a long and busy period of my life. It would not have been completed without the encouragement and/or input of a number of people. Early on Milton Friedman reassured me that the core ideas were both original and important. I also received encouragement and/or input from Armen Alchian, Pete Boettke, Serguey Braguinsky, Bruce Caldwell, David Colander, John Drobak, Robert Frank, Jack Hirshleifer, Michael Jensen, Deirdre McCloskey, Elinor Ostrom, Robert Putnam, Russell Roberts, James Reische, and Hilton Root. From beginning to end, Douglass North dared me to think boldly. James Buchanan read most of the first draft and gave me invaluable advice for improving both its substance and style. Finally, I would like to thank Jack Repcheck, whose encouragement, input, and support was crucial.

The late Henry (Harry) F. Langenberg supported my work in various ways. Harry was a remarkable man who opened many doors for me. John Prentis also took a strong interest in my work and straightened many paths for me. He, like my father, is the epitome of a *good man*.

I want to thank Stephen Dietrich, who taught me much about the publishing world and put me in contact with the right people. I want to thank Joe Anemone for suggesting many years ago that the concept of trust was the key. Mike Allison, Ray Bowen, Clinton Greene, Dave Hakes, Tom Ireland, Jim Otteson, Bob Sorensen, Herb Werner, Larry White, Anne Winkler, and Tom Wyrick have listened patiently to the arguments in this book and helped me discard the 99% that was chaff. One could not have better friends.

I would like to acknowledge my parents, who are incapable of moral prevarication and are fine examples of persons who abide by the moral foundation. I would like to acknowledge my sons, Matt and Chris, who suffered endless lectures on many road trips, and by doing so helped me sort things out in my own mind. They also challenged me with some very difficult questions. Finally, I'd like thank my wife, Angela, whose unflappable faith in me gave me faith in myself. There is no greater gift.

The Moral Foundation
of Economic Behavior

CHAPTER 1

Introduction

▓

The economist must go beyond the assumption of "economic man" precisely because of the economic advantage of not behaving like economic man—an advantage that presumably explains why the world is not populated solely by economic men.—Jack Hirshleifer, 1987, p. 322

What role does morality play in the functioning of a market economy? While it is difficult to imagine a highly immoral society sustaining a well-functioning market economic system, abundant anecdotal evidence also suggests that a high level of morality does not guarantee economic success. The relationship between morality and economic performance, if such a relationship even exists, is evidently not a simple one.

The purpose of this book is to improve our understanding of the relationship between morality and economic performance by explaining why some moral beliefs are more likely to lead a society to a condition of general prosperity than others. This is no small issue because nearly anything a society might value—moral or otherwise—is more easily achieved if it is rich.[1] I explain why the fullest development and most efficient operation of a market economy, one capable of *maximizing* general prosperity, requires a "moral foundation" in the form of a preponderance of people holding moral beliefs that possess certain characteristics. These characteristics are matters of content rather than moral earnestness, and they induce people to think about morality in a way that makes them unwilling to behave in an opportunistic manner even when there is no chance of detection and even when (and this turns out to be very important) there is no possibility of harming anyone. I show that this, in turn, averts what is normally an inevitable tradeoff between group size and transaction costs, which produces an insurmountable obstacle to the maximization of general prosperity.

So how does one go about identifying the required characteristics? The obvious approach would be to compare characteristics of existing and past moral beliefs to the levels of economic performance of their respective societies. But such an approach risks overlooking characteristics that are not present in existing moral beliefs or were not present in past ones. The approach I adopt in this book avoids this problem by undertaking an open-ended thought experiment launched by the following question: *If a society's sole objective is to maximize general prosperity and it can choose its own moral beliefs, what kinds of moral beliefs would it choose?*

Surprisingly, I found that the characteristics that moral beliefs must have if they are to provide the best possible foundation for the development and operation of a market economy have nothing to do with moral earnestness, a society's general level of morality, or even the set of moral values in the value system. This strongly suggests that poor people in poor societies are not poor because they or their societies are insufficiently moral or because they value the wrong things.[2]

Instead, what I found really matters is how people *think about* morality because that is what makes it possible for people to genuinely trust others, even those whom they know don't particularly care about them.[3] How people think about morality is, in turn, determined by how moral beliefs logically structure the relationship between moral values in the value system. Since there is a great deal of consistency in the list of moral values across societies, it is how moral beliefs logically structure the relationship between moral values in the value system that turns out to be of paramount importance.[4]

The moral foundation supports economic behavior at both micro and macro levels of social organization. It supports economic behavior at the micro level because it minimizes any individual's fear that he will be opportunistically victimized by any other transaction partner. For obvious reasons, we all prefer trustworthy transaction partners to untrustworthy ones. The greater the proportion of trustworthy people in a society, the lower transaction costs will generally be and, therefore, the larger will be the set of transactions through which the gains from specialization can be effectuated, which is the key to maximizing general prosperity.[5]

The moral foundation also supports economic behavior at the macro level because some institutions and organizational forms are themselves dependent on us being able to rationally expect others to behave in a trustworthy manner in most cases. By producing an environment within which such institutions and organizational forms can exist and function to fullest effect, the moral foundation further maximizes the set of transactions through which the gains from specialization can be effectuated.[6] The fullest possible development of a market system is, therefore, simply the maximization of the set of viable institutions and organizational forms.

Evidence on the relationship between trust and aggregate economic performance is broadly supportive of the proposition that trust matters, going at least as far back as Banfield's (1958) seminal work on the limitations of family-related trust. More recently, La Porta, Lopez-de-Silanes, Shleifer, and Vishny (1997) found strong evidence in support of Fukuyama's (1995) thesis in their cross-country analysis of the relationship between trust and the kind of large organizations that are needed to fuel economic growth. Knack and Keefer (1997) compared measures of trust to economic performance over a sample of 29 countries and found that trust was clearly related to economic performance. Zak and Knack (2001) found that measures of institutions that should support trust in their model were clearly related to economic growth.

In empirical work, trust behavior is increasingly being linked to culture and moral beliefs by accounting for differences in regional history (Guiso, Sapienza, Zingales 2006; Tabellini 2008ab; Guiso, Sapienza, Zingales 2008abc, 2009, 2010; Grosjean, 2011). Over the period of 1935–2000, Algan and Cahuc (2010) also found that even after controlling for country fixed effects and changes in institutions, "Inherited trust turns out to explain a significant share of the economic backwardness of developing countries and an important share of economic difference between developed countries over the twentieth century" (p. 2086). This finding strongly suggests that trust behavior is not solely a product of well-crafted institutions. It is also strongly affected by culture.

Banerjee, Bowie and Pavone (2006, p. 303) summarize much of the theoretical literature nicely:

> A growing literature of trust underscores its importance to economic life (e.g., Gambetta, 1988; Misztal, 1996; Rousseau et al., 1998; Smith et al. 1995). Trust seems to be beneficial to firms and organizations: it lowers agency and transaction costs (Frank, 1988; Jones, 1995), promotes efficient market exchanges (Arrow, 1974; Smith et al., 1995), improves co-operation (Mayer et al., 1995; Ring and Van de Van, 1992; Smith et al., 1995) and indeed enhances firms' ability to adapt to complexity and change (Korsgaard et al., 1995; McAllister, 1995). Trust also is described as an essential ingredient for innovation (Hosmer, 1994) and scientific collaboration.

All of this is hardly surprising. If a relatively high trust country like the United States suddenly became a low trust one, most of us would expect that in short order much economic activity would grind to a halt. One could argue that over time we would adjust to having a low trust environment by creating new institutions and organizational forms to substitute for trust. But it is unfathomable that this would be less costly than having a preponderance of people in our society unwilling to behave in an opportunistic manner in the first place.

Despite there being a great deal of empirical work suggesting a correlation between trust and economic performance, and theoretical work on the causal connection between trust and the functioning of market economies, many thoughtful skeptics remain. This is especially true for transaction cost economics (TCE) scholars who view institutions as the *sine qua non* of market economies.[7] Since institutions work through incentives that are external to individuals, this naturally leads to the view that what appears to be trust behavior is not really genuine trust at all, but is instead just a prudent response to incentives. TCE scholars argue further that genuine trust is unnecessary either because institutions are sufficient to combat opportunism or because factors inherent in social relationships provide sufficient incentive (e.g., repeat play effects) to do so. TCE scholars therefore contend that with respect to economic analysis, trust is a superfluous concept that for the most part just "promotes confusion" (Williamson, 1993, p. 469).

I shall argue that the TCE critique is right about conventional economic theories of trust not being about genuine trust but is wrong about the relevance of genuine trust in principle, because it fails to recognize a problem that I call *third-degree opportunism*. In a nutshell, an agent engages in third-degree opportunism when he takes advantage of the fact that he knows the full set of possible actions, while the principal does not, because of the *localization of knowledge*. To be specific, the agent selects an action that the principal will regard as the best one only because the principal is unaware that the agent knows of a better one.[8] The Nobel Prize winning economist Friedrich Hayek (1945) was the first economist to explain precisely how the price system facilitates an efficient allocation of resources across the whole of society by alleviating the problem of local knowledge. The price system does this by replacing central *planning* with a central *mechanism*—prices that reflect the social opportunity cost of using any resource, which induces agents to adjust their use of said resource in a socially efficient way without needing to know what anyone else is doing or why.

I contend that there is an equally important local knowledge problem that exists within nodes of cooperation—especially, but not limited to, large firms that must contend with unpredictably changing conditions. I explain why, to have any chance of general prosperity at all, firms must be able to grow large. But to *maximize* general prosperity such large firms must also be able to efficiently employ resources by making full use of localized knowledge within them.[9] The larger the firm, the more complex the production process, and the more uncertain is the environment, the more localized knowledge is, and therefore the more important it is that such knowledge be employed efficiently if general prosperity is to be maximized. This is a potentially serious problem because, as I will explain later, the very circumstances that increase the localization of knowledge also increase the frequency of opportunities to engage in third-degree opportunism. The crux of the problem is that efficient use of localized knowledge—not just within firms but also with regard to economic activity more generally—requires the ability to trust those who possess it not to take advantage of the information advantage they enjoy to engage in third-degree opportunism.

When a person believes there is no chance of being detected if he behaves in an opportunistic manner, we have an instance of what Robert Frank calls a "golden opportunity." Obviously, the more knowledge is localized the more frequently golden opportunities arise. Golden opportunities to engage in third-degree opportunism are by definition beyond the reach of institutional mechanisms that work through external incentives. It follows that to facilitate efficient decision making within nodes of cooperation a society needs some kind of internalized mechanism to discourage opportunism. Feelings of guilt aroused from the belief that certain behaviors are morally wrong can provide such a mechanism, since if one feels sufficiently guilty about behaving opportunistically, the net payoff of a given opportunistic act will be negative.

Given the centrality of the need to effectuate the gains from specialized production and the extreme localization of knowledge that inevitably results from it, I submit that an inability to extend genuine trust acts as a brake on development, potentially producing as daunting an obstacle to maximizing general prosperity as is the inability to effectuate efficient decentralized decision making through market pricing, as described by Hayek (1945). It follows directly that the greater is our ability to extend genuine trust, the more fully local knowledge can be employed and therefore the more prosperous a society can be.

Let me stress that the point of this book is not to challenge the importance of institutions. On the contrary, trust is important in large part because of the effect it has on the viability of institutions and their efficient function. In my view trust is more of a complement to than a substitute for institutions (Kuran 2009). What I am challenging is not the importance of institutions; it is, rather, the belief that concepts like culture, social capital, trust, and morality have nothing to offer to serious social scientists.

Genuine Trust

Although Adam Smith was a moral philosopher, economists throughout much of the twentieth century have tried to model moral behavior in general, and trust in particular, as nothing more than an exercise in the rational pursuit of enlightened self-interest. While this approach has produced sharp models, many have correctly pointed out that it robs the words *morality* and *trust* of their essential meaning.[10] What existing models explain is, therefore, not trust as most people think of the word, but what Toshio Yamagishi (1999, 2000) has defined as *assurance*, which is merely the expectation that a particular person has sufficient incentive not to behave opportunistically in a given circumstance.

In my view, existing models actually do a very good job describing how "trust-like behavior" (assurance) emerges among most people, most of the time, in most of the world, throughout most of human history. But most societies throughout most of human history did not (and do not) enjoy a condition of general prosperity. As a result, building models based on positive analysis of *what is* risks developing a theory of the most common forms of trust-like behavior that have, apparently, failed to get the job done. Even today, societies that enjoy *general* prosperity are rare, so the most common forms of trust-like behavior across societies and over the course of human history are not likely to have played an important role in making general prosperity possible where it now exists.

I will, therefore, also explain why the fullest development and most efficient operation of a market economy cannot be achieved from trustworthiness that is derived from common factors such as hardwired moral intuitions, strategic factors inherent in relationships, or even institutions. This casts doubt on the relevance of new theories of trustworthiness and trust based on evolutionary psychology, as well as theories in which trustworthiness is simply a prudent response to incentives. I explain why these approaches do not work where trustworthiness is needed most—large group contexts required to effectuate the fullest possible gains from specialization.

If conventional explanations for trust behavior are generally inadequate, then how does one explain it? Robert Frank has suggested an alternative approach to modeling trust that holds promise for understanding how trust behavior can produce general prosperity. Frank contends that *genuine* trust is necessarily based on the rational expectation of unconditional trustworthiness, rather than the expectation of mere prudence. Other social scientists, such as Karen Cook, Russell Hardin, Margaret Levi, and Elinor Ostrom, have also argued that the extension of trust must be based on the rational expectation of trustworthiness. But they differ from Frank because they theorize that such trustworthiness is, in turn, properly explained by some sort of incentive mechanism.

According to Frank, this kind of approach will necessarily fail to produce trustworthiness precisely where it is most meaningful and needed; that is, with respect to "golden opportunities" in which one believes there is no chance of detection. This idea is particularly pertinent to what follows, because golden opportunities to engage in third-degree opportunism frequently arise in large group contexts because of the very specialization that occasions them. So to be willing to extend trust in circumstances in which golden opportunities are frequent, one must believe that the decision-maker who possesses local knowledge is unconditionally trustworthy. According to Frank's argument, this means one must believe that the trusted party is trustworthy because his or her trustworthiness is derived from moral tastes rather than incentives.

Frank's logic is inescapable. Moreover, the basis for trustworthiness that he envisions is more relevant the larger the groups are within which we organize economic activity, the more complex they are, and the faster and more unpredictable technological and institutional change is, because all of these factors increase the frequency of golden opportunities. In other words, although Frank's approach might not be terribly relevant to most of the trust behavior in most of the world throughout most of human history because TCE trust critics were largely right about the sufficiency of institutions in those contexts, Frank's approach might nevertheless be particularly relevant to understanding the kind of trust behavior that is most pertinent to the fullest development and most efficient operation of market economies. But while Frank demonstrated why moral restraint must be derived from moral tastes, he did not address the question of what kinds of moral tastes would do this best. In this book I directly address this question by identifying the characteristics that moral beliefs must have if they are to instantiate moral tastes that produce moral restraint where it is needed most to maximize general prosperity.

Neoclassical economics has been a triumph for mankind, but its incentive-based explanations for morality and trust ring false. Too often people are moral when rational calculation implies that the payoff to immoral behavior is higher. This appears to imply that neoclassical economics has to accept that at least one of its core assumptions is wrong: either people don't maximize payoffs, or they are irrational, or both. But this turns out to be a byproduct of a strong "distaste for taste explanations." Although this distaste exists for good reason, it is not a fundamental tenet of neoclassical economics. It turns out that if we consider the possibility that moral behavior of the sort that is of most relevance to the *fullest* development and *most efficient* operation of a market economy is in fact derived from moral tastes, then the neoclassical approach can be preserved and the kind of economy that neoclassical economics seeks to explain can most fully exist.

There is abundant empirical evidence that demonstrates that most societies are not by any reasonable measure high trust societies (I review such evidence in detail in Chapter 9). The arguments advanced in what follows and the characteristics I ultimately identify turn out to be consistent with this finding. I shall conclude that societies that enjoy high levels of trust are relatively rare for good reason. They are rare because moral beliefs that possess the required characteristics are rare, and such beliefs are rare because they are not directly derived from our hardwired moral intuitions (which would tend to produce consistency across human societies) but they are, instead, based on abstract ideas that often conflict with such intuitions. This should not be surprising. Our hardwired moral intuitions evolved in small groups, so there is no reason why they should be able to sustain trust in the context of large group economic activity required for achieving a condition of general prosperity.

Group Size

The size of groups within which human cooperation can occur is as important as any other single issue in the social sciences. The very word *social* is directly related to the size of the groups within which people live, work, and exchange. As economists from Adam Smith to Paul Krugman have argued, the size of the groups within which economic activity takes place is crucial because the ability to realize the gains from specialization is directly related to group size.[11]

Although prosperity is directly related to the ability to cooperate effectively in large groups so as to enjoy the fullest possible benefits of specialization, group size worsens the problem of opportunism. This is because larger groups create more opportunities to behave opportunistically while weakening the ability of our hardwired moral intuitions to limit opportunism at the same time. Opportunism therefore acts as a brake on group size. As a result, in most societies, through most of human history, most economic activity beyond mere spot market exchanges only took place in relatively small groups. Since many societies understood the benefits of size to the process of development, many devised institutions to combat opportunism. But while these institutions played an important role in the history of economic development and the rise of civilization, they are of little value in combating opportunism when knowledge is highly local in nature, such as is the case for a decision-maker in a very large firm that employs a complex production process.

Since being unconditionally trustworthy is antithetical to being opportunistic, it follows that a society filled with unconditionally trustworthy individuals will have the lowest transaction costs of all, and this will be truer the larger the groups within which economic activity is organized. This releases the brake that opportunism places on group size and thereby increases the set of transactions through which the gains from specialization can be realized.

Recently much attention has been focused on the difficulty of effectuating trust and cooperation in large groups. It is natural to think of large group trust as a scaling-up of small group trust (alternatively, extending the radius of circles of trust). But in this book I explain why large group or "generalized trust" cannot, in fact, just be scaled-up from small group trust.[12] This is because mechanisms that support small group trust break down with group size, so something that differs not just in degree but in kind is needed to support large group trust. One possibility, suggested by Peter Turchin (2006), is that some societies have figured out how to get individuals to be willing to self-sacrifice for the common good by exploiting our ability to think in symbols to engage in tribalism on a larger scale. He even goes so far as to argue that our penchant for symbolism may have evolved for this very reason. We will find that this approach either has limited reach or creates a new set of problems.

Naturalism and Universals

Just as many (certainly not all) social scientists endeavor to explain as much as they can as an exercise in the rational promotion of one's own welfare, they are, like all scientists, also eager to explain phenomena as generally as possible. They are, therefore, in a never-ending hunt for universal explanations. For this reason there has been intense interest in recent years in searching for hardwired factors that support trust behavior and moral behavior. This hunt for universals naturally leads to an emphasis on naturalistic approaches since human behavior becomes more universal the further we drill down.

There is no question that we have significantly improved our understanding of moral behavior by exploring the nature of the hardwired psychological mechanisms that support moral decision making.[13] No matter how philosophically compelling any given theory of morality is, if it conflicts with the psychological mechanisms that humans actually possess it will be merely an academic exercise. Similarly, a thought experiment aimed at identifying characteristics that moral beliefs must have, if they are to most fully support the development and operation of a market economy, must take into account how human beings that fill a market economy actually think and behave. This does not contradict the ontological nature of the question that launched our thought experiment, because no rational society would choose moral beliefs for itself that didn't have a chance of actually working because they were inconsistent with how humans actually think and behave. Any hypothesized moral behavior must, therefore, plausibly manifest itself through the psychological hardwiring that humans actually possess. To paraphrase Kant, to be meaningful "a moral principle must be capable of being followed by normal mortals."[14]

But if our consideration of moral behavior is limited to only those explanations that are universal and therefore limited to aspects of moral behavior that are largely hardwired, we might very well end up with the natural condition of man within which such universal traits evolved. The natural condition of man is to live and cooperate in small groups, which means the natural condition of man is to be impoverished. On the other hand, abstract ideas are powerful precisely because they are flexible. The ability to think abstractly is hardwired but the ideas themselves are not, which is why they are not universal and why they can confer evolutionary advantages to one group over another. I submit that while abstract moral ideas often contradict our natural sense of morality and vary widely from society to society, the one thing many of them have in common is that they help us overcome our small group nature by providing behavioral guideposts that facilitate effective cooperation in large groups.

This point is closely related to one often made by Nobel Prize winners Douglass North and Vernon Smith. Both have argued that an important step in the economic development of any society is being able to move from only being able to support personal exchange to being able to support impersonal exchange. A completely small group sense of morality is adequate for personal exchange, but becomes increasingly inadequate as exchange and cooperation becomes increasingly impersonal because it is conducted in increasingly larger group contexts. Economic activity in a large, modern, complex market economy overwhelmingly involves impersonal exchange and this, I will show, is better supported by certain kinds of abstract moral beliefs than by moral beliefs that merely codify our natural, hardwired, intuitive, small group sense of morality.

This suggests that there is a deep conflict in all human societies: general prosperity requires cooperation in large groups, but we are indisputably a small group species.[15] We are therefore maladapted for achieving a condition of general prosperity. The challenge for any society is, therefore, to figure out a way that its small group citizens can transcend their small group nature to effectuate gains that are only possible vis-à-vis cooperation in large group contexts. This is therefore perhaps the most important puzzle for the social sciences to solve, for when a society enjoys a high level of general prosperity, nearly all other problems become easier to solve.

Culture

An important point of this book is that culture, specifically moral beliefs, powerfully affects a society's ability to organize cooperative behavior in large groups and therefore should be of interest to all *social* scientists. We are a small group species but the good life requires large group cooperation. I explain why, to maximize general prosperity, it is necessary to make genuine trust possible even between people who don't particularly care about one another and even in very large groups. This requires moral beliefs that must be taught and learned and, as such, they are matters of culture and not genes, geography, or institutions. Aspects of our behavior that are derived directly from genes that we all share obviously cannot explain differences in economic performance across societies. Conversely, being matters of culture, moral beliefs can potentially explain persistent differences in economic performance across societies.

Douglass North (1994, 2005) has argued that to understand economic history we have to understand institutions and how beliefs complement them and affect the subsequent evolution of them. In his own words:

> Learning . . . is an incremental process filtered by the culture of a society which determines the perceived payoffs, but there is no guarantee that the cumulative past experience of a society will necessarily fit them to solve new problems. Societies that get "stuck" embody belief systems and institutions that fail to confront and solve new problems of societal complexity. (North, 1994, p. 364)

For North, then, the development of society is inextricably bound up in its institutions and its beliefs, which would obviously include its moral beliefs. Guido Tabellini (2007) has similarly argued that the mechanism through which "distant political and economic history shapes the functioning of current institutions" goes beyond economic incentives and lies largely with morality.

Many social scientists believe that it is important to distinguish between "shame cultures" and "guilt cultures." Deepak Lal (1998) has argued that one of the primary reasons for the success of the West over "the Rest" is that whereas most societies have cultures in which self-regulation is largely a matter of shame, those in the West have cultures in which self-regulation is largely a matter of guilt. Many others have also explored the nature and possible implications of the difference between shame cultures and guilt cultures.[16] In the analysis developed in this book, the key problem is having a society in which individuals can trust others even in circumstances in which golden opportunities are likely to arise. This points to an important advantage of a guilt culture over a shame culture, because feelings of guilt can be experienced even if there is no possibility of detection, as is the case with golden opportunities. The distinction between shame and guilt is explored further in subsequent chapters, and the implications of the analysis in this book regarding this distinction is discussed in the conclusion.

I hope it is apparent by now that by "moral beliefs" I do not mean specific religious narratives that instantiate moral beliefs. Moreover, I do not claim and my analysis does not imply that there is anything inherently more moral about the kinds of moral beliefs that most fully support the development and operation of market economies and are therefore most likely to maximize general prosperity. It is possible that moral beliefs that provide the best moral foundation for the development and operation of a market economy are also the least moral ones as judged by some as-yet-undiscovered objective measure of morality. It is also possible that very different religious narratives can produce moral beliefs that possess the same set of key characteristics.

Many social scientists have turned their attention to topics like social capital, trust, and religion, all of which are obviously closely related to culture.[17] So arguing that culture is an important part of understanding how market economies develop and function is not a novel insight. David Landes (2000, p. 2) has even gone so far as to state that "If we learn anything from the history of economic development, it is that culture makes almost all the difference." But he has also spoken at length about the hazards of advancing cultural explanations of social behavior.[18] Given the temptation to write off poor societies on the basis of culture, it is probably good that cultural explanations are viewed with skepticism.

Of particular concern in appealing to cultural explanations for development patterns is the suggestion that variation in material success can be explained by variation in the level of morality. Religious leaders in many societies have made these kinds of arguments over the years, but there are at least two problems with doing so. First, on what basis do we rank societies by level of morality? Such a ranking requires some kind of standard, and the selection of the standard inevitably determines the ranking. Who picks the standard? On what basis is it chosen? That there are differences in moral beliefs across societies is obvious, but that there are differences in the level of morality across societies is far from obvious. Second, there are substantial differences in the religious beliefs of highly successful groups even within very prosperous societies. Protestant Christians have done extremely well in America but so have Jews, yet Jews explicitly reject the central tenet of Christian faith.

There are other reasons why many social scientists are reluctant to employ cultural explanations. They understand that it is an easy default explanation that, because of its exogenous nature, requires no further study.[19] But while it is this very exogenous nature of cultural explanations that concerns many social scientists, I will explain why it is precisely because moral beliefs are taken as given *at the point of decision making* that unconditional trustworthiness is credible and therefore the extension of genuine trust is rational. At the same time, at the macro level, it is the exogenous nature of moral beliefs that makes it possible for a society to overcome an otherwise insurmountable obstacle to becoming a truly high trust society, namely skyrocketing returns to behaving opportunistically in response to the emergence of generalized trust.

More generally, if our consideration of moral behavior as it relates to trust is limited by a desire to avoid exogenous explanations, then we might inadvertently throw the baby out with the bathwater. If it is from its very exogenous nature that culture derives its explanatory power, then shoehorning any acceptable theory of trust behavior into being an exercise of enlightened self-interest risks eliminating from consideration *the only possible explanation* for how rational, genuine trust can exist across the whole of truly large group societies so as to most fully support the development and operation of a market economy and thereby maximize general prosperity.

Of course, advancing a cultural explanation for any human social phenomenon also risks inviting charges of chauvinism. But in my view we have no choice but to ignore the possibility of being the target of such accusations. Just because culture has all too often been offered up as a facile and even disingenuous explanation for some phenomenon does not mean that it cannot ever be a valid explanation. Similarly, just because exogenous explanations are often a lazy theorist's form of *Deus ex machina* does not mean that there is nothing about human behavior or human society that is not appropriately explained by exogenous factors.

Thankfully, an increasing number of social scientists have accepted the premise that culture and the closely related concept of social capital are just too likely to be important to be ignored. In a number of important papers, Guiso, Sapienza, and Zingales (2003, 2004ab, 2006, 2008abc, 2010) and Tabellini (2007, 2008ab) have left little doubt that trust matters, and that to have a high trust society it takes more than institutions—it also takes the right kind of culture. Moreover, Butler, Giuliano, and Guiso (2009) found that immigrants from high trust countries are more likely to be cheated by opportunists than those from low trust countries, suggesting that cultural beliefs also strongly affect decision priors associated with extending trust.

Focusing on the transmission of preferences from parents to children, Tabellini (2010) found that bad political climate and culture are persistently epiphenomenal, resulting in societies with persistently lower levels of generalized trust. Nunn and Wantchekon (2009) found evidence of persistent differences in trust behavior among regions in Africa. Luttmer and Singhal (2011) found that one's preference for policies to effectuate redistribution are ". . . strongly affected by preferences in their countries of birth . . ." and are ". . . statistically significant, economically important, and robust to rich controls for economic factors . . ." (p. 176). A common thread is a persistent but decaying effect, which is precisely what one would expect of a cultural explanation.

It is hard to think of a concept like individualism being a matter of institutions rather than culture. Therefore, perhaps the most remarkable evidence of the power of culture to affect economic performance comes from Yuriy Gorodnichenko and Gerard Roland (2010). They presented a model showing that while an ethic of individualism produces dynamic effects on growth, an ethic of collectivism produces only static gains. They also found evidence that individualism significantly contributes to long-run growth. In a subsequent paper (Gorodnichenko and Roland, 2011) they explored the effect that other factors might have on long-run growth and found that individualism was the most important and robustly significant factor of all.

From the vantage of one who has already worked through the thought experiment you are about to undertake, a very plausible conclusion one can draw is that human history might be best understood as largely being a drama based on the ability of culture and institutions to facilitate effective cooperation in the largest social groups. We know that human history begins with only small groups, and we know that large group societies have since absorbed virtually all of the small ones. The only exceptions are hunter-gatherer bands that persist precisely because they are so remote as to avoid direct competition with large group societies. But drawing this conclusion is no cause for celebrating the end of history, for even those who flourish today by living in the most advanced and prosperous large group societies are still indisputably members of a small group species. Like gravity, their small group genes never stop calling them back to the small group fold, and therefore never cease undermining the cultural and institutional foundations of large group society. In my view this is why we, as a species, have never been able to fully put tribalism to bed. This may also help explain why it is the case that after a society finds a way to develop a thriving, prosperous, large group market society, the siren song of the genes of those who comprise it almost immediately turns their attention to dismantling the cultural and institutional foundations of its success.[20]

Overview of the Main Argument

In Chapter 2 I begin by explaining why specialization is the key to prosperity. I then argue that opportunism is a daunting obstacle to general prosperity because it drives up transaction costs and thereby impedes the realization of the gains from specialization. I explain that it is so daunting precisely because it is perfectly rational. I then categorize opportunism into three types and explain why what I call third-degree opportunism is an underappreciated problem that has important implications for economic activity organized in large group contexts such as (but not limited to) large firms.

In Chapter 3 I explain why the gains from specialization are directly related to the size of groups within which economic activity occurs. I then explain how size worsens the problem of opportunism by intensifying commons dilemma incentives associated with opportunism and by increasing the localization of knowledge, which increases opportunities—in many cases golden opportunities—to engage in third-degree opportunism. This is the point at which the concepts of genuine trust and morality come into play, because prudential restraint will not impede opportunism in the case of golden opportunities. Only moral restraint can do so, most likely through feelings of guilt.

In Chapter 4 I take up the issue of moral values because it is our moral values that determine what we feel guilty about. I explain why differences in moral values across societies are unlikely to be able to explain differences in economic perfor-mance, because there is very little difference in moral values across societies with respect to economic activity. I then argue that in a market economy, transactions are voluntary and therefore inherently efficient, so exhortations to undertake positive moral actions are not important for supporting economic activity. What really matters are prohibitions against taking negative moral actions, because they combat opportunism by precluding it and thereby help keep transaction costs low.

In Chapter 5 I provide an analysis of the relationship between the concepts of empathy, sympathy, and guilt. I then propose a simple theory for how guilt arising from sympathy actuated by empathy due to harming others produces a natural reluctance to undertake negative moral actions.

In Chapter 6 I argue that this natural reluctance to harm others is inadequate for supporting the full development and efficient operation of a market economy. The reason why is that group size weakens our natural reluctance to refrain from harming others. Our hardwired, harm-based sense of moral restraint is not scal-able because it is subject to what I call "the empathy problem." The larger the group over which the costs of opportunism are spread, the less likely there is anyone with whom to empathize, sympathize, and therefore feel guilty about harming. So for restraint to always be operative, even in large group situations, it must also be principled in nature. Unfortunately, hardwired moral restraint is small group in nature because we evolved in small groups, but the good life requires effective cooperation in large groups.

In Chapter 7 I argue that while moral tastes that comport with principled moral restraint solve the empathy problem, doing so is only a necessary condition for supporting genuine trust behavior because one can feel even guiltier about failing to take positive moral actions. To solve this "greater good rationalization problem," the obedience of moral prohibitions against negative moral actions (which combats opportunism) must take precedence over the obedience of moral exhortations for positive moral actions. Moral beliefs that solve both problems produce what I call an "ethic of duty-based moral restraint." So how much people care about others and/or their level of moral earnestness doesn't matter nearly as much as how people think about morality, for how they think about morality determines what they feel guilty about in the first place.[21]

In Chapter 8 I argue that for an ethic of duty-based moral restraint to be sus-tainable, it must not be undermined by an ethic of duty-based moral advocacy. So while negative moral actions have to be governed by nonconsequentialist moral thinking, positive moral actions have to be governed by consequentialist moral thinking. I define nonconsequentialist moral restraint coupled with consequentialist moral advocacy as the moral foundation of economic behavior. If an individual possesses the moral foundation with sufficient conviction, then he is unconditionally trustworthy so it is rational for others to extend genuine trust to him. If a society is composed of a sufficiently high proportion of unconditionally trustworthy people, then it will enjoy the benefits of being a high trust society. Moral beliefs that comport with the moral foundation of economic behavior therefore make it possible for us to trust each other at the micro level and make trust-dependent institutions viable at the macro level.

In Chapter 9 I compare trust behavior derived from moral beliefs that comport with the moral foundation to conventional theories of trust. I find that whereas conventional theories of trust do not square well with existing empirical evidence on trust behavior, a high trust society sustained by moral beliefs that comport with the moral foundation does.

In Chapter 10 I argue that moral beliefs that can support a high trust society are most plausibly instantiated in sufficient concentration, conviction, and consistency across the whole of a society by being passed from generation to generation through teaching and learning—that is, by culture. I explain that culture doesn't just solve this particular problem; it solves a fundamental problem associated with rational decision making that can only be solved by a mechanism like culture. So culture doesn't just matter because moral beliefs matter and they are part of culture; culture also matters instrumentally, too.

In Chapter 11 I discuss the implications this exercise has for the institutions versus culture debate. I then discuss implications for future theoretical work, as well as future empirical work. I then offer some speculations on the implications this work has for helping impoverished societies become prosperous and for preserving existing market economies by understanding why it is in our small group nature to undermine the large group mechanisms that make them possible.

CHAPTER 2

Opportunism

Opportunism . . . extends simple self-interest seeking to include self-interest seeking with guile. It is not necessary that all agents be regarded as opportunistic in identical degree. It suffices that those who are less opportunistic than others are difficult to ascertain ex ante and that, even among the less opportunistic, most have their price.—Oliver Williamson, 1979, p. 234n.

Introduction

In *The Wealth of Nations*, Adam Smith (1776) argued that a necessary condition for achieving general prosperity is increasing productivity through the division of labor. The basic idea is that when labor is divided so workers focus on learning and perfecting one skill rather than performing all of the skills needed for every step of production, everyone is made dramatically more productive so much more output can be produced *per person.*[1] Smith argued further that specialization effectuated not just within firms but also across the whole of society is the key to achieving general prosperity. This is perhaps the most universally accepted idea in economics of the last two centuries.

But there is a catch.

Specialization is completely impossible without transacting. We must be able to exchange the one thing we produce and/or the one thing we do for all the other things we don't produce and/or all the other tasks that must be done. So when it comes to maximizing prosperity, the ability to transact with others is every bit as important as the ability to maximize the realization of the gains from specialization.

The hallmark of a free market economy is that nearly all transactions are voluntary. For a transaction to be voluntary, it must be expected to be mutually beneficial. This requires that the value of the goods traded or produced exceeds the value of what would have prevailed before the transaction. In this way, each and every transaction that is mutually beneficial increases the amount, or value, or both, of output *per person*, which is the key to increasing general prosperity. At the same time, transactions that add to prosperity will by nature be mutually beneficial and, therefore, will need no additional impetus to be undertaken.

There are many different kinds of transactions that can support many different modes of specialization and thereby facilitate different net positive contributions to general prosperity. Obviously, the greater the scope of transactions through which the gains from specialization can be realized, the more specialized and therefore the more prosperous a society can be. A necessary condition for *maximizing* prosperity is, therefore, having an environment that supports the widest possible scope of transactions, as this will support the greatest possible degree of specialization. Conversely, anything that impedes transactions necessarily impedes realizing the gains from specialization and therefore acts as an impediment to the maximization of prosperity.

In all but the simplest spot market transactions there are obvious, explicit costs associated with achieving the transaction that have nothing to do with producing the output itself (e.g., paying a sales tax). There are also less obvious, implicit costs, such as opening ourselves up to the possibility of becoming a victim of opportunism. The expected cost of opportunism with respect to any given transaction is therefore a "transaction cost" that will be accounted for in any rational individual's decision to enter into it. Since for a transaction to be mutually beneficial the total expected gain to be derived from it must exceed the total expected cost, it follows that the higher transaction costs are, the more impoverished a society will tend to be.

So the fundamental moral problem facing a society that wishes to benefit from the fullest development and most efficient operation of a market economy is not that its people don't care enough about each other and therefore don't do enough to promote each other's welfare. The fundamental moral problem facing a society that wishes to benefit from the fullest development and most efficient operation of a market economy is that people are simply too willing to take advantage of each other—too willing to behave opportunistically. It is hardly an overstatement to claim that opportunism is the greatest single impediment to the development and operation of a market economy capable of producing a condition of general prosperity.[2]

Institutional theorists have emphasized that throughout much of human history opportunistic behavior has undermined property rights, thereby acting as an impediment to economic development and creating the need for institutions to provide clear "rules of the game" (North 1991, p. 27). In a society in which most citizens and the government are opportunistic, there are weak incentives for entrepreneurial behavior. People must believe that their property rights will be respected to be willing to expend effort, to bear risk, and to delay consumption so as to invest in ways that ultimately increase productivity. People must believe that the rules of the game won't be changed after they have made fixed investments.

Impartial enforcement of contracts is also essential for the fullest development and efficient operation of a market economy. In a society in which citizens and the government are opportunistic and therefore cannot be trusted, it is not rational to expect that contracts will be impartially enforced by courts when disputes arise. This makes it impossible to use to use contracts to their fullest extent, thereby increasing transaction costs.

Organization theorists view the problem of post-contractual opportunism, in the forms of shirking and hold-up, as central to the theory of vertical integration (Crawford, Klein and Alchian 1978; Williamson 1975, 1985; Hart and Moore 1990) and the theory of the firm (Alchian and Demsetz 1972; Holmstrom 1982; Hart 1995). Information and insurance theorists view the problem of pre-contractual opportunism, in the form of adverse selection, as central to devising efficient institutional arrangements under conditions of asymmetric information (Rothschild and Stiglitz 1976; Akerlof 1970). Political theorists such as Gordon Tullock and Mancur Olson have made seminal contributions to our understanding of the political economy of opportunism through their work on rent-seeking and special interest politics.

Despite ample work that points to the effects of opportunism, its effect on society is still generally underappreciated because much of the cost of opportunism is unobserved, taking the form of transactions that were never attempted, institutions that were never created, institutional arrangements that were never tried, and organizational governance structures that were never formed. In those societies in which opportunism is unchecked, widespread poverty is guaranteed because the transactions needed to fully realize the gains from specialization are a fool's wager so most of the transactions through which the gains from specialization are realized don't happen.

The problem of high transaction costs in impoverished societies is, therefore, not rooted in the fact that people in such societies lack intelligence, education, sophistication, or lawyers. Moreover, the absence of "nuts and bolts" institutions that prosperous societies take for granted is not evidence of a lack of understanding of what the crucial institutions are, the inability to create such institutions, or the lack of advice from nations that already have them. Impoverished societies need only adopt institutions whose templates have been eagerly supplied by those who have perfected them, thereby skipping the need to discover such institutions on their own.[3] But today, many less-developed countries do not adopt them because it is pointless to do so because of widespread opportunism. The absence of "nuts and bolts" institutions is not evidence of lack of knowledge or will; it is evidence of a lack of demand.

The problem of high transaction costs in impoverished societies—in any society, for that matter—is, instead, opportunism, broadly construed. Economic history has shown that the "nuts and bolts" institutions that lubricate economic activity by reducing the non-opportunistic aspects of transaction costs can be devised or copied and implemented quickly if there is money to be made from doing so. But there is little or no money to be made from doing so if opportunism is unchecked. The institutions that matter most in such societies are therefore those that combat opportunism.[4] Is there any doubt that a society filled with individuals who would never behave in an opportunistic manner would be able to create all of the nuts and bolts institutions they need, especially if templates for those institutions were available to be copied?

Defining Opportunism

Webster's Dictionary defines opportunism as "the practice of grasping at opportunities without regard for moral considerations || the practice of adjusting one's policy in the light of each new situation as it arises, not according to principle or a plan." The second definition merely captures the idea of acting flexibly, decisively, and creatively, of behaving in an "opportune" manner. In what follows, I will never use the word *opportunism* to convey the morally neutral idea of acting in an opportune manner. In what follows I will adopt the following definition of opportunism, which is slightly harsher than the first definition above: *opportunism is acting to promote one's welfare by taking advantage of a trust extended by an individual, group, or society as a whole.*

Although taking advantage of a trust often causes harm, the key idea here is not harm *per se*, but the violation of a trust. We say that B violates a trust between A and B when, given the nature of the relationship between A and B, B knows that A would have expected and preferred B not to have acted in a particular way in a particular circumstance because B is obliged to refrain from such action in that circumstance.

One can harm without behaving as an opportunist and one can behave as an opportunist without doing harm, so harm is neither a necessary nor a sufficient condition for an act to be an act of opportunism. If I play loud music in my backyard within legal limits but it is during a neighbor's barbecue, I do harm but I am not behaving as an opportunist. Such harm is more properly thought of as a negative externality, not as an instance of opportunism. Even if harm is intended, an act that harms but does not violate a trust is still not an act of opportunism. For example, in the context of a chess game in which both players understand that their relationship is one of conflict and not mutual benefit, person B promoting his interest by doing harm to A in the form of taking A's knight is not an example of opportunism as the term is used generally, or is used here. As long as it occurred within the agreed-upon rules of the game, it is simply part of the game.

Conversely, someone who lies to an insurance company by exaggerating a claim has promoted his welfare by violating a trust, and therefore has acted as an opportunist, but in many cases this kind of behavior perceptibly harms no one. This turns out to be a very common problem associated with economic activity that is organized in very large groups, and that presents a fundamental obstacle to the full development of a market economy. This problem will be discussed thoroughly in Chapter 6.

This definition stresses that behaving in an opportunistic way is essentially the equivalent of behaving in an untrustworthy way.[5] This comports with conventional use of the word *opportunism*. If A believes that B will opportunistically victimize him if given a good chance to do so, then A will regard B as untrustworthy and will be less willing to transact with B. Conversely, if A knows that B will never opportunistically exploit A, then it will be rational for A to trust B because A knows that B will always behave in a trustworthy way.[6] Trustworthiness is therefore antithetical to opportunism. Where there is no fear of opportunism, there is no reason to fear extending trust.

Oliver Williamson has given much thought to both opportunism and trust. According to Williamson (1985): "[opportunism is] self-interest seeking with guile (which) includes . . . more blatant forms, such as lying, stealing, and cheating . . . (but) more often involves subtle forms of deceit." The idea that opportunism is a violation of trust clearly comports with the word *deceit*. One would suspect that a focus on opportunism would produce an appreciation for the concepts of trust and trustworthiness. But it should be noted that Williamson is very skeptical of the concept of trust. This skepticism is well founded, but I believe it is partly due to not accounting for problems caused by a new form of opportunism that I discuss later in this chapter.

Choosing to Behave Opportunistically

Individuals do not act on every chance to behave opportunistically, and they differ in their likelihood of behaving opportunistically in any given situation. Some people seem to never opportunistically exploit others. In some societies such individuals are common while in other societies they are rare. To understand opportunistic behavior as well as the individual and social factors that govern it, we must consider how people differ in their willingness to behave opportunistically.

If we limit our attention to rational opportunism, then it follows that opportunistic behavior will be mediated by the benefits and costs associated with taking opportunistic actions. Differences in the frequency of opportunism across societies or individuals are, therefore, not the result of differences in the strength of a taste for opportunism *per se*; they are the result of differences in the benefits and costs of such behavior. In other words, opportunism is an equilibrium phenomenon, with the number of potential opportunists and the range of circumstances in which a given opportunist will choose to act opportunistically being governed by pertinent benefits and costs.[7]

The benefit of a given act of opportunism can be put simply: B opportunistically exploits A by doing x to get z, because B derives utility from z. Whether z is a good or a service or a job or a mate or status is irrelevant. What ultimately drives opportunism is the strength of one's desire for something. We behave opportunistically, ultimately, because we want what we want so badly.

There are also costs associated with behaving opportunistically. Indeed, one can feel compelled to act precisely because one believes the cost to be unusually low in a particular instance. As is true of rational behavior generally, rational opportunism is simply a matter of comparing the benefits to the costs of any particular "window of opportunity" that involves the violation of a trust. We now consider four costs associated with opportunistic behavior.

When *A* discovers that *B* has opportunistically exploited him, *A* may retaliate. Retaliation must generally go beyond effectuating restitution if it is to discourage future exploitation, so retaliation must leave the opportunist clearly worse off than before the act of opportunism.[8] This also means that retaliation by the victim may precipitate a subsequent reprisal by the opportunist, who might be an opportunist precisely because he believes himself to be more powerful than others. As a result, there is good reason to believe that the impulse to retaliate is rooted in emotions that serve the purpose of making the threat of retaliation credible. Indeed, Robert Frank (1987, 1988) and Jack Hirshleifer (1987) have argued that unless retaliation is rooted in emotions that supersede rationality, opportunists can take advantage of the rationality of their victims. If one accepts this argument, then the universality of our capacity for anger can be taken as evidence of the ubiquity of opportunism over the course of human evolution.

Another potential cost of opportunistic behavior is the loss of one's reputation. If *A* discovers that *B* has cheated him, then *A* can tell *C*, *D*, and so forth. This could prove very costly to *B*. Avner Grief's (1993) work on the Maghribi traders demonstrates the power of such information. In some cases it can lead to the complete ruin of an opportunist's livelihood. This cost of opportunism is powerful when the terms of the transaction are very clear so third parties are likely to conclude that the charge of opportunism was not merely the result of a misunderstanding. Conversely, the more unstructured is the transaction, the less likely that a third party will construe such information as definitive. Finally, this cost is not limited to foregone future transactions. If one values the opinions of others, then the loss of one's good reputation can result in feelings of shame. It is, of course, well known that some societies invest much in conditioning children to be responsive to shaming (Lal 1998).

These three costs—retaliation, ruined reputation for being an honest transaction partner, and feelings of shame—all require that the opportunist's act be discovered. But there is an important cost associated with opportunism that is realized even if opportunism is undiscovered. This is the cost of experiencing feelings of guilt from doing something we believe to be wrong, including but not limited to believing we have harmed someone.

Empathy is a universal trait of normally functioning individuals. From empathy naturally comes at least a small measure of sympathy, even for complete strangers. Empathy is the ability to identify with the emotional state of others, whereas sympathy is the emotional reaction that results from such identification. Therefore, if B opportunistically exploits A, he naturally empathizes with A's pain, so the empathetic response normally also produces feelings of sympathy. Since B knows that he is responsible for what happed to A, his feelings of sympathy, in turn, also produce feelings of guilt. All normally functioning humans know that there is nothing trivial or imaginary about the cost of feeling guilty, even from harming complete strangers.

Some benefits and some costs of opportunistic behavior are affected by the characteristics of society, so there are cross-sectional differences in the degree of opportunism among societies. In some societies, for example, telling a lie is considered generally imprudent but not particularly immoral, so in such societies the level of guilt from lying is very low, while in other societies lying carries much stronger feelings of guilt even if one's intentions are unselfish. But the benefits and costs of opportunistic behavior also differ across individuals, so there is also cross-sectional variation in the frequency and severity of opportunistic behavior among individuals within any given society. As a result, even in the most trustworthy societies there are prisons, and even in the least trustworthy societies there are saints.

A MODEL OF RATIONAL OPPORTUNISM

When an action does not involve opportunism, its value to the decision maker is simply determined by the utility derived from what was obtained by taking the action. This level of utility is assumed to already account for all the non-opportunistic costs associated with undertaking the action. For example, the utility derived from going to a movie is to be understood henceforth to mean the utility of the net payoff—the utility of the movie minus the disutility associated with the cost of the tickets, gas, lost wages, and so forth.

When an action does not involve opportunism, there are no retaliation, reputation, shame, or guilt costs to consider. In this case, any positive net utility is enough to induce the individual to undertake the action since we have implicitly accounted for the ordinary explicit and implicit costs associated with the action. If, however, an action under consideration is opportunistic in nature, then a rational decision maker will consider the four aforementioned costs associated with opportunism.

Let x represent an opportunistic action, z the net payoff (any combination of money, goods, services, or direct pleasure, less any non-opportunistic costs) that results from undertaking x, and $U()$ the utility derived from consuming z. Choosing to undertake an opportunistic action affects net utility, $V()$, through the benefits of the opportunistic action and the costs discussed above. Consider embezzling $1000 or asking your best friend's girlfriend for a date. Either act results in a gain, as measured by the vector z and valued by $U()$, but both acts also entail costs.[9]

Whether one undertakes such an act is simply a matter of whether the benefits of doing so, measured in utility units, exceeds the cost of doing so, measured in utility units. For a given opportunistic act, x_i, we can therefore define the net utility resulting from action i as:

$$V(x_i) = U(z(x_i)) - C(x_i),$$

where $C()$ accounts for the costs in utility units of taking action x_i.[10] The $C()$ term includes but is not limited to the expected cost of retaliation, the expected cost of a ruined reputation, the expected cost of feeling embarrassed, the expected cost of being shamed, and the expected cost of feeling guilty.[11]

Modeling morality as an exercise in rational decision making strikes many as callous and inappropriate. But such a reaction is mistaken if we account for guilt. This does not mean that guilt is a necessary condition for moral behavior. It is conceivable that people who have no capacity for guilt can be inspired to be virtuous. Over the course of this book, my argument will be that nearly all humans feel guilty when they do things they believe to be wrong, and that guilt provides a very plausible avenue through which to model moral behavior that is consistent with rational choice. Instead of a framework in which rationality implicitly obviates genuine morality, I offer a rational framework through which we can more fruitfully study morality, wherein one can be both rational and moral. If there is a problem with the *current* economic model of rational choice as it relates to moral behavior, it is simply that it generally does not account for the cost of guilt and therefore does not account for the reasons why people might experience feelings of guilt and thereby be morally self-restrained from behaving opportunistically.

The Ubiquity of Opportunism

As with love and war, our opportunistic nature is a recurring theme in literature, such as Shakespeare's *Macbeth* and Dostoyevsky's *Brothers Karamazov*. Even when opportunistic behavior is not observed, the threat of it often lurks just below the surface, held in check by fear of punishment, being shamed, or experiencing feelings of guilt.[12] Our predilection to behave opportunistically, and our fear of becoming a victim of someone else's opportunism, has shaped much of the world as we know it.

This presents a puzzle. I have already explained that opportunism drives up transaction costs and how this, in turn, destroys a society's ability to increase its general prosperity. But if opportunism is so bad for society as a whole, why is it so common? The fundamental problem is that even if all members of a group understand the harm that opportunism does to the group as a whole and therefore agree that it would be best if everyone refrained from it, in most societies maintaining such an agreement would be virtually impossible because it would still be in the individual's best interest to choose to behave opportunistically. The crux of the problem is that what is good for the individual is bad for the group as a whole.

In short, in many cases opportunism is governed by incentives that game theorists would say constitutes a variant of a particular kind of social dilemma known as the commons dilemma.

The *Tragedy of the Commons* problem was first proposed by Garret Hardin in his famous article in 1968. The basic problem in Hardin's example, and indeed the problem associated with opportunistic behavior in general, is that when a given action produces a benefit that is realized solely by the decision maker while producing costs that are shared by all members of the group, the private action of the decision maker will produce too much of that behavior to be socially optimal. In such circumstances, when people do what is best for them as individuals they are not doing what is best for the group as a whole. It is a dilemma because when everyone in the group does this at the same time, everyone ends up worse off. In Hardin's example, a commons is ruined by unchecked grazing. We consider now the possibility that in a market economy a low transaction cost environment is ruined by unchecked opportunism.

Note that I have characterized opportunism as *a variant* of the commons dilemma because, strictly speaking, the commons dilemma involves a socially desirable act (grazing cows) that, when pursued to excess, produces an adverse social outcome (overgrazing to the detriment of all). With opportunism as defined here, however, there is no level of the act that is desirable, so it differs from a standard commons story. But as a mathematical matter this simply means that the socially optimal level of the act is zero, so any positive amount is viewed as an adverse social outcome.

AN EXAMPLE

Suppose there are 1000 people in a society, and when there is no agreement to refrain from opportunism, $5000 worth of total output is produced per period, which translates to an average payoff of $5 worth of output per person. In this case there are many transactions that are not viable because of the expectation of opportunism. If, however, the members of the society never acted as opportunists, then transaction costs would fall dramatically so the range of viable transactions would rise dramatically. At the same time, institutions that could not exist in a highly opportunistic society could exist, could function properly, and could thereby indirectly decrease transaction costs even further. The surpluses associated with each of these new transactions would pile up, thereby increasing the total value of output for society. Finally, the society would also enjoy a windfall in the form of conserving resources that would otherwise go toward safeguarding against opportunistic behavior. Suppose that because of all of these gains, if all members of the society could somehow stick to an agreement to refrain from opportunism, output would increase to $100,000. Obviously, it follows that the average payoff rises to $100, a twentyfold increase.[13]

Now consider the incentives facing a single individual given that everyone else sticks to the agreement to refrain from opportunism. Suppose that if he acts on a particular chance to be opportunistic, he gains an additional $50. The larger the society is, the less likely that such an act, in isolation, will change the general transaction cost environment noticeably, and the less likely it will cause more resources to be devoted to safeguarding against opportunism. If we assume that the one act of opportunism only reduces total output by the $50 taken by the opportunist, then his share of the social payoff will be (100,000–50)/1000 + 50 = $149.95. So by incurring a shared cost of five cents, he gains $50 worth of unshared benefit. At the margin he does substantially better than the $100 he receives when he and everyone else sticks to the agreement, so if all that matters is material payoffs, it is in his best interest to act on such an opportunity. The problem, of course, is that when everyone makes this choice, the result is a high transaction cost environment that is only capable of producing $5000 of total output per period, or $5 worth of output per person.

Note that it is precisely because the harm done by any individual act of opportunism is miniscule when compared to the whole of society that this problem exists, because this is what makes the cost to him (and any other individual, for that matter) imperceptible at the margin.[14] The crux of the problem is that this is true of everyone, but if everyone chooses to be an opportunist, then we have an entirely different environment, one of markedly higher transaction costs and therefore lower output. Conversely, no individual, by refraining from opportunism, can change the outcome, so it is pointless to even try. Through their individual actions they can neither create a high transaction cost environment from a low transaction cost environment, nor can they create a low transaction cost environment from a high transaction cost environment. In either case, in this example if any given individual is to refrain from opportunism, and if refraining is to be rational, it will have to be for some other reason than the material payoff.[15]

Above we considered an entire society, but this argument could also be applied to specific organizations within a society such as a large firm. Suppose there are two ways of organizing production in a large firm. The first is much more productive but is not possible if most people behave opportunistically. The second is much less productive but can work even if most people behave opportunistically. In any given firm, a single individual choosing to undertake a given opportunistic act will not likely turn a firm of the first type into a firm of the second type. So at the margin, it pays those who work in firms of the first type to be opportunistic, but since this is true for everyone, this ultimately turns firms of the first type into firms of the second type, thereby reducing the profitability of any given firm that began as a firm of the first type. This has social implications as well, because if all firms in a given society could have been of the first type, there would have been many more goods and services to divide among society's members than if all firms were of the second type.

One might object that even in such a situation one's concern for one's fellow members of society should be enough limit opportunism, so it is not so clear that opportunism constitutes a commons dilemma. This would be especially true in small groups but it can also be true in large groups. One may, after all, also care about the welfare of strangers. But this possibility is already accounted for in the model of rational opportunism by virtue of including guilt costs in the computation of net payoff. It is indeed perfectly rational for some people to refrain from opportunism.[16] Even in highly opportunistic societies, some people do not always behave opportunistically even when they know that can get away with it, and some people never behave opportunistically at all. This is especially true when the harm done to another is significant, even if the harmed individual is a stranger.

But these counterexamples do not invalidate the commons dilemma characterization of opportunism because in these cases opportunism is not a dilemma. In these cases the individual's feelings of guilt produce costs that reduce the payoff sufficiently so as to make it irrational for the individual to behave opportunistically. As such, the true payoff structure required to produce a commons dilemma doesn't exist after accounting for guilt, so there is no dilemma and therefore no problem to overcome.

One might argue that it is hard to believe that members of a group—particularly a small group—couldn't figure out how to work out an agreement to assure that they don't suffer the inefficient outcome. This is especially true if there are many future periods to consider and people don't discount future benefits greatly. Those familiar with game theory know that, in general, the "Folk Theorem" tells us that the prospect of repeated interaction does indeed increase the likelihood that an agreement to refrain from playing "defect" in a repeated prisoners' dilemma game will be honored, even though it is rational to play "defect" in a one-period setting. In a commons dilemma game that models opportunistic behavior, the prospect of repeated interaction should also increase the likelihood that an agreement to refrain from behaving opportunistically will be honored, even if it would have been rational to behave opportunistically in a one-period setting. In the next chapter I will explain why the repeat play effects that are the *sine qua non* of the Folk Theorem weaken with group size. In short, it is indeed quite plausible that the commons dilemma can be overcome in small groups but, as we will learn in the next chapter, if economic activity is limited to small groups poverty is assured. So this point, while true, is not terribly relevant for fully developed market economies capable of maximizing general prosperity.

RATIONALITY AND THE COMMONS DILEMMA

A possible objection to the discussion above is that the commons dilemma is internally inconsistent because there is a lower payoff for everyone, including the opportunist himself, in the equilibrium state it predicts. It is, of course, true that even though A's single act of opportunism does not perceptibly harm anyone, when everyone behaves in this way actual harm does occur, even to A. But it is nevertheless true that the individual's specific act under consideration does not bring about that outcome. Through what he controls—his own actions only—the individual is powerless to bring about the inefficient outcome and, if it were to already exist, the individual is equally powerless to remove it. From the individual's perspective, then, the equilibrium outcome is a moot point, so the individual might as well not be the only sucker who is sticking to the agreement thereby reducing his welfare even more.

It is indeed true that if society as a whole could meaningfully "act" and it did not choose to refrain from opportunism, this would certainly be an irrational choice. Similarly, if an individual could act to bring about such an outcome generally, but chose not to, such an individual would certainly be irrational. But neither of these possibilities is on the table. The fact that opportunism produces essentially no harm at the margin but nevertheless produces great harm in equilibrium is irrelevant to one's individual actions unless one, through his own individual action, can alter the equilibrium outcome, which he can't. It's called a "dilemma" for a reason.

My point, therefore, is not that some societies are able to overcome the irrationality of such dilemmas and are therefore less opportunistic and more prosperous than those societies that cannot do so, because there is nothing irrational about such dilemmas. My point, which I will develop more fully later, is that in some societies a specific opportunistic act generally constitutes a commons dilemma, whereas in other societies it does not. In those societies where such an act constitutes a commons dilemma, some or all individuals will behave opportunistically because it is completely rational for them to do so. In those societies where the exact same act, in the exact same circumstance, is not undertaken, it is not because the dilemma has been overcome. The dilemma doesn't even exist in the first place because the cost of such actions for individuals in such a society has eliminated the commons dilemma altogether by making the net payoff to opportunism negative.

The connection between rationality and social dilemmas in general is the subject of much debate and confusion. Many equate the idea of efficiency with the idea of rationality. But, as Ken Binmore (2005) has argued, those who do so miss the point of such dilemmas entirely. It is precisely because the optimal course of action is completely rational for the one choosing the action, *despite* the fact that it leads to an inferior outcome in the long run for nearly everyone, that we call it a dilemma. This confusion likely results from the practice of taking society as the unit of analysis even though it is individuals who choose whether to act opportunistically or not.

Others argue that such social dilemmas imply that there is a fundamental conflict between rational and moral behavior. In other words, if people weren't so rational in the neoclassical, calculating, self-interest maximizing sense of the word, then society could avoid getting stuck in the inefficient equilibrium. The solution is therefore to somehow overcome our tendency to behave as rationally as neoclassical assumptions about human behavior imply that we do, or to make us moral enough to render the issue moot.

This suggests that the key to overcoming social dilemmas in general may lie in getting people to overcome their baser instincts; getting them to care more about others, exhorting them to always strive to do the right thing, perhaps to abandon their individualism and to focus more on the welfare of the group as a whole, and so forth. In short, the rationality of behavior within social dilemmas is taken to be a kind of moral lesson on the inadequacy of *homo economicus*. But this implicitly assumes that rational decision making only considers material payoffs. There is no reason why an individual couldn't care enough about others to make opportunism categorically irrational. In such a case there is no dilemma in the first place, because feelings of guilt drive the net payoff to opportunism too low for it to be the dominant strategy. This, in turn, suggests that the key is again encouraging people to care enough about their fellow man. But we shall find out later that even this argument turns out to have a fatal flaw. Indeed, such an approach might be worse than ineffective, it might actually backfire.

I therefore view the commons dilemma equilibrium associated with opportunistic behavior to be a consequence of perfectly rational behavior, which is precisely why opportunism is so ubiquitous and overcoming it is so difficult. But there is no reason to view this rationality in contradistinction to moral behavior, or to presume that the solution must involve irrationality in the form of emotions or irrationally held beliefs. Rationality, properly understood, is amoral; not moral or immoral. Perhaps some people just happen to possess moral tastes that make them feel guiltier about behaving in opportunistic ways than others and, for them, the net payoff of some acts of opportunism is negative so opportunism is irrational. If some societies are filled with such people it is important for us to figure out why—particularly what it is about their specific kinds of moral beliefs that allows them to overcome the problem of opportunism.

Types of Opportunism

In this section I consider three types of opportunism based on the nature of the relationship between the transacting parties involved, which I shall argue is a critical factor in determining whether a given action is opportunistic. Relationships between transacting parties are characterized as contracts, which can be informal or formal, implicit or explicit, open-ended or exhaustively stipulated. Of particular interest in this and the next chapter are relational contracts and how a particular form of opportunism, what I call third-degree opportunism, destroys the basis for trust that makes it possible to use them to fullest effect.

FIRST-DEGREE OPPORTUNISM

First-degree opportunism involves taking advantage of the imperfect enforceability of contracts by reneging on contracts—B takes advantage of A by taking advantage of the fact that contracts are not perfectly enforceable. This can result from information asymmetries (e.g., shirking or managerial self-dealing). This can also result from an insufficient threat of sanction, in which case B reneges on a contractual obligation to A either because B knows it will not be in A's best interest to press for a sanction (e.g., a home contractor that does not rectify a problem after being paid because he knows the cost of litigation for the injured party exceeds the benefit of rectifying the problem), or because the expected cost of the sanction is too low (e.g., if thieves are only forced to return what they stole, then the expected cost of sanction is too low to discourage theft) or the likelihood of detection is too low (e.g., horse thieves are always hanged but almost never caught).

The reneged contract could have been explicit (you signed an agreement not to disclose the terms of a law settlement, but you tell a friend) or implicit (you aren't helpful to a customer although you know you are expected to be); it can be an institutional arrangement in the form of a private contract (you renege on providing a promised service after receiving payment) or it can be a part of the institutional environment, in that it is part of a social contract (you steal a car from a stranger). Because an essential element of any meaningful contract is consideration, reneging generally harms the other party so reneging is not a mutually agreed-upon action. Normally when B reneges on a contract with A, it follows that B gains from the benefits derived from A's past or continued commitment to live up to his contractual promise, while B avoids the cost of fulfilling his commitment. Reneging on a contract is therefore a violation of a trust.

Although our principal interest is in opportunism in the context of voluntary transactions, it is possible for B to engage in first-degree opportunism with respect to A even if they do not transact in any way. First-degree opportunism is often a matter of violating a trust with respect to a social contract. If B steals something from A but A and B don't know each other, then while it is true that B is not reneging on a specific contract between A and B, B is nevertheless still reneging on a contract in the sense that A and B are both common parties to a social contract that prohibits theft. Both A and B benefit from belonging to a society with such a social contract, and these benefits arise from others—including complete strangers—giving up benefits they could derive from stealing, which can be viewed as a form of contractual consideration.[17]

Shirking is a particularly important form of first-degree opportunism. When an agent shirks, he reneges on a contract by providing less than the promised level of effort. Most forms of first-degree opportunism are acts of commission, upon which a detection and punishment scheme can be based. If police officers observe B stealing A's property or come upon compelling evidence to that effect, they then know to arrest him. This makes most forms of first-degree opportunism amenable to institutional sanctions, because they provide a specific predicate action that can be observed and then sanctioned. Moreover, because most forms of first-degree opportunism leave the individual clearly worse off than before, they engender a powerful emotional reaction on the part of the victim, which makes significant sanctioning by the victim himself a credible threat.

Shirking, however, often does not involve an explicit act that can be observed; it is often a non-act that can at best only be inferred, and since its costs are largely counterfactual in nature there might not be observable harm done to the victim. As a result, the "detection and punishment" approach that works well to limit most forms of first-degree opportunism does not work well with shirking, so proactive monitoring is a better option. Alchian and Demsetz (1972) viewed shirking to be such a fundamental problem in market economies that they argued that it provided a demand for an organizational governance structure to undertake monitoring—that is, it constitutes a compelling theory of the firm.

The final example of first-degree opportunism I offer here is reneging on a contract by failing to return a favor. When *A* does *B* a favor and both understand that the basis of that favor is not benevolence but reciprocity, *A* expects the favor to be repaid. The favor need not be repaid immediately or in kind, but it must be repaid nonetheless. If *B* neglects to repay such a favor, *B* has effectively reneged on a contract. Humans and even some animals (e.g., vampire bats) are very careful about keeping track of whether favors have been repaid. The cost of not returning a favor is normally a refusal to extend additional favors. When this does not constitute a very costly sanction, reciprocity requires a great deal of trust. A good example of this is any situation in which repeat dealing is unlikely.

For an opportunistic act to be rational, the expected cost of retaliation must be netted out from the expected payoff. Since first-degree opportunism often leaves the victim clearly worse off, retaliation is an important consideration and sanctions for such behavior tend to be very strong. Most forms of first-degree opportunism are therefore either criminally or civilly actionable, and are therefore well dealt with through formal institutional and organizational mechanisms.

SECOND-DEGREE OPPORTUNISM

Second-degree opportunism involves taking advantage of the incompleteness of contracts because most contracts cannot anticipate every possible eventuality, and therefore cannot explicitly stipulate a response that would have been voluntarily agreed to by all parties *ex ante*. For example, *B* exploits contractual incompleteness to expropriate more than an equal share of the surplus at the expense of *A, ex post*.

When an unanticipated event arises that is not covered in the contract, and this event creates a windfall benefit or harm that is directly related to the contract (in other words, had the contract not existed the windfall benefit or harm would not have existed), then it is to no party's credit or fault that it occurred. Since it is unusual for parties to a contract to agree to unequal division of any transaction surplus *ex ante*, second-degree opportunism generally involves an event that was not foreseen and therefore was not accounted for in the original contract but that confers either an increase in bargaining power or provides a pretext for deception to one party.

With second-degree opportunism there is a transaction involved and either an implicit or explicit contract that mediates it. The contract, even if implicit, is formal in the sense that the expectations of all parties are fairly clear, and any given party understands that the other party or parties involved are not concerned about promoting their welfare. Second-degree opportunism is, therefore, typically a matter of violating a trust with respect to a formal, arms-length contract—that is, a contract as traditionally understood. Second-degree opportunism captures an important sense of the word *opportunism*—taking advantage of a situation in a way that is not illegal but is nevertheless not what you would expect from a transaction partner who is completely fair minded. It is a violation of trust, in that the spirit of the contract is violated even if the letter of the contract is not.

Careful thinkers are understandably wary of phrases like "the spirit of the contract," so what, exactly, does it mean for the spirit of the contract to be broken? Let me offer a way of thinking about this issue. Consider a particular eventuality that is not anticipated by either party to a contract. Suppose that if both parties had in fact been aware of the possibility of that eventuality before the contract was written, they would have agreed to respond to it in a particular way. Now suppose the aforementioned eventuality occurs but both parties were not, in fact, aware of the possibility of it occurring when the contract was agreed to. If B does not respond in the way described by the thought experiment above but, instead, chooses to respond in a way that takes advantage of the event at A's expense (either absolutely or counterfactually), then B is taking advantage of A by taking advantage of A's inability to foresee the eventuality.

Whether a transaction partner would have actually agreed, *ex ante*, to deal with an eventuality in a particular way is private information because only he knows the utility costs or benefits to him of alternative approaches. What maximizes their surplus (and is therefore efficient) is a function of the cost and benefits experienced by all parties of the various approaches and some of the relevant costs and benefits may be subjective. So sometimes what looks like second-degree opportunism to one party might not actually be, and vice versa. When one party is repeatedly associated with such misunderstandings, ill will results and the relationship may be terminated. The existence of relationship-specific assets makes this more costly, which is one reason why relationship-specific assets play a prominent role in theories of vertically integrated production. One such scenario that has been studied extensively by economists is that of post-contractual hold-up made possible by the existence of specific physical capital, and an unpredicted event that leads to a change in the relative bargaining power of the two parties (e.g., the disappearance of an alternative use for the capital allows the transaction partner to demand better terms because he knows the other party can no longer sell his capital for more than scrap value) (Klein, Crawford and Alchian, 1978).[18]

In cases when the most efficient course of action is self-evident to all parties, *ex post*, but how benefits or costs should be shared is not, second-degree opportunism can still occur if there was an implicit agreement that all parties will share equally in the benefits or costs resulting from unforeseen eventualities, but one party nevertheless chose to take advantage of an increase in his relative bargaining power to promote his welfare at his transaction partner's expense (Klein, Crawford, and Alchian 1978; Hart and Moore 1990; Hart 1995). A proposal of an unequal division of a surplus in the ultimatum game can be viewed as an act of second-degree opportunism if one believes that the social contract requires that we should always divide surpluses evenly. Unequal divisions of the surplus are common for one-shot trades. Indeed, neoclassical economic theory predicts that in one-shot ultimatum games one will propose an unequal division of the surplus. Unequal divisions are less common for cooperative transactions because cooperation is much more likely to involve repeat play, which tends to produce an even division of surplus. Strictly speaking, however, if B were to hold out for more than an equal share of the surplus and A were to agree to such terms, no opportunism occurs because there is no violation of trust—unless, of course, in the context of the relationship between A and B there is an agreement never to seek more than an equal share of the surplus. The fact that this is rare does not change the logic of the example.

Those who engage in second-degree opportunism can sometimes reduce the welfare level of their victims in ways that are completely legal (e.g., opportunistic tort lawyers and plaintiffs). The most common sanction is the refusal to transact in the future or the breaking off a transaction relationship. As noted above, asset specificity can make this very costly, so in societies with highly opportunistic cultures we would expect there to be a reluctance to make investments in relationship-specific assets unless there was a prior investment in the relationship itself.[19] In the case of personal injury lawsuits, the plaintiff often does not know the defendant, so repeat play provides little disincentive for engaging second-degree opportunism of this sort. This kind of opportunism is very destructive in that it undermines the willingness to extend trust to strangers. It is also a powerful reminder that one can be law-abiding and opportunistic at the same time.

THIRD-DEGREE OPPORTUNISM

Third-degree opportunism involves taking advantage of discretion that exists in a relational contract. Relational contracts are contracts that lack specificity because the circumstances of the transactions involved are so unpredictable that flexibility is of paramount importance. Rather than prescribe specific actions in response to specific circumstances like traditional contracts, relational contracts define the nature of the relationship within which discretion exists for making decisions and taking action.[20] Williamson (1975) stressed the implications that relational contracts have for establishing firm boundaries emphasizing, in effect, ". . . that the advantage of firms over markets lies in the firm's ability to enforce relational contracts . . ." (Baker, Gibbons and Murphy, 2002, pp. 46–47).[21]

Third-degree opportunism involves modifying how existing transactions are conducted, or proposing entirely new ones, to achieve a higher payoff for oneself by violating a trust. The most obvious example involves decision makers taking advantage of the discretion provided to them to engage in day-to-day problem solving under unpredictably changing circumstances. Suppose *A* (a principal) hires *B* (an agent) to make decisions on behalf of a firm owned by *A*. By taking such a job, *B* normally either explicitly or implicitly promises to make decisions so as to maximize *A*'s welfare, which typically simply means maximizing profit. If *B* knowingly chooses an action that is better for *B* than the best possible action for *A*, then *B* has reneged on an implicit contract and has therefore engaged in third-degree opportunism. A trust is violated in that *B* understood that *A* trusted *B* to always make decisions in a way that maximized profit.

This is most problematic with respect to counterfactual losses due to self-serving decisions that result in an increase in profit, but nevertheless fail to increase profit by as much as some other action that is known only to the decision maker. In the next chapter I will explain why the more localized knowledge is within the firm, the more common is this occurrence. Self-serving decisions that reduce the absolute level of profit are much less problematic, since a lower profit level is likely to draw attention. The more daunting problem is, obviously, decisions that increase profit at the margin, but not by as much as possible, because of a bias toward self-serving decisions on the part of the decision maker.[22]

This is an admittedly unusual way to think of decision making in the context of relational contracts because relational contracts are normally viewed as mechanisms through which efficient behavior is self-enforcing. Previous work on relational contracts implicitly assumes that people can't be genuinely trusted. But self-enforcement is obviously not the reason why relational contracts exist—it is an attribute that many believe such contracts must possess to be viable. The ultimate reason for mediating economic activity through a relational rather than traditional contract is flexibility. If relational contracts weren't more flexible, their enforceability would be irrelevant.

Perhaps conventional theorists are missing the most crucial issue regarding relational contracts because they *presume* people can't be genuinely trusted. What if the real issue is this: the more fully decision makers can be trusted to not engage in opportunism when golden opportunities present themselves, the more fully decision-making discretion can be delegated so as to maximize flexibility. In other words, relational contracts can be used to fullest effect if, and only if, they can be used in situations where self-enforcement is inherently impossible. In this case an issue that is potentially every bit as important as the question of how self-enforcement is effectuated is the question of how exogenous factors work to make relational contracts that are not self-enforcing possible, because such contracts would afford flexibility precisely where it is needed most.

One cannot simply assert that relational contracts need not be self-enforcing. But it is equally true that one cannot simply assert that golden opportunities will always be acted on, so relational contracts must necessarily be self-enforcing. By presuming genuine trust is meaningless, the conventional approach overlooks the possibility that genuine trust might be an important part of the theory of relational contracts. We will find in the next chapter that the value of such genuine trust would be greatest in circumstances in which golden opportunities frequently arise—that is, very large and complex firms that are the engines of prosperity.

Third-degree opportunism sets a high bar for extending trust. Even the threat of litigation upon discovery of having engaged in third-degree opportunism is a weak deterrent because a failure to do one's best, especially in light of unforeseen circumstances, is not something that can normally be demonstrated objectively to a third party. Therefore, in a context in which third-degree opportunities are likely to arise, the principal must be able to completely trust the agent to do his best on the principal's behalf by always choosing actions that maximize the principal's welfare. Such trust does not necessarily require that the agent care about the principal's welfare; only that the agent feels he must do as he has promised by always choosing the most profitable action known to him, even if not known to anyone else.

Summary

General prosperity is impossible without specialization, but specialization is impossible without transactions. Transactions, in turn, inevitably open the door to opportunistic victimization. The resulting fear of opportunistic victimization can drive transaction costs so high that many transactions are discouraged. This is devastating because it is through transactions that the gains from specialization are realized. The higher are transaction costs generally, the smaller is the set of feasible transactions, the more limited transaction behavior will therefore be, and hence the lower will be the gains from specialization, so the less prosperous the society will be.

The fear of opportunism also results in resources being devoted to safeguarding against it. The risk of employee theft may, for example, require hiring extra managers to monitor workers. The risk of a transaction partner taking advantage of contractual incompleteness may require hiring more lawyers to write more comprehensive contracts and retaining them to enforce such contracts later. In this way, using resources to safeguard against opportunism reduces the net payoff of many transactions, making some no longer viable. At the same time, any resources devoted to safeguarding transactions that still occur leave less total output for the same number of people in society, which is obviously less efficient.[23] In the long run everyone loses. It follows that if the threat of opportunism were to disappear, resources that were no longer needed for safeguarding against opportunism would constitute a windfall that could be shared by all members of society.

By choking off transactions that facilitate realizing the gains from specialization, opportunism impedes the maximization of general prosperity. Evidence of opportunistic behavior need not be apparent for this to be true, for much of the cost of opportunism takes the form of transactions that are not attempted, as well as the absence of institutions and governance structures that never existed and therefore are not missed. With the exception of those who are members of the elite, no matter how talented an individual is, prospering in an impoverished society is impossible. So unless one is sure to be a member of the elite, a rational person would eagerly trade the immediate gains of being able to behave opportunistically for the ability to live in a prosperous society without the ability to opportunistically exploit others. Yet in most societies, behaving opportunistically is rational. This paradoxical result is explained by recognizing that, at the margin of decision making, opportunism constitutes a commons dilemma.

An important question is why some societies are more opportunistic than others. A natural explanation is that some societies have developed more effective institutions to limit opportunism. It is certainly true that societies with effective institutions do better than those with ineffective institutions, but what if the existence of some institutions is itself a product of being able to control opportunism? And what if there are transactions that are important to the development and operation of a market economy, and they are beyond the reach of institutions? I have argued in this chapter that third-degree opportunism often presents this very kind of challenge. In the next chapter we will see that this is a problem that gets worse—much worse—in precisely the contexts that matter most for maximizing general prosperity.

In the next chapter we explore how opportunism, particularly third-degree opportunism, can impede economic development by impeding the emergence of trust-dependent institutions as well as the emergence of firms that are both large and entrepreneurial in nature. We will find that to have large, adaptable, innovative, and entrepreneurial firms, opportunism must also be limited through internalized moral restraint made possible by feelings of guilt. For this reason, we will see that guilt plays a very important role in the arguments that follow.

Appendix

The canonical commons dilemma game is given by the following.[24] In an *n* player social dilemma, every agent gets a *REWARD* as long as there are no more than *M* defectors. The payoff that defectors get is always higher than the payoff obtained by those who cooperate, so *DEFECT* > *COOPERATE*. However, every player is better off if they all cooperate than if they all defect, so *COOPERATE* + *REWARD* > *DEFECT*. The table below shows the payoff matrix for a particular agent:

Table 2.1   The Commons Game

	Fewer than *M* others defect	Exactly *M* others defect	More than *M* others defect
Individual cooperates	*COOPERATE* + *REWARD*	*COOPERATE* + *REWARD*	*COOPERATE*
Individual defects	*DEFECT* + *REWARD*	*DEFECT*	*DEFECT*

The social cost of opportunism involves a kind of "tipping point" equilibrium. The tipping point is this: when a sufficiently high proportion of the population is not opportunistic so that with few exceptions we can presume that even strangers can be trusted, there are qualitative changes to society that produce a significantly lower level of transaction costs generally. Specifically, with a sufficiently high proportion of the population (M/n) playing COOPERATE, the society will have:

1. Lower transaction costs derived from the ability to presume others, even total strangers, are unconditionally trustworthy.
2. The existence and proper function of highly trust-dependent "nuts and bolts" type institutions that lower transaction costs even further.
3. A windfall of additional consumption derived from conserving resources that would have otherwise been devoted to safeguarding against opportunism.
4. A windfall of additional consumption made possible by being able to enjoy the benefits of having large yet thoroughly entrepreneurial firms.

The benefit to having more than M of n members of society play COOPERATE is that the increase in aggregate output due to the four effects above can be divided among all n members of society to produce an additional payoff of REWARD for everyone. But any individual nevertheless does better playing DEFECT. So what's rational at the margin is what produces the worst outcome in equilibrium. No individual through his actions or inactions can bring about a high trust regime, and no individual through his actions or inactions can undo it once it exists.

CHAPTER 3

Group Size

. . . civilization has largely been made possible by subjugating the innate animal instincts to the non-rational customs which made possible the formation of larger orderly groups of gradually increasing size.—Friedrich Hayek, 1979, p. 155

Introduction

The size of social groups within which activity can be organized is no small detail of human history, and it is one of the most important objects of study in social science (Seabright, 2004). Indeed, the word *social* becomes a more fitting adjective the larger is the group under consideration. A social scientist obviously has more things to study on Manhattan Island than on Robinson Crusoe's. Many things modern humans hold dear are products of a complex, sophisticated, *large group* society. It is obvious that much of what makes life in many modern societies so desirable are things that are not possible in a society that cannot cooperate outside of small groups.

The fact that so much goodness is the result of the ability to cooperate effectively in large groups presents a very fundamental problem. Since the split between the human and chimpanzee line over 5 million years ago, over 99.9% of our evolution occurred *exclusively* in the context of very small social groups.[1] Genetic evidence shows that humans have been around in their current form for at least 80,000 years, and even for nearly all of this time (certainly over 99%) most humans lived in very small social groups. Of course, all of us still live in small groups today, but in modern market societies these small groups are also parts of very large groups. Through most of human history, however, the largest group within which any human could be said to engage in meaningful social interaction was itself a small group (far less than 200 people). This means the kind of behavior that most dramatically improves the quality of life necessarily occurs in a context for which we are likely maladapted.[2] We are indisputably a small group species, but some of us have apparently figured out how to overcome our small group nature to cooperate effectively in large groups.

Why is the ability to coordinate behavior in large groups so important? Over 200 years since the publication of *The Wealth of Nations*, the essential message of Adam Smith remains valid: group size dramatically increases average productivity, and therefore general prosperity, by increasing the ability to specialize. This is why there are no prosperous societies that conduct all of their economic activity in the context of small groups. Since achieving a condition of general prosperity is ultimately a matter of increasing the amount of goods and services produced per capita, and most goods and services are produced by firms, of particular interest here is the ability to effectively organize production in large firms. But the principles apply to the ability to organize economic activity in large groups generally.

The complex, sophisticated, large group society that has produced so much good for humans is easily taken for granted by those who were born in and never leave such societies, but it should not be. Such societies are the exception and not the rule over the course of human history. Group size is such a fundamentally important factor in evolution that there are large literatures devoted to it in biology and the social sciences. The importance of group size to understanding human evolution is now widely accepted. In his pioneering work on group size, Robin Dunbar has shown why human groups inevitably hit a wall at approximately 150 persons, providing evidence for what we all already knew: we are a small group species.[3] The disappearance of many large group civilizations over the course of human history also suggests that sustaining cooperation in large groups is not something that comes easily to humans.

In what follows I show that the process of development is impeded by a daunting tradeoff: group size increases the benefits from specialization but it also worsens the problem of opportunism. This is because group size intensifies commons dilemma incentives to behave opportunistically, while increasing opportunities for opportunism at the same time. I then discuss how societies have learned to cope with this tradeoff between the benefits of size and the cost of opportunism. The institutions that have emerged to overcome this tradeoff made the rise of civilization possible, but they do not insure achieving a condition of general prosperity.

Benefits of Size

Evidence that group size matters is all around us. With respect to virtually any context for any kind of activity that occurs in families, neighborhoods, organizations, churches, firms, governments, armies, and society as a whole, bigger is nearly always better. The fact that some activities are best pursued in small groups does not change this because we can be members of small groups and large groups at the same time. Why, exactly, is it so important to be able to organize economic activity in large groups?

SPREADING FIXED COSTS

Nearly all production requires three things: throughputs, labor, and capital.[4] Labor uses capital to transform throughputs into output. Capital costs do not vary as closely with output as do throughput or labor costs. Indeed, in nearly all forms of production there are costs that do not vary with output, which we call *fixed costs*. Obviously, the greater the level of production the lower is the average fixed cost per unit. It follows, then, that undertaking any activity in a very large group often confers the advantage of enjoying lower average fixed costs per unit than in a small group.

Another benefit of bearing lower average fixed costs is that larger groups are able to do things that smaller ones cannot, because different activities involve different kinds of fixed costs. For example, one reason why a large church might be better than a small one is because it can afford a larger variety of programs than smaller churches can, since there are more people over which to spread the fixed costs of each individual program. This is a common feature of many organizations and is completely obvious to those who run such organizations.

SPECIALIZATION AND MASS PRODUCTION

The larger is the group, the more fully the gains from specialization can be realized. This is because tasks can be more finely divided among workers, which leads to greater gains from specialization. This simple idea is the central point Adam Smith made in *The Wealth of Nations*. Even non-economists are familiar with this argument, as well as the name we have given the phenomenon—*economies of scale*. So convincing has the historical evidence proven to be that the idea of economies of scale is now widely regarded as common sense.

There has been a resurgence of interest in Adam Smith's ideas regarding the effects of size on production and prosperity. Buchanan and Yoon (1994) have argued that while Ricardo's theory of comparative advantage has drawn the most attention as an explanation for the benefits of trade, Smith's theory of division of labor is more fundamental. *New Trade Theory* models also emphasize economies of scale (e.g., Helpman and Krugman, 1985; see Krugman, 1995 for a review of the relevant literature). This approach has solved a number of puzzles in the trade and development literatures that could not be answered by traditional models.

SPECIALIZATION AND INNOVATION

Specialization can also increase innovation. In many cases inventions and innovations can dramatically reduce the average cost of production, which makes it possible for a society to enjoy an increase in general prosperity. While there are many factors that affect innovative behavior, Adam Smith explained how specialization affects innovation. According to Smith:

> ... the invention of all those machines by which labour is so much facilitated and abridged, seems to have been originally owing to the division of labour. Men are much more likely to discover easier and readier methods of attaining any object, when the whole attention of their minds is directed towards that single object, than when it is dissipated among a great variety of things.[5]

As true as this was when Smith was writing, it is almost certainly truer now. Brain power is limited, so one is most likely to improve a given machine or process the more one's attention is limited to it. The growing technological sophistication of production processes and machines would appear to only intensify this effect, as would the growing level of complexity of production generally. For one to have the best chance of solving a new problem in the most efficient way, one must be as familiar as possible with the details of the particular processes, personnel, and machines involved.

One lesson of economic history is that mass production changed everything. Prior to mass production skilled craftsmen produced a variety of goods, but their firms were very small. Productivity was, by today's standards, very low and so prices, by today's standards, were very high. Prices were so high that much of what skilled craftsmen produced could only be afforded by those who were very rich. As a result, very few people were employed before the 1850s outside of agriculture. Mass production dramatically increased the productivity of labor, resulting in more goods per capita. This increased the demand for labor, which inevitably increased wages as firms competed to employ workers who were now able to produce far more output than before.

The history of the West comports well with Smith. Even today there are no prosperous societies that conduct all of their economic activity in small groups. Conversely, all prosperous societies are filled with large firms. Societies that are not able to undertake production in large firms are simply unable to enjoy sufficient levels of specialization to make prosperity possible. This does not mean that having large firms is sufficient—large Soviet and Chinese manufacturing firms circa 1970 certainly failed to produce general prosperity—but it strongly suggests that large firms are necessary.

Economic historians have noted that the rise of the railroads led to a stunning increase in industrialization and, soon thereafter, a stunning increase in general prosperity. This is because the railroads dramatically lowered transportation costs and therefore increased the size of markets that firms could serve. Alfred Chandler (1977) pointed out that before the 1840s, there was no such thing as middle managers. They simply didn't exist because no firms were large enough to need them. Of course, before the 1840s there was no such thing as general prosperity, either, even in the United States. Only after production became widely based on mass production was there a dramatic increase in the productivity of the average worker. This, in turn, made it possible for output to rise sufficiently relative to population to make general prosperity possible.

The larger volume of economic activity also created new pressures for institutions to evolve, or be created, to deal with problems they never had to deal with before. New institutions, in turn, fueled growth by making it possible to organize economic activity in completely new ways within and across very large groups, thereby further increasing the gains from specialization. The explosion of per capita income in the West from the mid nineteenth century to the present correlated directly with increases in the size and sophistication of government institutions, market institutions, financial markets, banks, and, most importantly, with the size of firms.

GROUP SIZE AND INSTITUTIONS

Institutions are central to understanding how economic systems make general prosperity possible because they decrease transaction costs, thereby increasing the set of transactions through which the gains from specialization can be effectuated. Some institutions cannot exist without other institutions in place. For example, it is hard to imagine a firm investing in a new kind of capital in the absence of contracts and property rights that insure that if the new capital proved highly profitable, the firm would actually benefit. It is equally hard to imagine such contracts being used in a society that does not possess a competent and impartial civil justice system.

It is easy to see why there is no civil justice system in hunter-gatherer bands— they are simply too small to afford one. Large tribes might have a justice system— a leader who acts as a judge—but impartiality is hard to imagine in such cases. This is why most of the institutions that we take for granted today that support market activity do not and cannot exist in small group societies. Institutions that support economic organizations (e.g., the existence of police to protect property, the existence of a NYSE to coordinate trading of stocks, the existence of civil courts to enforce contracts, and the existence of government to protect property rights and provide public goods) are costly, but the cost of using them varies little with the volume of transactions. Large societies are therefore able to spread the cost of having such institutions over many more transactions than small societies are, thereby lowering their average cost per transaction.

As is the case with capital in the production process, society can use many institutions over and over at little or no additional cost (in many cases an institution is just a pattern being followed, like a template is followed by machinist). The problem is that this also means that if a society does not use a given institution that is costly to maintain (e.g., property registration offices or civil courts) very much, it may prove too expensive for the total benefits it confers. So even if a hunter-gatherer band could conceive of using contracts, this would likely be moot because there would not be enough transactions over which to divide the cost of having the requisite support institutions in place. Larger societies have many more transactions, so what is untenable in a small society is no problem in a large society. It follows directly that the larger the society, the greater the number of institutions that will be viable. Since market societies require many institutions to support market activity, it follows that one necessary condition for maximizing general prosperity is for society to be a large society.[6]

Cost of Size

Although bigger is usually better, bigger is also harder. Large males are more likely to defeat small males in hand-to-hand combat, but they are more likely to starve to death during famines. Large firms enjoy economies of scale, but are more likely than small firms to suffer from the problem of the left hand not knowing what the right hand is doing. Largeness confers benefits but it also entails costs, so the size of organisms, organizations, firms, social groups, villages, tribes, and even entire societies is best thought of as being determined by a balancing of the benefits and costs of size. Of particular interest here is the possibility that increased group size worsens the problem of opportunism.

Larger group size worsens the problem of opportunism in at least three ways. First, although the Folk Theorem tells us that repeated interaction can often alleviate social dilemmas, this becomes less likely the larger the group involved. Second, the larger the group within which economic activity is organized, the more opportunities there will be to engage in opportunism with little or no chance of detection. Third, our natural reluctance to behave opportunistically tends to weaken with group size. So, incredibly, group size worsens the commons dilemma, increases opportunities for opportunism, and undermines our natural reluctance to behave opportunistically! Below I will discuss the first two problems. A discussion of the third problem, which is of central importance to this book, will have to wait until Chapters 5 and 6.

HOW GROUP SIZE WORSENS THE COMMONS DILEMMA

In small groups, even if opportunistic behavior cannot be directly observed it is often not a problem because the reduction in the opportunist's share of the total output will be expected to exceed the private gain from behaving opportunistically. In this case, combating opportunism is not necessary because undertaking opportunistic action is not rational. The efficient solution is therefore self-enforcing. But as group size increases, the effect of any given act of opportunism on the opportunist's share of total output will generally fall, thereby reducing the likelihood that this effect will be sufficient to discourage opportunism.[7]

In the previous chapter I noted that if the conditions of the Folk Theorem are met, the expectation of gains from future interactions might overcome the problem of opportunism even in circumstances that would constitute an insurmountable social dilemma in a one-period setting.[8] Since we actually live in a multi-period world, the Folk Theorem seems to suggest that opportunism might not be as daunting a problem as it first appears. In what follows I will explain that while this is likely to be true in small groups, repeat play effects that are the *sine qua non* of the Folk Theorem tend to weaken with group size.

Repeat play effects work by driving up the expected cost of opportunism at the moment of decision by reducing gains that would have otherwise been expected to be realized in the future. But for repeat play effects to work, those contemplating opportunistic behavior must believe they face a chance of not benefiting from future gains. This requires that they believe it is possible for those who refrain from behaving opportunistically to determine whether someone else has broken the agreement. The most obvious way to do this is to catch the opportunist in the act. With sufficiently strong sanctions, this produces an effective deterrent for many forms of opportunism. What about acts of opportunism that cannot be directly observed?

In a pathbreaking paper, Bengt Holmstrom (1982) studied a very common form of opportunism—shirking—in the context of a team in which its members cannot observe each others' effort. The level of effort each must put forth to achieve the efficient outcome is known by all of the members, but any member can improve his own net payoff more by shirking. The problem, of course, is that if they all choose to shirk then they all end up getting much less than if they had all stuck to the agreement. Holmstrom argued that this might point to a fundamental role for a team owner, which is to serve as a residual claimant who credibly denies payment to all team members if output falls below the level that would have resulted if all team members had stuck to the agreement not to shirk.

This means that even if the group is not small enough to produce a self-enforcing solution, and even if it is impossible to directly observe opportunistic behavior, it might nevertheless be possible that the reduction in total output due to one act of opportunism by one individual will be sufficient to alert others that the agreement to refrain from opportunism has been broken. If this results in an abandonment of the agreement or suffering a sufficiently high penalty, then under certain conditions this might make sticking to the agreement rational.

Holmstrom's (1982) approach of inferring shirking from a reduction in total output provides an intriguing mechanism through which repeat play effects overcome the commons dilemma associated with opportunism, even for opportunistic acts that cannot be directly observed. But the larger is the group involved, the more implausible it is that a single opportunistic act will produce a sufficiently clear indication that the agreement has been broken. This is because as the number of individuals in the group grows, the individual's situation within the group looks increasingly more like the situation discussed in the previous chapter regarding a society that is so large that no specific act of opportunism by any individual could possibly be detected from its effect on total output. So there is a group size, n, beyond which a given act of opportunism is rational because fluctuations in output due to random factors are enough to cover the reduction in output due to a specific act of opportunism, so there is no signal to the other n-1 members of the group (or monitor or owner) that any individual has reneged on the agreement to refrain from opportunism.[9] In short, powerful as it is, the Folk Theorem is less likely to be relevant the larger is the group in question.

One could argue that over a long enough period of time, even very weak signals might produce a statistically significant pattern from which opportunism can be inferred. This is true in principle, but there is nothing to assure that a sufficiently clear pattern will emerge before it is too late. Some golden opportunities produce payoffs that can make an opportunist rich for life. At some point the opportunist will not care if someone may become suspicious.

HOW GROUP SIZE AFFECTS OPPORTUNITIES FOR OPPORTUNISM

The specialization of economic activity throughout a market society inevitably increases the localization of knowledge. Hayek (1945) argued that this localization of knowledge is *the* fundamental problem that the price system solves. In short, paying market prices forces decision makers to account for the *social* opportunity cost of using any given resource, so economic activity can be decentralized without fear that some will discard a resource that others are scrambling to find. Those who desperately need it drive its price up, thereby inducing those who have it to make it available.

The beauty of the price system, according to Hayek, is that one need not have any knowledge of how others might use a resource to pay the market price for using it, yet by paying that market price along with everyone else we can, as a society, be assured that it is put to most effective use. This means that market prices make it possible to conduct economic activity in a decentralized yet efficient manner. Resources are used in light of local knowledge, while accounting for the social opportunity cost of their use, too. Since decentralization is obviously an epiphenomenon of specialization, it follows that maximizing general prosperity without a price system to overcome the local knowledge problem is impossible. Hayek argued that, given the complexity of production and trade in a large and highly specialized society, the price system addresses the problem of local knowledge much more effectively than central planning of economic activity could.

In small groups the localization of knowledge presents only a minor problem, so central planning normally maximizes efficiency and market pricing is unnecessary, in many cases even impossible.[10] The larger the society, however, the more difficult it becomes to know what everyone is doing, how they are doing it, and why they are doing it at a given point in time. For resources to be most efficiently used, the social opportunity cost of using them must accounted for by those who know the answers to the what, how, why, and when questions above—that is, by those who possess the relevant local knowledge.

Although group size intensifies the problem of local knowledge, it *improves* the functioning of markets and therefore the ability of market prices to cope with the problem of local knowledge. Larger societies have many more buyers and many more sellers for any given good, which makes possible competitive market pricing, which leads to efficient resource allocation as described by standard neoclassical analysis. Hayek argued that there was an even deeper way to think of what was going on, that competitive market pricing results in prices that provide the most accurate information possible about the social opportunity cost of using any given resource at any point in time. So, large societies have an increasingly difficult problem of local knowledge to deal with across the whole of society, but an increasingly effective mechanism with which to deal with it—market pricing.

In my view, there is another important local knowledge to be dealt with—the local knowledge problem *within* groups, particularly firms. Within very small groups or firms this problem is likely to be minimal. Consider a blacksmith, circa 1800, who employs his son and two nephews as apprentices. In such a firm, every important decision can be made by the owner because he knows everything that can possibly be known that is relevant to decision making. But it only takes a slightly larger firm for it to be impossible for him to possess all the knowledge needed to make the best possible decision in every instance. The larger the firm, the more complex the production process, and the more uncertain is the environment, the more knowledge tends to be localized.

Size improves the function of market pricing across the whole of society, so it is not inimical to solving the local knowledge problem as it is normally envisioned. But within firms market prices generally don't tell decision makers what to do in the face of continuously changing circumstances. According to Coase (1937), firms exist precisely because many forms of production involve transactions for which there are no market prices to guide action. So within firms the fact that size improves market pricing is of little help in solving the local knowledge problem. Another option is coordinating production activity through formal contracts, but with respect to most production this is so impractical that production is better mediated by relational contracts (Baker et al., 2002; Williamson, 1975).

This is not to suggest that market prices play no role in decision making within firms. When simply purchasing a throughput, for example, the market price is very close to the firm's opportunity cost of choosing that action, so the optimal decision-making process is very close to the cost-benefit analysis performed by a consumer when choosing levels of consumption in light of his tastes, prices, and income. But in many cases within firms, decision making also involves an element of problem solving. In such cases, market prices for the relevant resources only establish boundaries within which decisions are made. Such decisions must then be made in light of knowledge of competing ends that constitute opportunity costs that are affected by, but not equivalent to, the market prices of the resources involved.

Within firms prices often differ sharply from opportunity cost. For example, markets tell us that engineers cost more to employ than janitors, but if a window is broken and the janitor is busy attending to an overflowing toilet, markets don't tell us that the opportunity cost of having the engineer sweep up the glass in that instance is lower than having the janitor do so. A manager who possesses local knowledge in the form of knowing that the janitor is currently attending to an overflowing toilet, and knowing that the engineer has nothing to do because he is between projects, will therefore know to direct the engineer to sweep up the glass even though market prices alone would suggest just the opposite.

So while market prices work well across the whole of society to induce efficient decisions, they cannot solve the local knowledge problem within large firms because there aren't prices to guide any but the simplest of decisions (e.g., which brand of toner to buy for a printer). Therefore paying market prices for resources is a necessary condition for efficient resource use within firms, but it is not sufficient because there are other opportunity costs to be considered that are often only known by those who possess the relevant local knowledge. This means that while the local knowledge problem across the whole of society becomes easier to solve with larger group size, the local knowledge problem within firms becomes harder to solve.

To insure the efficient use of local knowledge within firms, what is needed is a way to get those who possess it to employ it efficiently. Traditional contracts are not enough. Traditional contracts state what all parties are expected to do and how they are to do it. They are by nature specific, which makes them amenable to third-party enforcement. The more specific they are the higher is the level of assurance that parties will get what they expected. But increased contractual specificity comes at the cost of inflexibility. The more localized knowledge is, the more costly inflexibility is. So to insure the efficient use of local knowledge, there is no avoiding the need to delegate decision-making authority to those who possess it. In this way the firm can effectuate decentralized planning within firms, analogous to how market pricing effectuates decentralized planning throughout the whole of society.

To *maximize* general prosperity a society needs to be filled with firms that are large enough to exhaust the gains from economies of scale, but within which all decisions are made so as to maximize profit. The farther a firm is from having profit maximization as the sole objective guiding behavior *throughout its entire hierarchy,* the less socially efficient it will be and the less it will promote general prosperity. Although firms can effectuate the sole objective of profit maximization by completely centralizing all decision making and subordinating it to that objective, this wastes local knowledge distributed throughout the firm. Conversely, decentralized decision making can overcome the local knowledge problem, but in many cases it is not likely to result in decisions that are guided by the sole objective of profit maximization because decision makers will exploit their decision-making authority to behave opportunistically.[11]

The larger is the production unit, the more complex the production process, and the more rapid is the pace of change, the greater is the benefit of directing activity through relational rather than formal contracts. The more flexible relational contacts are, the more likely they can make the fullest use of local knowledge by fully delegating decision-making authority and the greater efficiency gains will be. But this inevitably opens the firm up to third-degree opportunism on the part of those given such authority. Because of such fear, the inability to fully delegate decision-making authority to those who possess local knowledge acts as a check on the size of groups within which efficient economic cooperation takes place.

For a society to maximize general prosperity, it needs to be filled with firms that maximize the gains from economies of scale without sacrificing the gains from efficient use of knowledge. In other words, what is needed is decision making that is utterly entrepreneurial throughout firm hierarchy of even very large firms. The solution is to get those who possess local knowledge to use it so as to fully maximize profit. In such firms, all decisions are made to maximize profit while making full use of all local knowledge because decision makers are given the flexibility (decision-making discretion and authority) to do so.

Institutions and Prudential Restraint

The rise of agriculture is often heralded as a watershed event in the rise of human civilization, but it was only a necessary condition for the emergence of a society that could conduct economic activity efficiently in large groups. Societies that adopted agriculture but that were ineffective at dealing with opportunism were far less productive, and therefore far less able to defend themselves, since they could not cooperate effectively. There were, no doubt, many such societies over the course of human history, but for obvious reasons we know little about them.

Conversely, those agriculturally based societies that we know the most about were apparently able to limit opportunism sufficiently to be able to cooperate effectively in large groups. How did they do this? They did so through institutions, broadly construed.[12] The benefits of large-scale society that were made possible by agriculture appear to have set off an institutional arms race among societies, in the sense that societies that did not develop sufficiently effective institutions to limit opportunism often became targets of conquest for societies that did.[13] So by combating opportunism in ever larger group settings, institutions induced the continuing advancement of human civilization.

As societies and the groups organized within them grew larger, emphasis shifted increasingly to formal institutions because incentives associated with informal institutions (e.g., incentives derived from mutual affection, mutual monitoring, and repeat play) became weaker as groups grew larger. The Roman Empire, for example, was very large and remains influential not so much from its art, literature, culture, or moral beliefs, as from its *formal* institutions of commerce and government that are evident in many of our formal institutions even today. So it is not surprising that the study of the advancement of human civilization has focused on how all forms of activity were organized in increasingly larger groups, made possible through the development of increasingly sophisticated *formal* institutions.

How do formal institutions limit opportunism? According to the modern theory of institutions, decision makers are assumed to be rational so they respond to incentives.[14] Institutions combat opportunism by producing incentives that discourage opportunistic behavior. Heretofore, the analysis of formal and informal institutions has been based on incentives derived from sanctions that are triggered when opportunism is detected.[15] Detection can result from passive observation, from active monitoring, or can be inferred from a pattern of performance. If the probability of detection is high enough and/or punishment is severe enough, then opportunism will be irrational.

Like neoclassical economics generally, the modern theory of institutions does not assume that individuals forgo opportunities to engage in opportunism because they are benevolent, public spirited, or otherwise morally restrained. Institutions address opportunism by producing incentives that make it rational for the individual to refrain from opportunism. Although moral beliefs might reduce the strength of incentives needed to check opportunism, institutions do not require morality on the part of decision makers to be effective. All that is needed is for the individual in question to recognize the benefits of self-imposed restraint. Institutions therefore effectuate prudential rather than moral restraint.[16] Prudential restraint is simply a matter of choosing to forgo acting on an opportunity to behave opportunistically because the expected cost of an opportunistic action is so high that behaving opportunistically in that instance is not rational.[17]

Some are offended by the emphasis on prudential rather than moral restraint that is implicit in economic analysis, and mistakenly infer that this means that economists don't believe morality is important. In reality, the emphasis on prudential restraint is derived from a desire for modeling parsimony and tractability. A model that works in the absence of moral restraint has its advantages. While moral beliefs differ greatly across societies, rational choice is applicable to all societies, and social scientists prefer theories that are widely applicable. The modest yet plausible assumption that people are primarily concerned with promoting their own interests, and are fairly rational in doing so, is an assumption that is much more likely to be true for all societies than any assumption regarding any particular moral belief.

Prudential restraint effectuated by institutionally produced incentives has an Achilles heel. Institutions work by driving up the expected cost of opportunism. This means that if the chance of being caught is believed to be zero by the decision maker, then no matter how costly the sanction is or how patient or risk-averse the decision maker is, it would be irrational for the decision maker to not behave opportunistically if his only reason for restraint is prudence. The very calculating nature that is posited to produce prudential restraint, even in the absence of moral restraint, also means that individuals will always act on golden opportunities. So, in situations in which the decision maker believes there is no chance of detection, prudential restraint will not check opportunism. Unfortunately, the more localized knowledge is, the more likely there will be circumstances in which the decision maker believes there is no chance of detection. Since knowledge becomes more localized with increasing group size, while the maximization of general prosperity requires cooperation in very large groups, this is not merely an academic point.

Third-Degree Opportunism and Trust

In the previous chapter I defined third-degree opportunism as reneging on a relational contract by taking advantage of discretion delegated therein. The localization of knowledge implies that the delegation of decision-making discretion and authority inevitably gives decision makers the ability to promote their welfare at the expense of the firm. So the same factors that make "high discretion" relational contracts so valuable also increase opportunities for decision makers who possess local knowledge to act on it in self-serving ways. It follows that firms that make the fullest use of local knowledge by giving decision makers who possess local knowledge the greatest degree of discretion open themselves most fully to third-degree opportunism.

Here is the crux of the main problem. Institutions work by effectuating prudential restraint in response to external incentives. For institutions to work, something has to be observed or inferred to have happened to trigger a response that changes the payoffs involved. But when knowledge is highly localized, failure to take the correct action is often impossible to observe or infer because such a conclusion requires knowledge of counterfactual choices and outcomes that are only known to those who possess the relevant local knowledge.

Consider a decision maker who needs to choose a course of action in response to a change in circumstances. In many cases the principal would not even be aware such a choice is required. But for the sake of argument, let's suppose that in this case the principal is aware of the need for such a choice and knows of two actions, b and c, that could be chosen. Suppose that c is more profitable, and we indicate this by saying $c > b$.

The more localized knowledge is, the more likely it is that the set of actions known to the decision maker will be larger than b and c. It might, for example, also contain an action like a that is unknown to the principal, and for which it is the case that $c > b > a$. An action such as a is largely irrelevant, since it is even less profitable than the two actions that are known by the principal. If the decision maker chooses a, he knows that even if he is not observed doing so, the owners will nevertheless be able to infer that he is either incompetent or engaging in opportunism.

In contrast, consider an action such as d, which is the most profitable action of all, so we have $d > c > b > a$—but suppose d is only known to the decision maker. If the decision maker prefers c to d, then he is more likely to choose c over d the more confident he is that the principal will never know of the existence of d. Moreover, if his unwillingness to behave opportunistically has nothing to do with morality because he is only prudentially restrained, and if he is certain that the principal will never become aware that he selected c over d, then he will *always* choose c over d because it would be irrational for him not to do so.

In most cases the decision maker cannot be certain he will never be discovered to have taken advantage of his discretion by choosing an action like c over an action like d. If the likelihood is judged to be sufficiently low, however, it will be *prudent* to behave opportunistically by choosing c. Whether a decision maker will choose to behave opportunistically in such a case depends on the size of the payoff, the size of the sanction if discovered, the risk of discovery, the decision maker's level of risk-aversion, the decision maker's rate of time preference, and other factors.

Firms can take action to minimize this problem. They can mete out highly punitive sanctions, hire only managers who are very patient (so they do not discount future losses highly), hire only managers who are very risk-averse (so any positive chance of detection is likely to be enough to discourage opportunism), and they can tie the decision maker's compensation to measures of firm performance.

These approaches have serious drawbacks. Since it is possible to wrongly conclude that a decision maker is behaving opportunistically, driving up the severity of punishment can drive up a decision maker's risk exposure. The more risk-averse the decision maker is, the more likely this risk exposure will induce his decisions to be made to minimize the likelihood of making a mistake, or of being wrongly accused of self-serving behavior, rather than made to maximize expected profitability. Employing decision makers who are highly risk-averse is a prescription for bureaucratic rather than entrepreneurial decision making.

Performance based compensation is no panacea. The larger the firm and the farther from top-level management a decision maker is, the more irrelevant are incentives derived from performance-based pay because the marginal effect on firm profits of any decision they make will be swamped by the marginal effects of other decision makers.[18] Even in smaller firms, or with performance measures that are more focused (e.g., sales goals rather than profits), there is the additional problem that other random factors also affect firm performance, so the decision maker bears this additional risk which, in turn, requires more compensation than otherwise. Conversely, not relying on performance-based compensation, because one can trust that the best decision will be made because the decision maker is trustworthy, results in decision making that is more entrepreneurial in nature up and down the firm's hierarchy.

There is another way that firms can protect themselves from third-degree opportunism. A hallmark of institutions is that they produce regularity in transaction behavior. Institutions therefore discourage individuals from behaving opportunistically in part by regularizing activity through routines, rules, and procedures that make it difficult, and in some cases impossible, to engage in opportunism. When transaction behavior follows a set routine, assurance is derived in part from the fact that everyone appears to be doing things as expected, the way they were done before, when no one was victimized by opportunistic behavior. It is, after all, hard to engage in opportunism if one sticks to a routine that evolved precisely because opportunism is so difficult when that routine is followed. By fastidiously sticking to established routines, individuals are able to signal that they have no opportunistic intentions.

The problem is that limiting decision-making discretion by regularizing economic activity through strict procedures, routines, rules, and so forth reduces the firm's ability to quickly adapt to changing circumstances by acting on local knowledge. This is the very problem that delegating discretion through relational contracts was meant to solve. Such measures force firms to ignore local knowledge that could produce better decisions. The larger the firm, the more problematic this is. Large firms will, therefore, inevitably be bureaucratic firms. There will be no large yet *thoroughly* entrepreneurial firms.[19]

Institutions are tremendously important, but the prudential restraint they effectuate is simply not sufficient to deal with the problem of third-degree opportunism, a problem made worse by the large group size upon which general prosperity depends. So the more effectively a society can address the problem of opportunism, the larger it and the groups, organizations, and firms that comprise it can grow, while also making decisions in an entrepreneurial manner throughout their hierarchies.

GOLDEN OPPORTUNITIES AND TRUST

If a decision maker is convinced that he will not be detected if he chooses an action like c rather than an action like d, then institutional approaches will be rendered moot if the only reason why he is reluctant to behave opportunistically is that it is imprudent to do so. Such a decision maker will always act on any golden opportunity. Golden opportunities are of particular importance to the study of trust precisely because they cannot be addressed by institutions. In societies in which trustworthiness can only be based on prudential restraint, it follows that firms cannot combat golden opportunities that naturally arise in the context of relational contracts. This dramatically limits the ability to use relational contracts to fullest effect in such societies, because decision makers cannot be trusted with the authority to act on the local knowledge they possess.

Robert Frank (1988) was the first social scientist to clearly point out the limitations of prudential restraint in his book, *Passions Within Reason*. He explained that since prudential restraint works through external incentives that require some possibility of detection, as a matter of logic it cannot deal with golden opportunities. Since genuine trust is really about being able to depend on others even if they may be presented golden opportunities, this means that genuine trust cannot be based solely on the rational expectation of prudential restraint. Frank concluded that genuine trust must, therefore, ultimately be based on the rational expectation of trustworthiness derived from moral tastes that produce moral, rather than merely prudential, restraint.

In societies in which trustworthiness can only be based on prudential restraint, relational contracts will not be sufficiently flexible to afford the efficient use of local knowledge where it is needed most—in large firms that undertake highly complex production under conditions of uncertainty. As a result, social welfare losses will result that are analogous to the losses described by Hayek in his discussion of how market pricing alleviates the problem of local knowledge across the whole of society. The flexibility of relational contracts is antithetical to the regularity that is the hallmark of institutions. This, in conjunction with principals' inability to evaluate the functional competency and moral propriety of decisions, is why relational contracts are so dependent on trustworthiness. To employ relational contracts to fullest effect a society must somehow find a way to sustain trustworthiness that goes beyond prudential restraint.

Since size, complexity, and uncertainty all contribute to the localization of knowledge, it follows that the inability to use relational contracts to fullest effect forces a tradeoff between size, complexity, and uncertainty. This has the effect of limiting the size of the firm, especially if the production process is complex and/or the environment is highly uncertain. It follows that if opportunism is only combated via prudential restraint based on external incentives, then firms will, on average, be smaller, less complex, more regimented, and more bureaucratic than otherwise. Similarly, since size contributes to each of these problems, it follows that the larger firms are, the simpler their production process will have to be and/or the less flexible their procedures and decision making will have to be and/or the more risk-averse their decision makers will have to be.

This may explain why in many societies the only large firms that exist are those whose production is not complex, such as firms that produce intermediate goods. It follows that if it was rational to always expect trustworthiness on the part of decision makers, these tradeoffs could be avoided. This is a fundamental problem for economic development because if large firms are only viable with respect to noncomplex production, then the ability to create prosperity through multi-stage production is severely curtailed.

In order to avoid the tradeoff between size, production complexity, and uncertainty, what is needed is a means of eliminating the commons dilemma incentives that drive the problem of third-degree opportunism. This makes it possible for firm owners to mediate activity within firms through relational contracts, because they can trust decision makers not to take advantage of golden opportunities that inevitably present themselves when knowledge is highly localized. What is needed, then, is a basis for trust derived from the rational expectation that decision makers will be trustworthy irrespective of incentives, for anything less leaves the door open for third-degree opportunism, particularly in the case of golden opportunities.

If a way can be found to produce such trustworthiness, then firms can be large, engage in complex production, cope with uncertainty, and employ decision makers who are not especially risk-averse, because their reluctance to behave opportunistically is not derived from external incentives but from moral restraint based on the belief that opportunism is simply wrong. Analogous to how prices alleviate the problem of local knowledge across the whole of society, such morally grounded trustworthiness could potentially alleviate the problem of local knowledge within firms, thereby making it possible to employ relational contracts to fullest effect.[20]

Conversely, in societies in which prudential restraint is all one can hope for, there will be little third-degree opportunism, but not because people lack the inclination to behave opportunistically. It will be because in such societies, firms employ governance structures that do not afford the discretion needed to engage in third-degree opportunism. Routines will be precisely scripted and managers will possess far less discretion. Managerial decisions that do not comport with well-established routines and guidelines will be viewed with suspicion. But the price for combating third-degree opportunism in this way is every bit as huge as it is hard to see. It is huge because it represents a monumental loss of efficiency through failure to fully make use of local knowledge possessed by decision makers. The larger is the firm and the more complex is the production process, the truer this is.

Consider, for example, the economic environment in the United States. Despite having a sophisticated legal system with ample resources for contract enforcement, if all citizens woke up one morning feeling no compunction to refrain from opportunism, much economic activity would grind to a halt as every golden opportunity would be acted on. Although over time institutions would respond with more detailed contracts, tighter laws, more lawyers, more vigorous enforcement, and stronger punishments to act as a substitute for the absence of moral restraint, this would come at a high cost. In my view, because the potential harm done by opportunists is so great, we tend to give it a great amount of attention. But in doing so we are inclined to underestimate how much we actually trust each other—especially relative to how much people trust each other in most of the rest of the world. We also underestimate how dependent we are on the ability to trust each other to engage in daily economic activity.

In most of the world the idea of working in a firm in which nearly everyone is trusted with a great deal of discretion is unfathomable. In most of the world, third-degree opportunism is combated through institutional preclusion, yet firms no doubt think they are entrepreneurial because they are so focused on profit.

They are not aware of their lack of flexibility, adaptability, or innovativeness, because they were not raised in a society in which such things are taken for granted. Knowing no better, they likely think themselves to be very entrepreneurial because they equate entrepreneurship with profit seeking.

To summarize, if firm owners can trust their decision makers to not take advantage of their discretionary decision authority, then very large firms can undertake very complex production under conditions of uncertainty without sacrificing efficiency by throwing away local knowledge. Just as market prices alleviated the problem of local knowledge across the whole of society, relational contracts that confer discretionary decision authority to those who possess local knowledge alleviate the problem of local knowledge within firms. The connection between solving this problem and prosperity is very fundamental, for it is specialized production that makes prosperity possible but it is specialization that inevitably leads to the localization of knowledge.

The Solution

How can firms combat third-degree opportunism so decision makers can be delegated sufficient decision-making discretion and authority to make full use of the local knowledge they possess? The answer is that the unwillingness to behave opportunistically must come from something other than prudential restraint.

Recall that for a given opportunistic act, x_i, we can define the net utility resulting from action i as:

$$V(x_i) = U(z(x_i)) - C(x_i),$$

where $C()$ accounts for the cost in utility units of taking action x_i. The $C()$ term accounts for the effects of incentives derived from the expected cost of retaliation, of a ruined reputation, and perhaps even of feelings of embarrassment and shame. All of these potential costs require detection to trigger sanctions. This puts much of third-degree opportunism beyond the reach of institutions, especially when the likelihood of detection is very low or zero, as it is in the case of golden opportunities.

Prudential restraint clearly works through external incentives derived from the cost side of the rational choice model. Frank's point really comes down to saying that for restraint to be applicable to golden opportunities, it cannot be a matter of incentives because they require external triggers, so it must therefore be derived from the other side of the rational choice model; that is, through tastes. In short, "moral restraint" essentially means "beyond merely prudential restraint." The key idea is that because moral tastes are antecedent to rational decision making, they have nothing to do with external incentives and therefore nothing to do with prudence or rationality.

Suppose that individuals possess moral tastes that correspond to their believing that a given action is not merely ill-advised, it is morally wrong. Frank argued that someone who held such tastes and who also experienced involuntary emotions of guilt whenever he did things he believed to be morally wrong, would effectively assure others that he can be trusted. This is especially true if such emotions involuntarily produced signals that others could observe (e.g., a person who has a reputation for blushing even when fibbing in a joke is someone others will be likely to assume is telling the truth when he doesn't blush). Since one need not be caught to experience feelings of guilt, if emotional signals that betray feelings of guilt are involuntary, then we have a mechanism that works even if golden opportunities might arise.

Let's now push this argument a little further. For example, suppose that

$$C(x_i) = C_p(x_i) + C_M(x_i),$$

where C_p represents costs that even a merely prudent person would consider because they are derived from incentives produced by the expected costs of external mechanisms (e.g., the expected cost of sanction, the expected cost of retaliation, the expected cost of a ruined reputation, and feelings of shame). The C_p therefore produces prudential restraint. The C_M term, however, represents costs derived from feelings of guilt for having behaved in what one believes to be an immoral way. The C_M term can potentially provide a basis for trust that can reduce the threat of third-degree opportunism even when a golden opportunity presents itself.

It is irrational for one to behave opportunistically if he knows the disutility he will endure from experiencing involuntary feelings of guilt will more than offset the utility he expects to gain from the payoff *even if there is a zero probability of detection*. Such an individual can be rationally regarded by others as being unconditionally trustworthy because, given his moral tastes, it is rational for him to refrain from acting even on golden opportunities. One way to solve the problem of third-degree opportunism, then, is to eliminate the commons dilemma altogether by driving the C_M term so high that such opportunism is simply irrational. This is a very fundamental and comprehensive solution to the problem of opportunism, because driving up the C_M term works for all forms of opportunism and golden opportunities. If decision makers can be made to feel sufficiently guilty for behaving in opportunistic ways, firms will be able to trust decision makers throughout the firm's hierarchy to make the best decision on behalf of the firm, even when it is impossible for higher-level managers to question it.

Recall that the inability to genuinely trust decision makers effectively forces a tradeoff between firm size and *efficient* use of local knowledge. This is why in low trust societies we can find entrepreneurial firms but they will be small, and we can find large firms but they will be bureaucratic, but we will find no large and *thoroughly entrepreneurial* firms. But if those who possess local knowledge can be trusted to refrain from acting on golden opportunities, there is hope that even large firms will make full use of local knowledge by delegating decision-making authority up and down the firm's hierarchy without fear that their inability to monitor decision makers won't come back to haunt them. More generally, this produces a society that is qualitatively different, in that it is uniquely suited for large group cooperation under changing conditions.

I have explained why there is no substitute for eliminating the commons dilemma associated with opportunistic behavior through internalized moral restraint. Moral tastes are therefore of potentially fundamental importance to the development and operation of a market society, and should therefore be of great interest to all social scientists. Robert Frank made this point over two decades ago. Now, the question is what kinds of moral beliefs are required to do this to fullest effect? Answering this question is a surprisingly difficult task. The next four chapters explain why.

CHAPTER 4

Moral Values

> . . . *persons motivated to pursue self-interest are often for that reason doomed to fail. They fail because they cannot solve commitment problems. These problems can often be solved by persons known to have abandoned the quest for maximum material advantage. The emotions that lead people to behave in seemingly irrational ways can thus indirectly lead to greater material well-being.*—Robert Frank, 1988, p. 258

Introduction

Larger group size increases the gains from specialization, and therefore the level of general prosperity, but it also worsens the problem of opportunism. In the last chapter, I argued that what was needed to address this problem was moral rather than prudential restraint, because only an internalized form of restraint can address golden opportunities. I proposed guilt as a plausible psychological mechanism for producing such internalized restrain. But to feel guilty about doing something, one has to believe it is wrong. Since it is our moral values that determine what we regard as wrong, I now turn to the issue of moral values.

Although I am not telling a story to fit the facts, this does not mean that there are no constraints whatsoever on how to proceed. It accomplishes nothing to answer questions by assuming the existence of psychological mechanisms that humans do not possess, or by assuming behavior that conflicts significantly with psychological mechanisms that humans do possess. Identifying a particular kind of moral belief that best supports the development and operation of a market economy, if it requires people to think or act in ways that are contrary to their basic nature, is nothing more than an academic exercise. It is, therefore, imperative that our thought experiment obey the constraint of taking humans as they actually are, and not as we posit or wish them to be.[1]

I posit that in most cases what keeps us from behaving opportunistically, even in circumstances in which we believe there is no chance of being caught, is that we know we will feel guilty if we do so. We will feel guilty because we regard such behavior as wrong. But guilt is generally ignored in economic models of behavior. This is not because models of rational behavior cannot accommodate guilt; guilt simply has not received much attention. This is curious, for as any normally functioning human knows, the cost of experiencing feelings of guilt can be terrible indeed.

Perhaps guilt has not received much attention from those who study economic behavior because guilt is an emotional response. Since we normally view emotionalism as being antithetical to rationality, it seems unnatural to think of guilt in the context of rational decision making. But if feelings of guilt are not rationally chosen by the individual any more than one's favorite color is, then there is no conflict or contradiction. In such a case, guilt is antecedent to rational decision making and therefore the psychological mechanisms of guilt are primary to the process of rational decision making.

It follows, then, that there is nothing irrational about experiencing feelings of guilt or responding to feelings of guilt, just as there is nothing irrational about eating candy because it gives us pleasure to do so. We eat candy that we know is not good for us because our taste for candy is antecedent to rational decision making. Of course, this begs the question of where such moral tastes might come from (more to the point, where such moral beliefs might come from), but we must set aside that important question for now. We will return to it in Chapter 10.

If person A, *for a given set of transactions*, believes that opportunism is irrational for B because the expected guilt costs borne by B will be too high, then it is rational for A to conclude that B can be trusted over that set of transactions even if it is impossible to determine later what B actually did. Guilt can therefore provide a basis for trust even with respect to relational contracts, within which golden opportunities frequently arise because decision makers have been entrusted with discretion in order to support entrepreneurial rather than bureaucratic decision making. In short, the big problem facing societies that want to maximize general prosperity is opportunism and the big solution to that problem is guilt.[2] What we feel guilty about, and why we feel guilty about it, matters a great deal. Moral beliefs are of central importance because moral beliefs answer these questions. In what follows, I will explore how value systems determine what we feel guilty about. In later chapters I will explain why a value system must be logically organized in a rather specific way to produce feelings of guilt where it is needed most.

Value Systems

The phrase *value system* is often used but rarely defined. There is no generally accepted definition. Ideological values are generally recognized to be an important part of any society's value system. Here our focus is on moral values, not ideological ones, so we limit our attention to what would more accurately be called *the moral value system*. In addition, the kind of economic behavior that promotes general prosperity is social in nature. Realizing the gains from specialization requires that we cooperate and exchange with others. A prosperous market economy is largely a social enterprise. As a result, moral values that do not pertain to social behavior are not important for understanding the role morality plays in the development and operation of market economy. We therefore further limit our attention to *social* moral values.[3]

There are two parts to any social moral value system: the moral values that comprise it, and the nature of the relationships among them. It is natural to think of differences between social moral value systems as being principally a matter of differences in social moral values. There is no doubt that in many cases, something that is positively valued in one society (e.g., circumcising Jewish males) might not be positively valued in another (circumcising males in hunter-gather societies). Similarly, something that is negatively valued in one society (cutting one's hair and thereby angering the rain god) might not be negatively valued in another (societies that do not believe there is a connection between hair length and rain). Historically there has been much emphasis on such differences, and many continue to view differences in social moral value systems as primarily a matter of differences in their respective sets of social moral values.[4]

Increasingly, however, social scientists believe that these differences are not nearly as important as the way value systems relate moral values to one another. This should be particularly true with respect to economic activity, because in the context of normal economic activity the same sets of actions are generally viewed negatively and positively across nearly all societies. But there can still be substantial differences in *how strongly* members of a given society or culture feel about the same specific moral values. Significant differences also exist with respect to the moral beliefs that give rise to the set of moral values. In other words, even though people from every society may agree that stealing is wrong, the rationale given for why it is wrong varies substantially across societies and cultures.[5] In any case, it is now generally accepted that if there are interesting differences to be found between value systems, they are more likely to be found in differences in how moral beliefs affect the logical structure of the value system, and thereby affect the relationships among moral values.

Conventional wisdom today emphasizes the ordering of moral values by strength of moral importance or urgency, so the presumption is that moral behavior differs across societies because there are differences in the ordering and weighting of the moral values that we all share. This is certainly less chauvinistic than believing that societies are differentiated by differences in their sets of moral values. But I shall argue later that this "modern" approach is nevertheless based on an overly simple framework, one that is nothing more than a logical extension of our hardwired moral intuitions.

Modern approaches that, I will argue later, are derived rather directly from our hardwired moral sensibilities, implicitly treat moral values as differing only in algebraic sign and moral weight. Moral values are therefore implicitly arrayed on a number line, where those that correspond to not undertaking negative moral actions are to the left of zero, and those that correspond to undertaking positive moral actions are to the right of zero. Moral values that pertain to discouraging acts that are negative in nature are, therefore, functionally nothing more than the negation of moral values that pertain to encouraging acts that are positive in nature. Modern theories contend that which actions are viewed as positive or negative is very similar across societies. This is a very plausible supposition with regard to economic behavior.

But this also means that differences in moral value systems are largely due to differences in where moral values are placed on a single number line relative to one another. The modern approach therefore implicitly frames moral thinking in a way that inevitably leads one to the conclusion that the way to solve any specific problem of moral choice is by increasing moral earnestness with respect to the relevant moral value. This amounts to the popular exhortation to try harder to "do the right thing." But social behavior is complex, and the circumstances within which such behavior happens are constantly changing in unpredictable ways. So it is impossible for a one-dimensional ordering of moral values to cover all possible events without producing outcomes that are either ridiculous, or that conflict profoundly with our hardwired moral intuitions. Often, the ordering produces outcomes we refuse to accept, so the modern approach inevitably requires that many scenarios be viewed as dilemmas that can only be dealt with subjectively or as exceptions. This produces so many "exceptions" in the modern approach that the meaning of the word is stretched beyond recognition.

This emphasis on moral dilemmas that require subjective moral judgments, or require endless exceptions, creates the impression that proper moral reasoning is inherently subtle, nuanced, and sophisticated. This presents a major problem for modern theories of morality, because not everyone is able or inclined to devote a scholar's attention to moral decision making. It seems that for any moral belief, and value system derived therefrom, to work well—to provide clear standards of behavior that nearly all understand and can expect others to understand—it must produce the same set of moral conclusions over a very wide set of circumstances and people.

In Chapters 5–7, I explain why insufficient moral sophistication is not the problem that a society needs to solve to enjoy a condition of general prosperity. We will find that the need for nuanced moral reasoning in the modern approach is actually a byproduct of a specific theory of morality, one that is as common as it is old, one that comes naturally to us because it is derived directly from hardwired moral intuitions. Furthermore, these hardwired moral intuitions constitute atavisms in the modern, market economy within which much economic activity must occur in very large groups so as to enjoy the gains from economies of scale. As such, the modern approach provides an inadequate foundation for the fullest development and most efficient operation of a market economy. It is the application of a primitive approach to moral reasoning to our complex and large group world that produces the need for discussion of countless dilemmas and exceptions.

The emphasis on weighting in the modern approach also suggests that differences in economic performance across societies are the result of differences in the average level of moral earnestness of the individuals in those societies. If the only differences between value systems are the weights assigned to moral values, and if morality plays an important role in development and operation of an economy capable of producing general prosperity, then one must conclude that what explains differences in the economic performance of societies is that some societies are just not as moral as others. Since such a conclusion is painful, advocates of the modern approach generally discourage frank discussion of how cultural differences might explain performance differences.

A Framework for Analyzing Social Moral Values

Which moral values matter most for achieving the condition of general prosperity? As noted above, the kind of economic behavior that contributes most to prosperity is social in nature. Our attention is therefore fixed on how an individual's behavior affects the welfare of others, because others are not likely to be concerned with behavior that does not affect their welfare in any way. Behavior that does not affect the welfare of others is taken to be morally neutral, and is ignored in what follows.

Since our attention is directed to those behaviors that increase or decrease the welfare of others, the set of social moral values naturally divides itself into two mutually exclusive and exhaustive subsets. The first subset contains those moral values that encourage *positive moral actions*, which I define as actions that are generally regarded as "nice, good, right, or moral" because they nearly always increase the welfare of others. Moral values that exhort us to undertake positive moral actions are called *moral exhortations*. Colloquially, they are the "moral do's."

The second subset contains those moral values that discourage *negative moral actions*, which I define as actions that are generally regarded as "mean, evil, wrong, or immoral" because they nearly always reduce the welfare of others. Moral values that prohibit us from taking negative moral actions are called *moral prohibitions*. Colloquially, they are the "moral don'ts." In a nutshell, being moral *in a social context* is about doing the moral do's, and not doing the moral don'ts.[6]

ADAM SMITH AND THE EMERGENCE OF SOCIAL MORAL VALUES

Our actions increase, decrease, or leave unchanged the welfare of others, so specific actions can be categorized as those that are, respectively, positive, negative, or neutral. What is the nature of the relationship between these actions and moral values *per se*? In *The Theory of Moral Sentiments*, Adam Smith provided a framework for understanding how moral standards emerge with which people in a given society can evaluate the moral behavior of others and themselves.[7] An argument similar to Smith's is employed here to explain how moral values emerge to encourage positive moral actions and discourage negative moral actions, and to explain why differences between value systems are not likely the result of differences in the set of moral values that comprise them.

Suppose B undertakes an action, y, and as a result, A's welfare is increased. Individual A naturally comes to regard B as a good person, as do others who observed B's action. The greater the cost born by B to do y, the stronger is this conclusion. The idea of goodness is attached to B, and B is deemed to be "good." Over time, however, it becomes obvious that the welfare of those around whoever does y is nearly always increased. Over time, too, the recipients of such benefits begin to associate the quality of goodness with y itself. The idea of goodness therefore becomes increasingly attached to y. So while the reason we came to regard y as a positive moral action was ultimately consequentialist in nature, even in those cases when doing y does *not* improve welfare we still view y itself in a positive light. In other words, we effectively adopt a moral rule of thumb that categorizes y as a positive moral act, even though in some cases it may turn out that the affected party's welfare is actually decreased.

Consider sharing food. Sharing food with those who are hungry does not always help others, of course, but it nearly always does. So, given our cognitive limitations, it is efficient to adopt a moral rule of thumb that regards sharing food with those who are hungry as a positive moral action, rather than treating every opportunity to share food as an open moral question. Parents know that while there may be exceptions to this rule of thumb, treating every instance as an open question is too likely to invite confusion. In short, the moral rule of thumb that "food sharing is good" keeps things simple.

Conversely, suppose B undertakes an action, x, and as a result, A's welfare is decreased. Individual A naturally comes to regard B as a bad person, as do others who observed B's action. The more harm that doing x causes A, the stronger is this conclusion. The idea of badness is attached to B, and B is deemed to be "bad." Over time, however, it becomes obvious that regardless of who does x, the welfare of those around the actor is nearly always decreased. Over time, those harmed by x begin to also associate the quality of badness with x itself. The idea of badness therefore becomes increasingly attached to x. So while the reason we came to regard x as a negative moral action was ultimately consequentialist in nature, we still tend to view x itself in a negative light, even in those rare cases when doing x does no harm. In other words, we effectively adopt a moral rule of thumb categorizing x as a negative moral act, even though in some cases it may turn out that the affected party's welfare is actually increased.

Consider stealing. Stealing does not always harm others, of course, but it nearly always does. So, given our cognitive limitations, it is efficient to adopt a moral rule of thumb that regards stealing from others as a negative moral action, rather than treating every opportunity to steal as an open moral question. Parents know that while there may be exceptions to this rule of thumb, treating every instance as an open question invites confusion. In short, the moral rule of thumb that "stealing is bad" keeps things simple. After all, in the small group society in which these norms evolved, stealing probably did harm another person at least 99% of the time. In contrast to positive moral actions, parents have a particularly strong incentive to insure that their offspring internalize moral values that regard actions that generally reduce the welfare of others as categorically wrong, because it is easy to underestimate the likelihood of detection and the cost of losing one's good reputation. All parents know that children and young adults tend to underestimate both.

The discussion above explains how a consensus can emerge to regard a given set of actions as positive moral actions or negative moral actions. The actions themselves come to be regarded as good or bad, respectively, because they nearly always bring about good outcomes or bad outcomes, respectively, for others. Since the same actions tend to bring about good outcomes in nearly all societies (sharing food, giving to charities, helping a neighbor, etc.) and the same actions tend to bring about bad outcomes in nearly all societies (lying, stealing, murder, etc.), the set of positive moral actions and the set of negative moral actions is nearly identical across most societies. But a list of positive and negative *moral actions* does not a set of *moral values* make. Moral values are not just about categorizing behavior—they are about assigning weights (value) to various kinds of actions. Smith's framework also sheds light on this process.

When B acts in a way that benefits those around B, the welfare of those around B is increased. This is good for those around B, and those around B naturally approve of such actions because they stand to benefit from such behavior in the future. Smith argued that people are naturally predisposed to be very sensitive to such expressions of approval.[8] Smith's argument comports with principles of behaviorism, since expressions of approval by those around B effectively reinforce such actions to increase their frequency. Such actions (e.g., B defends his tribe from murderous raiders) may be rewarded through positive reinforcement (e.g., B is accorded high social status or given control over more of the tribe's resources), or may be rewarded through negative reinforcement (e.g., the removal of unpleasant responsibilities—a hero does not take out the trash).[9]

Conversely, when B acts in a way that harms those around B, the welfare of those around B is decreased. This is bad for those around B, and those around B naturally disapprove of such actions. Smith argued that people were also very sensitive to expressions of disapproval. Obviously, if the harm done to those around B is substantial, disapproval can take the form of outright retaliation. In general, the stronger the expression of disapproval by those around B toward B, the more likely retaliation will occur so B would do well to pay close attention to expressions of disapproval. This also comports with the principles of behaviorism since those around B will punish B for taking such harmful actions, in an attempt to reduce their frequency. Such actions (e.g., B steals seed corn from a common store in the middle of a harsh winter) may be punished through positive punishment (e.g., being publicly whipped) or through negative punishment (e.g., the removal of normal rights and privileges—house arrest).

It is not difficult to imagine that the welfare effect on others of certain types of behaviors inevitably leads them to respond in ways that lead to conditioning effects that alter the frequency of those behaviors. But whereas behaviorism only asserts that a greater frequency of positive moral action will result from approval, Smith would argue that it is in our nature to want to be the kind of person whose own sense of morality is in harmony with the moral sensibilities of those around us. For this reason, we naturally internalize these sentiments in the form of moral values.

The reinforcement of positive moral actions through approval will also affect the person's sense of what is morally appropriate, not only for others but also for the individual himself with respect to how he evaluates his own actions. His own "internal spectator" will begin to provide approval even when others aren't looking and, in so doing, positive moral actions will become a source of happiness and esteem even when others aren't looking. In short, the individual will develop tastes that comport with what others generally regard as positive moral action. In this way, a pattern of consistent approval by others of our positive moral actions has the effect of inducing us to adopt exhortations to undertake such actions as our own internalized moral values. Similarly, a pattern of consistent disapproval by others of our negative moral actions has the effect of inducing us to adopt exhortations to refrain from undertaking such actions as our own internalized moral values.

The strength and frequency of approval for the former, and the strength and frequency of disapproval for the latter, will directly affect the moral weight associated with any given action, effectively transforming it from a list of permissible and impermissible actions to a list of moral values. Parents understand this, which is why they engage in moral training. Parents want their children to be successful, and to be valued by those around them (which is more likely to happen if they undertake positive moral actions), as well as want them to avoid the costs of retaliation and a ruined reputation (which is more likely to happen if they undertake negative moral actions). Parents therefore inculcate moral values that support these actions, striving to make such moral values a part of their child's character—that is, a product of their child's moral tastes—and they strengthen and cultivate these tastes to make them robust.

To summarize, over time, certain actions are seen to *nearly always* help those around the actor and are therefore encouraged by them, while others are seen to *nearly always* harm those around the actor and are therefore discouraged by them. One way individuals stay out of trouble is to just follow established moral rules of thumb that prohibit taking actions that are recognized by everyone to nearly always harm others. In this way, something like stealing becomes part of the set of negative moral actions. There are circumstances in which stealing is not wrong, but it is more efficient to have a rule of thumb that says it is inherently wrong, and then deal with exceptions as they arise, than it is to say every instance of stealing is an open moral question. Parents know this and teach their children accordingly.

Properties of Moral Exhortations and Moral Prohibitions

I noted above that conventional approaches to the study of value systems tend to lead us to view positive moral actions as merely the negation of negative moral actions. It should be emphasized here that this a consequence of the approach employed in modern analysis, not a consequence of the nature of moral actions *per se*. What differentiates moral actions is not whether they are expressed in positive or negative language, but whether an action can be expected to increase or decrease the welfare of others.[10] In what follows, I discuss the properties of moral exhortations and moral prohibitions, to highlight important differences between them, differences that will prove important later.

MORAL EXHORTATIONS

Moral exhortations tell us what we should do if we are to be moral. To be meaningful, moral exhortations must encourage us to do things for others that are costly to us (if they aren't costly, or the benefit to us exceeds the cost, then there is no need for a moral invocation; such actions are compelled by prudent self-interest). Moral exhortations do not prescribe specific actions. For example, the moral exhortations to "be generous" or "be compassionate" may induce you to give a beggar money, but they do not tell you how much to give. These moral exhortations only tell you it is good to give him something because it is good to be generous and compassionate. Beyond that, these moral exhortations only tell you that it is perhaps better to give him more rather than less, while leaving unanswered the question of how generous is generous enough. Moral exhortations therefore do not entail specific, well-defined acts like "always salute a superior officer."

As a general matter, moral exhortations do not tell us how much of a positive moral action is required to fulfill a generally accepted standard of moral propriety. There are different levels of generosity, and what *A* might think is appropriately generous in a given circumstance, *B* might find inadequate or excessive. Because moral exhortations are matters of degree, there is simply no objective basis for determining the proper place to stop on the continuum of generosity. People can honestly disagree over what constitutes a proper level of generosity in any given circumstance; there is no basis for saying one opinion is right and the other wrong. How generous is *generous enough* is therefore fundamentally subjective. It really is just an opinion. It might be a thoughtful opinion, a sincere opinion, an educated opinion, an earnest opinion, an opinion we strongly approve of, but it is still ultimately just an opinion, a matter of personal taste.

So even if there is widespread agreement across and within societies about what should be morally exhorted because there is agreement as to what constitutes the set of positive moral actions, there may be substantial disagreement across societies— and even within societies, among close friends, and among family members—as to how much is enough in any given circumstance. Encouraging one to be *completely* generous is meaningless, because generosity is unbounded, but resources are finite. Indeed, to be generous to the extent of using all of one's resources implies that no resources will be put toward the obedience of other moral exhortations. Because moral exhortations require action, and action requires resources, moral exhortations force us to choose between competing positive moral actions.

What accounts for differences in such moral judgments regarding moral exhortations? It is tempting to view such differences in intensity of desire to promote the welfare of others as being reflective of nothing more than differences in the morality of individuals. But while some people may be more generally concerned about the welfare of others, even among those who have the same level of concern there can be substantial disagreement regarding which positive moral actions are appropriate in a given circumstance. For example, even if A and B are equally moral, by whatever measure one cares to apply, A might think it is much more important to feed the poor today than it is to protect the environment for future generations, while B thinks the opposite is true. There is simply no objective basis for saying one is right and the other is wrong.

It would therefore be mistaken to infer that a lower level of giving to a needy person by B than by A is an indication that B has a lower level of general morality. Instead, it may merely be an indication of differences in moral tastes. Where B stops on the continuum of moral action is therefore not only affected by his level of morality as reflected by his general level of concern for others, it is also affected by the relative importance of that *specific* positive moral action to other positive moral actions by its relative weight among the set of all of B's moral values. There is simply no objective basis for defining either the general level of concern for others or the relative importance of any given positive moral value. The level of positive moral action that is appropriate in any given circumstance is by nature subjective, so it is generally inaccurate to infer one's general level of moral earnestness from such actions.

MORAL PROHIBITIONS

Moral prohibitions tell us what we shouldn't do if we are to be moral. Unlike moral exhortations, one either obeys or disobeys any given moral prohibition, so moral prohibitions are not matters of degree. Whereas moral exhortations do not prescribe specific positive moral actions, moral prohibitions rather sharply proscribe very specific negative moral actions. For example, the moral prohibition "don't steal" tells one clearly not to steal. Unlike the moral exhortation "be kind," there is no quibbling about whether the prohibition was obeyed or not. Unlike kindness, one either stole or did not; it is not a matter of degree. Because they are qualitative in nature, it is therefore possible for moral prohibitions to provide an objective moral standard for appropriate moral behavior.

There may be disagreement about the level of harm, and therefore the proper level of punishment for having disobeyed a given moral prohibition. But a difference in the level of harm does not mean that the violation of a prohibition is not qualitative, and therefore not objective. There may also be disagreement about whether the available evidence is sufficient to conclude that a moral prohibition has been violated. But the fact that evidence can be a matter of degree (two eye witnesses are more compelling than one) does not mean that the violation itself is a matter of degree. Under perfect information, there will be no debate about whether a moral prohibition was obeyed or not; fulfilling the moral requirement to obey the prohibition is categorical and clear. Under perfect information, reasonable people will not disagree over whether A stole something from C. There can be disagreement over the *moral weight* that should be attributed to these actions, but that is not a debate over what is immoral, it is a debate over how immoral the action is. Conversely, even under perfect information, in many cases reasonable people can disagree over whether A was sufficiently generous to C.

There is also no objective basis for asserting that a failure to obey a moral exhortation constitutes an instance of immoral behavior; it just means that the individual involved is less moral than he might have otherwise been. Failure to obey a moral prohibition, however, does constitute an objective instance of immoral behavior. But while you can make yourself more moral by pursuing a moral exhortations more fully, you cannot make yourself more moral by obeying moral prohibitions more fully because they are categorical—they are either obeyed, or not. With respect to moral prohibitions, then, you are either moral because you obeyed the prohibition, or immoral because you did not. With respect to moral exhortations, however, there is no objective basis for asserting that you are immoral, but doing more positive moral acts (or pursuing the same set to greater degree) is obviously more moral than doing less.

Because positive moral action requires resources, and resources are finite, moral exhortations force us to choose, so except in very rare circumstances, it is not possible to have a universal standard for behavior with respect to moral exhortations. An important exception is a situation in which *not* undertaking a positive moral action would be construed as depraved indifference. But a closer look at the nature of such a situation reveals that this is basically an exception that proves the rule. It is precisely those actions that produce large benefits to others (specifically in the form of averting harm), at little or no cost to the actor, that we regard as imperative even though they are positive in nature. This is because even if one were completely unconcerned about any other person's welfare, any non-zero probability of reciprocation would imply that the dominant strategy would still be to provide help in such a circumstance. Not providing help would, therefore, be most revealing indeed.[11]

In any case, the fact that resources are required to undertake positive moral actions, and we therefore cannot reasonably expect everyone to abide by a specific standard of behavior, is not a problem for moral prohibitions. Moral prohibitions require inaction, not action. Whereas action requires resources, inaction does not. One can therefore "not lie" to an infinitely long list of individuals without running out of resources. Obeying moral prohibitions may be costly in the sense that one forgoes the chance to engage in opportunism, but it is always feasible, so a universal standard is possible and expecting others to live up to it is meaningful.

Implications for Economic Behavior—
Moral Exhortations

What role might economic exhortations play with respect to economic behavior? The only way an economic transaction can increase the welfare of all parties to it is when it produces a surplus. By surplus, I mean the value of the transaction exceeds the sum of the opportunity costs to all parties involved.

Transactions can be either based on the gains from cooperation or the gains from exchange. Consider A and B, who can cooperate with one another to produce something. Alone A makes 10 units and alone B makes 10 units, but if they cooperate they make 26 units. The value of cooperating (the surplus) is six units of output—their cooperative output minus the sum of outputs from producing in isolation $(10 + 10 = 20)$.[12] Now consider the surplus associated with exchange. Suppose A has one unit of X, which he values at $10, and B has one unit of Y, which he values at $10. If A values one Y at $14 and B values one X at $14, by exchanging, both give up something worth $10 to get something worth $14. The surplus of this transaction is obviously 8 $(= 28–10–10)$.[13]

It is through such surpluses that the value of output is increased per capita, so it is through such surpluses that a society can increase its general prosperity. Put another way, transactions facilitate specialization, which increases productivity, thereby making it possible to produce more output per capita than otherwise. The gains from specialization are therefore realized through transactions.

It is the expectation of a surplus that provides the impetus for voluntary transactions. The larger is the surplus, the more each party's welfare can be increased by the transaction so the stronger are incentives for all parties to it to undertake it. This also means that those transactions that produce the largest increase in output per capita are the transactions we are most strongly induced to undertake. Conversely, transactions that are not expected to produce a surplus will not be undertaken if transactions are voluntary.

Clearly, voluntary transactions must be expected to produce a surplus, and therefore provide ample incentive to be undertaken. Given the performance of market economies relative to all known alternatives, the economic transactions that typically occur in them apparently do provide ample incentive to be undertaken. This does not mean that every transaction that could have contributed to general prosperity was necessarily undertaken. Perhaps some transactions that did not occur could have increased net social welfare if they had been encouraged through moral exhortations. But for that to be the case—that there is a transaction that would not be undertaken, but would nevertheless add to net social welfare—we would have to explain why economic agents were less able to identify opportunities to improve their own welfare than were those who argue that such moral encouragement is needed.

What about market failure? In this case, there may be transactions that are not undertaken even though they would have added to social welfare, or there are transactions being undertaken that reduce social welfare at the margin. Given the performance of market economies relative to all known alternatives, the evidence suggests that either: (1) market economies are so much more efficient than any alternative that even if market failures are not addressed, they outperform alternatives; or (2) market economies have done a reasonably good job of addressing market failures through collective action to regulate economic activity. In either case, one could argue that there are even larger gains to be had by doing a better job of addressing market failure. But this does not constitute a compelling argument for using market exhortations to do so, especially since there is no reason to believe the strength of moral earnestness necessarily leads to the appropriate level of the positive moral actions required to solve market failure problems.

Should economic transactions be encouraged in any way, or should they be left to the pursuit of self-interest by the set of potential transaction parties because that is sufficient to maximize social welfare? Economic transactions are morally desirable to the extent that they increase social welfare. But the gain derived from the surplus that occasions them is sufficient to induce socially desirable transactions to occur, since any possible reason not to do so would have already been accounted for as an opportunity cost in the calculation of the surplus. In other words, the gains derived from each party's share of the surplus directly increases that party's welfare, and is already accounted for by that party, so if the transaction is indeed economically efficient, there is no need for additional encouragement in the form of moral exhortations.

What if there are potential gains that a particular transaction party is not aware of? In such a case, the solution would be to point out such potential gains. Other parties to the transaction have ample incentive to do this since a failure to do so will cost them potential rewards. What if all parties to a transaction fail to recognize potential gains? In this case, the proper response is for whoever is convinced that this is true to point it out to all potential transaction parties. If they remain unconvinced, the question becomes why the agent who pointed it out is unable to convince those who will benefit.

In short, since what is morally positive about economic transactions is the surplus they produce, and this surplus is precisely what induces the transaction, there is nothing for moral exhortations to do. Mutual gain made possible by a surplus provides ample incentive for *efficient* transactions to occur. No moral encouragement is necessary. So unless there is a market failure problem in need of solving, moral exhortations solve a problem that does not exist in the context of ordinary economic activity.[14] Hence, they are either superfluous, because they don't change the outcome, or inefficient, because they do.

The preceding discussion should not be construed to imply that moral exhortations are not an important part of a decent society. I would not want to live in a society in which no one felt inclined to take positive moral actions because no one cares about others. Just because a person need only be concerned with his own welfare for the efficient outcome to be reached when transactions are voluntary, it does not follow that people are only concerned about their own welfare or that they *should* only be concerned about their own welfare. I should hope that most people do, in fact, care about the welfare of others, even strangers. As is clear from many passages in his *Theory of Moral Sentiments*, Adam Smith certainly did.

But with *economic* transactions, no additional moral encouragement is needed for the outcomes to occur that do the best job maximizing general prosperity. Additional moral encouragement, by altering the pattern of resource allocation, likely *reduces* social welfare because there will be fewer resources available to undertake positive moral actions. It follows that benevolence is most efficaciously pursued in the long run if, when we are moved to behave benevolently, we do so as a consumption activity—that is, through how individuals, groups, or even society as a whole spends resources that have already been earned—rather than in the context of production and commerce.

THE EFFECT OF GROUP SIZE

The larger is the group, and therefore the farther is the average social distance between people in the group, the more likely that everyone in the group ends up happier if we don't risk wasting resources by trying to promote the welfare of others in the conduct of ordinary business. We should, instead, maximize the material payoffs by maximizing profit (subject to obeying moral prohibitions) and, using the increased income that results, fund greater charitable efforts that are pursued as matters of consumption and not production.

For example, hiring A rather than B because A needs a job more, even though B is much better qualified, results in less output produced by A and B combined. It is therefore more efficient to not hire A, leave him instead to be employed in a more socially optimal occupation, and then give him, via an act of consumption, some of the difference in overall output that results. This difference is, by construction, necessarily large enough to leave A better off than hiring him to do something that market prices imply he is not best suited for.

Finally, the desire to undertake positive moral actions might result in the wrong person or the wrong firm being favorably treated for no other reason than low social distance. This is a fancy way of saying that a practice of "doing good" through economic transactions often results in favoritism. Most people know that this is quickly perceived as unjust by those who are not favored, and it can have a devastating effect on morale. Most people would prefer working for a firm or boss who is relatively indifferent to their personal needs, and therefore engages in little positive moral action on their behalf, but who is completely honest and fair in all things.

Implications for Economic Behavior—
Moral Prohibitions

With respect to economic behavior, there is nothing for moral exhortations to do, no problem for them to solve. What concerns us about the moral character of our transaction partners is not that they aren't sufficiently willing to promote our interest. We don't need them to. The surplus that occasions the transaction produces mutual benefit, irrespective of benevolence. Beyond actions that are contractually stipulated, the only thing we require of our transaction partners is *inaction*—that they not opportunistically exploit us.

The expectation of opportunistic exploitation is viewed as a risk of undertaking transactions, and the cost of bearing such risk is clearly a transaction cost. This transaction cost can dramatically reduce the scope of viable transactions. In this way, socially beneficial transactions can be impeded by the mere expectation of immoral behavior in the form of opportunism. In any society in which opportunism is widespread, one does not have far to look to find evidence of its crippling effect on economic activity and, hence, on prosperity.

The risk of opportunistic exploitation makes moral prohibitions relevant to economic activity because it is impossible to engage in opportunism through any transaction if one never disobeys a moral prohibition against violating a trust. Opportunism is, by definition, the violation of a trust. Since transaction costs rise directly with expected opportunistic behavior, it follows that obedience of moral prohibitions directly reduces transaction costs by precluding opportunism. So while there is nothing for moral exhortations to do, there is plenty for moral prohibitions to do. All three forms of opportunism discussed in Chapter 2 are effectively precluded by obedience to a sufficiently comprehensive set of moral prohibitions.[15]

FIRST-DEGREE OPPORTUNISM

Recall that first-degree opportunism is taking advantage of others by reneging on a contract. This includes reneging on social contracts, so criminal behavior is properly viewed as first-degree opportunism. With respect to economic transactions, first-degree opportunism can, in some cases, potentially destroy all incentive for transactions to occur, because the harm done to a transaction partner can easily exceed the surplus value of the transaction. As economies developed, people had more property to protect and it became efficient to pool resources for provide for formal institutions that could continuously combat first-degree opportunism. Only the smallest societies lack such institutions.

Even a society that is wealthy enough to afford very effective formal institutions to protect property rights by combating first-degree opportunism will provide little peace of mind to property owners unless virtually every citizen possesses moral values that lead him/her to view first-degree opportunism as wrong. Those who own property in societies that highly value the obedience of moral prohibitions should not underestimate the benefits of moral restraint on the part of their neighbors. They bear little risk that others will circumvent formal institutions to take property indirectly, or reduce the value of property by abusing it or appropriating rents produced by it. Any adult who has angered a nasty teenager bent on making his life miserable knows that the police cannot be everywhere, all the time, and neither can he. A society in which all people are inclined to destroy property in such a way is a society in which little effort will be put forth to maintain property, or to obtain resources to own it in the first place.

Formal institutions are often politically limited in their ability to discourage opportunistic behavior. In the ancient world, severe punishments were often meted out because there were insufficient resources for careful monitoring. The problem is that even minor acts of opportunism can add up to dramatically increase transaction costs in the aggregate, producing economic death by a thousand cuts. Formal enforcement institutions will be insufficient if, given a high potential reward to the opportunist and a low probability of detection, a sanction that is severe enough to deter opportunism is too severe to be politically tenable.

These issues are moot, however, if the willingness to obey moral prohibitions is so strong and widespread that there is little fear of first-degree opportunism, and therefore little need for enforcement institutions—because people will not be inclined to take others' property or renege on contracts generally, social or otherwise. A strong willingness to obey moral prohibitions is a more comprehensive deterrent than formal institutions, because the best assurance against the erosion of property rights through opportunistic behavior is that individuals are not willing to take such actions in the first place.

SECOND-DEGREE OPPORTUNISM

Second-degree opportunism is taking advantage of the fact that contracts are incomplete because they cannot anticipate every possible eventuality, and therefore cannot stipulate a response that would have been mutually agreed to by all parties *ex ante* under perfect foresight. In this case, A exploits contractual incompleteness by taking more than an equal share of the true surplus at the expense of B, *ex post*. This type of opportunism normally involves taking advantage of a situation in a way that is not illegal, but is not what you would expect from a transaction partner who is completely fair-minded.

Contracts can stipulate required actions, remedies for failure to act, and remedies for actions that are forbidden by agreement. Since even carefully written contracts cannot anticipate every possible contingency, moral prohibitions reduce the risk of using contracts by eliminating the fear that an unforeseen event will produce windfall benefits or costs that will not be shared equally because the event confers a bargaining advantage to the other party or parties. Not sharing windfall benefits or costs equally is to act in a way that you would have agreed *not* to act if such an agreement had been required for the contract to be accepted *ex ante*. Acting in such a way, therefore, is disobeying the spirit of the contract.

Those who obey the overarching moral prohibition against behaving opportunistically in any way will always endeavor to abide not only by the letter of the contract, but also by the spirit of the contract. Being able to trust that transaction partners will not take advantage of contractual incompleteness makes contractually coordinated commerce less risky, and thereby reduces transaction costs by avoiding conflicts that must be resolved in civil courts that are costly to use. Because of this, contracts can be written in a more flexible form, to the benefit of all parties, because one is confident that the other transaction party will deal fairly with unforeseen eventualities.

THIRD-DEGREE OPPORTUNISM

Third-degree opportunism is taking advantage of discretion that exists in a relational contract. The greater the decision-making authority held by those who possess local knowledge, the more flexibility decision makerers have to make the best use of such local knowledge. The problem is that the more knowledge is localized, the more likely it is that those who possess it can engage in third-degree opportunism if they have sufficient discretion. In cases where knowledge is so localized that there is no chance of detection, a golden opportunity exists so for restraint to be meaningful in such cases it must be internalized.

Moral restraint derived from a desire to obey all moral prohibitions makes it possible to use relational contracts to their fullest effect, because if decision makers can be expected to always obey moral prohibitions, there is no reason to fear becoming a victim of third-degree opportunism. Put directly, knowing that decision makers will obey moral prohibitions means knowing they will keep their word to make decisions in a way that best advances the principal's interests, rather than in ways that best advance their own. In this way, the steadfast obedience of moral prohibitions makes it possible to use relational contracts to their fullest effect, because the extension of trust to those who possess local knowledge is perfectly rational.

Relational contracts, within which those who possess local knowledge are given the widest possible latitude, support maximum entrepreneurial flexibility, adaptability, and innovation. This allows a society to overcome the normal trade-off between group size and efficient use of local knowledge. Such societies can enjoy the benefits of having firms that are both large and entrepreneurial throughout their hierarchies, because the objective of profit maximization can be entrusted to those who could get away with self-serving decision making but feel morally constrained from doing so.

MORAL PROHIBITIONS AND TRUST

If a desire to obey moral prohibitions precludes all acts of opportunism for a given individual over a given set of transactions, then the individual can be expected to behave in a trustworthy manner with respect to that set of transactions even if he is not specifically rewarded for doing so. For example, if A believes that B will never disobey moral prohibitions over a given set of transactions, because doing so will make B feel too guilty, then this is effectively equivalent to A believing that B will never behave opportunistically with respect to that set of transactions. This, in turn, means that A will regard B as being completely trustworthy over that set of transactions, since the essence of being trustworthy is never taking advantage of a trust that has been extended to you. In this way, moral prohibitions make the emergence of rational, genuine trust possible. The more strongly B feels compelled to obey moral prohibitions, the wider is the scope of transactions over which A will regard B to be completely trustworthy.

Unlike moral exhortations, moral prohibitions provide very clear expectations for what one can expect of others, and vice versa, and this contributes to having a high trust environment across the whole of society. The larger is the society and therefore the more likely we can potentially benefit from transacting with complete strangers, the truer it is that we would prefer transaction partners whose moral beliefs stress obedience of moral prohibitions over obedience of moral exhortations. We simply don't need our potential transaction partners to treat us benevolently.

Moral prohibitions provide an objective, qualitative, categorical, and universal moral standard for social behavior. Such a standard can emerge spontaneously and work automatically, because it does not require any central authority to make value judgments. Obedience of the standard is not a matter of degree and is therefore not a matter of subjective judgment. There is no objective basis for how strongly one must feel compelled to obey moral exhortations to be regarded as moral—and, more to the point, trustworthy—but one who disobeys moral prohibitions by engaging in opportunism is clearly immoral and untrustworthy.

A high trust society, made possible by the widespread obedience of moral prohibitions, allows large firms to make efficient use of local knowledge. This means society can enjoy the benefits of economies of scale without sacrificing the benefits of entrepreneurial coordination, initiative, problem solving, innovation, and creativity. In addition, a high trust society also enjoys a windfall benefit, because safeguarding costs will be lower than otherwise. Unfortunately, less developed countries suffer the most from first-degree opportunism, so they must waste precious resources on formal mechanisms to hold such opportunism in check.

MORAL PROHIBITIONS AND STANDARDS FOR BEHAVIOR

The ability of people in a society to police each other is directly related to the existence of standards for behavior that everyone understands. I will now briefly discuss why moral exhortations are unable to provide such standards, but moral prohibitions provide very clear standards indeed.

Moral exhortations suffer from two problems. First, they encourage taking some form of action, and taking action requires resources. This is problematic because people have different levels of resources to work with, so we can't possibly expect everyone to undertake the same set of positive moral actions in a given circumstance. Second, moral exhortations only tell us what to value; they don't tell us what to do or what not do in every circumstance. They are therefore subjective with regard to required moral behavior, because there is no objective basis for discerning to what degree any given exhortation should be obeyed. These two problems make it impossible to have a meaningful standard for moral behavior that everyone can expect of everyone in nearly every circumstance, because it is impossible for everyone to agree on what is required.

Things are very different for moral prohibitions. Whereas moral exhortations require actions, and therefore require resources, moral prohibitions require *inaction*. So as a practical matter, we can expect everyone to always to obey moral prohibitions.[16] Moreover, moral prohibitions differ in logical function, in a way that makes them more amenable to providing a consistent standard for moral behavior that everyone can agree on. Because moral prohibitions require non-acts, they are categorical and therefore objective and well defined. "Be generous" only points us in a direction, and reasonable people can disagree over whether one was, in fact, generous enough to be deemed generous in a given circumstance. But "don't steal" tells us precisely what not to do, and we have either done it or not done it. Most importantly, while it is impossible to envision everyone agreeing on how generous to be in most circumstances, nearly everyone agrees that one should not undertake negative moral actions, and that those who do have done wrong.

Unlike moral exhortations, then, moral prohibitions allow everyone to conclude at the same time that someone has not lived up to a clear and shared standard for moral behavior. This produces a consensus of disapproval from everyone. With moral exhortations, we don't know what we can expect from others, but with moral prohibitions we know exactly what we can practicably expect from others and what others can practicably expect from us. When everyone can agree that a given action is wrong, and therefore requires disapproval, people can police themselves, and children can learn moral standards from observing adult behavior.

Because modern theories of morality do not fully appreciate the differences in logical function between exhortations and prohibitions, they produce little in the way of practicable standards for moral behavior. Indeed, most modern theorists insouciantly reject uniform standards for moral behavior as simple-minded and incapable of dealing with the nuances of actual life. In their view, the moral gravity of competing moral actions (both positive and negative) is what is decisive, and these are matters of personal judgment of the moral decision maker. So even if negative moral actions themselves are well defined, the moral weight put on them is not—nor is the moral weight put on whatever positive moral actions might be made possible by disobeying prohibitions. This makes moral behavior inescapably subjective, and in so doing makes people effectively moral free agents. As such, we won't know what we can and cannot expect from others.

Many firms have been caught engaging in questionable practices because of a competitive race to the bottom of ethical behavior. Modern moral theorists normally attribute this lack of morality to excessive greed and/or insufficient moral earnestness on the part of decision makers. But another possibility is that clear moral standards act as focal points through which people of integrity can, in effect, collude with one another to avert a competitive race to the bottom. Clear moral standards make it possible for firm managers and owners to behave morally with far less fear that doing so amounts to choosing a sucker's payoff. Conversely, the absence of clear moral standards for behavior can make managers feel that they are morally compelled to disobey moral prohibitions in order to pursue required positive moral actions (e.g., tell a small lie so as not to fire an employee). It can also make them feel that if they don't ever cross the line, they simply cannot compete with all other firms that do cross the line.

MORAL PROHIBITIONS AND INSTITUTIONS

To the extent that moral prohibitions support a high trust environment across the whole of society (precisely how this might come about will explained in later chapters), highly trust-dependent "nuts and bolts" institutions can emerge and flourish. "Nuts and bolts" type institutions are those that are not designed to directly combat opportunism, but exist instead to lubricate transaction activity. Moral prohibitions therefore also reduce transaction costs indirectly, thereby by expanding the scope of institutions that are themselves dependent on a society being a high trust one.

For example, a deed recording office is necessary for secure property rights, but is completely meaningless if no one trusts the government with such information. Moreover, the more impartial and competent are mechanisms of third-party dispute resolution, the lower is the risk of using contracts. In a society in which everyone obeys moral prohibitions, institutions such as civil courts that oversee dispute resolution and enforcement of remedies can be trusted not to take advantage of their discretion to engage in opportunism through information gained by such proceedings.

Conclusion

The moral problem that societies must solve, if they are to enjoy the benefits of efficiently organizing economic activity in large groups, is *not* getting people to care more about each other, or getting them to do nice things for one another. The problem that societies must solve is combating their willingness to take advantage of each other, to behave opportunistically. By driving up feelings of guilt associated with behaving opportunistically, the payoff to opportunism can be driven so low as to make it an irrational choice. In this way, the commons dilemma associated with opportunistic behavior can be eliminated.

But what we feel guilty about makes all the difference. Feeling guilty about failing to obey moral exhortations to undertake positive moral actions does nothing to support efficient transaction behavior, since efficient transactions have ample incentive to occur anyway. However, feeling guilty about not obeying moral prohibitions against taking negative moral actions, such as behaving opportunistically, lowers transaction costs and thereby dramatically increases the scope of transactions through which the gains from specialization can be realized. To maximize prosperity we need to feel guilty about taking negative moral actions, not about *not taking* positive moral actions.

A society of individuals who strongly value obeying moral prohibitions is a society of individuals who expect to feel very guilty when they undertake negative moral actions. Such a society will enjoy low transaction costs and conserve on resources that other societies must devote to safeguarding against opportunism. Such a society has the reason to create, and the ability to sustain, institutions that support property rights and the use of contracts, which strengthens incentives for effort, problem solving, initiative, innovation, and invention, while at the same time increasing the scope of viable transactions through which to effectuate the gains from specialization. Such a society can combat third-degree opportunism, and can therefore make the fullest possible use of relational contracts, because decision makers can be trusted not to abuse the discretion afforded by highly flexible relational contracts. This, in turn, avoids the normal tradeoff between size and efficient use of local knowledge, thereby allowing society to have large yet thoroughly entrepreneurial firms. These are the engines of *general* prosperity.

In a large society, the only practicable moral expectation of strangers is that moral prohibitions will be obeyed. The value system can therefore create economic value by inculcating in the population the belief that the following rule of behavior must always be followed: do not disobey moral prohibitions. In this way, the threat of opportunism can be neutralized; it is impossible to behave in an opportunistic manner because opportunism is inherently a negative moral action. Moreover, when an individual obeys all moral prohibitions, the only way he can improve his welfare through his interaction with others is by engaging in truly mutually beneficial transactions. He can, therefore, use others as a means to the end of promoting his own welfare if—and only if—they agree to it. And this they will do only if they expect that their own welfare will be increased in the process. A person who obeys all moral prohibitions therefore inevitably improves the welfare of everyone with whom he transacts.

The discussion above is clearly in "if, then" form. *If* moral prohibitions are always obeyed *then* opportunism will not occur, so transaction costs will be low. But what is to assure us that these "if, then" arguments are not "if pigs had wings, then they could fly" arguments? The capacity for guilt is a psychological mechanism that we already possess, and one that can be plausibly put to work to effectuate sufficient moral restraint even with respect to golden opportunities.

In the next three chapters I will explain that while guilt plays a key role, it is not enough to simply drive up feelings of guilt by placing a very high moral weight on obeying moral prohibitions. In the social contexts that matter most for generating general prosperity—economic activity undertaken in large groups—*why* we believe it is wrong to disobey moral prohibitions also matters, and is even more important than our level of moral earnestness. Indeed, if we don't have the right kind of moral beliefs, no amount of moral earnestness will be sufficient to produce moral restraint where it is needed most. Indeed, trying to solve the problem by increasing moral earnestness may even make matters worse.

CHAPTER 5

Harm-Based Moral Restraint

How selfish soever man may be supposed, there are evidently some principles in his nature, which interest him in the fortune of others, and render their happiness necessary to him, though he derives nothing from it except the pleasure of seeing it.—Adam Smith, 1759, p. 1

Introduction

Why do so many otherwise honest people cheat on their taxes or exaggerate their expense accounts? Most who do such things are otherwise good people, people we might personally trust even if we knew they did such things. In my view, the reason why so many otherwise honest people behave in these ways is that such behavior does not *feel* wrong because it does not automatically evoke feelings of guilt the way stealing a starving child's bread would. This is because in such cases there is no harmed individual with whom to empathize and therefore feel sorry for, and therefore feel guilty about.[1]

This is why we frequently trust someone like Cindy, whom we know to have exaggerated an insurance claim, to babysit our children. We believe that she believes that it is one thing to harm a faceless organization, but it is quite another to harm another human being. We implicitly understand that it is in Cindy's basic human nature to be sympathetic with regard to the welfare of our children, and to be able to empathize with what they are feeling so as to be aware of their needs. As such, we presume that *she* can be trusted with *them*; yet, ironically, if she were our employee during the day we might not trust her with something far less important, like an expense account. At some level we understand that it's not her level of morality that is the problem—it's how she thinks about morality that matters.

Empathizing and sympathizing with others is such a deeply rooted moral capability that when it conflicts with abstract moral beliefs, empathy and sympathy usually win. Consider the dilemma facing Huck in Mark Twain's *The Adventures of Huckleberry Finn*. Every source of moral authority in his life taught Huck to view

Jim, a runaway slave, as someone else's property. It was therefore Huck's moral duty to return Jim to his rightful owner. Huck was even convinced that if he failed to do so, his soul would be damned for eternity. But his empathetic nature got the best of him. He decided not to return Jim. I submit that the reason why we all cheer when we read this passage is that in our hearts, this is the conclusion we all hope Huck reaches; it *feels* so right because it comports with our hardwired moral intuitions.[2]

Our capacities for empathy and sympathy help to keep us moral by telling us in our gut that there are some things you should always do and there are some things you should never do—indeed, never even contemplate. When our capacity for empathy for our fellow human beings is suppressed, our capacity for sympathy is rendered moot and true horror becomes possible.

In the last chapter we switched from discussing the nature of the moral problem confronting any society that wishes to maximize general prosperity to the question of how moral values might solve the problem. I argued that what is needed to overcome the tradeoff between group size and efficient use of local knowledge is moral restraint, not moral advocacy—so what matters is not obeying moral exhortations to undertake positive moral actions, but obeying moral prohibitions against taking negative moral actions. This suggests that if individuals in a society feel strongly enough that they should obey moral prohibitions, the problem of opportunism can be alleviated.

This raises an obvious question: precisely why do people feel obliged to obey moral prohibitions in the first place? In this chapter I will argue that throughout the world most people, most of the time, obey most moral prohibitions because they possess an implicit theory of morality that is an inevitable product of hardwired capacities that all normally functioning humans possess. The crux of this implicit theory of morality is that the reason we are naturally willing to obey moral prohibitions is because we are naturally unwilling to harm others. I call this natural unwillingness to harm others *harm-based moral restraint*.[3]

Jerome Kagan (1984) and Robert Frank (1988) have stressed that moral behavior may differ greatly across individuals and societies, but it is nevertheless derived from a small set of basic emotional capacities.[4] In *Moral Minds*, Marc Hauser (2006) has argued that much of our basic morality is not derived from abstract moral beliefs, but is in our basic human nature—our genetic hardwiring. In this chapter I discuss how three fundamentally important psychological/ emotional capacities—the capacity to empathize, sympathize, and feel guilty— are related to one another and work together to produce our natural, harm-based sense of moral restraint.

EMPATHY, SYMPATHY, AND GUILT

Empathy is defined in Webster's Dictionary as "the power to enter into the feeling or spirit of others." The essence of empathy is using one's imagination to put oneself in the other person's place, in his shoes so to speak, to understand how it would feel to be in his situation. There are obviously great benefits to being aware of how others feel generally, and to being able to predict how others will respond to changing circumstances, to the actions of other individuals, and, most importantly, to our actions.

Empathy goes beyond merely being aware of how others feel. I may infer from your crying that you are upset, but I may have no idea what you are upset about or how badly you feel. Empathy is about being acutely aware of another person's state because you are able to simulate what they are experiencing in your mind. You are, in some sense, feeling it too, and you therefore understand more clearly why they feel as they do. Feeling like another person feels because you imagine what it would be like to be in that person's situation is precisely what it means to empathize.[5]

Recent brain research suggests that our ability to perceive what others perceive, to even feel what others feel, is biologically grounded in "mirror neurons" that were first discovered to function by allowing us to read other people's movements. Daniel Glaser of University College London notes that now some researchers think that ". . . we move differently when we're happy or when we're sad. And, in fact, we can empathize to some extent with the way people are feeling by reading their movements in a special way."[6] Empathy also involves interpreting what we know others are experiencing through what developmental psychologists and cognitive scientists call an implicit "theory of the mind" that humans are uniquely able to devise. This is an ability not possessed by monkeys, and exists in only limited form in apes (Povinelli and Bering, 2002; Singer and Fehr, 2005).

Sympathy is defined in Webster's Dictionary as "sharing in the emotions of others, especially the sharing of grief, pain, etc." Since sharing in the emotions of others is very close to *entering into the feeling of others*, it is easy to see why sympathy and empathy are often used synonymously. Early usage of the word *sympathy* stressed the idea of consonance or harmony of emotions (this is how Adam Smith used the term; see Otteson, 2002). Increasingly, however, the word *sympathy* conveys the idea of *caring about* how others feel.[7]

It is, of course, hard to sympathize with someone if you are not fully aware of how it feels to be in their situation. Conversely, we are most likely to attempt to empathize with those we care about. But while we often feel most sympathetic toward those with whom we most acutely empathize, one need not necessarily care about someone in order to empathize with him. "Entering into" does not equal "caring." Successful con men are so notorious for having the ability to gauge how others respond to their actions that if we find another person who appears to be highly conscious of how we feel or what we think, we naturally suspect that he might be a con man. But con men obviously do not care very much about the harm they bring to their victims. Conversely, we all know lovable dolts who care deeply about others, but are oblivious to how their actions affect them.

Guilt is defined in Webster's Dictionary as "the fact of having committed a legal offense ‖ the fact of having transgressed the moral law ‖ a feeling of culpability."

As put nicely by Fessler and Haley (2003, p. 16), "Guilt focuses attention on the action and the harm that has been done to the other party, inflicts subjective discomfort on the actor via its strongly aversive valence."

The sense of the word *guilt* as used here will stress that guilt is an involuntary emotional response to knowing that one is responsible for having done something wrong. A key feature of guilt is that it is an *involuntary* emotional response. Thanks to the pioneering work of Jack Hirshleifer and Robert Frank, the role that emotions play in mediating economic behavior is now widely understood, as is the need for guilt to be an involuntary emotional response if it is to act as a credible commitment device.[8]

We do not choose to feel guilty, although we choose the actions that end up making us feel guilty. The involuntary emotions of guilt go beyond the reduction in our own utility that comes from empathizing and sympathizing with those who are harmed in some way. If harm comes to someone I care about, then my welfare is reduced, but I do not feel guilty if I had nothing to do with it. In my view, *our natural sense of guilt* is an additional emotional reaction that is triggered by sympathy in conjunction with culpability.[9] If a bad event occurs to you and I have nothing to do with it whatsoever, I may feel badly but I do not feel guilty. But if the same event occurred as a result of my own self-serving action (intentional or not), then even if the goal was not to harm you, I would feel even worse because I would also feel guilty.

In Chapter 2 the concept of guilt was accounted for in the model of rational opportunism as a cost. In the model developed in this chapter, our natural sense of moral restraint works as follows: a negative moral action is considered because it is expected to produce a positive material payoff for the actor. But because we have a capacity for empathy, we identify with how the victim will feel in response to our action. If we also sympathize with the victim, then we will care about the pain he is experiencing and this will reduce our own utility directly. But in addition to this direct effect, there is the guilt effect. Because we are culpable, we will also feel guilty. As a result, our own utility is reduced by more if we are also culpable.

On the surface, rational choice theory appears hostile to the concepts of empathy, sympathy, and guilt, because rational choice theory assumes that behavior is driven by the maximization of self-interest, which certainly sounds more selfish than empathetic or sympathetic.[10] But a person can be rational, self-interested, and unselfish at the same time if his own happiness is affected by the happiness or welfare of others. Most people care about others, and this does not contradict the idea that they behave rationally by maximizing their own utility; in such cases, it is in their best interest to improve the welfare of others because doing so makes them happy. In principle, this can be handled mathematically by including the happiness or welfare of others in the individual's utility function. Ken Binmore (2005, p. 101) puts it directly, stating: "Nobody denies the existence of other-regarding preferences. . . . People are said to have a sympathetic utility function, with arguments that directly represent the welfare of others."

Origins of Sympathy, Empathy, and Guilt

Our ability to empathize and sympathize with others, and our capacity for experiencing involuntary feelings of guilt, are central to our ability to cooperate with one another. They are also fundamental parts of what makes us human. Conversely, inhumane treatment of others becomes increasingly unlikely the more strongly we empathize and sympathize with others and, therefore, the more likely we will expect to feel guilty about knowingly taking actions that might bring about harm. I personally take great comfort in the idea that our basic human decency is a fundamental part of who we are.

These mechanisms are so strong and so universal that it seems unnecessary to point out that they almost certainly are hardwired behavioral mechanisms and therefore products of biological evolution. Since I suspect most readers are already prepared to accept that they are hardwired, the discussion that follows will be brief and by no means exhaustive. One could easily write an entire book devoted to the biological foundations of sympathy, empathy, and guilt.[11] So why is it important to discuss the possibility that they are hardwired and not merely cultural attributes? If they are products of biological evolution, then since we have lived and interacted in large groups only very recently in our evolutionary history, it follows that the traits that support these capabilities necessarily evolved in a small group context. It then follows that our *natural* hardwired sense of moral restraint is therefore a *small group* sense of moral restraint.

We begin with an important concept in evolutionary psychology that acknowledges the importance of group size in human evolution. It is the concept of the *Environment of Evolutionary Adaptedness* (EEA), which captures the idea that much of our hardwiring is a product of evolutionary adaptation to the circumstances of small group life. About group size in the EEA, Paul Rubin (2002, p. 27) has argued:

> One important difference between the EEA and modern societies that has ramifications in many contexts is the difference in scale in the societies. Societies in the EEA were small—perhaps 25 to 150 persons . . . mechanisms ensuring cooperation in small environments where interactions are face-to-face are quite different from mechanisms needed in large rather impersonal environments such as our contemporary world . . . some methods of decision making carried over from the EEA are often not well suited to decision making in larger environments.

As noted in Chapter 3, prosperity is impossible if economic activity is limited to small groups, but we are fundamentally a small group species for whom small group moral sensibilities come naturally. This is problematic for any society that wants to avoid widespread poverty, let alone maximize general prosperity.

The importance of group size to understanding human evolution is now widely accepted. Robin Dunbar's finding that human group size tends to be limited to about 150 individuals is now so well known that "Dunbar's Number" has become a familiar locution among social scientists. Even when we find ourselves in large groups, we naturally form small groups within them (Rubin, 2002). One possible reason for this is that moral sensibilities play an important role in facilitating co-operation and maintaining group harmony, but our natural moral sensibilities break down in larger groups. By forming smaller groups we are again comfortable because the moral mechanisms that support social behavior and protect us from opportunistic predation are again effective.

SYMPATHY

One benefit of evolving a capacity for mutual affection is that we depend on other humans for survival so it pays to keep them alive. One way our genes induce us to keep them alive is to make us care about them. For example, suppose that a particular hunter-gatherer band has exactly four adult males who are capable of hunting, and that four adult males can kill a mammoth with a low probability of injury and a high probability of success but three cannot. This leads to an evolutionary reward for traits that induces them to care about keeping each other alive. One way genes can accomplish this is to make them sympathize with each other.[12] In very small groups, of course, the effect of losing just one person can be substantial.

This comports with the fact that we tend to be more sympathetic toward those we know well than those we do not know, because those we know well are likely to be those we are either related to or those with whom we jointly produce surpluses that increase the chances of our survival and the chances of survival of our descendants. Conversely, someone we don't know is almost certainly not related to us and is someone whose continued existence is not likely to affect the likelihood of our survival significantly. Therefore being hardwired to care about those around us whom we know (not strangers from rival tribes who might want to kill us) works to keep those who benefit us (through higher personal payoffs from shared surpluses) alive so we can continue to benefit from cooperative surpluses that emerge between us and them.

The benefits of sympathy go beyond keeping others in our group alive and thereby increasing our own payoffs. Individuals who are highly sympathetic are most likely to help those who need help most, and are likely to inflict harm on those who have harmed those we care about most. As Binmore (2005) has argued, this can lead to a more efficient group overall by effectuating a more efficient allocation of resources.

Within groups, individuals who are sympathetic are also better equipped to be good reciprocators and will therefore benefit more from cooperation and exchange. If someone grants us a favor, we know that their welfare is reduced at the margin for having done so. If we care about that person, we are saddened by their welfare being reduced, so we seek to restore it because doing so will produce feelings of happiness for us. This produces reciprocation, but not because of any strategic calculation in the thought process of the reciprocator. This seems a more plausible explanation for reciprocity than theories that posit strategic calculations on the part of reciprocating agents (although the two approaches are not mutually exclusive). It comports with reciprocity among animals such as vampire bats that clearly are not engaging in conscious strategic decision making (even if their genes are doing so in "as though" fashion). I will have more to say about weaknesses of conventional theories of reciprocity—particularly generalized reciprocity—in Chapter 9.

A capacity for sympathy may also serve as a moderating factor with respect to opportunistic behavior. Opportunism increases payoffs for opportunists at the expense of victims. So, as mechanisms that supported opportunistic exploitation of others evolved in humans, other mechanisms that supported retaliation against opportunists likely evolved in response. Obviously, an individual who does not care about those around him is more likely to end up bearing costs of retaliation than an individual who cares so much about those around him that he never attempts to opportunistically exploit them. Feelings of sympathy have the effect of internalizing costs that opportunism imposes on others. This raises the bar on what will be judged to be worthwhile acts of opportunism, thereby lowering the frequency of opportunism. When average payoffs from opportunism are low because opportunism is occurring more frequently than is optimal, the return to evolving stronger feelings of sympathy should therefore rise. So sympathy might also help us be prudent opportunists, rather than reckless and short-lived ones.

Because opportunism can be directed at strangers, and even strangers might retaliate, it follows that there are also benefits to caring about those whom we don't know personally. Caring about what happens to those whose social distance from us is great helps keep us out of trouble with respect to face-to-face dealings with strangers, by internalizing the costs of opportunistic action. Strangers are also less likely to victimize us if they feel we wouldn't victimize them because we appear to be at least minimally concerned about their welfare. The best way to appear to be this way is, of course, to actually feel this way.

EMPATHY

New models based on recent brain research evidence have been developed to show how using one's imagination to consider what another is experiencing arouses neurological responses that facilitate actually feeling what another is feeling (e.g., Preston and de Waal, 2002). Singer, Seymour, O'Doherty, Kaube, Dolan and Frith (2004) suggest that empathy is a hardwired, intuitive capability, since the empathetic response to stimuli tends to be "rather automatic and does not require active engagement of some explicit judgments about others' feelings." As Singer and Fehr (2005) note, the key point is that this response is *automatic*. This suggests that it is a rather fundamental mechanism that may subconsciously color our perceptions in a powerful way.

Unlike sympathy, empathy is not about caring about how another feels. Empathy is about being fully aware of how another feels because we are able to use our imagination to simulate their experience and thereby arouse neurological triggers that allow us to feel what the other person is feeling. We may or may not care about what they are feeling. Even if we don't care about those around us, there are obviously advantages to being aware of how others will respond to our actions. Those who are keenly empathetic do better than those who are not, because there are obvious benefits to knowing which of our actions are likely to be positively perceived and which are likely to be negatively perceived by others.

Empathizing also allows us to gain insight into precisely how others feel and why they feel the way they do. How strongly they feel is closely related to the effect our actions might have on their welfare. The more empathetic one is, then, the more efficiently one can promote and protect the welfare of those he is related to, and those whose existence increases the likelihood of his survival. Conversely, those who are not empathetic will often fail to help those in need when they really need it, or will waste resources helping those who are not really in need.

Similarly, others draw inferences about an individual's level of regard for them from the individual's actions. If an individual is not very empathetic, he may not realize how much his actions may have reduced the utility of others and therefore might send the signal that he does not sympathize as much with others as he, in fact, does. For example, suppose that Sue's dog is hit by a car. Bob has never owned a pet and therefore has little understanding of how attached people can be to their pets, so when Sue reports what has happened, Bob appears indifferent and changes the subject to baseball. From such behavior, Sue might infer that Bob simply doesn't care about her hurt feelings and therefore must not care about her, either. The inability to empathize can lead to others discounting one's degree of sympathy and therefore one's trustworthiness.

Individuals can also benefit from an acute sense of empathy since it facilitates reciprocal behavior at the best possible terms. Those who are very empathetic are better at securing high-valued future favors by granting low-cost ones that are highly valued because they were granted where and when they were needed most. By recognizing low-cost opportunities to dramatically improve the welfare of others, those who are acutely empathetic know how to give up little to potentially gain much.[13]

We can do a better job keeping those alive who increase the likelihood of our own continued survival if we understand their wants, needs, and feelings. Those who are keenly attuned to how changes in environment affect others know when to comfort them or help them. Being empathetic therefore improves the precision with which feelings of sympathy are actuated to help those who need it most. This increases efficiency by increasing the likelihood that resources are directed to where they will do the most good, thereby creating an evolutionary advantage for those groups composed of individuals who possess an acute sense of empathy. Ken Binmore (2005) has similarly argued that the existence of empathetic preferences facilitates the simulation of the original position (in the sense of Rawls), thereby producing utilitarian outcomes that are more efficient and therefore evolutionarily rewarded. Contrariwise, "If Adam and Eve are autistic or unable to empathize successfully with each other for other reasons, then the device of the original position won't work for them" (Binmore, 2005, p. 28).

In short, groups composed of individuals who were acutely empathetic were much more perceptive about other members' wants, needs, and feelings, and were therefore able to more efficiently assign tasks, divide resources, and provide help when needed. The resulting increase in efficiency led to higher group payoffs. This led to more successful reproduction for members of the group relative to members of other groups. With respect to direct group-on-group competition, it also led to the domination, conquering, and destruction of groups less able to empathize and therefore efficiently allocate resources.

Finally, the capacity for empathy may have also evolved in part because empathizing makes individuals better opportunists. Being able to understand how others will feel in response to one's actions allows opportunists to be more efficient opportunists by helping them determine which gambles are worth taking. When deciding whether to take advantage of another person, the expected strength of his retaliation goes into the estimation of the expected costs of such action. The strength of retaliation varies directly with the reduction in the victim's utility, which is best estimated by one who is very empathetic. Those individuals who could accurately gauge the likelihood and severity of retaliation made better decisions about with whom, when, and how to engage in opportunism. Those who engaged in no opportunism and those who engaged in reckless opportunism both suffered lower payoffs, on average, than those who had the ability to engage in skillful opportunism, because they possessed an acute sense of empathy and they could accurately gauge the strength of retaliation.

GUILT

Over three decades ago Robert Trivers (1971) argued that a capacity for guilt may have evolved to help people maintain good reputations. Robert Frank (1988) has also argued that guilt may act as a self-control mechanism, noting that even "Darwin was well aware of the belief that symptoms of guilt prevent people from cheating" and arguing that feelings like guilt and anger "shift the relevant future payoffs into the current moment" when decisions are actually made. According to Fessler and Haley (2003, p. 16): ". . . just as anticipation of another's anger often leads actors to refrain from intentionally transgressing, anticipation of their own guilt often leads them to refrain from intentionally defecting."

Here I consider the possibility that our capacity for guilt evolved as a mechanism to attach negative emotions to being directly responsible for bringing harm to others, so as to internalize these expected costs into our decision-making efforts when considering acts of opportunism. It is natural to presume that a capacity for empathizing and sympathizing would already solve the problem of internalizing the expected costs of retaliation from opportunistic behavior so a reasonable question is this: *what is the value added of evolving yet another emotional capacity to go along with empathy and sympathy?*

An additional mechanism to account for culpability makes evolutionary sense because rational retaliation would necessarily vary directly with intentionality. Guilt ties disutility directly to such intentionality.[14] Guilt, therefore, induces us to take account of how our behavior will affect others through learning (if you did a bad act on purpose, you now know how guilty you will feel if you do it again in the future) in a way that directly accounts for intentionality and explicitly ignores random factors over which the actor has no control.

Those who are harmed respond very differently to harm that is unintentional than they do to harm that is either intentional or a consequence of reckless indifference. Moreover, the more responsibility a person bears for the outcome, the more strongly harmed individuals feel compelled to retaliate and the more severe retaliation will be. If someone kills our child but it was clearly a pure accident, we might even reach out to that person to assure him that it was not his fault and that there are no hard feelings. But we would be enraged by even a minor act of opportunism that was directed toward our child even if it produced little actual harm.

Those who have a capacity for empathy and sympathy, but who do not have a capacity for guilt, would treat the first situation as having much higher expected costs for them than the second when, in fact, the exact opposite is the case. This suggests that guilt is a meaningful addition to empathy and sympathy, because the strength of retaliation is tied directly to intentionality. If one has a capacity for empathy and sympathy, but not a capacity for guilt, one will not account for the effect of intentionality on the expected severity of retaliation if one's actions are detected.

Opportunistic acts are intentional (even if harm *per se* is not the goal, as it generally isn't), so having an additional capacity for feeling guilt is valuable because it internalizes costs that calculated opportunistic actions impose on victims of opportunism and therefore leads to more efficient opportunism. In other words, our capacity for guilt may have evolved in part to mediate opportunistic behavior. Perhaps it is a testament to how important opportunism is that guilt is such a powerful and widespread emotion. Perhaps this is why we see little evidence of a capacity for guilt among animals that are only opportunistic via hardwired instinct, even though many animals appear to have capacities for empathy and sympathy.[15]

My claim is that guilt functions differently than empathy and sympathy because it accounts for intentionality, and therefore gives individuals a mechanism that more accurately accounts for the cost of retaliation, since the severity of retaliation will vary directly with intentionality. But couldn't the same outcome be accomplished by having a capacity for sympathy that is so strong that one would never be willing to consider opportunism in the first place? This appears to be an implicit assumption of those who stress making us care more for one another in moral training to effectuate better moral outcomes.

Suppose an individual has no capacity for guilt, but engages in little opportunism because his sympathy response is so strong that he rarely wants to act on opportunities for exploitation because he doesn't want to do harm to anyone. The problem with having opportunism mediated by sympathy alone is that the increase in the strength of the sympathetic response would threaten to paralyze him with emotional pain arising from sympathizing with the daily harm that comes to those around him. He would be overwhelmed with sorrow, and the larger the group the truer this would be. Another problem with having a very strong sympathetic response is that sympathy can be a liability when it comes to fighting enemies, which is precisely why armies attempt to dehumanize their enemies. Dehumanizing an enemy weakens empathizing, and weakened empathy removes any reason for sympathy.

If, however, the individual possesses a capacity for guilt, then strong feelings of sympathy could be limited only to those who are close to him, which is efficient for the reasons discussed above. So by having a capacity for guilt, unpleasant emotions that impede our ability to function are limited to where they produce the greatest net return: sympathizing with harm to those related to us, or those whose survival figures heavily into our own survival. Feelings of guilt are then strong, but limited to actions that are likely to engender very costly retaliation because of their intentionality or reckless disregard. Guilt therefore allows us to tie our strongest negative emotions precisely to those actions over which we have control, because they are most likely to induce strong retaliation.

AN ILLUSTRATION OF HARM-BASED MORAL RESTRAINT

In Chapter 2, guilt was accounted for in the model of rational opportunism by adding a cost term. I now propose that our natural sense of moral restraint works as follows: a negative moral action is considered because it is expected to produce a positive material payoff. Because we have a capacity for empathy, we identify with how the victim will feel in response to our action. Because we have a capacity for sympathy, we also care about the pain the victim experiences, and this reduces our own utility directly. But in addition to this reduction in utility, there is yet another due to having a capacity for guilt. Because we are also culpable, we also feel guilty. As a result, our own utility is reduced by even more. If feelings of guilt are sufficiently strong—and therefore sufficiently costly, thereby reducing utility at the margin by a sufficiently large amount—then such feelings will make such action irrational, and thereby produce moral restraint. If it is rational to expect moral restraint in the form of a reluctance to behave opportunistically, then it is rational to expect trustworthiness and therefore rational to extend trust. The relationship between opportunistic actions, empathy, sympathy, guilt, moral restraint, trustworthiness, and ultimately trust, can now be summarized as follows:

A self-serving action is considered that will likely bring harm to one or more individuals
↓
Empathizing with the harmed individual or individuals → feelings of sympathy
↓
Feelings of sympathy + culpability → involuntary feelings of guilt
↓
Sufficiently strong feelings of guilt → moral restraint
↓
Moral restraint precludes opportunism
↓
Trustworthiness
↓
Trust

Modeling Harm-Based Moral Restraint

To simplify matters, let's set aside the issue of prudential restraint by assuming that the opportunistic actions considered below are in response to what the individual believes to be golden opportunities. In this case, there is no chance of being detected, so costs associated with institutional sanctions, the cost of a ruined reputation, the psychic cost of experiencing feelings of shame, etc., are all irrelevant and therefore can be ignored. Let's also assume there are no direct costs associated with opportunism (e.g., in the case of a burglar, he already owns all the tools he needs and he is off work and bored anyway). Given these assumptions, the only way to thwart opportunism is through an internalized mechanism such as internalized moral restraint.

Suppose that B considers taking a negative moral action, x_1, with respect to A. This action reduces A's utility by $\Delta U_A(x_1)$, which is the reduction in A's utility resulting from harm caused by B taking negative moral action x_1. Of course, B cannot know the form of A's utility function, but B nevertheless forms some kind of an expectation of the reduction in utility that results from his action. Let's represent B's belief about the effect of x_1 on A's welfare as the mathematical expectation of this effect; that is, as $E[\Delta U_A(x_1)]$, the *perceived harm* to A from doing x_1. The more that B knows about A's preferences, and the more accurate is B's ability to empathize with others in general, the closer $E[\Delta U_A(x_1)]$ will be to $\Delta U_A(x_1)$.

To say that B sympathizes with A is to say that B cares about A. This means that B's utility is affected by A's utility. A simple way to convey this idea is to add A's utility level to B's utility function. In other words, we can write

$$U_B(\cdot) = U(\ldots, \theta_A E[U_A(x_1)], \ldots)$$

where $\theta_A \geq \theta_0 > 0$. In economic parlance, this is just a very simple way of capturing interpersonal utility effects by saying, in effect, that if B believes that A's welfare has been decreased, then B's welfare will be decreased, too. If $\theta_A = 0$, then B is completely indifferent to A's welfare and the $\theta_A E[U_A(x_1)]$ term above vanishes from B's utility function regardless of how much A is affected by B's actions.

As long as $\theta_A > 0$, the $\theta_A E[U_A(x_1)]$ expression simply says that if B believes that A's welfare has been increased, then B's welfare will be increased, too. This is why parents take their children to Disney World—it makes them happy to see their children made happy. We obviously care more about the welfare of some people than others. The value of θ for our children is likely much higher than the value of θ for our neighbor, even if we like our neighbor very much. The parameter θ_A is therefore a measure of how strongly B cares about A and therefore how much B sympathizes with A's condition. If B cares about A's welfare exactly as much as his own, then $\theta_A = 1$. It is plausible that in some circumstances θ_A could exceed one (e.g., caring more about your only child than yourself) or be less than zero for someone you hate and therefore enjoy seeing harmed.

For simplicity, I will use the phrase "feeling guilty" to refer to the total expected reduction in utility resulting from taking a negative moral action. How strongly we feel guilty about harming others is a function of empathy and sympathy. Because B empathizes with A, B understands the harm that A is suffering. As noted earlier, it is possible for someone to sympathize with another but be lacking in empathy (a lovable oaf). This would be reflected in the $E[U_A(x_1)]$ term being a zero even though the $\Delta U_A(x_1)$ term is positive. It is also possible for someone to be empathetic but lacking in sympathy with respect to a particular person (a skilled con man, a bounty hunter). This would be reflected by $\theta_A = 0$.

The assumption that $\theta_0 > 0$ conveys the idea that there is a lower bound to our regard for others, even complete strangers. I believe this to be a very realistic assumption.[16] We often do small things for complete strangers quite automatically, even if there is no chance for reciprocation in the future if we do, and no threat of retaliation if we don't. It could be argued that such behavior may still be driven by reciprocity because in the EEA, those who appeared to be strangers at a point in time might pop up again in the future. I don't dispute this point, I merely think that such reciprocity would require a mechanism that is nearly automatic and works when such reciprocity is generally efficient. One way to accomplish this is through hardwired traits or moral values that result in us having at least a small amount of concern for others. My point is simply that the assumption that $\theta_0 > 0$ is quite plausible.[17] In any case, the analysis proceeds without difficulty even if $\theta_0 = 0$.

We can now think about how our natural, harm-based sense of moral restraint, through the mechanisms of empathy and sympathy, manifests itself in terms of the discussion above. Someone like B considers undertaking an opportunistic action (x_1) that promotes his welfare at the expense of A. Because we assume that B has a capacity for empathy, B understands that action x_1 will harm A and forms an expectation of the effect of the action. In B's estimation, A's harm will be $E[\Delta U_A(x_1)]$ (the perceived harm). If B cares about A's welfare, then $\theta_A > 0$ and the reduction in A's welfare will also produce a reduction in B's welfare equal to $\theta_A E[\Delta U_A(x_1)]$ (the *relevant* perceived harm).

Let us now account for the effect of feelings of guilt. Actions vary in their degree of culpability. I shall assume that the higher the degree of culpability, the greater will be the guilt response. Of course guilt is also directly related to how much we care about the person who was harmed. This suggests a simple modification to the expression above to account for guilt. Define $g_B(x)$ as B's guilt response function. Let $g_B(x)$ have a range of $[1, \infty]$. Multiplying it by $\theta_A E[\Delta U_A(x)]$ we have an expression for B's total utility cost of undertaking x_1, which is $g_B(x_1)\theta_A E[\Delta U_A(x_1)]$. An action that carries no sense of culpability will produce no additional feelings of guilt, so $g_B = 1$ and there is no effect beyond our feelings of sympathy for the harmed individual. If, however, the harm was the fault of B's behavior, then $g_B > 1$. The higher the degree of culpability, the larger g_B will be and therefore the more disutility results from the reduction in A's utility, so the more B's welfare will also be reduced.[18]

In Chapter 2, I posited that rational opportunism is governed by comparing the benefits and costs of opportunistic action, its effect on *net* utility. In other words:

$$V(x) = U(z(x)) - C(x),$$

where the $C(x)$ term accounted for the cost of many factors. Since we are limiting our attention to golden opportunities, we need only consider that the cost of experiencing involuntary feelings of guilt from harming those we care about. This expression can now be rewritten from the perspective of B as:

$$V_B(x) = U_B(z(x)) - g_B(x)\theta_A E[\Delta U_A(x)].$$

Will B undertake a specific negative moral action such as x_1? The expression above gives us a precise way of answering this question if B's sense of moral restraint is solely harm-based in nature. If B is rational, B will contemplate whether to undertake x_1 by weighing the benefits and costs of undertaking x_1. The benefit to B of undertaking x_1 is simply $U_B(z(x))$. Since B's sense of moral restraint is harm-based in nature, the cost to B of undertaking x_1 is determined by B's ability to perceive that A has been harmed, $E[\Delta U_A(x_1)]$, the cost of sympathizing with that perceived harm, $\theta_A E[\Delta U_A(x_1)]$, which is scaled up by the additional cost of feeling guilty, $g_B(x_1)\theta_A E[\Delta U_A(x_1)]$.

In short, if the first term is larger than the second, then the answer is yes—*B* will undertake x_1 with respect to *A*. Obviously, the larger is the first term, the more likely the answer will be yes. However, the larger is the second term (that is, the larger are the values of $E[\Delta U_A(x)]$, θ_A, or $g_B(x)$), the more likely the answer will be no. Note that in this model there is no conflict between the concept of rational choice and the possibility that our actions are governed in part by our emotions. With respect to most people in most of the world most of the time, the answer is "no" because the vast majority of us care at least a little about other people, even complete strangers, and so we feel guilty about doing things that harm them.

There is nothing irrational about people generally drawing this conclusion as long as their feelings are derived from moral tastes that are primary to the process of decision making. We don't choose to feel guilty when we act as opportunists any more than we choose to feel pleasure when we eat chocolate. We feel guilty because when we harm others it is part of our basic human nature to feel guilty. In the context of a rational decision-making model, feelings of guilt are ultimately based on moral tastes that are primary to rational decision making. Some of these moral tastes are likely hardwired, but that hardwiring can likely be amplified by moral beliefs and moral training. Some religions are notorious for doing just that very thing.

Our natural sense of moral restraint is, therefore, derived from the cost of experiencing feelings of guilt outweighing the benefits of the gains from opportunism. Of course, occasionally opportunities come along that produce large benefits (a large value for $U(z(x))$ that either harms others very little or harms others we do not care about harming or enjoy harming). In such cases, choosing to behave opportunistically is completely rational, so if moral restraint is derived solely from a reluctance to do harm, then opportunism will occur.

Conclusion

The account given here of our natural, harm-based sense of moral restraint comports well with the work of Adam Smith. Like Smith, I have attempted to give an account based on how people actually think about morality, not how they should think. This was therefore an utterly empirically driven exercise in an effort to develop a positive theory, not a philosophical or ideological exercise in the development of normative theory. Although Smith's work did have normative content (he was not shy about stating flatly the desirability of a society that embraced benevolence, for example), the framework he presented in *The Theory of Moral Sentiments* and then applied in *The Wealth of Nations* was a framework derived from claims about how people actually behave, not how they should behave or how we might wish they behaved. As a result, this analysis is not inconsistent with actual human nature.

CHAPTER 6

The Empathy Problem

If you just learn a single trick, Scout, you'll get along a lot better with all kinds of folks. You never really understand a person until you consider things from his point of view . . . Until you climb inside of his skin and walk around in it.—Atticus Finch in Harper Lee's *To Kill a Mockingbird*, 1960, p. 30

Introduction

In this chapter, I identify a fundamental problem that large group size poses for combating opportunism through harm-based moral restraint. I will show that if one's implicit theory of morality maintains that wrongfulness is derived solely from harm, then in large groups many acts of opportunism will simply not *feel* wrong. This is because in large groups it is often the case that no perceptible harm will come to any person because it is spread over too many people to affect any individual's welfare perceptibly. As such, there is no harmed person to empathize with, sympathize with, or feel guilty about. This is a very important point, for it is because of this "empathy problem" that neither increasing our concern for others nor increasing our predilection for feeling guilty will effectively combat opportunism where doing so matters most.[1]

Consider a single mother of three who has to work two jobs to earn $25,000 per year. Even she would not notice the loss of 20 cents if she did not observe the loss directly. What is going here is very simple. Life is filled with many random factors. Therefore, we often cannot even perceive relatively small losses unless they are pointed out to us directly. This is for good reason. To be so fastidious as to be able to notice all of them would be inefficient, as it would put us at risk of being so preoccupied with minor problems that we will miss large problems.

When harm from opportunism is spread over most members of a large group, then something like the above occurs. The *empathy problem* refers to the phenomenon of negative moral acts not feeling wrong if moral restraint is solely harm-based in nature and the cost of such acts is spread over so many people that no one is perceptibly harmed. This is a problem because to an individual, embezzling $1,000 from the corporation that employs him represents a significant improvement in his welfare, but since not a single shareholder has his wealth reduced by even a cent as a result, no feelings of guilt are aroused. Similarly, when an individual inflates an insurance claim by $10,000, no person on the planet is actually harmed at the margin. "The Insurance Company" is harmed, but it is owned by a great many persons, none of whom are perceptibly harmed as individuals. The crux of the problem is that if moral restraint is limited to harm-based moral restraint, then when the harm from opportunism is spread over so many people that there is no person with whom to empathize, there is no one to sympathize with and therefore nothing to feel guilty about.

This is such a simple and obvious problem that one wonders why more hasn't been made of it. One possible reason is that modeling it mathematically in a straightforward way tends to mask its effect. Although the harm per person falls with the size of the group, the number of persons harmed rises proportionately at the same time. At first, this appears to produce an equivalent mathematical effect—100 people harmed by a $1 each, or 1 person harmed by $100, is still $100 of total harm. This is certainly true, of course, but it leaves out important details about the psychological mechanisms that actually give rise to harm-based moral restraint. In reality, no matter how many terms are in a sum, if none of the terms are perceived, so that they are all effectively regarded as zeroes, then the total perceived effect on the part of the opportunist will also be zero. So the fact that a great many people are harmed ends up not offsetting the fact that the harm done at the margin is small.[2] This comports with Gneezy's (2005) observation that a focus on the harm done to an individual may explain why ". . . people are more accepting of fraudulent behavior directed at large organizations or rich counterparts than at individuals: the monetary cost may be identical, but the damage to the individual is perceived as greater" (p. 391).

In the movie *Office Space,* a plan is hatched to skim digits from transactions that would normally be rounded. If you were a "victim" of this scheme you would have had to transact dozens of times just to have the harm add up to one cent. This does not mean you are not worse off, of course, but that is beside the point. The point is that the person stealing the pennies would know that your utility level has not fallen, so you won't feel badly, so the opportunist has no bad feeling to empathize with at the margin. Increasing the number of people who are not perceptibly harmed doesn't change this result, even though it does pile up an impressive sum of money for the opportunist.

In the previous chapter, I explained why we might be naturally inclined to obey moral prohibitions that provide moral restraint in those instances where prudential restraint derived from repeat play effects, social relations, or formal institutions is insufficient. In this chapter I now explain why, to be effective in large groups, *the actual content of moral beliefs also matters.* In short, our implicit moral theory for why it is wrong to disobey moral prohibitions must go beyond the consequences our actions have on the welfare of others, because in large groups the practical effect of such consequences often disappear.[3] This should surprise no one. Our utterly consequentialist harm-based sense of moral restraint has no reason to work well in large group contexts, because it evolved in very small social groups.

A Model of the Empathy Problem[4]

In many cases, opportunistic actions impose harm that is spread among the members of an entire group. For example, when a team member shirks, the harm may be spread among all team members in the form of lower total output. When a person embezzles money from a corporate firm, the harm that results is borne by all of the firm's shareholders. When a person exaggerates a deduction on his income taxes, the harm that results is borne by all of the nation's taxpayers.

Let's therefore consider a single act of opportunism whose harm is spread equally over all of the members of a group. As we consider groups of increasing size, the number of individuals over which the harm from a given negative moral action is divided is increased. Obviously, for any single act of opportunism undertaken by B, the harm experienced by any other individual with whom B can empathize grows closer to zero as n grows larger. At some point the harm done is imperceptible, so the common query, "Who's it going to hurt?" can be honestly answered, "No one."

The golden rule is often touted as the ultimate moral calculus. The golden rule demonstrates the power of empathy. But even the golden rule is susceptible to the empathy problem. If by doing x_1 person B is able to promote his welfare and harms no one in the process, he can rationalize that were he an "A" (someone in the group over which the cost of opportunism is spread) he would not be harmed, and therefore would not object. This is indeed what happens when someone supports another's cheating of an insurance company because "nobody gets hurt," even though that supporting individual pays premiums to or owns stock in the company being scammed. The crux of the problem is that insurance premiums will not rise and stock prices will not fall—not even by one penny—because of *that* particular instance of cheating.

Note also that harm-based moral restraint disappears in such cases, regardless of how prone an individual is to feeling guilty (that is, no matter how large the $g(x)$ term is). This implies that inculcating a stronger predilection for feeling guilty does not solve the problem, because if one's theory of wrongfulness is based solely on harm, then being culpable for an action that produces no harm means there is nothing to feel guilty about. So no matter how large $g(x_1)$ is, if n is sufficiently large, and harm is spread evenly over all members of the group, B will know he is responsible for the outcome but will not feel not feel guilty about it.

For negative moral acts, x, undertaken in a group of size n, we can incorporate the discussion above into the model by rewriting net utility as:

$$V(x, n) = U(z(x)) - C(x, n) = U(z(x)) - g(x)h(x, n),$$

where $h(x, n) = \theta_A E[\Delta U_A(x_1, n)]$, the *relevant* perceived harm to A given B's concern for A's welfare ($\theta_A > 0$). Recall that since we are limiting our attention to golden opportunities, we ignore the expected cost of retaliation or a ruined reputation. The key point is that U(), which accounts for the benefits of undertaking an opportunistic action, is not a function of n, but h() is. As the number of people over which harm is spread increases, the harm suffered by any individual with whom the opportunist can empathize vanishes, so cost in the form of experiencing feelings of guilt vanishes. Again, how much one cares about the individuals involved is irrelevant, because if they cannot even perceive a change in welfare, then clearly no harm has come to them. How prone one is to feeling guilty is similarly irrelevant. Note that this result does not require any heroic assumptions about the nature of individual preferences or knowledge of preferences. One need not know the utility function for every individual to know that as $n \rightarrow \infty$ moral restraint vanishes, if one's moral restraint is ultimately derived from feelings of sympathy and guilt derived from doing harm.[5]

Let us now consider how you might actually think through the rationalization of opportunism when empathy effects are driven to zero. You really want something, but to get it you have to do x_1. You don't want to do x_1 because x_1 is a negative moral act and, being a moral person, you try to stick to moral rules of thumb. You know that when you deviate from moral rules of thumb you normally feel guilty. So you generally don't do things like x_1 because of the feelings of guilt you expect to experience.

But wait a minute. Why do you regard x_1 as wrong in the first place? If you regard it as wrong solely because of the harm it *normally* causes—because your implicit moral theory of wrongfulness is solely harm-based—then things you deem as wrong are wrong because they harm others. If you know with certainty that no one will be harmed by doing x_1 in this particular circumstance, then even though doing x_1 is generally wrong, and a prohibition against doing x_1 is therefore a good rule of thumb, the *spirit* of the rule is not violated by doing x_1 in this instance because clearly no one will be harmed. Given your implicit moral theory of wrongfulness, this is clearly a valid exception to the rule.[6] This does not mean x_1 drops from the list of negative moral acts. You still understand that doing x_1 is *generally* wrong. It simply means that *in this instance* you believe that you are confronted with a genuine exception to the moral rule of thumb. Doing x_1, therefore, simply does not *feel* wrong *in this instance*. After all, who's it going to hurt?

You might even still feel a little guilty about doing x_1 because of your habit of mind, but you will experience far less guilt than if you knew your actions would actually harm someone. As long as the utility loss from experiencing that twinge of guilt is outweighed by the utility gain from the spoils of undertaking x_1, you will still undertake x_1. This example is precisely the problem we face in large groups. As a rule of thumb we regard x_1 as a negative moral act. As such, we think it is wrong and we know we are not supposed to do it. We don't give much thought to why we believe it to be wrong. But if we believe that what makes x_1 wrong in the first place is solely the harm it causes others, then in a circumstance in which no person is harmed (taking paper home from our large employer) we have a clear exception to our moral rule of thumb against doing x_1.

This has important implications for opportunistic behavior in general. All opportunistic acts ultimately involve taking advantage of a trust. Taking advantage of a trust is a negative moral act. We don't give much thought to why we believe this, but in reality this carries moral force with most people because taking advantage of a trust nearly always results in harm. As a result, a general prohibition against taking advantage of a trust is a moral rule of thumb in all societies. But if your implicit theory of morality maintains that wrongfulness is itself ultimately derived solely from a prohibition against doing harm, then if taking advantage of a trust in a particular circumstance is expected to harm no one, you will believe that you are confronted with a genuine exception to the rule. You therefore won't feel very guilty, in that instance, about behaving in an opportunistic manner.

This result is hardly shocking or surprising. It comports with our personal life experiences and is exemplified repeatedly in our literature. In *The Adventures of Huckleberry Finn*, for example, Huck's acts of complicity with petty con artists show that his moral restraint was largely limited to his natural reluctance to harm others. So as long as the con artists harmed a great many by very little, his conscience was not terribly burdened. But when the king and duke were going to take everything left to a man's daughters and nieces, it was too much for him to bear. Why? In this case he could directly empathize with the harm he was doing to actual people because the harm was no longer divided over many people.[7]

Given his willingness to mock those driven by facile eagerness to obey rules, I suspect Mark Twain would have us believe that a man whose conscience is driven by rules rather than sympathy is a less moral man. I would be inclined to agree, as far as that goes. But we will find shortly that while the *sine qua non* of our basic decency may be ultimately derived from sympathy actuated by empathy, this is merely the foundation for a decent society as a whole. A foundation does not a house make, and we will soon find that because of the empathy problem, harm-based moral restraint is simply not enough for a society to enjoy the full fruits of prosperity.

As was pointed out in Chapter 2, even if a single opportunistic action undertaken by a single opportunist inflicts no perceptible harm at the margin, when *everyone* behaves as an opportunist great harm is done to everyone. When every employee of a large firm embezzles just a little, the cumulative effect is devastating. The crux of the problem is that at no individual has the power to change the outcome through his own moral restraint. Indeed, any single opportunistic act taken by an individual does not by itself bring about the general result. As we saw in

Chapter 2, opportunism is a pervasive problem for human societies precisely because it is often quite rational, given the nature of the incentives involved.

The empathy problem makes matters worse, because when n is very large it is often the case that there isn't any perceptible harm done to any victim. But if everyone always behaves opportunistically when they think they can get away with it, then the combined effect is devastating. It can be rational yet harmful because, as demonstrated in Chapter 2, that is the nature of the commons dilemma associated with opportunistic behavior. The effect that the empathy problem has on the commons dilemma problem, in terms of its canonical matrix payoffs, is presented in the Appendix.

TWO ILLUSTRATIONS OF THE COST OF THE EMPATHY PROBLEM

To see how a diminished ability to empathize with harmed individuals can reduce general prosperity, let's first consider what happens when firms are limited in size because moral restraint is solely harm-based. Suppose that for firms of size $n > n^*$ workers, empathy effects are so weak that behaving opportunistically is generally optimal for workers, so agreements to refrain from opportunism inevitably break down for the reasons discussed in Chapter 2. Now suppose that each of two societies is made up of 100 individuals and they produce one good, whose output is measured by Q. Suppose it is more efficient to produce a great deal of this good in one firm than it is to produce a small amount in many smaller firms. In other words, bigger as better, as argued by Adam Smith and as discussed in Chapter 3. To reflect this, let $Q = L^2$ in both societies, where L is the number of workers. Increasing returns is reflected by the exponent on L being greater than one. Now suppose that in the first society, people are unable to solve the empathy problem for firms larger than 10 individuals so $n^* = 10$. In the second society, the empathy problem is better solved so groups can be as large as 100. In the first society output is $10(10^2) = 1000$. In the second society output is $1(100^2) = 10,000$. If the first society could solve its empathy problem as well as the second society has, then its output would rise tenfold.[8]

Here is another example. I used to frequently get advertisements for cable television splitters that enable one to get premium channels for free. Since the signal is being sent anyway, the marginal cost imposed on the cable company is zero, so I would not harm anyone if I were to buy the splitter. Suppose everyone is willing to pay $30 a month for premium cable channels. Suppose the cable company has to pay the premium channel suppliers a flat fee of $100,000 per month for the right to provide these channels, and it charges $20 per month to its customers. If all 10,000 people in the subscription area want the premium channels, then the cable company can profitably provide what all the customers want and are willing to pay for. What costs the cable company $100,000 a month to provide, it can sell for $200,000 a month to its customers.

Now suppose anyone can buy a cable TV device for $50 that allows free access to premium channels with no chance of detection. If moral restraint is solely harm-based in nature, then no one would pay the $20 per month to buy the premium channels—they would all buy the device because it pays for itself in three months. But in this case, the cable company will not be able to cover the $100,000 it needs to get the signal in the first place, so the result is that no one gets the premium channels. This leaves everyone worse off (the cable company makes no additional profit, and each customer fails to get something for $20 per month that is actually worth $30 to him). To argue that harm is in fact done in equilibrium is to completely miss the point about why social dilemmas in general are so daunting. An individual's decision to buy a device for himself does not bring about the terrible outcome, because at the margin the loss in revenue is not sufficient to cause the cable company to terminate premium channel service.

Other Problems Associated with Harm-Based Moral Restraint

DIFFERENCES IN INCOME OR WEALTH

Harm-based moral restraint likely weakens the richer is the victim relative to the opportunist and/or those benefited by the opportunistic act. If utility is diminishing with respect to income and wealth, then the richer is the victim, the less the victim is harmed for any given amount taken. For this reason, it is simply difficult to empathize with those who possess much more wealth or earn much more income than we do. Consider a poor man who robs a billionaire of $10,000. If his moral restraint is derived solely from a reluctance to harm others, then he will not feel particularly guilty, because he knows the reduction in the billionaire's wealth is imperceptible to the billionaire. But even though he is poor himself, he might feel terribly guilty about cheating a homeless person out of $10. Moreover, the more disparities in income/wealth are believed to be random or the winnings of a zero-sum game, the easier it is to rationalize theft. In other words, empathy/guilt effects are reduced by such beliefs—we wouldn't likely feel as guilty about stealing what is believed to be either an arbitrary or possibly ill-gotten gain.[9]

This may present a problem for poor people who want to move up the income ladder, because it makes it hard for rich people to trust them. If (rich) A believes that (poor) B's moral restraint is solely harm-based, then A will not genuinely trust B unless he has a strong personal connection to B. Since many high-paying jobs and careers require being genuinely trusted by others, this can be a daunting impediment to economic advancement by those who are poor. To the extent that poor people are discriminated against in this way, poor people are more likely to become discouraged and demoralized, concluding that "the system" is unfair and thereby more easily rationalizing future opportunism.

DIFFERENCES IN TIME HORIZON

The ability to empathize with others can also be weakened when the benefits of opportunism are realized in a time horizon that differs from the time horizon over which harm is experienced by victims. In the 1980s many people who were otherwise moral copied computer programs purchased by others even though doing so was illegal. The problem was that when people copied software it harmed no one at *that* margin. The cost to software producers of a single individual copying their software is essentially zero to them, so that individual knows he has not harmed them in any way. No harm was suffered by the software manufacturer, so there was no one to empathize with and therefore nothing to feel guilty about. To those who lacked a principled reluctance to copy software illegally, it simply didn't feel wrong.

But doesn't the software firm lose the profit it would have otherwise earned? The answer is no, if the opportunist can convince himself that he would not have otherwise bought the product. This, of course, is an easy thing for an opportunist to convince himself of, and he has ample incentive for doing so. Moreover, even if the opportunist knew that he was willing to buy the software at the market price, he could rationalize that the software firm could have improved his welfare at zero marginal cost, but refused to. Instead, the firm engaged in what the individual regards as opportunistic hold-up, by making him pay for something that costs the firm nothing to give away by allowing unlimited copying.[10]

We have all heard this kind of rationalization before and many of us made such rationalizations in our youth. It is a fallacious rationalization, of course, because it considers the issue in an artificially narrow way (if everyone copies software illegally, then, similar to the earlier example about cable splitters, software creation becomes an unprofitable business so we all are harmed by not having software produced). One does not have to be evil to make such rationalizations—one need only desire the object and possess an implicit theory of morality that fails to make it feel wrong.

FIXED VERSUS VARIABLE COSTS

A closely related problem is political opportunism that takes advantage of the fact that most voters do not understand the distinction between fixed and variable costs. If we possess only harm-based moral restraint, then the benefits that accrue to society from the production and sale of high fixed-cost, low variable-cost goods, such as drugs, will disappear if such goods are under-produced because government only allows drug companies to charge a small amount above variable costs to keep the company from going bankrupt. The problem is that such a policy often results in revenues falling far short of covering prior development costs.

This is essentially an act of social bait and switch. The firm makes long-term investments because it believes it will make large profits over many years, only to discover that once the investment is in place the government delivers a political benefit to voters who are eager to rationalize a policy that reduces current drug prices. The problem is that once this lesson has been learned by drug companies, investment in developing new drugs drops dramatically, so products we can't even yet conceive of fail to ever emerge. Political opportunists are never held responsible, because no one misses drugs that never came to be.

The problem is really that the time scales over which the decision is made to buy or illegally copy software, or to buy a drug, is different than the time scales over which investments are made that make software or drugs possible. In the moment of opportunistic appropriation, the assets are fixed and therefore moot. If people could, at that moment of self-serving rationalization, fully appreciate the entire time scale associated with production of these kinds of goods, then it would no longer appear to them that the marginal cost imposed on the seller of their actions is zero.

COUNTERFACTUAL LOSSES

Our ability to empathize and therefore sympathize with others is also diminished when harm is counterfactual in nature. Suppose B undertakes an act that does not reduce A's welfare from what it is presently, but fails to increase it by as much as some other action would have. In many cases we are not obliged to increase the welfare others, and certainly not to increase it as much as possible. But in cases where, in return for something of value like a job, B has promised to do his best to *maximize* A's welfare, then failure by B to take the most beneficial action because a different action produces more benefits for B amounts to reneging on a contract. As such, it is an act of third-degree opportunism as defined in Chapter 2.

The reason why empathy effects are likely to be low or nonexistent with respect to counterfactual harm is that it is hard to think of a person as being harmed when his welfare has not been reduced, and it is especially hard when his welfare has actually been increased. In this case, harm does not fit the normal pattern of cause and effect (B does x to A [cause], therefore A's welfare falls [effect], so it follows that B harmed A by doing x). Suppose, for example, that a store manager considers taking advantage of an opportunity to steal $500 from the store's owner. This was the kind of moral dilemma faced by Ethan Allen Hawley in John Steinbeck's *The Winter of Our Discontent*. If he is the manager of a very small store, empathy effects are generally strong enough to keep the manager from stealing directly from the store's owner and thereby reducing his welfare.

But suppose the manager could choose actions x_1 or x_2 in response to an event, and neither action is known to the owner, as the choice constitutes local knowledge possessed only by the store manager. What if x_1 and x_2 solve the problem so well that in both cases profit rises, but x_1 makes it rise even more than x_2, while x_2 produces more benefit to the manager than x_1? In this case, the harm done to the owner by the manager's choice of x_2 is counterfactual in nature, so the manager might not feel guilty. His choice of x_2 did not reduce the owner's welfare from what it was—indeed, it increased it. In other words, putting himself in the store owner's shoes, he could rationalize that if he were the owner he would not be made unhappy by the outcome because his welfare would have actually been increased at the margin.[11]

But shouldn't the manager's ability to empathize with the store owner lead him to imagine himself as a store owner, and conjecture that if he were, he would want the manager to choose the most profitable action? Perhaps. But this alone is not enough to produce harm-based moral restraint. Unless the difference between x_1 and x_2 is large, it is still the case that there will be little harm to sympathize with, and therefore feel guilty about. In some cases, of course, the level of sympathy the store manager has for the owner might be so great that the manager will always choose the most profitable action. This is certainly plausible if the store manager and owner are very close, which may explain why in most of the world a store owner will only delegate significant decision-making discretion to a relative or close friend.

The weak or nonexistent empathy response to counterfactual harm is of particular relevance to the use of relational contracts for which third-degree opportunism is a problem. Recall that the larger is the firm, the more localized is knowledge and therefore the more important are relational contracts. But relational contracts create innumerable opportunities for third-degree opportunism that produce harm that is often only counterfactual in nature, because the self-serving action still increases profit at the margin.

In large firms that are crucial for achieving general prosperity, the use of relational contracts is particularly important to deal with the local knowledge problem in a way that supports entrepreneurial decision making throughout the firm. But the local knowledge problem that occasions their use and the flexibility they afford produces many more opportunities for third-degree opportunism than otherwise—many of which produce only counterfactual losses. In such cases if moral restraint is based solely on a reluctance to do harm, then moral restraint will be virtually non-existent.

Solving the Empathy Problem

Most humans have understood for a very long time that there are tremendous benefits to being able to organize social, political, economic, and military activity in large groups. In Chapter 3 I explained why a fundamental obstacle to large group cooperation is the problem of increasingly localized knowledge. Now we know that there is another, even more fundamental problem. Since our natural, harm-based sense of moral restraint withers in large groups, humans had to address the empathy problem in order to build large civilizations.

Some moral concepts may have evolved in part, therefore, to solve the empathy problem by supplementing harm-based moral restraint. For example, before societies had formal governments they were able to organize social, political, economic, and military activity into larger groups by addressing the problem of opportunism informally. Public shaming, for example, was often used to sanction those who were caught behaving opportunistically (Lal, 1998). The possibility of having to experience shame and feelings of embarrassment drives up the expected cost of undertaking negative moral actions, even in those cases in which no one could possibly be perceptibly harmed. So a social norm of shaming those who are discovered to have been behaving opportunistically can be viewed as a means of overcoming the empathy problem.

In even larger groups, opportunism that is not suppressed by self-restraint in the form of harm-based moral restraint, or by incentive effects due to shaming, was often suppressed by institutions that either preclude it through strict routines and procedures, or deter it through prudential restraint derived from incentives produced by monitoring and punishment. These are particularly effective means of combating first-degree opportunism because it involves potentially observable acts. With first-degree opportunism, harm is usually not counterfactual in nature, as is common with third-degree opportunism.

But as successful as these approaches were, they had serious shortcomings. Shaming has little effect in a society that is so large that people are effectively anonymous. This left formal institutions to take up the slack—but the harsh punishments that were common in all civilizations just a century ago are, for the most part, politically impossible in modern democratic societies. Judges and juries are normally inclined to punish opportunists in proportion to the damage done to people (judges and juries are, after all, hardwired to automatically conjecture that such punishment is just). This means that for expected costs to be sufficiently high to discourage opportunism, the reduction in harshness of punishment must be made up for by increasing the probability of detection. But in many poor societies this is simply not possible.

An even more fundamental problem is that of third-degree opportunism. Relational contracts are the key to addressing the problem of local knowledge in large groups, but relational contracts are highly susceptible to third-degree opportunism, which is by nature largely beyond the reach of institutions. This means that societies that are limited to relying on institutions to combat opportunism will face a tradeoff between firm size and the efficient use of local knowledge and, therefore, a tradeoff between the benefits of scale and the benefits of entrepreneurial rather than bureaucratic direction throughout firms. As I noted in Chapter 3, this may explain why most civilizations have been able to produce large organizations or entrepreneurial organizations, but not large *and* entrepreneurial organizations.

In Chapter 4 I argued that moral restraint could provide a way out of this problem. Recall that agents will not, by definition, be discouraged from acting on golden opportunities if their restraint is solely prudential in nature. Moral restraint overcomes this problem—it does not even require the possibility of detection because moral restraint is internalized. This renders moot the inability to detect golden opportunities. But in this chapter I have shown why even moral restraint is not necessarily enough. This is because if moral restraint is based solely on a reluctance to do harm, it will often wither in large group settings.

Can't societies circumvent this problem by dividing large groups into many small groups? Rubin (2002, p. 125) has pointed out that in large groups we tend to divide ourselves into smaller groups. Within large firms, for example, many workers are organized in small teams. Could this be the result of a need to solve the empathy problem through subdivision of large groups into smaller ones to actuate our natural, harm-based sense of moral restraint? Kandel and Lazear (1992) have indeed argued that this may be explained as an effort to harness the power of guilt to minimize shirking. By having some of each team member's reward earned at the team level, and also keeping the team small, shirking noticeably harms one's teammates—thereby actuating harm-based moral restraint.

But shirking is only one form of opportunism, and it is not even the most problematic form, since it can often be addressed with external mechanisms that don't weaken with group size. As we learned from Chapter 3, the most problematic form of opportunism in large organizations is third-degree opportunism, since it usually cannot be addressed by external mechanisms and it can potentially make the use of relational contracts impossible. Dividing workers into teams is especially impertinent to the problem of third-degree opportunism for a decision maker in a very large firm. This is because harm is generally counterfactual in nature, so in many cases not choosing the best possible action does not actually reduce any team member's welfare from its current state.

Moreover, the empathy problem has little to do with the size of the group within which cooperative production activity takes place. What really matters is the size of the group over which the costs of opportunism are spread. Dividing workers into teams will do nothing to limit opportunistic consumption of health insurance that is provided by the firm, or to limit petty theft from other units of the firm. So while dividing workers into teams may deal with some forms of opportunism, particularly shirking, it does not come close to fully addressing the empathy problem.

The most obvious means of effectuating moral restraint that is strong enough to address the empathy problem is to drive up regard for others. We generally do not, after all, take advantage of those we care deeply about. In a recent book, *The Empathy Gap*, J. D. Trout (2009) makes essentially this argument, echoing a common view that appears to be gaining in popularity. So couldn't a sufficiently strong desire to be a nice person overcome this problem? A desire to be nice certainly makes one more willing to undertake positive moral actions and less willing to undertake negative moral actions. As such, it could induce people to try to be more empathetic, so they are nice to greater effect. But if one's unwillingness to take negative moral actions is based solely on a reluctance to harm others, then if no one is perceptibly harmed, we are right back to the empathy problem.

With no perceptible harm there is nothing to empathize with, no reason to feel sympathy, and therefore no reason to feel guilty. Therefore increasing B's regard for others in general, by increasing θ_0 (the lower bound for θ in a given group), does not solve the problem. If no one is perceptibly harmed in the first place, then the level of sympathy for others is simply irrelevant so driving up θ_0 is irrelevant—the harm-based moral restraint story never gets off the ground. Driving up regard for others doesn't change the fact that our natural sense of moral restraint breaks down precisely where it is needed most—economic activity organized in the context of large groups.

So moral restraint is not enough—the *kind of moral restraint* people have also matters. Harm-based moral restraint is clearly insufficient in many large group settings. Is there some other way to make people reluctant to undertake negative moral acts when they believe there is little or no chance of being caught? One possibility would be to teach people moral beliefs that compel them to not undertake negative moral acts because they believe undertaking them is wrong as a matter of principle, and is therefore wrong irrespective of the harm they may do to others. This would produce what one might call *principled moral restraint*.

Principled Moral Restraint

My claim is that if the empathy problem is not addressed, it presents a daunting obstacle to the process of economic development and thereby impedes the maximization of general prosperity. The good news is that it can be plausibly overcome with moral beliefs that deem undertaking negative moral actions as inherently wrong, and therefore wrong as a matter of principle, and therefore wrong even if no harm is done to others.

Principled moral restraint is particularly relevant to combating the problem of opportunism. One generally recognized negative moral action is that of breaking one's word. If no one ever broke his or her word, including when it is implicitly given in the context of a social contract, then opportunism simply ceases to be a problem for society. But even if breaking one's word is recognized as being generally wrong, if the implicit theory of wrongfulness is based on harm, and in a particular instance no one is perceptibly harmed, in that instance breaking one's word won't feel wrong. It will feel like a legitimate exception. The key to solving the problem of opportunism in a general way, then, is to make breaking one's word *always feel wrong* because it is inherently wrong and therefore is wrong as a matter of principle.

But regardless of the nature of the arguments that might be made for having principled moral restraint, such restraint must ultimately be effectuated through the psychological mechanisms humans actually have—otherwise, we risk developing a theory of moral restraint that is based on unsound assumptions about human behavior.[12] This is why I carefully developed a theory of moral restraint based on hardwired moral intuitions in Chapter 5. I will now explain how principled moral restraint can plausibly work through a psychological mechanism that humans already possess: feelings of guilt attached, by moral beliefs, to negative moral acts themselves. This is not an heroic assumption—just ask anyone who foregoes an opportunity to improve his own welfare when he could have done so with no chance of detection, and without harming anyone else, and invariably that person will say something like ". . . honestly, it didn't even occur to me, but even if it had, I still wouldn't have done it because it still would have been wrong."

If the feelings of guilt an individual expects to experience from doing something he believes to be wrong as a matter of principle are sufficiently strong, then the resulting guilt cost will make undertaking any negative moral act irrational, even in such a large group that harm-based moral restraint is rendered inoperative. This can be added to our model of rational opportunism in a very straightforward way. Recall that if moral restraint is solely harm-based, and therefore solely *consequentialist* in nature, net utility can be expressed as:

$$V(x, n) = U(z(x)) - C(x, n) = U(z(x)) - g(x)h(x, n).$$

Recall that as n grows larger, the effect on $U()$ of undertaking x is unchanged, but the cost of experiencing feelings of guilt vanish. In this case, the commons dilemma associated with opportunism can only be overcome with external mechanisms, and those mechanisms will inevitably prove insufficient to provide moral restraint with respect to golden opportunities.

We can now incorporate principled moral restraint to solve the empathy problem directly, thereby alleviating the problem of third-degree opportunism in large groups such as large firms. Suppose people possess moral beliefs that attach feelings of guilt to the decision to undertake negative moral actions irrespective of harm done to others because, according to their moral beliefs, disobeying moral prohibitions against negative moral actions is wrong as a matter of principle. In this case there is a separate channel of guilt, so we must distinguish between guilt derived from being responsible for having done harm and guilt derived from the act itself. Such a *nonconsequentialist* source of guilt can be added, as follows, with a term that reflects guilt associated with negative moral acts irrespective of harm; that is:

$$V(x, n) = U(z(x)) - g(x)h(x, n) - g^p(x).$$

The main point is that while g can often be rendered moot by a sufficiently large n, g^p is unaffected by n because this form of guilt is attached to the act itself. This can dramatically reduce the risk of opportunistic exploitation in the context of large groups. The $C(x, n)$ term now becomes

$$C(x, n) = g(x)\theta_1 E[\Delta U_1(x)] + g(x)\theta_2 E[\Delta U_2(x)] + \ldots + g(x)\theta_n E[\Delta U_n(x)] + g^p(x).$$

But for $n > n^*$, we have:

$$C(x, n > n^*) = g(x)\theta_1[0] + g(x)\theta_2[0] + \ldots + g(x)\theta_n[0] + g^p(x) = g^p(x).$$

Obviously, if $g^p(x_1)$ is sufficiently large for a given individual, then it will be irrational for that individual to undertake negative moral action x_1 regardless of how large n is. Therefore, the empathy problem can be solved through moral beliefs that tie guilt directly to x_1 by making $g^p(x_1)$ sufficiently high. By doing so, the commons dilemma associated with opportunism disappears.[13] It follows that from society's point of view, a key to enjoying the lowest possible transaction costs is to make g^p as high as possible, for as many people as possible, over the largest set of negative moral actions possible. Of particular importance would be to make g^p as high as possible for the negative moral act of breaking one's word, as this provides an overarching mechanism to combat all forms of opportunism.

An obvious way to drive up g^p is to drive up moral conviction. One does not need much conviction to obey hardwired moral intuitions because in normally functioning adults, their gut already tells them that hurting others is wrong. Abstract moral ideas that provide the basis for believing that a given type of act is inherently wrong, however, likely require much more conviction because our hardwired moral intuitions give us little to go on. It is one thing to refrain from stealing \$10,000 because you are not willing to harm another person. It is quite another to refrain from stealing \$10,000 if you know with certainty that no specific person—not even a complete stranger—will be harmed in any way. In this latter case, if one knows one cannot be detected, one must, with great conviction, believe that stealing is inherently wrong if sufficient principled moral restraint is to be effectuated.

Religious beliefs can obviously play a role in driving up conviction, and perhaps this may be one reason why religion is such an important part of human history.[14] It may also be a reason why, in large societies, religions are noticeably more abstract and value oriented.[15] Many religions deem x_1 to be wrong because God said it is wrong. Since God is the ultimate moral authority, such a pronouncement makes it inherently wrong, and therefore wrong as a matter of principle, and therefore wrong even if no harm is done. Religious beliefs could have also improved the function of formal institutions by providing a moral basis for meting out punishments that are excessive given the nature of the transgression, but that are necessary given the difficulty of increasing expected costs through increased probability of detection. It is easier to hang someone for a minor crime if you believe it is your moral duty to do so because God commands that you do so.

A person goes beyond the *consequentialist*, harm-based approach to moral restraint when he adds a *nonconsequentialist*, principled approach to moral restraint. He regards the act as being wrong as a matter of principle and therefore feels guilty about undertaking the act even if no one is harmed in any way. But if the expected guilt cost is nevertheless low, and the benefit arising from opportunism is high, then he will still act in an opportunistic manner—even though the reason for feeling guilty was that he believed the act was wrong as a matter of principle. In short, principled moral restraint does not necessarily imply sufficient moral restraint to fully discourage opportunism.

This is very realistic. Even criminals who defend their actions by arguing that no one was harmed will often agree that what they did was still wrong as a matter of principle and that they feel some guilt for having done it. But they did it anyway because they wanted what they wanted so badly. The expected utility gained from the expected payoff of the opportunistic act simply outweighed the expected utility lost from experiencing feelings of guilt for having done wrong.

Conclusion

Our ability to empathize and therefore sympathize with others is not just the basis of our natural sense of moral restraint—it is the very foundation of basic human decency. It is a deep part of who we are. I personally find great comfort in the idea that an important part of our goodness is written in our genes.

In Chapter 3 I argued that prudential restraint effectuated by externally produced incentives is not enough to minimize transaction costs and thereby maximize general prosperity. To most fully deal with the local knowledge problem, it follows that moral restraint is also required to overcome the problem of third-degree opportunism because relational contracts open the door to third-degree opportunism.

In this chapter I have argued that even moral restraint is often not enough because harm-based moral restraint is not *scalable*. This is because the larger is the group over which the costs of opportunism are spread, the more likely no actual harm is done to anyone with whom we can empathize, sympathize, and therefore feel guilty about harming. If moral restraint is solely harm-based, it winds up withering in the large groups whose local knowledge problems occasioned the need for relational contracts in the first place. Because of the empathy problem, to discourage opportunism where doing so matters most—in the context of large group economic activity—we need more than harm-based moral restraint. We need principled moral restraint. This again points to the fact that we should not take too much solace from naturalistic arguments made in books by thoughtful authors such as Fukuyama (1999), Hauser (2006), Shermer (2008), and Trout (2009). The universal factors they seek in their efforts to explain moral behavior are very important, but they are simply not enough.

This chapter is titled "The Empathy Problem" and not "The Sympathy Problem" for a very good reason. Contrary to what many modern moral theorists appear to believe, a high trust society cannot be produced by simply increasing our regard for others. How much we care about others is simply irrelevant if no harm is done to them in the first place. Therefore, striving to increase moral earnestness by driving up the θ_0 and g() terms for all members of society is a misguided application of small group thinking to a large group problem. Indeed, in Chapter 8 I will explain why attempts to produce moral restraint by increasing moral earnestness may actually backfire, if moral restraint is limited to that which comes most naturally to us.

Finally, let me emphasize yet again that the discussion above should in no way be taken to suggest that our ability to empathize and sympathize with others is not important. Empathy and sympathy are not enough to achieve a large and generally prosperous society, but they are absolutely essential to having a decent society. While general prosperity requires moral sensibilities based on abstract moral ideas, the greatest horrors of human history were made possible by leaders that used abstract ideas to supersede what their citizens' natural moral instincts told them very clearly was wrong.

Appendix

Recall from the Appendix of Chapter 2 that the canonical commons dilemma game is given by the following:[16]

Table 6.1 The Commons Game

	Fewer than M others defect	Exactly M others defect	More than M others defect
Individual cooperates	COOPERATE + REWARD	COOPERATE + REWARD	COOPERATE
Individual defects	DEFECT + REWARD	DEFECT	DEFECT

All n players get a REWARD as long as there are no more than M defectors, but the payoff that defectors get (DEFECT) is always higher than the payoff obtained by those who cooperate (COOPERATE). However, every player is better off if they all cooperate than if they all defect, because COOPERATE + REWARD > DEFECT. The existence of a REWARD payoff term produces a kind of "tipping point" equilibrium, in that when a sufficiently high proportion of the population is not opportunistic, there are qualitative changes to society that produce a significantly lower level of transaction costs generally. The problem is that any individual nevertheless does better playing *DEFECT*. So what's rational at the margin is what produces the worst outcome in equilibrium.

An important but heretofore unrecognized element of the commons dilemma problem associated with opportunism is that because of the empathy problem, the absolute number of players, n, can affect the payoffs. Specifically,

1. The smaller n is, the more likely it is the case that:
   a. Choosing *COOPERATE* is self-enforcing so there is no dilemma in the first place.
   b. Choosing *DEFECT* will significantly harm some persons and the resulting guilt costs will be sufficient to drive the net payoff of choosing *DEFECT* too low for *DEFECT* to be the dominant strategy. In this case, harm-based moral restraint is sufficient to overcome the commons dilemma.
2. Conversely, the larger n is, the more likely it is the case that:
   a. No one will be perceptibly harmed by choosing *DEFECT*.
   b. If moral restraint is solely harm-based, no guilt will be experienced, and therefore the net payoff from *DEFECT* will be unaffected. A tragedy of the commons outcome may occur even if people are highly moral. In this case, harm-based moral restraint is insufficient to overcome the commons dilemma.

CHAPTER 7

Duty-Based Moral Restraint

We do not behave opportunistically in each and every encounter; we do not act in accordance with some 'as-if' cost-benefit reckoning . . . Many of us do not steal, even if we should be certain that there is no possibility of discovery, apprehension, and punishment.—James Buchanan, 1994, p. 63

Introduction

In many societies moral reasoning is complicated, subtle, and nuanced, because placing a value on all the costs and benefits involved is difficult, subjective, and varies with ever-changing circumstances. But in the kind of societies James Buchanan was speaking of in the quote above, moral reasoning is not complicated—it is largely a matter of right and wrong, not shades of gray requiring endless nuanced analysis. In these societies, moral expectations are simple and modest.[1]

In the previous chapter I explained why harm-based moral restraint is inadequate where moral restraint is needed most—in large group settings such as large firms and in the context of impersonal exchange. This is the *empathy problem*, and because of the central importance that economies of scale play in making general prosperity possible, it constitutes a fundamental obstacle to the development and operation of a market economy. By attaching feelings of guilt directly to having undertaken a negative moral act, however, principled moral restraint can solve the empathy problem.

This chapter explains why moral beliefs must logically structure the value system in a specific way to overcome another problem that is every bit as daunting as the empathy problem. I call this *the greater good rationalization problem*. I will show how a particular kind of moral restraint—duty-based moral restraint—overcomes both the empathy and greater good rationalization problems, and leads to beneficial changes in social, political, and commercial institutions by changing how people think about morality. To be specific, habits of mind produced by an ethic of duty-based moral restraint produce a social norm of always behaving in a trustworthy manner. This, in turn, makes it rational to extend trust others—even complete strangers—in most situations, producing a high trust society that minimizes transaction costs and thereby maximizes general prosperity.

The Greater Good Rationalization Problem

We naturally think of opportunism as an act of selfishness. But there is another reason why people are tempted to behave opportunistically. Suppose B cares so deeply about his spouse, children, grandchildren, close friends, etc., that while he would never engage in opportunism on his own behalf, he might do so if it protects them from harm or increases their welfare. Many otherwise moral people would, for example, steal food to feed their children if they were starving. The problem is that A might therefore fear B's opportunism even if A believes B to be a very decent guy.

The basic idea behind greater good rationalization is the belief that a negative moral act is not necessarily immoral if it is undertaken as a means to a positive moral end. The most obvious form of greater good rationalization takes the following form: B cheats A to help C and feels morally justified in doing so, because the harm done to A is small relative to the benefit realized by C. I shall argue below that it is likely that we are hardwired to think in these terms. When caught behaving opportunistically, people often explain their behavior in such terms. Indeed, the word "rationalize" has almost become synonymous with making a greater good argument to excuse one's actions.

The crux of the problem is that while guilt provides a durable mechanism through which internalized moral restraint can be effectuated, we can also feel guilty about not doing what we believe we *should* do. So if A knows that B might feel guilty about failing to undertake a positive moral action, A must worry about becoming a victim of B's opportunism in B's effort to achieve some noble end at A's expense. It is therefore nearly impossible for A to regard B as being *unconditionally* trustworthy.[2] For A to be able to rationally extend trust to B, then, A must believe B will not opportunistically victimize him even if B believes that by doing so he can do great good while harming A but little.

It follows that if a person is known to possess moral beliefs that permit greater good rationalizations, his trustworthiness will be suspect. Those who might consider extending him trust know that he may conclude that it is not immoral to cheat them if he believes that the harm done to them is small, while the good done for others is large. Since those who might extend him trust can anticipate this possibility, they know it is unwise for them to treat him as being unconditionally trustworthy. This reduces the scope of transactions they can undertake with him. Only those who are very close to him can feel sure that he won't sacrifice their welfare as a means to achieving some greater good.

There is troubling evidence that greater good rationalization is contributing to an epidemic of student cheating in American education. There has always been student cheating, of course, but in the past most students who were caught agreed that what they did was wrong. But increasingly today, students report that they simply don't feel that it is wrong to cheat because it was done in an effort to help someone else.[3]

WHY PRINCIPLED MORAL RESTRAINT IS NOT ENOUGH

The fact that one's moral restraint is principled rather than harm-based in nature is not enough to solve the greater good rationalization problem. Principled moral restraint works by tying feelings of guilt directly to negative moral actions through the belief that some actions are inherently wrong. Principled moral restraint tells us why we should feel guilty, but just because one believes that doing something is inherently wrong does not mean that the resulting feelings of guilt will be strong enough to discourage the action. This is because there is no particular reason why the level of guilt one experiences for failing to undertake a positive moral action would not exceed the level guilt arising from taking the negative moral action that made it possible.

If the guilt B experiences from failing to promote the welfare of C is greater than the guilt B experiences from undertaking the required negative moral action, then it will be rational for B to behave opportunistically even if B believes the action is wrong as a matter of principle. Put another way, even principled moral restraint that is sufficient to solve the empathy problem with respect to self-serving opportunism is not necessarily sufficient to solve the greater good rationalization problem.

Obviously, the likelihood that an individual in any given circumstance will behave opportunistically as a result of a greater good rationalization is greater the more the value system emphasizes exhortations to undertake positive moral actions over prohibitions against taking negative moral actions. People who live in societies that emphasize moral exhortations while downplaying the importance of moral prohibitions are, therefore, more likely to become victims of opportunism than those who live in other societies. It follows directly that transaction costs will generally be higher in societies that emphasize moral exhortations over moral prohibitions.

Obviously, the more B cares about or feels responsible for C's welfare, the guiltier B will feel about failing to act to improve it when given the opportunity to do so. This is why it is so easy to rationalize nepotism, favoritism, and cronyism, and it is also why each so powerfully undermines trust in the broader society. Greater good rationalization might therefore be an important factor in undermining the emergence of a high trust society, because we are least suspicious of those whom we believe care about us. This has the effect of limiting the extension of trust only to those we know very well—a circle of trust—thereby contributing to economic tribalism.[4]

In short, even if *B* possesses principled moral restraint, we can become a victim of *B*'s opportunism through greater good rationalizations that may be a completely sincere exercise in virtue. Indeed, it could be argued that, according to a (consequentialist) utilitarian theory of morality, such action may even be morally required and economically efficient. The problem is that such greater good rationalizations nevertheless undermine the possibility of having a norm of unconditional trustworthiness and are therefore inconsistent with having a high trust society. Even if the impulses involved are genuine, those who expect to be opportunistically victimized will not extend trust. This drives up transaction costs. From the perspective of a society that wishes to maximize general prosperity, this is a fundamental problem indeed.

FROM GREATER GOOD RATIONALIZATION TO SELF-SERVING OPPORTUNISM

Greater good rationalization can also produce habits of mind that are likely to support the rationalization of self-serving acts of opportunism. How guilty *B* feels for choosing not to improve *C*'s welfare is subjective. *B* alone knows how much he values any given positive moral act in any given circumstance. Unfortunately, this makes it easy for *B* to conclude that he will (or should) feel guiltier about not acting to improve the welfare of others than how guilty he will feel about the negative moral act that makes it possible. This is especially true when what is good for *C* also happens to be good for the decision maker. For example, *B* could say to himself, "I would feel guilty if I cheated my coworker out of a promotion. But not cheating my coworker out of the promotion also means that I will not be doing my best to support my family. I'd rather cheat my coworker than not put my family first."

Since there is no objective basis for weighing the good that is made possible by a negative moral action or the bad resulting from it, it is the individual considering the opportunistic action who ultimately weighs the good against the bad. This consequentialist, benefit-cost calculation occurs completely in the mind of the individual who stands to benefit (either directly or indirectly via interpersonal utility effects). This often leads to the moral conclusion that one should behave opportunistically when it is prudent for him to do so. For many people, then, moral restraint is sometimes no more restraining than prudential restraint.

Greater good rationalization can also be ultimately self-serving in the following way: *B* can do x, which is a negative moral act, and by doing x, improve *C*'s welfare. In the future *C* now feels indebted to *B* and therefore obliged to return the favor by doing y to help *B* directly, or by doing something harmful *A*, who is *B*'s rival. If *B* was only willing to do x because he expected *C* to feel indebted, then what he justifies in his own mind as an act of benevolence might actually be a cynical manipulation of *C*'s predilection to return favors. Through future returned favors, benefactors can therefore benefit indirectly from disobeying moral prohibitions.

Yet another way in which greater good rationalizations can be ultimately self-serving is that *B* takes advantage of *A*, but *B* reasons that he should not feel guilty because he plans to repay *A* with a favor that will more than compensate *A*. The weight put on the negative moral act and the weight put on the future favor are both determined in the mind of *B*, the opportunist. As a result, *B* might repay *A* with a favor that *A* (if *A* knew what happened) would contend is far less valuable than the harm done to him. Moreover, if conflict later emerges between *A* and *B*, then *B* might decide that part of his retaliation will be to not return the favor owed to *A*. This is a tempting approach for *B* since it will save resources without engendering retaliation from *A* since *A* did not know he was entitled to the repayment of a favor in the first place.

One can also rationalize a negative moral act taken today with a promise *one makes to oneself* to undertake positive moral acts in the future. The problem, again, is that all the moral valuations involved are chosen by the opportunist himself. This means that in any given period, virtually anything can be rationalized. Such rationalizations are, of course, most problematic with respect to golden opportunities, since there is no possibility of punishment or negative reinforcement for disobeying moral prohibitions, but there is the possibility of positive reinforcement for undertaking the positive moral acts involved. Such rationalizations also become more problematic the larger is the group involved because of the empathy problem and the greater number of spectators to express approval for positive moral actions that won't be concealed.

These examples are hardly farfetched. People frequently rationalize self-serving opportunism via greater good arguments, especially when the negative moral act does little damage, but the positive moral act that is made possible by it produces a significant improvement in the welfare of those who benefit. If such rationalizations are viewed as legitimate by most people, a norm of unconditional trustworthiness will be impossible, so people will generally feel that it is foolish to extend trust outside their circle of trust. Even if the motives involved are pure, this dramatically reduces the scope of viable transactions through which to effectuate the gains from specialization. The end result is a society whose value system produces a penny-wise but pound-foolish form of morality.

Can't moral standards solve the greater good rationalization problem? Not likely. Even if there is complete agreement as to the appropriate moral weight for every moral act in every circumstance, the set of all possible future circumstances cannot be known *a priori*. This means that moral weights are still effectively subjective because we cannot predict how a particular person will weigh a given action in a circumstance no one has thought of yet. This is why it is one thing to trust someone in a highly structured transaction relationship, but quite another to trust someone in a flexible transaction relationship under constantly changing circumstances, such as is required in the context of a relational contract.[5]

If internalized moral restraint takes the form of the individual's own conscience, then what matters is his personal moral valuation of x relative to y in a given circumstance, where the set of future possible circumstances cannot be known beforehand. We therefore cannot know that we will not become a victim of that individual's greater good rationalizations. So if a society is to enjoy the benefits of having the lowest possible transaction costs by making unconditional trustworthiness possible where it matters most, then both the empathy problem and the greater good rationalization problem must be addressed.

Finally, in Chapter 6 I explained why, because of the empathy problem, opportunism cannot be successfully combated by increasing our regard for others, by increasing θ_0. From our discussion above, it follows that such an approach to addressing the general problem of opportunism may actually worsen the greater good rationalization problem. This is because the larger is θ_0, the greater is the weight placed on positive moral actions, so the guiltier one will feel from failing to take positive moral actions. The larger the group, the stronger this effect will be, since in very large groups the ability of θ_0 to thwart opportunism is essentially zero because empathy effects will also be zero while at the same time the esteem derived from the approval of others will be even higher.

The Lexical Primacy of Moral Prohibitions

Since the root of the greater good rationalization problem is the trading off of positive moral actions against negative moral actions, what is ultimately needed is a bright line between moral values that encourage us to undertake positive moral actions and moral values that discourage us from taking negative moral actions. Otherwise, it will be all too easy for us to convince ourselves that the value of doing positive moral act y is so high that we are justified in doing x as a means to that end.

Many social scientists now believe that our hardwired moral intuitions naturally lead us to think of morality in a utilitarian manner because it effectuates an efficient pattern of resource allocation in small groups—which is precisely the environment in which our hardwired moral intuitions evolved. We therefore naturally employ a cost-benefit approach to moral reasoning. This produces a one-dimensional approach to moral reasoning, in the sense that both positive and negative moral actions are distributed on the same number line. As such, the only qualitative difference between moral values is algebraic sign (with negative moral actions to the left of zero and positive moral actions to the right of zero). The quantitative difference between moral actions is simply the moral weight we place on them (their absolute value).

The problem is that value systems that effectively relate moral values to one another in this way inevitably promote greater good rationalization, because the moral propriety of any action is inevitably determined by a cost-benefit calculation. Since it is the decision maker who stands to benefit from opportunism (either directly or indirectly) and the moral weight of each positive moral action is necessarily subjective in nature, it is all too easy for him to convince himself that acts of opportunism that are prudent are also morally acceptable. This means that with the exception of those with whom you have very close ties, you can trust almost no one not to take advantage of you if by doing so he harms you only a small amount but benefits others a great amount. It should be clear that a necessary condition for addressing the greater good rationalization problem is to impede the trading off of positive and negative moral actions.

In economic theory, indifference curves between two goods are normally negatively sloped and convex. But the more an individual regards two goods as being close substitutes for one another, the closer to linear his indifference curves will be and the more likely the individual will be willing to exchange one for the other. Figure 7.1a illustrates indifference curves for two goods, X and Y, if they are *perfect* substitutes.

Conversely, the truer it is that consuming one good is only desirable if another good can also be consumed, the less likely one will be willing to exchange one for the other. Such goods are said to be complements of one another. They are goods we tend consume together, so getting more of one and less of the other doesn't make much sense. A well known example of perfect complements is right and left shoes. We are not willing to exchange in our left shoes to get more right shoes for obvious reasons. Figure 7.1b illustrates indifference for two goods, X and Y, if they are *perfect* complements.

It might appear that the bright line we seek to establish between moral prohibitions and moral exhortations would be logically analogous to having positive and negative moral values be perfect complements, but this is not correct. Addressing the greater good rationalization problem by avoiding the trading off of the obedience of moral exhortations for the obedience of moral prohibitions is necessary, but not sufficient. Because combating opportunism is of paramount importance, it is

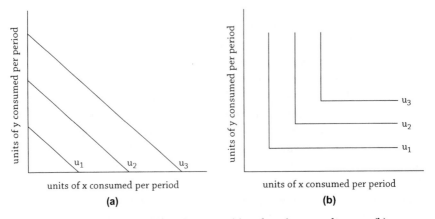

Figure 7.1. Illustration of perfect substitutes (a) and perfect complements (b). Because $U_3 > U_2 > U_1$, moving northeast in either panel means the individual jumps to higher levels of utility. But whereas more of X *or* Y will result in higher levels of utility for perfect substitutes (panel a), more of both X *and* Y is required to reach higher levels of utility for perfect complements (panel b).

obeying moral prohibitions against negative moral actions that matters (recall that in Chapter 4 I argued that obeying moral exhortations may even reduce efficiency). This means that in addition to thwarting the trading off of positive moral actions against negative moral actions, we also want to insure that the obedience of moral prohibitions *always* takes precedence, that it *always* comes first.

Economists have identified a preference relation that captures the idea of the consumption of one thing taking strict precedence over another so, for example, it is only after a certain amount of one good (e.g., water) is consumed that the consumption of another good (e.g., video games) begins to add to utility. Such preferences are called lexicographic preferences. Figure 7.2 illustrates lexicographic preferences for goods X and Y, where the consumption of good X can be said to be *lexically primary* to the consumption of good Y.

Unlike perfectly complementary preferences, lexicographic preferences also imply the existence of a hierarchy that is antithetical to the idea that X and Y *must* be consumed or experienced together. I posit that the disobedience of moral prohibitions can be made effectively unworthy of consideration by moral beliefs that make the obedience of moral prohibitions lexically primary to the obedience of moral exhortations in the value system. In this way, the value system can change how people think about morality, essentially taking the disobedience of moral prohibitions "off the table."

Elizabeth Anderson, in *Value in Ethics and Economics* (1993, p. 67) summarizes the concept of lexicographic preferences quite well, and also illustrates the usefulness of this idea in other philosophical contexts:

> Lexical orderings offer the most popular way of representing a hierarchy of goods. A person lexically prefers *C* to *B* if she is unwilling to give up any amount of *C* for any amount of *B*. *Lexical orderings prohibit tradeoffs of one*

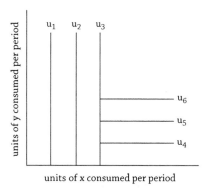

Figure 7.2. Lexicographic preferences. In this case the individual derives no utility from the consumption of Y whatsoever until a minimum threshold of X consumption is achieved. Once past that threshold, however, utility can rise as more Y is consumed.

good against another. Rawls's claim that rights to basic liberties must not be traded off against greater economic benefits, Dworkin's claim that rights "trump" claims to advance aggregate social welfare, and Nozick's claim that individual rights operate as "side-constraints" on others' actions can all be represented by lexical rankings of rights over other goods (Rawls 1971, p. 61; Nozick 1974, pp. 29–33; Dworkin 1977, p. xi). [emphasis added][6]

Her characterization is perfectly valid as far as it goes, but lexicographic preferences do more than just prohibit tradeoffs. They also establish that one thing takes precedence over the other. A lexical ordering of the set of all moral prohibitions and all moral exhortations, therefore, solves two problems at once. It eliminates the trading off of obedience of moral exhortations for the obedience of moral prohibitions and, by virtue of making the obedience of moral prohibitions lexically primary to the obedience of moral exhortations, it insures that the obedience of moral prohibitions comes first.

THE TWO PARTS TO BEING MORAL

If one's obedience of moral prohibitions is lexically primary to one's obedience of moral exhortations, then one's morality rises with positive moral actions if, and only if, one obeys all moral prohibitions against taking negative moral

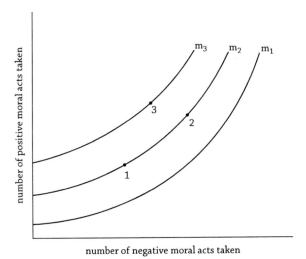

Figure 7.3. Relative moral merit when moral values/tastes regard positive and negative moral actions as substitutes. Note that while I have drawn the level curves in convex fashion, all that really matters is that the level curves be positively sloped. Since reasonable people can disagree about how positive and negative moral actions should be weighted to determine moral merit, moral standards for behavior are essentially meaningless.

actions. Obedience of moral exhortations is laudable, commendable, and praiseworthy, but nevertheless optional—one is not immoral even if one undertakes zero positive moral actions. The obedience of moral prohibitions, however, is anything but optional.

Figure 7.3 illustrates the default utilitarian approach, in which positive moral actions can be traded against negative moral actions. The moral merit of any combination of actions is given by m with subscripts corresponding to relative moral merit. In Figure 7.3, Point 2 involves more negative moral actions than Point 1, but since it also involves more positive moral actions, it generates the same moral merit as Point 1. In this way, positive moral actions can be traded for negative moral actions. A comparison of points like 1 and 3 illustrates the problem of greater good rationalization: by undertaking enough additional positive moral actions, one can conclude, even when taking additional negative moral actions, that one is more moral than before.

Figure 7.4 illustrates the idea that there are two distinct parts to being moral, with the obedience of moral prohibitions taking strict precedence over the obedience of moral exhortations. In Figure 7.4, points like 1 and 2 never produce the same moral merit. Indeed, quite the opposite occurs: increasing the amount of negative moral actions reduces moral merit regardless of how many more positive moral actions are taken. No matter how much additional positive moral action one takes (no matter how far Point 2 is pushed up), if one undertakes more negative moral actions and possesses moral beliefs that comport with the moral values/tastes exemplified in Figure 7.4, one will be less, not more, moral.

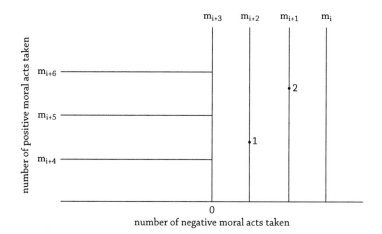

Figure 7.4. Relative moral merit when moral values/tastes regard the obedience of moral prohibitions as lexically primary to the obedience of moral exhortations. People need not agree on how moral actions should be weighted in determining moral merit to enjoy the benefits of having the modest but clear standard of never engaging in negative moral action.

What this means is that if both *A* and *B* never undertake any negative moral actions, neither is immoral. Even if *A* never lifts a finger for anyone and *B* is incredibly benevolent, it is simply incorrect to say *B* is moral and *A* is immoral. They are both categorically *not immoral*. Of course being categorically not immoral does not mean being as moral as one can be. Some moral people can be *more* moral than other moral people, because undertaking positive moral actions increases morality at the margin. It is therefore potentially correct to say that while neither *A* nor *B* are immoral, *A* is nevertheless *more moral* than *B*. Finally, if *C* has undertaken a negative moral act—even just one—then no matter how many positive moral acts *C* has undertaken, *C* is categorically immoral while *A* is categorically not immoral. We might all agree that *C* is nicer or more benevolent than *A*, but that is a separate issue.

So if the obedience of moral prohibitions is lexically primary to the obedience of moral exhortations in the value system, then that individual's morality is a two-part construct—one part qualitative and the other part quantitative. To be a moral person, one must *first not be immoral* by obeying all moral prohibitions against negative moral actions. If this first condition is not met, the individual in question is immoral regardless of how many positive moral actions he or she takes.[7] No person who has undertaken a negative moral action can be more moral than another person who hasn't, no matter how many positive moral acts the former has taken relative to the latter. Therefore, it is if and only if the first condition is met that we will even consider a person's degree of morality as it is evidenced by the number and quality of his or her positive moral actions.

Conversely, in a value system that treats moral prohibitions and moral exhortations as substitutes, there is no objective basis for claiming that *A* is moral in the sense of not being immoral, because one can argue that failure to undertake positive moral actions also constitutes a case for claiming that someone is immoral. Since there is no objective basis for weighing the morality of actions, this means that how moral is moral enough to be generally regarded as being moral is by nature subjective. So no one (except, perhaps, Mother Theresa) is above being accused by others of being immoral. This has the effect of robbing the concept of morality of any meaningful standard by which to assess the moral propriety of our actions, or to evaluate the moral propriety of the actions of others.[8]

EFFICACIOUS HABITS OF MIND

If a society chooses moral beliefs to maximize general prosperity, it follows from the discussion above that it would do well to adopt moral beliefs that structure the value system to induce people to treat the obedience of moral prohibitions as lexically primary to the obedience of moral exhortations. This would lead them to always conclude that it is imperative that they obey moral prohibitions regardless of how noble the positive moral ends of disobeying moral prohibitions might be.

How might such a habit of mind arise? A habit of mind that views disobedience of moral prohibitions as unworthy of consideration could be the result of the subconscious mind learning over time that considering negative moral acts is simply a waste of cognitive resources, because the answer is always no. This supports a social norm of unconditional trustworthiness, because the best way to insure that one never behaves opportunistically is for one to never be tempted to do so. And the best way to never be tempted is to never even consider it in the first place.

If you live in a society in which nearly everyone abides by a social norm of not even considering behaving as an opportunist, your grocer need not worry that you will shoplift. This is not because he can count on you always arriving at the same conclusion when you consider shoplifting (as the utilitarian cost-benefit calculation approach would suggest) but because when you go to the grocery store, shoplifting never even crosses your mind. This provides the ultimate assurance to the grocer that you will not engage in opportunism at his expense. This is neither a prudent response to external incentives nor a product of irrational thinking. It is a perfectly rational response to expected guilt costs. Reaching the same conclusion when such actions are considered, in turn, produces a completely rational subconscious moral rule of thumb to the effect of "don't waste time consciously thinking about whether I should disobey a moral prohibition, because the answer is always no."[9]

The idea that what starts out as a repeated moral calculation can ultimately become an automatic decision rule mirrors the moral development of children quite well. Even in societies where nearly all adults always obey all moral prohibitions, as small children most of them did not. As they got older, however, they were less tempted—in part because increasingly they did not even consider such acts. Their ability to appreciate abstract moral ideas had risen to a sufficient level for them to believe that it is indeed one's moral duty to always obey moral prohibitions. This process occurs whether punishment is in the form of external sanction or internalized guilt, but the advantage of the latter is that it remains in force even if the possibility of detection does not exist. Once the level of guilt becomes high enough so that the answer is always no, a completely rational moral rule of thumb emerges that effectuates a *de facto* qualitative distinction between exhortations and prohibitions, even though the underlying psychological mechanisms are quantitative in nature.

TYPES OF LEXICAL PRIMACY

Even if lexical primacy of moral prohibitions can solve the greater good rationalization problem, how do we know it can be effectuated through the psychological mechanisms people actually possess? I believe there are at least three ways in which the value system can produce lexical primacy of moral prohibitions over moral exhortations, and that can plausibly work through existing human psychological mechanisms and capabilities.

The first form of lexical primacy I call *de facto* lexical primacy. With *de facto* lexical primacy, moral decision making appears to work through an absolute formal logical mechanism that produces a lexical ordering when, in fact, it is simply the case that the level of guilt one feels from even the most minor negative moral action exceeds the level of guilt one would experience from failing to undertake a positive moral act that produces extraordinary benefits. So what appears to be a qualitative distinction (never disobey moral prohibitions) is, in reality, based on quantitative latent factors (the level of guilt from undertaking negative moral actions always exceeds the level of guilt from failing to undertake positive moral actions).

The second form of lexical primacy I call *de jure* lexical primacy. *De jure* is the subordination, by rule, of guilt from failing to take positive moral action to guilt from taking negative moral action. With *de jure* lexical primacy, when a person asks himself "should I do x (a negative moral act) so I can do y (a positive moral act)?" the answer is always no, because the individual believes that no matter how badly he will feel about not being able to do y, his moral value system requires that he should feel even guiltier about doing x.

De jure lexical primacy is superior to *de facto* lexical primacy because the set of all known actions does not exhaust the set of all future potential actions. *De jure* lexical primacy effectively lets people off the hook, as it were, for failing to undertake positive moral actions. They don't feel badly for not undertaking positive moral actions because they honestly believe they are not *supposed* to feel badly when such actions would require undertaking negative moral actions as a means to that end. On the contrary, they are supposed to feel good about such a decision, because it is what is morally required.

The third form of lexical primacy I call *perfect* lexical primacy. This is effectuated by the absence of any feelings of guilt whatsoever arising from failure to undertake any positive moral act under any circumstance.[10] So, while it is morally laudable to undertake positive moral actions, no one is morally compelled to do so. As a result, failing to take such actions is in no way immoral, even if there would be little or no cost involved. There is no reason to experience feelings of guilt for failing to undertake such actions in the first place, because not undertaking positive moral actions is simply not wrong.

This first appears to suggest that people will have no basis for undertaking positive moral actions, or that a society comprised of such individuals will lack all benevolence. This is incorrect. *Perfect* lexical primacy is simply the belief that benevolence is never an obligation or duty. As such, there is no reason to feel guilty for failing to take a positive moral action.

Just as *de jure* lexical primacy is superior to *de facto* lexical primacy, *perfect* lexical primacy is superior to *de jure* lexical primacy. You can't do more to combat greater good rationalization than never experiencing any feelings of guilt with respect to failing to take any positive moral act. In such a case any guilt at all associated with negative moral actions will assure that no greater good rationalization will occur. Finally, *de jure* lexical primacy also comports well with the concept of non-tuism.[11]

Duty-Based Moral Restraint

Let's summarize our thought experiment up to this point. Prudential restraint manifests itself through external incentives produced by strategic factors inherent in human relationships (e.g., repeat play effects), or through institutions that convince the decision maker that opportunism is an irrational choice given the expected costs involved. Moral restraint manifests itself through internally produced incentives—the cost of bearing feelings of guilt—that are derived from moral values that induce the decision maker to conclude that opportunism is wrong. It is natural to expect that moral restraint has little to do with rationality, but it actually comports perfectly with behaving in a rational manner because tastes are antecedent to rational decision making. Moral restraint, being derived from internalized moral tastes rather than external incentives, is able to combat opportunism even in cases where there is no chance of detection—that is, where golden opportunities are likely to arise.

Moral restraint solves the golden opportunity problem, but it turns out that *why* one feels morally restrained makes a big difference. Because of the empathy problem, harm-based moral restraint is insufficient in large group settings, so moral restraint must also be principled in nature. But even principled moral restraint is insufficient, because we can also feel guilty about failing to undertake positive moral actions. As a result, our moral intuition may tell us that it is morally proper to undertake a given negative moral act. This is the greater good rationalization problem. To address this problem, moral beliefs must structure the value system so as to make the obedience of moral prohibitions lexically primary to the obedience of moral exhortations.

So to make unconditional trustworthiness possible, something must structure the individual's value system in a way that produces principled moral restraint in conjunction with the lexical primacy of obedience of moral prohibitions. An individual who very strongly believes that undertaking negative moral actions is wrong as a matter of principle, *and who also believes* that obeying moral prohibitions is lexically primary to obeying moral exhortations, possesses what I shall call *an ethic of duty-based moral restraint.*

THE TWO PARTS OF DUTY-BASED MORAL RESTRAINT

The empathy problem and the greater good rationalization problem are distinct problems. Principled moral restraint doesn't solve the greater good rationalization problem, because one might feel even guiltier about failing to undertake a positive moral action than failing to refrain from behaving opportunistically. But lexical primacy of moral prohibitions doesn't solve the empathy problem, either, because even if you believe the obedience of moral prohibitions takes precedence over the obedience of moral exhortations, if moral restraint is derived solely from a reluctance to do harm, and no harm is done by doing x in a given circumstance, then doing x *in that particular circumstance* will appear to be a legitimate exception. As a result, the primacy of obeying moral prohibitions against taking negative moral acts is moot, because in this circumstance x is effectively not a negative moral act.

Without sufficiently strong principled moral restraint to overcome the empathy problem, and without lexical primacy of obedience of moral prohibitions to overcome the greater good rationalization problem, it simply cannot be said that the individual will always feel as though he must obey all moral prohibitions against taking negative moral actions. Both are required to produce the belief that one has no choice but to obey all moral prohibitions as a matter of moral duty. Sufficiently strong principled moral restraint must therefore be coupled with lexical primacy to produce duty-based moral restraint that, in turn, produces unconditional trustworthiness.

Many find it difficult to separate the closely related ideas of principle and duty, so let's press the point a little further. In any particular circumstance that requires one to make a moral decision, principled moral restraint pertains to *why* one thinks something is wrong. Duty, however, pertains to one's strength of conviction to act or not act as required. The underlying theory of morality for concluding that a given act is a positive or negative moral one is a separate issue. In other words, duty is not just a matter of principle; it implies that some things matter more than others. There are many things that I believe I should do, and there are many things that I believe I should not do. But there are very few things that I believe I *must not* do, and there are very few things that I believe I *must* do. Going from "should" to "must" is the essence of duty. Believing it is your moral duty to act or not act means much more than believing that doing the right thing will make you more moral at the margin.

Duty is a very old idea that figures prominently in Western culture, dating back at least to the ancient Greeks.[12] A more recent example, one that has been resurrected in various forms, is the account of Charles Goodnight delivering on an unusual promise made to his friend Oliver Loving. Goodnight promised Loving that no matter where he died, Goodnight would bury Loving in Texas.[13] Even given the high cost of fulfilling the promise, it was simply unfathomable to Goodnight to fail to honor it. His behavior had nothing to do with strategy, reputation, or sophisticated moral reasoning. Yet his behavior was in no way irrational, because given his moral beliefs the level of guilt he would have experienced from failing to keep his promise would have wiped out any possible benefits derived from not honoring the promise.

MORAL CONSTRAINTS

The traditional neoclassical theory of rational choice models an individual's choice of action (what to consume, how many hours to work, how much crime to commit, etc.) as a solution to a constrained optimization problem. In its simplest and most commonly used form, a person chooses to consume a certain amount of goods X and Y by maximizing an objective function (the individual's utility function) subject to a constraint function (the individual's budget constraint). In the traditional model, rational choice is therefore rather simple—it is a matter of balancing marginal benefits determined by tastes against marginal costs determined by prices and income.

It is only natural that neoclassical economists think of constraints on human behavior as being external to the decision maker, while they think of tastes as being internal and as defining objectives rather than constraints. The emphasis economists place on incentives reflects a belief that general explanations for behavior are likely to be derived from identifying changes in external constraints (e.g., changes in income, wealth, and prices). This emphasis on external constraints lends generality to the theory, because external constraints can be objectively measured and are more likely to apply to everyone, while tastes are highly subjective.[14]

My claim is that the maximization of utility can also be subject to self-imposed *internal* constraints that are matters of taste, but that do not function like tastes in the conventional model of consumer choice because their influence does not come through striving to achieve an objective. Such constraints effectively redact areas of the action space—actions that may be prudent, but that the individual regards as impermissible and therefore "off the table" because he believes it is his moral duty to not undertake them. In such a case, the decision is not framed as "I value not doing x" but rather, "I won't consider doing x." For such an individual, the correct way to view the effect of a moral value that relates to a negative moral action is that it establishes another constraint in the constrained optimization problem. As such, he regards such actions as no more worthy of his consideration than daydreaming about how he would spend a billion dollars he does not have and knows he will never have.

What difference does it make if moral restraint is the result of an individual strongly valuing being good, or is the result of an individual treating some actions as not worthy of consideration—as outside the legitimate action set? The difference is profound.

If an individual's moral beliefs and value system frame moral decision making in a way that views some actions as encouraged to varying degree, some actions as morally neutral, and some actions as discouraged to varying degree, then all moral values function like tastes in a utility function that simply places different weights on different goods and services. As in the case of goods in the consumer's utility maximization problem, this invites the trading of moral values against one another, including the trading of negative and positive moral values that are related to negative and positive moral actions, respectively. As we discussed earlier in this chapter, this invites greater good rationalization that undermines our ability to trust each other.

Money and prices obviously constrain the range of actions. But there is no reason why internalized moral self-restraint could not be equally constraining. These constraints can also function as norms if they are derived from commonly held moral beliefs. History is filled with examples of people who have endured torture and death because they were unwilling to undertake certain negative moral actions (e.g., renouncing one's faith, revealing the name of another person, revealing battle plans to the enemy, etc.). Because of how their moral beliefs structured their value system, moral prohibitions effectively functioned as mathematical constraints, with every bit as much logical force as budget lines defined by money and prices in the model of rational choice.

It is well known that neoclassical economics is inherently consequentialist in its approach to modeling human behavior. The central calculation is benefits minus costs. This naturally leads to a cost-benefit approach to moral thinking that completely ignores the concept of duty. Neoclassical economists might argue that the concept of duty can be easily accounted for in the traditional model by saying that having a duty to y or to not do x simply means one has a very strong taste to do y or to not do x relative to other tastes. But it should be clear from the discussion above that this is not logically equivalent to duty. Even strong tastes allow trading off, and don't establish strict hierarchical priority of one type of action over the other.

Steadfastly doing one's duty is consistent with an "always obey moral constraints" approach to morality. If a person believes it is his duty to never do x, and he abides by his duty, then that is equivalent to saying that for him doing x is outside his set of feasible actions. The fact that such a belief exists in his mind, and is not imposed externally, does not change the fact that the belief functions as a constraint. The lexical primacy of moral prohibitions, in conjunction with sufficiently strong principled moral restraint, effectively makes moral prohibitions against taking negative moral actions moral constraints—and, in so doing, comports perfectly with the obedience of moral prohibitions being regarded as a moral duty, and not merely a strongly encouraged moral choice.

DUTY VERSUS RULE FOLLOWING

In addition to distinguishing between consequentialist and nonconsequentialist theories of morality, moral theorists also distinguish between *rule* and *act* approaches to moral decision making. This naturally raises the question of how, precisely, does the discussion above relate to rule following? Put another way, is duty-based moral restraint nothing more than consistent rule following?

Rules effectuate coordination by producing clear expectations for behavior. A rule can pertain to moral restraint (you must not steal) or moral advocacy (you must help a drowning man), but it can also have nothing to do with morality (you must drive on the right side of the road). Whereas rules are about clarity and consistency to improve efficiency, duty pertains to the reason why and the conviction with which one follows rules. One can be a good rule follower with no sense of duty at all, and one can have a strong sense of duty but refuse to follow a rule if he believes the spirit of the rule is violated by the letter of the rule.

One way societies can improve the function of rules is to attempt to make the obedience of rules a moral issue. Consider a rule against an act that is not inherently immoral (e.g., raking leaves into the creek) but is subject to a coordination failure problem (when everyone rakes leaves into the creek, the result can be a clog that causes a flood when it rains heavily). In such a case, everyone is better off if everyone obeys a rule against raking leaves into the creek. But your highest payoff comes from everyone except you obeying the rule. In this case the creek never clogs because no individual has enough leaves to cause a problem, but you get to benefit from raking your leaves into the creek rather than hauling them to the curb. If a society can convince people that breaking a rule that solves this kind of problem is inherently wrong—because it is an act of hypocrisy, and hypocrisy is itself inherently wrong—then this commons dilemma can be overcome by making the following of a rule against dumping leaves a moral matter.

CONCERNS ABOUT DUTY

There are a number of potential problems with moral restraint being effectuated through a sense of duty. I review three in what follows and I will discuss several more in the next chapter.

The first potential problem is that duty-based moral restraint might be so impractical as to be infeasible. For positive moral actions, a duty approach to morality has the obvious problems of (1) feasibility (what if duty says "do y" but you don't have the required resources or duty says "do y_1 and do y_2," but you only have the resources for one?), and (2) efficiency (what if duty says "do y_1" but does not require doing y_2, yet the benefits enjoyed by the beneficiaries of positive moral action are much greater if y_2 is undertaken instead of y_1). All of these problems are derived from the fact that positive moral action nearly always requires resources. This forces choice between competing alternatives, but that is inconsistent with the concept of duty.

We do not, however, have this problem with duty-based moral restraint. Moral restraint is about inaction. Since "not doing x_1" does not generally reduce one's ability to "not do x_2," the obedience of moral prohibitions is non-rival.[15] Therefore, obeying any given moral prohibition does not come at the expense of obeying other prohibitions. As a result, requiring that one obey all moral prohibitions as a matter of duty is not subject to the fallacy of composition that the simultaneous obedience of all moral exhortations necessarily is. This non-rival nature of moral prohibitions is also important because it means that moral prohibitions can provide standards for moral behavior that moral exhortations cannot.

The second potential problem is that, given the role duty plays in Kant's theory of morality, duty-based moral restraint smacks of moral absolutism. This discomfort need not concern us here. For Kant, duty is the *sine qua non* of moral propriety. I make no claim about what is or is not ultimately moral, and therefore I make no claim about whether actions must be a matter of duty to be moral. My claim about duty is purely functional. Duty pertains to *how people think about morality*, not whether something is moral. Duty is only important because when an individual possesses an ethic of duty-based moral restraint, it is rational for others to regard him as unconditionally trustworthy. This provides a rational basis for extending trust, even in very large groups where both empathy effects and the likelihood of detection are low.

This is related to another concern, expressed by Binmore (2005) and by Doug North to me personally, which is that if the required moral beliefs for fully supporting the development and operation of a market system are absolute in nature, then the exercise is moot, because such moral beliefs are not consistent with psychological mechanisms that humans actually have. In Chapter 5 I anticipated this concern and worked through the thought experiment by constructing moral beliefs that could plausibly work through existing psychological mechanisms. In reality, duty-based moral restraint is ultimately derived from latent consequentialist factors (even if guilt is attached to negative moral acts themselves and not the harm they cause, the *level* of guilt still matters).[16]

The third potential problem is that in the past, the concept of duty has been employed to manipulate otherwise decent people into undertaking acts of horror. Moral, cultural, and ideological beliefs can sometimes have the effect of depersonalizing those outside of one's tribe or society. This is often a means to the end of pursuing some greater good, such as the Nazis claimed to be doing by improving the world through racial purification. Throughout human history, many horrors have been made possible by clever manipulators attaching a sense of duty to abstract moral, cultural, and ideological ideas in order to suppress our natural reluctance to harm each other, and therefore make us pawns in their causes.

In most cases, such manipulations are ultimately based on greater good rationalizations. But an ethic of duty-based moral restraint never allows such greater good rationalizations to get off the ground. Although duty-based moral restraint is functionally inflexible, this inflexibility is not an asset to those who wish to pit us against each other. Instead, it contributes to preserving our basic decency by making us completely uncompromising when it comes to being receptive to greater good arguments designed to get people to suppress what their gut is telling them they shouldn't do.

It is when people stop listening to their basic sense of humanity that horror becomes possible. Horror does not—indeed cannot—result from a steadfast refusal to undertake negative moral actions. Duty-based moral restraint, therefore, stands directly in the way of such horror. One who fully abides by an ethic of duty-based moral restraint says, after hearing of any sort of greater good rationalization for doing harm to others, "there are some things you just don't do, period."

Conclusion

Principled moral restraint solves the empathy problem by tying feelings of guilt directly to negative moral acts. But while solving the empathy problem is a necessary condition for one being unconditionally trustworthy in large groups, it is not sufficient. In this chapter I explained why moral beliefs must also solve the greater good rationalization problem, if a society is to maximize general prosperity. Otherwise, even very decent individuals will no longer be regarded as being unconditionally trustworthy. To do this, moral beliefs must logically structure the value system so that the obedience of moral prohibitions is treated as lexically primary to the obedience of moral exhortations.

De facto lexical primacy can arise from attaching a sufficiently high moral weight to obeying moral prohibitions relative to moral exhortations. *De jure* lexical primacy can arise from subordinating the obedience of moral exhortations to the obedience of moral prohibitions, via a moral rule of thumb that tells individuals that no matter how guilty they might feel about failing to undertake *any* positive moral action, they should always feel even guiltier about taking *any* negative moral action as a means to that end. *Perfect* lexical primacy can arise from believing that one should never feel guilty about failing to undertake any positive moral action, because one is not obligated to undertake any positive moral action.

Like principled moral restraint, *de jure* and *perfect* lexical primacy are abstract ideas that must be taught and learned. Harm-based moral restraint, on the other hand, is almost certainly biologically grounded. Although the cognitive and psychological capabilities that enable the creation, adoption, and teaching of abstract ideas are also hardwired, the ideas themselves are not. As a result, an ethic of duty-based moral restraint is fragile compared an ethic of harm-based moral restraint. This further suggests that any solace taken in the fact that we have hardwired moral sensibilities may be misguided, because there is no particular reason why our hardwired moral sensibilities will be up to the task of fully supporting the development and operation of a market society. There certainly is little evidence—anecdotal or otherwise—to support such a claim.

The main lesson of this chapter is that while wanting to be a moral person matters, how our moral beliefs frame the way we think about morality also matters. How moral conviction is directed is obviously primary to the level of conviction itself. If moral conviction is only based on our reluctance to harm others, then it will be subject to the empathy problem and will break down in the large groups without which general prosperity is impossible. If moral conviction is based only on principled moral restraint, then it will be subject to the greater good rationality problem. Indeed, if conviction is not girded by lexical primacy, greater conviction can lead to a lower level of trust by driving up the guilt people feel for failing to promote the welfare of those they care for, even if it involves cheating those who are outside their immediate "circle of trust."

More generally, there is a profound difference between having a value system that frames all moral choices as "shades of gray," and having a value system that frames moral choices about negative moral actions in "black and white" terms, while framing only moral choices about positive moral actions as "shades of gray."

In the former kind of value system there is no objective standard for weighing moral values, so moral choices are fundamentally subjective. Hence, there is no meaningful standard for moral behavior in the first place. Not surprisingly, therefore, there are few exceptions because it treats nearly all actions as morally open questions in the first place.

CHAPTER 8

The Moral Foundation

And upon this is founded that remarkable distinction between justice and all the other social virtues . . . that we feel ourselves to be under a stricter obligation to act according to justice, than agreeably to friendship, charity, or generosity; that the practice of these last mentioned virtues seems to be left in some measure to our own choice, but that, somehow or the other, we feel ourselves to be in a peculiar manner tied, bound, and obliged to the observation of justice.—Adam Smith, 1759, p. 79

Introduction

I have argued that there is an inescapable problem that any society must contend with if it wishes to flourish. To maximize general prosperity, people must be able to trust each other even in large group settings. But we are opportunistic by nature, and we are also a small group species, so there is no reason that our natural reluctance to behave as opportunists should work in large group settings.

In the last chapter, I explained why hardwired moral sensibilities must therefore be supplemented in any society that hopes to foster the fullest development and most efficient operation of a market economy to maximize general prosperity. This is best accomplished with an ethic of duty-based moral restraint that produces individuals we can rationally regard as being unconditionally trustworthy. The transaction cost of interacting with such individuals is much lower than it is for others. The higher the proportion of such individuals, the lower transaction costs are generally and, hence, the larger is the set of viable transactions. This includes maximizing the ability to use relational contracts which, in turn, maximizes the number of firms that can be both very large and thoroughly entrepreneurial at the same time.

An ethic of duty-based moral restraint implies that people must apply what is effectively a nonconsequentialist theory of moral propriety to the consideration of negative moral actions. It would be natural to suspect that it follows that the development and operation of a market economy is best supported by moral beliefs that are generally nonconsequentialist in nature. The purpose of this chapter is to explain why such a reasonable conclusion is wrong.

In this chapter I will show that the moral foundation of economic behavior requires even more than duty-based moral restraint—that it also requires that people apply a consequentialist theory of moral propriety to the consideration of positive moral actions. So whereas moral restraint with respect to negative moral actions must be perceived to be a moral duty, moral advocacy with respect to positive moral actions *must not be*. I explain why duty-based moral advocacy is impractical, inefficient, and harmful, because it inevitably undermines duty-based moral restraint, thereby making the extension of genuine trust irrational in large group settings. Conversely, when positive moral action is guided by a consequentialist theory of moral propriety, such action is normally efficient and does not undermine duty-based moral restraint.

Finally, I explain why the moral foundation can plausibly work through existing psychological mechanisms, and why it is compatible with market competition. I then explain why it is not nearly as uncharitable as it might first appear. Thankfully, we need not sell our souls to enjoy general prosperity. In reality, the moral foundation makes it possible to be charitable in ways that were unimaginable in most societies throughout human history. I then explain why the moral foundation is not nearly as complicated or as inflexible as it might first appear, and is hardly an exercise in moral absolutism.

Duty-Based Moral Advocacy

Moral advocacy pertains to endeavoring to take positive moral actions or encouraging others to do so. In Chapter 4 we discussed why, in the context of economic activity, exhortations to undertake positive moral actions are generally unnecessary. Voluntary transactions are mutually beneficial by nature, so they tend to promote social welfare very efficiently. So, while positive moral actions may be laudable, in the conduct of most forms of economic activity, they simply have nothing to do.[1] It follows that any additional impetus is generally at best superfluous (because it doesn't change the outcome) or is inefficient (because it does). Exhortations to undertake positive moral actions in this context amount to solving problems that do not exist and, in the attempt to do so, reducing the amount of resources available to solve problems that actually do exist.

This does not mean that there is no role for positive moral actions in a market society. There is nothing inherently inefficient about A deciding to use some of his resources to undertake positive moral actions because it gives A pleasure to do so. Similarly, when a person is persuaded that spending his money on a particular cause is morally desirable, if he values being a moral person he will expect to experience feelings of pleasure from doing so. Such a person will naturally attempt to spend his money in a way that produces the most pleasure—in this case, in a way that he believes will produce the most moral outcome. Such freely chosen charitable spending is therefore inherently efficient, just as spending money on a hamburger is, and there is no particular reason why it would impede the operation of a market economy.

Similarly, moral advocacy in the form of a person or group attempting to convince others of the moral merit of supporting a particular kind of positive moral action, perhaps through a charity, presents no particular problem for the development or operation of a market economy. As long as such advocacy is truthful, it can improve the efficiency with which individuals choose to give to charities. Moreover, one of the best things about having a market economy is that it makes it possible to be more charitable than otherwise, because nearly everyone in society has many more resources than required for subsistence. But, as with negative moral actions, *why* people undertake positive moral actions also matters. This is because their motivation for undertaking such actions can powerfully affect the development and operation of a market economy.

PROBLEMS WITH DUTY-BASED MORAL ADVOCACY

Duty is by nature uncompromising. When undertaken because of a perceived moral duty to do so, a positive moral action goes from being an "ought" to a "must." So if B believes that he has a moral duty to do y, then failure to do y is not just failing to behave in a way that is morally laudable, it is behaving in a way that is immoral, and therefore cause for feeling guilty. This causes two problems. The first problem is that duty-based moral advocacy is often inefficient for those who possess a consequentialist theory of the moral propriety of positive moral actions. The second problem is that it inevitably undermines an ethic of duty-based moral restraint which, in turn, undermines the ability to sustain a social norm of unconditional trustworthiness.

Inefficiency
The most obvious problem with duty-based moral advocacy is that it is generally inconsistent with efficiency. Positive moral action normally requires resources that cannot be used to undertake other positive moral actions, so any positive moral act usually comes at the expense of other positive moral acts. For a given positive moral act to be efficient, the resources used to achieve it must not have been able to produce a better moral outcome through some other act.

The problem is that if y_1 is viewed as a moral duty and y_3 is not, but in a given circumstance y_3 produces a more moral outcome, then taking y_1 instead of y_3 because y_1 was viewed as a duty wastes resources that can no longer achieve the more moral outcome. So duty-based advocacy can reduce welfare by reducing the efficiency with which resources are used to undertake positive moral action.

Note that this is also a problem for Turchin's (2006) insightful argument that a capacity for symbolic thinking may have evolved to facilitate cooperation in ever larger groups. If individuals are induced to make sacrifices to engage in pro-social behavior because of symbolic triggers, then what is to insure that these actions will be efficient? This does not mean that Turchin's (2006) argument is wrong. Evolution does not guaranteed absolute best, it only rewards the best among the set of existing alternatives. What we will find is that it does mean that societies that sustain large group cooperation by extending the reach of trib-alism through symbols are less efficient than those that do so by abiding by the moral foundation.

But aren't some positive moral acts inherently matters of duty? In such a case, moral propriety is not derived from doing good but from obedience *per se*, so such an act could just as easily have been regarded as the negation of a negative moral act because failing to do what you are supposed to is wrong. In other words, it makes no difference whether we regard circumcising infant boys as a positive moral act, or not circumcising infant boys as a negative moral act, if the reason for viewing the act as being moral is solely the result of an unconditional moral com-mand by an ultimate moral authority. Such positive moral acts are correctly regarded as duties, but are equally validly regarded as the negation of negative moral actions. Operationally, then, they amount to redactions of the action space that is observationally equivalent to the redactions associated with duty-based moral restraint.

Eroding Duty-Based Moral Restraint

An even more troubling problem with duty-based moral advocacy is that it inevi-tably erodes duty-based moral restraint. This is because if we find ourselves with insufficient resources to undertake a positive moral action we believe we have a duty to undertake, we will naturally consider undertaking negative moral acts as means to that end. Suppose B views all moral behavior as a matter of duty, so B possesses an ethic of duty-based moral advocacy with respect to positive moral actions $(y_1, y_2, \ldots, y_m)$ in addition to possessing an ethic of duty-based moral restraint with respect to negative moral actions $(x_1, x_2, \ldots, x_n)$. Now suppose that in a particular circumstance B *must do* y_1, but y_1 can only be accomplished in that circumstance by doing x_1 as a means to that end. In this case, B's moral duty to do y_1 implies that B *must do* x_1. But if B possesses duty-based moral restraint, then it is also B's moral duty to *not do* x_1, so B must do x_1 and must also not do x_1—a contradiction. Both duties cannot be simultaneously honored.

An ethic of duty-based moral advocacy goes beyond merely conflicting with an ethic of duty-based moral restraint—it actually undermines it and, in the process, undermines a social norm of unconditional trustworthiness. In a given circum-stance, how does one choose between competing moral duties? Such a choice in-evitably requires some kind of consequentialist evaluation. Comparing the relative strengths of duties ends up being effectively a consequentialist exercise. This makes moral restraint effectively consequentialist, and thereby opens up moral decision making to greater good rationalization.[2] Such rationalization might be sincere, but that is beside the point. The issue we are concerned with here is the ability to genuinely trust each other, and if A thinks that B might feel morally compelled to undertake a given positive moral action that can only be undertaken if B opportunistically victimizes A, then no matter how much regard A has for B's moral earnestness, or how much sympathy he has for B's moral quandary, A cannot trust B.

Conversely, when the willingness to undertake positive moral actions is solely derived from the pleasure that benefactors expect to enjoy from freely choosing to behave virtuously, while the unwillingness to undertake negative moral actions is largely a matter guilt manifested by involuntary emotions, a cognitive bright line is established between these two moral motivations. This helps to psychologically sustain lexical primacy of obedience of moral prohibitions over obedience of moral exhortations.

Duty-based moral advocacy therefore represents a serious threat to the obedience of moral prohibitions, because it can employ the guilt associated with failure to take positive moral actions to override the guilt associated with disobeying moral prohibitions. This undermines moral restraint by making the disobedience of moral prohibitions feel necessary and therefore right. Duty-based moral advocacy therefore makes it harder for us to genuinely trust each other unless we can depend on strong interpersonal utility effects. This limits trust to rather small "circles" of trust. Duty-based moral advocacy can therefore be expected to impede the emergence of a high trust society, and the introduction of such an ethic in an existing high trust society risks destroying trust and therefore prosperity and social harmony as well.

Inefficient Emotional Manipulation through Duty Arguments

Since we don't feel guilty about failing to do things that we believe we are morally free to choose not to do, many advocates attempt to cultivate the belief that taking positive moral actions associated with *their cause* is a moral duty, so one should feel guilty about not undertaking them. This allows advocates to separate their cause from others by painting the others as mere matters of taste, while theirs is a matter of duty. The problem is that all charitable causes have an incentive to do this, and when they all do, none ends up with more resources but all will have wasted resources in the attempt to do so.

One solution to this problem would be to hold moral beliefs that one should not feel guilty about failing to undertake any positive moral action, because positive moral actions are a matter of personal taste and therefore a private matter. Even better would be to believe that even the attempt to make others feel guilty about failing to support one's favorite cause is immoral because it amounts to emotional manipulation. This does not mean that a charity cannot be its own advocate and cannot argue for the moral propriety of supporting it over other charities. Such arguments, if made honestly, can also contribute to efficiency by conveying information that allows benefactors to more accurately compute the opportunity costs of their choices.

To summarize, the problem with duty-based moral advocacy is that it pits guilt derived from failing to undertake a given positive moral action against guilt derived from taking a negative moral act, thereby eroding duty-based moral restraint and increasing the likelihood of opportunistic victimization. For duty-based moral restraint to be meaningful, it is necessary that the obedience of moral exhortations not be a matter of duty. It is only when the latter is conjoined with the former that the former is not eroded, and a norm of unconditional trustworthiness is made possible.

The Moral Foundation

If the key to being able to regard someone as unconditionally trustworthy is that he or she possesses an ethic of duty-based moral restraint, but duty-based moral restraint is undermined by duty-based moral advocacy, then to best support the development and operation of a market economy, moral beliefs must produce a value system for which moral restraint is a matter of duty while moral advocacy is not. This means that moral restraint must be governed by a nonconsequentialist approach to moral decision making, while moral advocacy must be governed by a consequentialist approach to moral decision making.

As alluded to above, the concept of duty is very closely related to the concept of nonconsequentialism, and possessing a consequentialist ethic is antithetical to possessing a duty ethic. A society whose moral beliefs are based solely on a consequentialist theory of moral propriety is not one that will support duty-based moral restraint, while a society whose moral beliefs are based solely on a nonconsequentialist theory of moral propriety is not one that will reject duty-based moral advocacy.

It follows that if a society's moral beliefs are uniformly consequentialist or uniformly nonconsequentialist in nature, then that society won't best support the development and operation of a market economy, because people will not be able to trust each other enough to hold transaction costs to their lowest possible level. Such societies will therefore fail to maximize general prosperity and their people will fail to enjoy the benefit of not living in constant fear of opportunistic exploitation.

The moral foundation of economic behavior can now be stated thusly: *the moral foundation of economic behavior is a norm of unconditional trustworthiness made possible by a preponderance of people possessing an ethic of duty-based moral restraint while* not *regarding moral advocacy as a moral duty.* The moral foundation of economic behavior therefore involves moral beliefs that apply a nonconsequentialist theory of moral propriety to negative moral actions while applying a consequentialist theory of moral propriety to positive moral actions.

The moral foundation of economic behavior implies that for moral beliefs to best support the development and operation of a market economy, they must produce a kind of two-dimensional value system. This is best illustrated by a matrix that divides moral behavior into positive and negative moral actions, and also divides theories of morality into nonconsequentialist and consequentialist ones.

	Negative Moral Actions	Positive Moral Actions
Non-Consequentialist	✔	
Consequentialist		✔

In Chapters 2–5 we demonstrated that what matters for economic activity is refraining from undertaking negative moral actions, so our initial focus is on the column associated with negative moral action. But we learned in Chapters 6–7 that *why* we obey prohibitions against taking negative moral actions also matters; that only when moral restraint is regarded as a matter of duty will it produce unconditional trustworthiness where doing so matters most. This means that it is not enough to strongly value refraining from taking negative moral actions; we must possess a nonconsequentialist theory of moral propriety with respect to negative moral actions. This identifies the NW cell.

In this chapter we discovered that the theory of moral propriety governing positive moral actions affects the likelihood that duty-based moral restraint will be upheld. For duty-based moral restraint to not be undermined by a desire to undertake positive moral action, positive moral action *must not be* viewed as a matter of duty. Instead, a consequentialist theory of moral propriety must be applied to positive moral actions. So it follows that the SE cell—positive moral action governed by a moral theory that is consequentialist in nature—is essential to insuring that the NW cell is meaningful. Note that the SE cell also contributes in a positive way to supporting the NW cell. A society that does not waste its benevolence because it fails to consider the opportunity cost of its positive moral actions will have fewer people who are strongly tempted to disobey moral prohibitions.[3]

It is also instructive to think about the off-diagonal elements. A person who abides by the NE cell will be incompetently benevolent because he will fail to account for the opportunity cost of taking any given positive moral action so he will get a very low return on resources used to undertake those actions. A person who abides by the SW cell will find that others who know about his moral beliefs will find it impossible to genuinely trust him unless he happens to be connected to them in some way. A society in which most people abide by the SW cell would find that all trust-dependent transactions will be limited to small groups. Such a society will be less able to support positive moral actions because it will be significantly poorer than a society that abides by the moral foundation.

One might ask how the matrix above adds anything beyond making the obedience of moral prohibitions lexically primacy to the obedience of moral exhortations. Recall that lexical primacy of the obedience of moral prohibitions over the obedience of moral exhortations is a necessary condition for overcoming the greater good rationalization problem. But this is merely a description of the required logical structure of our moral tastes—it ignores the question of why such obedience is regarded as moral in the first place. This is important, because why people believe behavior is moral affects the likelihood that lexical primacy can actually be achieved and sustained.

The point of discussing the problems associated with duty-based moral advocacy is to show that lexical primacy will likely break down if the motivation for obeying exhortations to undertake positive moral actions is the belief that one has a duty to do so. So it is not enough to merely believe that obedience of moral prohibitions is lexically primary to the obedience of moral exhortations—one's theory of moral propriety for taking positive moral actions must not be duty-based, and therefore must be consequentialist, if it is not to render duty-based moral restraint meaningless by rendering lexical primacy meaningless.

Let me stress that I am not passing moral judgment on either consequentialist or nonconsequentialist theories of morality. It might very well be the case that, by some as yet undiscovered universally compelling theory of morality, morality is truly based on one of these approaches to the exclusion of the other. My claim here is only that either approach to moral decision making to the exclusion of the other is inconsistent with having a large group society within which we can genuinely trust each other and thereby most fully enjoy the benefits of a market economy.

We have, therefore, now reached the conclusion of the thought experiment that was launched by the question: *If a society's sole objective is to maximize general prosperity, and it could choose its own moral beliefs, what kinds of moral beliefs would it choose?* We now know that the answer is that such a society would choose to have its people possess moral beliefs that effectuate an ethic of duty-based moral restraint, while at the same time believing that moral advocacy must not be duty-based. In other words, such a society would choose to have as many of its people as possible abide by the moral foundation.

WHAT OTHERS HAVE TO SAY

Religious leaders have stressed the importance of distinguishing between moral values that encourage positive moral behavior and those that discourage negative moral behavior. The best example is the teaching of Hillel the Elder (הלל). Hillel is a towering figure in Judaism. He famously proclaimed:

> That which is hateful to you, do not do to your fellow [man]. That is the whole Torah; the rest is the explanation; go and learn.

Many have noted the similarity of Hillel's rule to the Christian golden rule, or even a generalized ethic of reciprocity. But note that this quote is not about reciprocity *per se*, because it is stated as a command and not a recommendation for how to effectuate cooperation. The intent of Hillel's rule appears to be much more about employing one's capacity for empathy to provide a personal moral compass for behavior. Hillel was also effectively saying that avoidance of harm is what the Torah is primarily about. Although it comes short of calling for a lexical ordering, clearly Hillel's rule is consistent with the idea that the obedience of moral prohibitions is more important than the obedience of moral exhortations. This is extraordinary in light of the strong emphasis on positive moral action in the Judaic conception of social justice.[4]

The Christian golden rule might suggest that Jesus favored a broadly consequentialist approach to moral behavior. But the distinction between obeying prohibitions against taking negative moral actions, and obeying exhortations to take positive moral actions, is implicit in the asymmetry of treatment of each of these behaviors in the New Testament. For example, whereas capital punishment is never denounced, which suggests tacit approval for such a measure in response to a serious negative moral act, nothing like capital punishment is ever advocated for failing to undertake positive moral action. On the contrary, Jesus appears to suggest that positive moral action, when taken out of a sense of dutiful rule following, is of little or no merit and is often just an exercise in moral vanity. Jesus emphasized the importance of positive moral actions being a product of one's personal moral character, rather than an exercise in approval seeking either from fellow citizens, church leaders, or even God.

Implicit in the Gospel is the idea that people should strive to possess such character rather than focus on the behavior itself. The general message appears to be that while Jesus expected obedience of *The Law*, such obedience was not nearly enough. Obeying *The Law* was therefore necessary, but not sufficient for being a moral person. But it does not follow from such an argument that being benevolent is therefore sufficient because obeying *The Law* is not necessary, nor does it follow that being benevolent is more important than obeying *The Law*.

Bernard Gert is a moral philosopher who has stressed that it is far more important to avoid behaving in evil ways than it is to behave benevolently. Common sense tells us that our ability to help others is very limited, because positive moral action requires resources and resources are limited. But our ability to harm others is extraordinary, because great harm can be done with few resources (even an imbecile with a cup of kerosene and a match can bring down a multimillion-dollar building). This means that we have a great ability to reduce others' utility, but we have comparatively little ability to increase others' utility. Given this asymmetry, it follows that a value system that favors harmony should focus more on discouraging wrong than on encouraging good (Gert, 2004).

Others went beyond arguing that the obedience of prohibitions is more important that the obedience of exhortations. Recall that the moral foundation requires duty-based moral restraint which, in turn, requires lexical primacy of obedience of moral prohibitions over obedience of moral exhortations. Such lexical primacy comports well with Adam Smith's famous distinction between justice and beneficence.

Smith's use of the word *justice* clearly pertains to refraining from taking negative moral actions or redressing them *ex post*. But as is evident from the following quote, Smith has little patience for those who limit their morality to justice:

> There is, no doubt, a propriety in the practice of justice, and it merits, upon that account, all the approbation which is due to propriety. But as it does no real positive good, it is entitled to very little gratitude. Mere justice is, upon most occasions, but a negative virtue, and only hinders us from hurting our neighbour. (Adam Smith, in *The Theory of Moral Sentiments*, 1976 [1759], p. 82)

But Smith nevertheless clearly views justice as more crucial than beneficence for a well-functioning society:

> Society may subsist among different men, as among different merchants, from a sense of its utility, without any mutual love or affection; and though no man in it should owe any obligation, or be bound in gratitude to any other, it may still be upheld by a mercenary exchange of good offices according to an agreed valuation. Society, however, cannot subsist among those who are at all times ready to hurt and injure one another . . .
>
> Beneficence, therefore, is less essential to the existence of society than justice. Society may subsist, though not in the most comfortable state, without beneficence; but the prevalence of injustice must utterly destroy it. (Adam Smith, in *The Theory of Moral Sentiments*, 1976 [1759], p. 86)

Smith's distinction between justice and beneficence is similar to the distinctions drawn in this book. But from the quote above and the quote that opened this chapter, it is clear that Smith has a harm-based theory of injustice in mind.[5] This is perfectly consistent with Smith's emphasis on empathy and sympathy in his *Theory of Moral Sentiments*. But what about negative moral acts that do not actually harm anyone because, perhaps, harm is spread over so many people that it is imperceptible? Ironically, Smith, who did more to improve our understanding of the benefits of human cooperation in large group contexts than any other person to ever live, in *The Wealth of Nations* did not recognize that there was an inevitable and fundamental obstacle to cooperation in that context—the empathy problem. While Smith clearly put justice ahead of beneficence, he did not make a case for principled moral restraint *per se*, and hence he did not make a case for duty-based moral restraint.[6]

One could say that Smith got it right, but he just didn't go far enough. But such an argument is not fair to Smith. This book ultimately attempts to answer a "what if" question. Smith's work, however, was fundamentally an empirical exercise. He was simply describing the nature of human moral behavior by identifying the process by which moral standards for human behavior *actually* arise. His descriptions of how people actually behave can be perfectly accurate, even if such behavior does not produce the best possible foundation for a market economy.

Many aspects of the theory of morality advanced by a follower of Smith, Immanuel Kant, are also related to the moral foundation as it is proposed here. There is an obvious similarity between the concept of duty employed here, and how it was employed by Kant. There is also an obvious similarity between Kant's distinction between perfect and imperfect duties, and the moral foundation's differential treatment of positive and negative moral actions.[7] But the analysis presented here differs from Kant in at least two substantive ways.

First, Kant argued that moral propriety is derived from duty.[8] I do not make this argument. My claim is simply that an ethic of duty-based moral restraint is a necessary condition for most fully supporting the development and operation of a market economy, and thereby maximizing general prosperity. Duty is simply a word that captures the thought of attaching sufficiently strong feelings of guilt to actions, and not just their consequences. In the moral foundation, duty is not a matter of "the good" but is instead a matter of "what works best." Duty matters because it leads to a better outcome because of how it affects the way people think about morality. Indeed, the moral foundation has at its core a deep irony—the consequentialist goal of maximizing general prosperity is best achieved by moral beliefs that induce people to regard moral restraint in clearly nonconsequentialist terms. This is hardly Kantian.

Second, Kant believed that positive moral acts undertaken because of interpersonal utility effects have no moral merit. For Kant, only those positive moral acts undertaken as a matter of duty are of moral merit. But such a view presents an intractable problem. If positive moral acts are only of moral merit if they are matters of duty, then what do we do if we have conflicting imperatives such as would happen if a particular positive moral act is compelled by duty but it can only be achieved by violating a moral prohibition? Insisting that the latter trumps the former essentially robs the former of its duty status and, by Kant's theory, means it is no longer good. Similarly, insisting that the former trumps the latter robs the latter of its duty status and again, by Kant's theory, means that it is no longer good. This is not a problem for the moral foundation.

Those familiar with John Rawls' *A Theory of Justice* (1971) have likely noticed that the lexical primacy of obedience of moral prohibitions over moral exhortations is reminiscent of the lexical primacy of Rawls' first principle to his second principle, in his concept of *justice as fairness*. Rawls' first principle concerns upholding individual liberty equally, while his second principle concerns the desirability of effectuating social justice through income/wealth redistribution that is of greatest benefit to the least advantaged members of society.

But whereas the moral foundation involves the lexical primacy of not undertaking negative moral actions to undertaking positive ones, Rawls' lexical ordering relates to what he considers to be two competing positive ends. As such, as long as one does not consider income/wealth redistribution an infringement on individual liberty, and therefore a violation of his first principle, Rawls' lexical ordering has nothing to do with making the obedience of moral prohibitions primary to the obedience of moral exhortations. As such, it does not eliminate the problem of greater good rationalization.

More generally, even if one is persuaded by the device of "the original position" and even if one also agrees with the ultimate morality of Rawls' concept of *justice as fairness,* that is quite irrelevant to the present exercise. Regardless of how ultimately moral Rawls' framework might be, it still risks undermining the ability of individuals to trust that other individuals, organizations, or the government will not promote the welfare of third parties at their expense. One could argue that this is what the social justice theory movement has in fact done in many Western societies.

Rawls' *A Theory of Justice* almost appears to be reverse engineered. It is filled with so many exceptions and qualifications that it often appears to be an elaborate story constructed to fit aspects of the real world he endorsed, while improving upon aspects he did not. Indeed, Kenneth Arrow (1973) and John Harsanyi (1975) argued that it appeared that Rawls developed the device of the "original position" to justify his two principles, and not the other way around as Rawls leads the reader to believe.

The moral foundation avoids these kinds of criticisms altogether, because of the nature of the exercise from which it was derived. But to be fair to Rawls, it should be stressed that he was struggling with a much more fundamental and difficult question than I am struggling with here. Rawls was addressing the question of how a society should decide what is just, and therefore what *should be* in the set of positive moral actions in the first place. I take that set as given, and only briefly address its composition at the individual rather than the social level (the social level being more pertinent to collective choice). My goal is simply to identify characteristics that the moral beliefs held by individuals must have in order to maximize general prosperity irrespective of whether such moral beliefs themselves are ultimately just or moral.

Finally, Buchanan's (2001) distinction between moral community and moral order is close to the distinction I have made here between our intuitive, small group sense of morality based on empathy and mutual affection, and our formal, large group sense of morality based on a principled desire to obey moral prohibitions. Consistent with the moral foundation, Buchanan's moral order is about following the rules, not about positive moral action. On p. 189 he states:

> The emergence of abstract rules of behavior describing moral order had the effect of expanding dramatically the range of possible interpersonal

dealings. Once rules embodying reciprocal trust came to be established, it was no longer necessary that both parties to a contract identify themselves with the same moral community of shared values and loyalties.

This is another way of saying that the formal rules of impersonal exchange do not require that our transaction partners reside in our "circle of trust" because they care about us or share our moral values. In this way, a moral order can help a society transcend the small group nature of those who comprise it.

Potential Problems with the Moral Foundation

THE MORAL FOUNDATION IS JUST AN ACADEMIC EXERCISE

A potentially serious problem with the moral foundation is that it is incompatible with the psychological mechanisms humans actually possess. This is not likely to be a problem, because I have already accounted for it. Although my analysis was not driven by a naturalistic approach, it was constrained by naturalism in that the exercise only considered moral beliefs that could plausibly work through psychological mechanisms that humans actually possess. Applying this constraint was a necessary element of this thought experiment, because no society would choose moral beliefs that have no chance of producing the intended result.

It is also possible that moral beliefs that comport with the moral foundation might not actually exist, or might never have existed in the past. But I do not find this possibility to be troublesome—indeed, I would find such a result to be quite intriguing and perhaps even enlightening. How could anyone who understands the central role that general prosperity plays in supporting human flourishing not want to know how far existing moral beliefs are from those that best support it?

THE MORAL FOUNDATION IS INCOMPATIBLE WITH MARKET COMPETITION

A hallmark of prosperous market economies is competition. But competition inevitably harms others. This is likely a reason why many people look upon market economies and capitalism with disfavor. Duty-based moral restraint, where prohibitions against taking negative moral actions are lexically primary to exhortations to take positive moral actions, would seem to be inconsistent with allowing market competition, and hence inconsistent with the moral foundation. But rather than call into question the moral respectability of market competition, the moral foundation actually strengthens it.

The moral foundation generates moral restraint not from an aversion to doing harm *per se*, but from an unwillingness to undertake negative moral actions as a matter of principle. As such, the moral foundation attaches guilt to negative moral actions themselves, rather than to the harm that may result. This does not mean that harm does not matter, but it does mean that if harm results from actions that do not belong to the set of negative moral actions, its existence does not constitute *ipso facto* evidence of such actions being immoral.

Competition that refers to actions aimed at prevailing over another party by doing harm to that party as a means to that end, by nature entails actions that all value systems regard as negative moral actions (sabotage, defamation, theft, murder, etc.). Such competition would therefore not be permitted under the moral foundation. One obviously does not need to have a general aversion to competition to regard such actions as immoral. But what about competition in which a person, firm, organization, etc., prevails over another party not by interfering with his, her, or its performance, but simply by performing better? In other words, rather than compete in a manner analogous to how a defensive end competes by sacking a quarterback in a football game (what biologists call interference competition), what about cases when people compete in a manner that is more analogous to one sprinter passing another sprinter in a footrace (what biologists call scramble competition)?[9]

Such competition does not involve negative moral actions, so it should produce no feelings of guilt. This is consistent with the view that wrongfulness is not equivalent to doing harm, which comports with a principled view of moral restraint in which certain actions are inherently wrong, irrespective of harm done. So if one inflicts harm unintentionally, and not through a negative moral action, one has not behaved immorally. At the same time, the only way to "win" when competition is limited to the scramble variety is to perform better than the competition, which induces greater effort. When transactions are limited to those that are strictly voluntary, and therefore mutually beneficial, greater effort leads to higher *average* payoffs. Moreover, greater effort tends to discourage those who are not talented in a given area from competing in that area in the first place. This, in turn, produces additional spillover benefits by inducing a more efficacious matching of talent and activities.

But even if no negative moral action is taken, someone loses the race, someone loses the account, someone fails to get the promotion, etc., etc. Is not this harm immoral in itself? Not necessarily. If a social contract exists to the effect that we will all accept the possibility of losing in market (scramble) competition (interference competition is not tolerated) in return for living in a more prosperous society made possible by such competition, then no trust is violated by market competition that produces harm in the form of some of us being the losers from time to time. This harm is real and we should certainly be compassionate about it, but there is no reason to feel any guiltier about it than feeling guilty about winning a football game or a bet with a friend. Think of it this way: would you rather be a frequent winner in an impoverished hunter-gatherer band, or would you rather be a frequent loser (as most of us are) in a modern market society?

In my view, such a contract implicitly exists in the most prosperous societies in the world precisely because there is an understanding that in the long run, even the losers are winners because of the benefits of living in a rapidly growing and creative society made possible by honest market competition. Honest market competition is therefore generally regarded as morally respectable in those societies, because they possess a social contract that says people are not obliged to avoid harming others as long as they do not engage in negative moral acts as a means to the end of winning. So rather than conflict with market competition, the moral foundation is consistent with it by providing a basis for concluding that such competition is a morally respectable activity.

David Teece (1992, p. 1) stated that the real challenge to a market economy is ". . . to find the right balance of competition and cooperation, and the appropriate institutional structures within which competition and cooperation ought to take place." By simultaneously making competition between firms morally respectable (which induces innovation and forces efficiency) and making trust within firms possible (which reduces the risk of working creatively with others), the moral foundation creates the conditions necessary for cooperation within firms to be induced in fullest measure.[10] This happens by, among other things, inducing greater innovation that facilitates competing with other firms in a socially beneficial way. If the moral foundation is in place, firms effectively become ships of cooperation in seas of competition, where the latter does not undermine the former, and indeed fosters *more* of the former.

THE MORAL FOUNDATION IS TOO UNCHARITABLE

At first it would appear that those who care deeply about the welfare of others might oppose the moral foundation because it explicitly makes positive moral action a secondary moral concern. But to believe that positive moral action is not a duty is not equivalent to saying that positive moral action should not be valued greatly. Even for a person who abides by the moral foundation, the potential strength of moral conviction associated with positive moral actions could be very high. One could abide by the moral foundation while sacrificing every creature comfort to give virtually everything he has to the poor. The moral foundation simply requires that he never undertake negative moral acts to facilitate engaging in such charity.

Positive moral action requires resources. The more prosperous a society is the more resources will be available to pay for positive moral actions. All the good intentions in the world are irrelevant if a society doesn't have sufficient resources to undertake positive moral actions. The moral foundation maximizes the ability to take positive moral action by maximizing general prosperity. Viewed in this way, even steadfast consequentialists should conclude that making moral restraint primary to moral advocacy is a morally justified means to the end of undertaking the highest possible level of positive moral action.

It is obvious that the richer a society is the more benevolent it can afford to be, but it is also true that at any given point in time a society may be able to improve the welfare of the needy even more by abandoning the moral foundation. This is especially true in a prosperous society that has already built up well functioning but trust-dependent market institutions. In such a society, disobeying a specific moral prohibition in order to pay for a given positive moral action will not destroy trust or the set of trust-dependent market institutions overnight, so the gain can be great while the cost remains relatively small (perhaps precisely zero). Evaluated from a consequentialist perspective, this might appear to justify disobeying moral prohibitions as a means to the end of obeying moral exhortations.

But while the erosion of trust may be imperceptible for any given negative moral act, the combined effect of everyone behaving in this way is to destroy trust. Employing such an approach to moral propriety, period after period, results in many fewer resources to pay for positive moral actions in the long run. Moreover, as the amount of resources available falls over time, there will be increasing demand by moral advocates to get an even larger proportion of the resources that still exist. This can contribute to the urgency to take even more drastic measures to provide for positive moral actions, hastening the downward spiral of a high trust society in the process.

A related effect is that strong property rights produce the strongest incentives for creativity, invention, and innovation. This results in the most rapid development of new technologies and institutions, which in turn increases productivity and general prosperity. New technologies and institutions also provide the foundation for subsequent technological and institutional development. For this reason, economic growth tends to be subject to positive feedback, so output per capita rises exponentially. It follows that even if in the current period more positive moral action can be undertaken by not abiding by the moral foundation, at some point in the future this will no longer be true, because failing to abide in the moral foundation will reduce trust that property rights will be respected and/or enforced by government, which will therefore reduce the rate of economic growth.

It follows further that failure to abide by the moral foundation doesn't make a society more benevolent in the long run, because it can't. Trying to do more good in the present period weakens incentives, and therefore the level of resources with which to do good in the future. Not abiding by the moral foundation therefore amounts to choosing to promote the welfare of today's poor at the expense of tomorrow's poor. There is no moral theory of which I am aware that contends that this is a morally appropriate tradeoff. To argue that favoring today's poor over tomorrow's poor is nevertheless justified, because each generation has had more goods than its predecessor, is empirically incorrect. Even in the richest countries in the West, it has only been in the last 150 years that there has been a clear trend upward in real output per capita so as to assure that most children will do better than their parents.

So consequentialist moral beliefs that put positive moral action first end up being penny-wise and pound-foolish unless one is willing to improve the welfare of today's poor at the expense of tomorrow's poor.[11] Consequentialism with respect to negative moral actions, in conjunction with nonconsequentialism with respect to positive moral actions, is even worse because it insures the inefficiency of what little positive moral action that can still be afforded. Conversely, the moral foundation—which requires a nonconsequentialist theory of morality applied to negative moral actions and a consequentialist theory of morality with respect to positive moral action—produces the most resources for charity in the long run. In such a society, no one need fear being made a victim of opportunism and there will also be the greatest possible amount of resources to care for the needy.

Actions that are deemed positive, and therefore morally laudable by our moral intuitions, simply have no reason not to be deemed positive by those who abide by the moral foundation. There is simply nothing uncharitable about the moral foundation. With respect to negative moral action, the moral foundation does not in any way conflict with harm-based moral restraint. On the contrary, it strengthens moral restraint generally. Horror does not result from making people more reluctant to undertake negative moral acts and from adding additional constraints on behavior. I would argue that we are most likely to engage in horror when our harm-based sense of moral restraint has been overridden by duty-based moral advocacy (e.g., the Nazis suppressing their natural sense of empathy to persecute Jews because they believed they had a duty to what they were ordered to do for the good of Germany).

No matter how much more attractive a society described by Hitler or Pol Pot might have appeared to the citizens of their respective countries, if everyone believed that moral exhortations must always be subordinated to moral prohibitions, then those citizens would have listened to their hardwired sense of empathy, which would have told them they were listening to evil. Under the moral foundation, no amount of abstract moral or ideological reasoning would have been able to overturn this conclusion, because positive moral actions made possible by negative moral actions are simply not considered legitimate. Therefore by making the obedience of moral prohibitions unconditional, the moral foundation strengthens our basic decency. It takes horrible actions that could be rationalized with greater good arguments completely off the table. Again, horror does not come from additional constraints. Horror comes from twisted greater good arguments. The moral foundation robs people of their ability to get the majority to adopt any greater good argument, twisted or otherwise.

To summarize, a nonconsequentialist theory of moral propriety, applied to moral prohibitions, produces the most resources to pay for positive moral actions. And a consequentialist theory of moral propriety, applied to moral exhortations, assures efficient deployment of such resources without undermining duty-based moral restraint. Again, this constitutes an interesting irony: the best moral outcome, according to a consequentialist who favors positive moral action above all else, is best achieved in the long run by having moral restraint governed by a nonconsequentialist view of moral propriety.

THE MORAL FOUNDATION IS TOO COMPLICATED

The moral foundation is the product of a complex thought experiment. The distinction between positive and negative moral actions and the distinction between consequentialist and nonconsequentialist theories of moral propriety must be considered together for the moral foundation to come into full logical relief. This raises an obvious question about its practical value. A thought experiment that answers a question with an answer that cannot practicably work is not a very useful thought experiment. A society obviously would not choose moral beliefs for itself that actual humans aren't smart enough to follow. So is the moral foundation too complicated to be practicable?

Although the derivation of the moral foundation involved arguments that were often indirect and subtle, its implications for moral behavior are actually quite simple. In short, not doing the moral "don'ts" is a matter of duty, while doing the moral "do's" is a matter of personal moral tastes. This is not a difficult framework to actually employ in moral decision making.

I would argue that the modern, *do the right thing* approach to moral thinking is quite the opposite. It is derived from a very simple framework that ends up producing unclear rules for moral behavior, because it is not up to the task of dealing with moral decision making in a modern, complex, large group society. Its application therefore requires endless nuanced reasoning, not because the underlying moral theory is sophisticated, but because it amounts to bringing a knife to a gunfight. In other words, modern moral theories appear sophisticated because they are so poorly suited for the modern world that they require sophisticated reasoning to take up the slack. Conversely, the moral foundation involves a more complicated underlying framework than theories of morality now being taught in most K–12 classrooms today, but it produces simpler rules for dealing with the kinds of moral decisions that arise in a modern, complex, large group society.

Consider a mechanic who has to work on an aircraft engine but only has a Sears Craftsman starter tool set to work with. Such tools are fine for simple household repair projects, but they are inadequate for working on an aircraft engine. Figuring out how to repair such an engine with such tools requires a great deal of cleverness on the part of the mechanic. To be assured that repairs will be done properly, it would be necessary for every aircraft mechanic to be a genius who desperately wants to do a good job. The more poorly adapted the tools, the more important it is that the mechanic be both intellectually gifted and earnest.

Now consider a mechanic who has all the advanced tools normally required to work on an aircraft engine. The mechanic might not have any appreciation for the level of engineering involved in their development, but because the tools are up to the task, their use is rather straightforward. Therefore even a very ordinary mechanic has no problem doing repairs. It is not necessary that the mechanic be intellectually gifted or particularly earnest about doing a good job.

It would be a mistake to conclude that because the first mechanic is working so hard and cleverly that his tools must be very advanced. It would also be a mistake to conclude that the second mechanic must be using simple tools that are not very advanced because their application is so straightforward. Quite the opposite is the case. It is because the tools used by the second mechanic are up to their task that their application is very straightforward. Similarly, because the moral foundation was derived through a thought experiment that explicitly considered what is needed to maximize general prosperity, it is up to the task of doing so and its application is rather straightforward.

Finally, with its emphasis on never disobeying moral prohibitions, the moral foundation provides a clear standard for behavior for being a moral person. The moral foundation demands nothing in the way of positive moral action, but it is unwavering in its demand for refraining from taking negative moral action. As such, the moral foundation involves a much lower but much clearer standard for moral behavior, one we know we can all live up to and one we know we can demand of everyone else, which is essential for internal consistency, universality, and sustainability.[12]

THE MORAL FOUNDATION IS TOO INFLEXIBLE

An advantage of the modern *do the right thing* approach to morality is that it is very flexible. An advantage of the moral foundation is that its rules for behavior are very simple. Does this mean that the simplicity of implementation of the moral foundation comes at the expense of flexibility? A related concern is that the moral foundation's emphasis on duty smacks of moral absolutism, which in some circumstances can drive a wedge between what is regarded as morally appropriate and what our gut tells us we should or shouldn't do.

A value system that comports with our hardwired moral intuitions is obviously more likely to work than one that does not. When duty-based moral restraint appears to produce an absurd outcome—one that our gut tells us is clearly not right—is there a basis for justifying an exception? In what follows, I will argue that the moral foundation implicitly provides a straightforward and objective way to identify legitimate exceptions, so duty-based moral restraint does not result in unconscionable inflexibility.

A Basis for Exceptions regarding Negative Moral Actions

A familiar objection to rule-based moral decision making is that the existence of exceptions demonstrates that the rule involved is internally inconsistent. Most scholars recognize that this is essentially a straw-man argument because there is a difference between having a rule for which there are exceptions and not having any rule at all. As but one reason why there is a difference, in the former case exceptions require some kind of justification, whereas in the latter case the full range of actions is already on the table. Still, it is undeniable that the greater the number of exceptions and/or the more *ad hoc* in nature arguments can be to justify them, the less meaningful a rule is.

Rules are by nature imperfect. So in a world of rules with no exceptions, we have orderly and predictable behavior but we also have many absurd outcomes. In a world in which there are no rules, moral decision making is governed only by intuitions and the details of the moment, so we largely avoid absurd outcomes. But we sacrifice orderliness and predictability, thereby paving the way to having a high transaction cost society. This might not concern those who don't understand how market economies work, and therefore how general prosperity comes about, but it should concern everyone else.

As is often the case in the real world, the best approach is not a perfect one. What works best, in the world we actually live in, is having rules but realizing that there will be exceptions. In a world of rules with exceptions, we have orderly and predictable behavior for the most part, but we can also avoid most of the absurd outcomes. It is precisely this approach to moral behavior that allows a police officer to decide not to write a ticket to a person who is speeding in order to get someone who is bleeding to death to the hospital.

Is there an objective basis for identifying genuine exceptions? This is crucial because without an objective basis for doing so, people will be able to engage in *ad hoc* exception making that is ultimately self-serving.[13] The moral foundation implicitly suggests the following criteria for justifying exceptions: if abiding by the letter of a moral prohibition effectively violates the spirit of that prohibition in a particular case, then a genuine exception exists in that case.

Because the moral foundation is derived from the ultimate objective of most fully supporting the development and operation of a market economy by most fully combating opportunism, any rule of behavior derived from it ultimately exists to combat opportunism. We therefore know the spirit of the rules derived from it, so we can therefore discern when the letter of such rules violates their spirit. Such exceptions are not merely *ad hoc* exceptions, and they are amenable to evaluation by others *ex post*.[14] As such, when our moral intuition tells us that obeying a moral prohibition in a particular circumstance is wrong, we can ask ourselves whether it is in any way opportunistic. If not, a true exception may exist that it is not *ad hoc* in nature. To allow an exception in such a case is in no way hypocritical.

We are all better off in the long run when such exceptions are granted and viewed as morally respectable. Such exceptions do not open the door to rationalizing negative moral actions that are directly or indirectly self-serving in nature. Conversely, when the justification of exceptions is *ad hoc*, and therefore is not itself governed by an objective rule for exception making such as I have described above, exceptions proliferate and thereby render rules meaningless. Rules work best when exceptions to them must also follow rules governing the making of exceptions.

Examples of ethical conundrums are popular among modern moral theorists because they appear to demonstrate why moral rules usually end up being too absolute because rules are by nature simple-minded. Absurdities that we cannot accept can be avoided by abandoning rules and letting our moral intuition tell us what to do. The problem is that this creates a *de facto* act-utilitarian standard for moral behavior. This amounts to avoiding a superficial problem of inelegance (dealing with occasional exceptions) by inviting a substantive problem (having a *de facto* act-utilitarian ethic that is incapable of sustaining unconditional trustworthiness or producing clear standards for behavior).

Many apparent conundrums simply melt away if one realizes that the fundamental problem society must address, if it wishes to flourish, is the problem of opportunism. Consider deception, for example. Deception is generally regarded as a negative moral action. But what if the only way B can get A to leave a burning house is to deceive A by telling him that his dog has already been saved? Would we want to live in a world in which A dies because B never tells a lie no matter what? Would it not be the case that A would be made worse off by dying, even though the emotions of the moment would lead him to charge in?

As an economist, I am aware of the need for humility here. People have different tastes, and it is easy to become convinced that you know what is best for someone else. Yet the fact that it is easy to make a mistake about such a matter does not mean we always make mistakes about such matters. This is especially true when the other party is likely experiencing strong emotions. Are there not cases when such a conclusion is not so much an indication of hubris as it is recognition of the exceptional nature of the circumstances involved? Is there really never a good reason for telling a "white lie" to talk a suicidal person off a ledge?

Finally, the famous "lying to the murderer" scenario proposed by Benjamin Constant produces no conundrum for the moral foundation. When a murderer asks a question that, if answered honestly, will result in an innocent person's death, even a person who is committed to an ethic of duty-based moral restraint can, without hypocrisy, conclude that lying is appropriate, because the reason duty-based moral restraint exists in the first place is not that it combats deception *per se*, but that it combats opportunism. In this case lying to the murderer does not in any way promote the liar's own interest (it may even reduce it if the murderer figures out he has been lied to). As such, the liar is not attempting to promote his own welfare. There is nothing hypocritical or inconsistent about lying to the murderer, even if one believes it is normally one's duty not to lie.

Let's now consider how one can employ the moral foundation to think through any unpleasant decision that is often viewed as a conundrum according to today's *do the right thing* approach to morality. Should a firm, for example, shut down a plant to increase profits, or remain open to save the jobs of its employees? Many would regard this as a difficult moral decision, but for those who abide by the moral foundation it is not. Those who are in a position to make decisions for the firm are there because at some point in the past they gave their word that they would run the firm to maximize its profits. To refuse to shut down a plant that is unprofitable is, therefore, disobeying a moral prohibition against breaking one's word as a means to the end of doing something nice for the workers. This is not permissible under the moral foundation.

Those who work for the firm are valuable to the firm precisely because they produce a profit. The firm is not bound to them, any more than the workers are bound to the firm, unless there is a contract to the contrary. There is a wage that is low enough that firms would be willing to guarantee lifetime employment, but workers apparently don't want it because they never even propose it. So if workers make moral arguments against a firm shutting down a plant, they are creating a moral obligation out of thin air. They are not offering to take a much lower wage and bind themselves to never leaving the firm if a better offer comes along.[15]

A Basis for Exceptions regarding Positive Moral Actions

In rare circumstances nearly everyone believes that it is immoral to fail to take a positive moral action. Nearly everyone believes that extending an oar to a drowning man is morally required. Doesn't this conflict with the moral foundation because it treats a positive moral act as a matter of duty? Does not this example therefore reveal a deep conflict between the moral foundation and our moral intuitions?

In some cases, failure to take a positive moral act (which is an act of omission) is tantamount to choosing to take a negative moral act (which is an act of commission). Moreover, this is more likely to be true the more self-evident it is that a given positive moral action should be taken, perhaps even must be taken. When an act of omission is effectively an act of commission (not extending an oar when one is handy), a compelling case can sometimes be made that we are morally obligated to help the drowning man because to not do so goes beyond allowing harm, it amounts to choosing to do harm. I will now argue that such cases are really not examples of positive moral action at all, but are better regarded as not taking negative moral actions.

Normally, not doing y does not perfectly equal doing x, because the doing of good and the doing of bad are not perfectly complementary sets. This is because in most cases when we think a person should do y because if he doesn't, harm will likely come to another person, we don't know with certainty that this will be the case. It is even possible that doing y might turn out to do more harm than doing nothing, because of unforeseen consequences. But in some rare cases the scenario is simple enough that one can say with virtual certainty that if a given positive moral action isn't taken, a particular adverse outcome will occur. In such cases what appears to be an act of omission is, for all practical purposes, an act of commission.

If in addition it is also true that taking such an action entails little or no cost to the actor, then not taking it amounts to revealing a desire to see harm done.[16] Although I have already shown that harm *per se* is neither a necessary nor sufficient condition for an act to be a negative one, an act that is taken for the sheer pleasure of seeing harm done is clearly a negative moral act. Inaction in such cases is therefore tantamount to deciding to undertake an action to bring about harm.

The lower the cost of acting, and the more likely it is that to not act will necessarily result in a harmful outcome, the more likely this is the correct inference. Indeed, if there is zero cost to acting it is the dominant strategy under uncertainty to help because of potential reciprocity, so to not help is to reveal a preference for harm. In reality, then, what looks like a decision to undertake a positive moral act is really a decision to not undertake a negative moral act. Since the moral foundation endorses the obedience of moral prohibitions against negative moral actions as a matter of duty, it follows that it would endorse the claim that extending an oar to a drowning man is a moral duty. It should be stressed that while these circumstances clearly exist in life, in the conduct of ordinary economic activity such circumstances are exceedingly rare and are easily recognized as genuine exceptions by people of good faith when they arise.

CHAPTER 9

Trust

Virtually every commercial transaction has within itself an element of
trust, certainly any transaction conducted over a period of time. It can be
plausibly argued that much of the economic backwardness in the world
can be explained by the lack of mutual confidence.—Kenneth Arrow,
1972, p. 357

Introduction

The last chapter brought our thought experiment to a close. The moral foundation
of economic behavior is unconditional trustworthiness made possible by a preponderance of people possessing an ethic of duty-based moral restraint that is not
undermined by an ethic of duty-based moral advocacy.

The purpose of this chapter is to determine whether there is any value added
from having undertaken this thought experiment. I will address the question of
how well trust, based on moral beliefs that comport with the moral foundation,
compares with existing theories of trust. I will explain why previous theoretical
work takes aim at the wrong target, modeling what is really assurance rather than
genuine trust, or modeling genuine trust that is inherently small group trust.
While these are important achievements in their own right, maximizing general
prosperity requires maximizing the effectiveness of large group cooperation,
which requires a basis for genuine trust in large group contexts.

In this chapter I will also explain why existing theories of trust do not square well
with existing empirical evidence, but trust based on A's rational expectation that B's
moral beliefs comport with the moral foundation does. Among other problems,
existing approaches are inconsistent with persistent findings from experimental
economics. Of particular interest is the persistent finding that people are simply too
eager to extend trust, and too unwilling to behave in an untrustworthy way, even
when it is rational to do so if trust behavior is governed solely by prudence.

This well-known finding has led to fascinating research into the possibility that
trust behavior is a manifestation of hardwired factors. There is no doubt that we

possess inherited traits that support trust behavior, but this is not the same thing as being hardwired to be unconditionally trustworthy or to extend genuine trust. If we are hardwired to be trustworthy and to be willing to extend trust, then why are there such profound differences in trust behavior across societies? Moreover, hardwired traits would have evolved largely in the context of small groups, so there is no particular reason why they should be able to support trust behavior in large groups. In Chapters 5 and 6 we learned why there are good reasons to suspect they won't. In short, traditional incentive-based approaches to trustworthiness don't support genuine trust, while newer hardwired approaches cannot explain measured variations in trust across societies and are likely only pertinent to small group contexts.

Is there any basis for unconditional trustworthiness that could give rise to what could be characterized as a "high trust society"? This is a subtler question than it might first appear. The thought experiment only identified necessary conditions for moral beliefs possessed by *B* to result in *A* being willing to rationally extend genuine trust to *B* at the micro level. This chapter will address the question of whether moral beliefs that comport with the moral foundation can plausibly give rise to genuine trust at the macro level as well—that is, to a preponderance of people across the whole of a society. This is often referred to in the literature as *generalized trust*.[1] We will find that the key to a society being able to enjoy the benefits of being a high trust society—of having genuine trust that is also generalized in nature—is the moral tastes of its individuals. Expanding on arguments first made by Robert Frank (1988), I will explain why nothing else can get the job done.

ARGUMENTS AND EVIDENCE FOR WHY TRUST MATTERS[2]

Janet Landa (1994) argued that trust arising from kin-based networks can emerge between economic actors to facilitate transactions, even in the absence of a framework of contract law and the formal institutions normally associated with supporting contractual enforcement. Francis Fukuyama (1995) argued that trust is crucial for the development of the kinds of organizations and institutions that are associated with economic prosperity. Dyer and Chu (2003), Sako (1998), and Zaheer et al. (1998) have similarly argued that trust is an important factor in "organizational-level strategic performance."[3] Fukuyama (1995) argued further that generalized trust is a substitute for the kind of trust that might be found in family firms. Covey (2008) provides numerous examples of how trust makes almost everything easier within and across firms.

La Porta, Lopez-de-Silanes, Shleifer, and Vishny (1997) found strong evidence in support of Fukuyama's (1995) thesis in their cross-country analysis of the relationship between trust and the kind of large organizations that are needed to fuel economic growth. Knack and Keefer (1997) compared measures of trust to economic performance over a sample of 29 countries, and found that trust was clearly related to economic growth—although the measures of social capital emphasized in Putnam et al. (1993), which were based on data on membership in social groups, were not related to either measures of trust or improved economic performance. Controlling for the level of law enforcement, Zak and Knack (2001) also found evidence that trust was related to economic growth. Guiso, Sapienza, and Zingales (2004) found that trust is related to the level of financial development across different parts of Italy, thereby indirectly affecting economic performance. Trust, as measured by the *World Values Survey*, is strongly and negatively related to cash holdings, suggesting that trust acts as a substitute for weak financial institutions. In short, there is much evidence to suggest that trust matters, and it is therefore important that we develop theories of trust behavior.[4]

Much attention has been paid to documenting the relationship between trust and economic performance, as well as to developing theories of trust behavior (Frank 1988; Hardin 1996; Zak and Knack 2001; Uslaner 2002; Macleod 2007; Goergen 2008). I submit that the importance of trust continues to be underestimated, and the role trust plays continues to be misunderstood, because the kind of trust that social scientists have studied is not the kind of trust that matters most. In what follows, I explain why the fullest development and most efficient operation of a market economy cannot be achieved from trustworthiness that is derived from hardwired moral intuitions, strategic factors inherent in human relationships, or institutions. This casts doubt on the relevance of theories of trust based on hardwired traits, as well as theories of trust in which trustworthiness is simply a prudent response to externally produced incentives.

Theories of Trust

ALTRUISTIC/MORALISTIC TRUST

Which is the most accurate description of a high trust society: a society filled with people eager to trust others because they have a strong preference for extending trust, or a society filled with people who are trustworthy?[5] The former position is taken by Uslaner (2002), who argues that societies that enjoy generalized trust do so because of a belief that extending trust is a moral imperative. This is sometimes called "moralistic trust" and is closely related to the idea of altruistic trust.[6]

Not surprisingly, the argument that a high trust society can be based on a moral imperative to extend trust has been met with skepticism. Hardin (1993, 1996, 2002), Ostrom (2003), and Levi (1998), among others, are skeptical about the possibility that the extension of trust can lead to an environment of generalized trust. They view the act of extending trust as a morally neutral response to the rational expectation of trustworthiness. As such, the extension of trust is not in any way morally praiseworthy (Hardin 1993). Baron (1998, p. 411) has drawn a similar distinction, that of the distinction between "trust as belief and trust as a norm," but notes that there may be feedbacks involved that make trust more complicated than it first appears.

Hardin, Ostrom, and Levi clearly have a point, but other work has demonstrated the power of trust preferences relative to beliefs about the other party's trustworthiness. Sapienza, Toldra, and Zingales (2007) address conflicting findings about trust in two important papers. Glaeser, Laibson, Scheinkmen, and Soutter (2000) questioned the validity of the well-known *World Values Survey* question regarding trust, because while it did correlate with trustworthiness, it did not correlate with sender behavior in trust games.[7] Fehr, Fischbacher, von Rosenbladt, Schupp, and Wagner (2003) found just the opposite to be the case for their sample. Sapienza, Toldra, and Zingales (2007) reconciled these results by employing a framework that experimentally accounts for both preferences regarding the extension of trust and beliefs about trustworthiness. They found that both preferences and beliefs matter, and that given differences in the samples involved, Glaeser et al. and Fehr et al.'s results can be reconciled.

It is not surprising that trust preferences matter at the decision margin in a trust game, but what does that tell us about trust behavior in the broader society over time? Consider what would happen if people had a strong preference for extending trust, but they happen to live in a society that is filled with untrustworthy people. In such a case, those who extend trust would constantly be victimized. The effects of operant conditioning alone would likely be sufficient to induce people to stop extending trust in the absence of clear evidence that the other party is indeed trustworthy. It is simply implausible to believe that any individual would continue to extend trust if he were repeatedly victimized by untrustworthy individuals. In any case, those who possess inherited traits and/or cultural beliefs that make them pessimistic about extending trust would enjoy higher payoffs than those who don't.

Now suppose that most people are not willing to extend trust, even though nearly all people in a given society are trustworthy in nearly all circumstances. In this case, the few who were willing to extend trust would enjoy higher payoffs through the benefits of engaging in the high trust transactions that the untrusting would pass up. Others would observe this and likely figure out that their pessimism is just too costly. In any case, those who possess inherited traits and/or cultural beliefs that make them optimistic about extending trust would enjoy higher payoffs than those who don't.

So trust in the absence of trustworthiness will almost certainly reduce the extension of trust over time, but trustworthiness in the absence of trust will almost certainly increase the extension of trust over time. We can therefore safely ignore theories of trust that are not based on the rational expectation of trustworthiness, because such trust behavior would be inherently unsustainable.[8]

RATIONAL TRUST

So when is it rational to extend trust? The answer, of course, is when it is rational to expect that the party to be trusted is trustworthy. There are a number of reasons why it might be rational for *A* to expect *B* to behave in a trustworthy manner. The most obvious reason is that A believes that B cares about his welfare. This is such an obvious point that Hardin (2002) and Guinnane (2005) have argued that it does not even constitute an interesting sense of the word *trust*.

In small group contexts (e.g., the family) it is perfectly rational to expect that others will behave in a trustworthy way toward you, if you believe they care about you. Such trustworthiness is unconditional, because it not based on the other party's self-interest. It is based, instead, on interpersonal utility effects that, if sufficiently strong, can withstand the greatest temptation. You can trust your parents not to steal from you because you know that they care so much about you that opportunism *at your expense* is unthinkable for them.

But while there is no shortage of rational trust based on the rational expectation of strong interpersonal utility effects in small groups like families, such interpersonal utility effects are fundamentally consequentialist in nature—we do or don't do something because of the effect it has another individual whose welfare we care about. But in Chapter 6 we learned why our capacity for empathy, sympathy, and guilt have limited ability to combat opportunism in large groups, *no matter how much we care about the welfare of those who comprise such groups*. This is because the larger the group over which the harm of opportunism is spread, the less likely there will be a harmed individual with whom to empathize, sympathize, and therefore feel guilty about harming. This means that genuine trust sustained by interpersonal utility effects is fundamentally a small group phenomenon. This is true no matter how strong interpersonal utility effects are. If the extension of genuine trust is to be rational in the context of large groups, it will require something beyond interpersonal utility effects or our hardwired reluctance to harm others. Since general prosperity is impossible if economic activity is limited to small groups, trust derived from either interpersonal utility effects or harm-based moral restraint simply won't get the job done.

To summarize, altruistic/moralistic trust is generally unsustainable. If a convincing theory of trust is to exist, it will have to be a theory of *rational* trust. This means that the core of any plausible theory of trust is a convincing theory of trustworthiness. One possibility is the rational expectation of strong interpersonal utility effects. Such trust is certainly genuine, but the larger the group, the more likely it will prove insufficient because of the empathy problem. A convincing theory of rational trust needs a convincing theory of trustworthiness that depends neither on interpersonal utility effects nor harm-based moral restraint.

Theories of Trustworthiness

For A to rationally conclude that B is trustworthy, A has to believe that B's trustworthiness is *not irrational*. This is because if B's trustworthiness were not consistent with rationality, it would by definition produce lower payoffs than otherwise, and would therefore not be credible or sustainable because it would conflict with the individual's self-interest. An obvious way to assure that B's trustworthiness is rational is to limit our attention to theories of trustworthiness that comport with a model of rational choice with respect to B's behavior.

For the case of an individual's behavior, the model of rational choice explains decision making as the result of maximizing an objective (defined by tastes that are internal to the individual, such as how strongly he likes chocolate relative to popcorn) while obeying constraints (defined by factors external to the individual, such as his income and market prices). The constraints that confront an individual affect his choice by altering the net rewards of alternative actions—that is, by changing incentives. This suggests that theories of rational trustworthiness must produce trustworthiness through one or both of these channels, so they can be usefully divided between theories based on incentives and theories based on tastes.

TRUSTWORTHINESS BASED ON INCENTIVES

Consider the possibility that an individual can be rationally expected to be trustworthy because concern for his own welfare provides ample incentive to refrain from opportunism. So A believes it is rational to extend trust to B, because A believes that B believes it is in B's own best interest to be trustworthy. Incentive-based theories of trustworthiness are not based on any moral imperative for A to extend trust, or any moral imperative for B to behave in a trustworthy way. Such theories are, instead, ultimately based on incentives.[9] In these models even treacherous people are trustworthy, because it is simply in their best interest to be so.

Social scientists, and economists in particular, are naturally inclined to view trust in such strategic or "calculative" terms, because they are eager to understand a behavior like trust in terms of universal economic forces rather than from idiosyncratic tastes in the form of moral imperatives to trust or be trustworthy. For them, the key to understanding trust and trustworthiness is discovering what it takes to make trustworthiness "incentive-compatible"—that is, what it takes for it to be in the trusted party's best interest to behave in a trustworthy way. The point of such models is to identify reasons why this might be true.

In some cases, incentives for behaving in a trustworthy manner are "spontaneously emergent" in the sense that they are derived from strategic factors inherent in human relationships. Spontaneously emergent incentives is essentially what Hardin (2002) was alluding to with his notion of "encapsulated interests." Economists prefer to call this "repeat play effects" (Gibbons 2001). But long before game theorists worked out the theory of repeated games, economists often argued that the cost of losing one's reputation produces powerful incentives for individuals to behave in a trustworthy manner. So, they argued, even something as sublime as being trustworthy could be explained as nothing more than an exercise in enlightened self-interest.

There are numerous models in economics based on the effects of repeated interaction (e.g., Arrow 1972; Klein and Leffler 1981; Kreps et al. 1982; Fudenberg and Maskin 1986; Abreu 1988; Dasgupta 1988; Kreps 1990; Grief 1993; Neilson 1999) that imply that repeat play can provide a basis for trustworthiness. Alluding to Axelrod's (1984) famous work on reciprocal altruism, Robert Frank (1988) refers to such theories as mere tit-for-tat theories that are rooted in prudence, meaning that people behave in a desirable way not because they are moral, but because they have sufficient incentive to do so, and are sufficiently rational to understand that fact. Oliver Williamson (1993) has pejoratively referred to trust based on the expectation of this kind of trustworthiness as merely "calculative trust." Toshio Yamagishi (1999, 2000) argues that such trustworthiness does not produce genuine trust, but what is more accurately described as "assurance."

Social capital theory provides a powerful framework for explaining how human societies can derive benefits from social organization that provides incentives for effective cooperation, in large part by supporting trust behavior. The concept of social capital is most closely identified with the work of Pierre Bourdieu, James Coleman, and Robert Putnam.[10] Coleman (1988, 1990) laid out the basic theoretical framework in an effort to close the gap between sociological and economic approaches. For extensive reviews of the social capital literature, see Portes (1998), Sobel (2002), Ostrom and Ahn (2003), and Durlauf and Fafchamps (2004).

Since Coleman (1988), trust has been considered a key component of social capital. The basic idea is that behavior within social groups will not be very effective if trust is low. Networks and trust do seem to go together. Dasgupta (2003) states: "Trust is the key to cooperation, *social capital is merely a means to creating trust*" [emphasis added]. According to this approach, social capital is not made up of networks *and/or* trust; social capital *is* the network itself, and such networks exist to support trustworthiness and, hence, the rational extension of trust. The value of networks (and, hence, social capital) is therefore derived largely from their ability to create trustworthiness through incentives.

Social capital in the form of social networks creates an environment of trust because within a social network, repeat play is more likely and the cost of losing one's reputation is high. If an individual is caught behaving in an untrustworthy manner in a social network, and this is conveyed to all other members of the network, the individual can be banned from further transactions within the network. This can drive the value of prior investments into such network relationships to zero. Historical evidence indeed suggests that social networks have proven to be extremely important mechanisms for reducing transaction costs (e.g., Maghribi traders, Japanese Zaibatsu, and Hassidic Jews in the Diamond trade).

Formal institutional mechanisms can also produce incentives for behaving in a trustworthy manner. This can occur directly by affecting the institutional environment, as in government enforced laws against fraud, or it can occur indirectly through institutional arrangements, as in government enforcement of contracts through the good faith doctrine. Formal institutional mechanisms can also indirectly produce incentives for behaving in a trustworthy manner through the regularization of economic activity. Many transactions follow a specific pattern by design, so as to preclude opportunism. For example, in the United States, consumer credit transactions often involve a number of disclosure statements that have the intended effect of closing opportunities for opportunism by either unscrupulous lenders or dishonest borrowers. We have, of course, learned the hard way what can happen when such institutional mechanisms are no longer followed.

Informal institutional mechanisms can also produce direct incentives for behaving in a trustworthy manner. One example is the now common practice of posting displeasure about poor service on the internet. Informal institutional mechanisms can also work indirectly, through the regularization of economic activity that results from evolved, rather than designed, transaction patterns. Obviously, transaction patterns that often open both parties to opportunism are less evolutionarily fit than those that rarely leave any room for opportunism. Examples of such regularization include the practice of giving a third party the money placed on a bet, the practice of drawing straws, or the practice of using escrow accounts even when not required by law.

Institutional practices within organizations also produce incentives for individuals to behave in a trustworthy manner. For example, firms hire managers to monitor workers to insure that they don't shirk or steal, use software to keep track of worker productivity, and give out bonuses based on measured performance. In addition, firms can use strict procedures to regularize activity in such a way as to minimize the opportunities for opportunism. This is the underlying reason for many accounting practices.

REVIEW OF THEORIES OF TRUSTWORTHINESS BASED ON INCENTIVES

All incentive-based theories of trustworthiness posit a credible commitment to refrain from behaving in an opportunistic manner through *externally* generated incentives and, hence, a credible commitment to behave in a trustworthy way. The basic idea is that one refrains from behaving in an opportunistic manner because of the expected cost of not doing so. But for such a cost to matter, the trusted party must believe there is at least some chance of being caught.

Robert Frank pointed out over two decades ago that this presents a fundamental problem for theories of trust based on a merely prudent form of restraint. If a person's unwillingness to behave in an opportunistic manner is derived solely from a desire to avoid the cost associated with detection, then a possibility of detection is required. This leads to a fundamental problem—the prudence problem—which is that trustworthiness derived solely from prudential restraint is meaningless for golden opportunities, by the very definition of a golden opportunity.

The essence of genuine, unconditional trustworthiness is doing as you promised, even if a golden opportunity presents itself. Decision makers in firms make the often explicit, and always implicit promise to make decisions that are in the best interest of the firm. Genuine trust is only possible when the party extending trust believes that the trusted party will keep this promise, even if golden opportunities arise for the decision maker to improve his own welfare at the trusting party's expense.

This is no small point. If trustworthiness is merely a prudent response to external incentives, then it will fail precisely where trustworthiness really matters. Many have pointed out that trustworthiness derived solely from external incentives is arguably not trustworthiness at all, and trust extended in the expectation of such incentives is not properly viewed as genuine trust. What is the value to *A* of being able to trust *B*, if *B*'s trustworthiness fails where it is actually needed? Indeed, it is irrational to expect not to be taken advantage of when golden opportunities arise if all that exists is prudential restraint. For this reason, in all but the most unusual of circumstances, the extension of *genuine trust* cannot be rational if it is solely based on prudential restraint.

Of particular importance is the inability of trustworthiness, derived solely from prudential restraint, to minimize the costs associated with third-degree opportunism. Recall that third-degree opportunism involves taking advantage of discretion that has been delegated to those who possess local knowledge in the context of a relational contract. In Chapter 3 we learned that this is a particularly troubling problem associated with local knowledge, and is intensified within firms by increasing size or complexity. In other words, the circumstances that make relational contracts valuable also tend to increase the likelihood of golden opportunities. The larger the firm, the more complicated the production process, and the faster the pace of unpredictable change, the truer this is.

It follows that a requirement for being able to employ relational contracts to efficiently use local knowledge is being able to trust decision makers not to act on golden opportunities that inevitably arise. But, by definition, no amount of prudential restraint will discourage a rational opportunist from acting on golden opportunities. There is no way to escape this conclusion. We can't assume that people are utterly and merely rational, and then turn around and assume they are not. It follows that if trustworthiness is derived solely from a rational response to incentives—prudential restraint—then the use of relational contracts will often be foolish. This impedes a society's ability to avert the normal tradeoff between size and entrepreneurial direction of firm behavior through the use of relational contracts.

Note further that if there is nothing to impede one's taking advantage of golden opportunities as they arise, then the organizational governance structures that are most likely to produce golden opportunities will be too costly to be viable. This is precisely what it means to say that one advantage of a high trust society is that it can support highly trust-dependent institutions and governance structures. More to the point, if we are to enjoy firms that are both large and entrepreneurial, because they can employ relational contracts to facilitate the efficient use of local knowledge, we need something other than prudential restraint to produce unconditional trustworthiness.

An important distinction in the trust literature is between trust extended to particular individuals or particular organizations, versus generalized trust (Ulsaner 2002). As Durlauf and Fafchamps (2004, p. 9) point out, how strangers are expected to react when trust is extended to them plays a crucial role in making generalized trust possible:

> "Sometimes, trust arises from repeated interpersonal interaction. Other times, it arises from general knowledge about the population of agents . . . The former can be called personalized trust and the latter generalized trust. The main difference between the two is that, for each pair of newly matched agents, the former takes time and effort to establish while the latter is instantaneous."

The idea of generalized trust is more accurately described if one replaces the word "instantaneous" with "presumed" in the quote above. *Rational* generalized trust exists when it is rational for people to adopt a rule of thumb that presumes others are trustworthy with respect to most transactions, unless there is specific evidence to the contrary. This does not mean that we have to literally believe that everyone is trustworthy. It only means we believe that untrustworthy people so rare that for all but the most exceptional of transactions we are better off presuming the other party is trustworthy.[11] Fukuyama (1995) and Yamagishi and Yamagishi (1994) have also emphasized the distinction between particularized and generalized trust, the latter referring to this distinction as the difference between personal trust and general trust.

We have already seen that while interpersonal utility effects can produce unconditional trustworthiness, and therefore support the rational extension of genuine trust, this mechanism becomes less plausible the larger the group over which the cost of opportunism can be spread. Interpersonal utility effects, therefore, can at best support only small group trust, and are incapable of producing generalized trust. What about conventional incentive-based theories of trustworthiness? Do any of these theories provide a plausible account of how generalized trust can arise for trust that is genuine in nature? In my view, the answer is no.

Although Hardin's (2002) notion of encapsulated interest provides a compelling explanation for much of the trust behavior we observe, it does not provide a plausible basis for generalized trust. If trust is limited to encapsulated interests, then strangers will not presumptively trust each other. Yet in many countries, they appear to, and their willingness to do so correlates with social, political, and economic performance (Knack and Keefer, 1997; Putnam 1993; 1995; 2000). This suggests that while Hardin's approach may explain the most common forms of trust quite well, it does not explain how the kind of trust that matters most actually works—that being the kind of trust that is required for the fullest development and most efficient operation of a market society.

There is, however, no compelling *a priori* reason for claiming that it is impossible for trustworthiness, based on incentives produced by social networks and institutions, to produce generalized trust. But it must be emphasized that while such trust might be generalized, it is still dependent on externally produced incentives to combat opportunism. So it would not be extended where there was a reasonable chance of golden opportunities (or even a remote chance if the potential cost of opportunism is great).

Prior efforts to explain generalized trust via institutional mechanisms have not been encouraging about the ability of such models to explain trust that is also genuine in nature. The most ambitious attempt to model trust behavior at the micro level, in such a way as to explain the existence of generalized trust at the macro level through the existence of supporting institutions, is Zak and Knack (2001). In their model, they considered fealty trust between principals and agents. Their paper is important because it empirically connects a formal model of particularized trust to a condition of generalized trust (as measured by the *World Values Survey*). There is no doubt that where institutions exist to strengthen the sanctioning of breaches of fealty trust, this form of trust works better than otherwise (this has been stressed by Ensminger, 2004). But because their model is based on repeat play, it does not model genuine trust.

Conventional incentive-based theories of trustworthiness, modeled on incentives produced by social networks, seem less likely to be able to produce generalized trust. One way to interpret the widely held view that social networks exist to create trust through repeated interactions is to conclude that social networks produce the greatest possible "radius of trust" from a small group basis for trust (Fukuyama 1995). But the larger is the group, the more likely that the expectation of repeat play will be zero, and the more likely that the strength of harm-based moral restraint will be zero. Moreover, the more fluid is membership in a social network, and the more uncertain is the nature of transactions involved, the more implausible it is that a social network can provide a basis for trustworthiness in a calculative sense (Coleman 1990; Hardin 1993, 2002). Lee and Persson (2011) have also developed a model that casts considerable doubt on the idea that generalized trust is just an extension of the radius of personalized (small group) trust.

More generally, regarding conventional incentive-based theories of trustworthiness that are based on spontaneously emergent factors inherent in human relationships, the incentive effects at work are particular to the individuals in the relationship. Repeat play effects, for example, attach unwillingness on the part of A to trust B again because of what B, in particular, did to A earlier. Such theories are theories of particularized trustworthiness and, hence, can only explain small group trust.

If the only incentive-based theories of trustworthiness that might produce generalized trust are incapable of producing genuine trust, is there any other way a society might have generalized trust that is also genuine in nature? One possibility is that a high trust society might be a manifestation of generalized reciprocity, which Putnam (2000, p. 134) argues is not just the basis for trust, it is indeed the foundation for all civilized life. According to Putnam, we all do better when we understand that "the touchstone of social capital is the principle of generalized reciprocity—I'll do this for you now, without expecting anything immediately in return and perhaps without even knowing you, confident that down the road you or someone else will return the favor." According to evolutionary psychologists, humans do indeed appear to have a natural disposition to reciprocate (Cosmides and Tooby 1992; Fehr and Gachter 1998; Fehr, Fishbacher, and Simon 2002; Dasgupta 2003; Seabright 2004).

There is little doubt that humans and other animals have hardwired traits that support reciprocal behavior by supporting a willingness to return favors. This, in turn, makes it possible to genuinely trust that others will return favors. But being predisposed to return favors at the micro level does not necessarily imply that generalized reciprocity will exist at the macro level. For one thing, any predilection we have for reciprocity would be based on traits that largely evolved in a small group context, so there is no particular reason why they would work in a large group context.

More fundamentally, because it is meaningless to return a favor to someone other than the one who granted the original favor, the concept of generalized reciprocity appears to contradict the very idea of reciprocity itself. Reciprocity is a matter of A repaying a favor to B because of something B did for A. But it is meaningless for A to repay a favor to B by A doing something *in return* for C. Such a convention defies logic, and why would B do something for A in the first place, if B knows he will likely be "repaid" by A doing something for C? Note that the larger the group involved, the less likely B would be fortunate enough to also be C. Even if people behaved in this way for some inexplicable reason, this would not be reciprocation.

Such behavior would only make sense if there were interpersonal utility effects between B and C—but that is a mutual affection story, not a reciprocity story. Moreover, we have already shown that interpersonal utility effects would not provide moral restraint with respect to golden opportunities in a large group context, and therefore cannot provide a basis for generalized trust in a large group society. In a large group society, many if not most would try to play the role of C—that is, enjoy the benefits of having trustworthy transaction partners without necessarily having to behave in a trustworthy way themselves.

In the real world, this free-rider problem does not exist, because generalized reciprocity is not a sustainable convention. In the real world, A wouldn't bother trying to repay B by repaying C, because there is no need to pay C and because A knows that if he doesn't repay the favor to B, then B will not grant favors to A in the future—even if he does "repay" C. There is no getting around reciprocity being personalized in nature. It is because A has an expectation of repeated interaction with B that it is rational for A to repay a favor to B, and that it is rational for B to extend favors to A in the first place.

A convention of generalized reciprocity would also be exploited by untrustworthy individuals. If A trusts B because A feels inclined to repay the favor of having been extended trust by some other stranger, such as C, then A can be exploited by B if B is untrustworthy. The larger the group, the less likely there will be a cost to B in the form of negative reciprocity. So unless nearly everyone is trustworthy in the first place, the repeated exploitation that results from this arrangement will necessarily end the extension of trust to strangers, even if one is predisposed to doing so out of a desire to reciprocate for trust granted by other strangers earlier. The only way to solve this problem is for nearly everyone to be trustworthy, but in that case there is no value added from the concept of generalized reciprocity. With a norm of trustworthiness, it is already rational to extend trust to most people in most circumstances.

Generalized trust is therefore more likely to be a rational response to the existence of generalized trustworthiness, than to the existence of generalized reciprocity. With a norm of trustworthiness A, B, and C already (rationally) believe that nearly everyone will behave in a trustworthy manner with respect to nearly every transaction. As Dagupta (2003) put it, ". . . you do not need to know each and every fellow citizen to arrive at rational beliefs, at a statistical level, about their intended behavior." Note that believing that one must always be *trustworthy* does not open a door for exploitation such as believing that one must always be *willing to extend trust* does.

The general problem for incentive-based trustworthiness is this: how can A be assured that a *randomly drawn* B will have an incentive to be trustworthy with respect to virtually any transaction A proposes? Any effort to gain such assurance is inconsistent with trust being presumptive in nature, and is therefore inconsistent with generalized trust. For trust to be generalized, trustworthiness must be generalized. And if trustworthiness is generalized, then the question of whether there is sufficient evidence of strong incentives for B to be trustworthy is moot.

To summarize, to maximize general prosperity by minimizing transaction costs, a society needs people to be trustworthy in a way that is impervious to golden opportunities and therefore elicits the extension of genuine trust from others. Genuine trust can be based on interpersonal utility effects in small groups, but to minimize transaction costs, genuine trust must also be generalized rather than merely particularized in nature. Generalized trust, if it is to be sustainable, is necessarily based on it being rational to presume that others—even strangers— are unconditionally trustworthy in all but the most exceptional of circumstances. So as a rule of thumb, we are inclined to extend trust with respect to most transactions because it is indeed rational to do so.

It remains to be shown that moral beliefs that comport with the moral foundation can produce trust behavior that is both genuine and generalized. But first we will review the empirical evidence to show that conventional theories cannot produce trust behavior that is both genuine and generalized. We will then see that moral beliefs that comport with the moral foundation can.

REVIEW OF THE EMPIRICAL EVIDENCE

Empirical work that looks for evidence of the effects of social capital on social, political, and economic performance tends to emphasize generalized trust over particularized trust (Putnam 1995, 2000; Knack and Keefer 1997; La Porta et al. 1997; Uslaner 2002; Tabellini 2008ab, Guiso, Sapienza, Zingales (2008abc, 2009, 2010); Algan and Cahuc 2010). Most employ a specific question from the *World Values Survey*, and this question is clearly aimed at measuring generalized trust.[12] There is, therefore, a disconnect between the empirical literature that examines the relationship between trust and economic performance at the macro level, and the theoretical literature that tries to model trust as an exercise in rational behavior at the micro level. Because existing theoretical models view trusting behavior as an exercise in providing the right incentives, trusting behavior is predicated on the specifics of the transaction partners involved, or the specifics of the transaction relationship. This means that such models are somewhat narrower than they might first appear, because what they explain is particularized rather than generalized trust. As such they are, in fact, models of small group trust.

As a result, the kind of trust considered in conventional incentive-based models is a kind of trust that would easily exist, and likely be even more important, in low trust societies than in high trust societies. Such models therefore have little to do with improving our understanding of the kind of trust that does the best job supporting the development and operation of market economies. These models, in other words, endeavor to explain a kind of trust that has nothing to do with explaining the existence of genuine trust that is also generalized.

There is also evidence that people are too trustworthy to support conventional incentive-based models of trustworthiness. A consistent empirical finding from experimental economics is that many people are trusting, and trustworthy, in one-shot games. These are games in which there is no effort to make either trust or trustworthiness incentive-compatible (Ensminger 2003; Camerer and Thaler 1995; Berg, Dickhaut, and McCabe 1995; Glaeser, Laibson, Scheinkman and Soutter 2000).[13] Indeed, McCabe, Rassenti, and Smith (1996) found that almost 50% of subjects attempt to cooperate even in a one-shot prisoner's dilemma game in which players were told they would be playing with a randomized and anonymous partner only once. The only conclusion that could be afforded by most game theory models of trust in response to this finding would be that about 50% of the population is either irrational or stupid, or that the subjects simply did not believe the experiments (which would contradict their being fully trusting). It seems much more likely that some kind of behavioral rule of thumb was being followed in these experiments, so the question of whether to act in a trustworthy fashion was, for many subjects at least, not really an open one.

More recent evidence from experimental economics also supports the view that trustworthiness may be less strategic than is commonly assumed in game theory models.[14] Cox (2002, 2003) used a triadic experimental design to separate trust and reciprocity from altruism. He found that in the strong social context variation of an investment game experiment, "67% of the amount returned by second movers to first movers can be attributed to other-regarding preferences." (Cox 2003, p. 25) In a recent paper by Carter and Castillo (2003) they devised a set of experiments that allowed the separation of the effects of trust and altruism in a random sample of South African communities. What they found was that while these effects are related, they are nevertheless quite distinct.

In general, we find high levels of trust across many cultures—much higher than would be predicted by Nash equilibrium. Why? One reason might be the ubiquity of small group trust. Economic experiments regarding trust involve a small number of individuals, usually only two players. Even if other players are anonymous, the scenario involved frames thinking in a small group way. The marginal effect of A's actions in such experiments are not diluted, so A knows that what he does will actually affect B's welfare. As a result, A empathizes with B even if B is anonymous, so A knows he will feel guilty about harming B if he acts opportunistically. Trust in this context may therefore only tell us that empathy effects are, in many cases for many people, enough to sustain higher levels of trust than predicted by strategic models. This tells us nothing about the presence, nature, or viability of generalized trust. For example, an experiment in which B interacts anonymously with A, and gives B the opportunity to redistribute ten dollars to himself at A's expense, tells us little about B's willingness to redistribute ten dollars to himself at the expense to 10,000 people of one-tenth of a cent each.

In experiments in which other-regarding preferences can be disentangled from incentive effects, findings suggest that at least some forms of trust come quite naturally to us through our desire to promote the welfare of others. This is hardly surprising. We are a small group species, so it is only logical that we instinctively look out for each other's interests. Could this be the factor that accounts for generalized trust in high trust societies? Not likely. Remember that no matter how strong other-regarding preferences are, the empathy problem will still exist if the sole basis for moral restraint is an unwillingness to harm others.

All incentive-based theories of trust and trustworthiness fail to produce moral restraint with respect to golden opportunities in the context of very large groups such as large firms. Moreover, all of the available empirical evidence points in the same direction: people behave in ways that are not fully consistent with trusting behavior being solely a matter of enlightened self-interest. The willingness to trust and, more important, the predilection to behave in a trustworthy manner, seems to involve something more than a rational response to incentives and, hence, something other than the constraint side of the rational choice model.

Trustworthiness Based on Moral Tastes

Trustworthiness based on incentives is not unconditional, and therefore cannot support the rational extension of genuine trust. I will now briefly expand on arguments presented in Chapter 7 to explain why, for trustworthiness to give rise to the rational extension of trust that is both genuine and generalized in nature, it must be derived from moral tastes.

In Chapter 7 I explained why—to give rise to unconditional trustworthiness and therefore make possible the rational extension of genuine trust to those whom we do not particularly care about—duty-based moral restraint must be a product of moral tastes. Let me reemphasize here that by moral tastes, I do not mean that the decision maker possesses a sufficiently strong desire to be moral (although moral conviction does matter, too). I mean that moral restraint is derived from the internal, preference side, rather than the external, incentive side of the model of rational choice.

But while duty-based moral restraint must not be a product of rational calculation, I will now explain why unconditional trustworthiness is nevertheless consistent with rational behavior *if* it is derived from moral tastes. Finally, I will argue that while genuine trust is not generalized if it is derived from moral tastes in the form of interpersonal utility effects, genuine trust can be generalized if the trustworthiness upon which it is predicated is itself derived from moral tastes instantiated by certain kinds of moral beliefs. So, unlike enlightened self-interest, moral beliefs can ultimately give rise to the rational extension of trust that is both genuine and generalized in nature.

GENUINE TRUST

Echoing Frank (1988), my claim here is that moral restraint derived from a mere exercise in enlightened self-interest is insufficient to produce unconditional trustworthiness. This "prudence problem" results from the fact that we cannot, as a prudent response to externally produced incentives alone, reach the conclusion that it is always in our best interest to be trustworthy, because in the case of golden opportunities it clearly is not. Golden opportunities are believed by the decision maker to carry no chance of detection, and therefore trustworthiness is most meaningful when golden opportunities are likely to arise. The essence of the prudence problem is that the very logic that produces moral restraint also *requires* acting on golden opportunities, for it would be irrational not to do so.

This means the incentive side of the rational choice model is not enough to support unconditional trustworthiness, and therefore won't get the job done in situations in which golden opportunities might arise. It follows that the only possibility for effectuating the moral foundation so as to produce unconditional trustworthiness is the other side of the rational choice model—tastes. Conventional incentive-based theories of trustworthiness are simply incapable of explaining the rational extension of genuine trust.

It should be pointed out that the problem isn't with incentives *per se*, but with moral restraint that is externalized in nature. Moral tastes can be thought of as producing moral restraint through internalized incentives in the form of guilt costs. As such, duty-based moral restraint derived from moral tastes is perfectly consistent with rational behavior at the micro level, because it would be irrational to act on a golden opportunity if one has moral tastes that give rise to powerful and involuntary emotions of guilt that are costly to experience. The key idea is that moral tastes are not chosen at the time of the decision to act opportunistically. At the time of decision, they are exogenous and are therefore not a matter of rationality.[15]

Duty-based moral restraint derived from moral tastes is therefore neither rational nor irrational; it is functionally *pre-rational*, because moral tastes are antecedent to rational decision making. This is important, because it is not rational to expect consistent trustworthiness from B if B's trustworthiness is itself irrational. Moral tastes provide a credible commitment to behave in a trustworthy manner to those who extend trust, even in situations in which golden opportunities are likely to arise, because the emotions of guilt that would result from being untrustworthy are no more voluntary than the feelings of pleasure that come from eating chocolate. Unconditional trustworthiness derived from duty-based moral restraint derived from moral tastes is, therefore, perfectly consistent with rationality.

Let me stress that I am not merely arguing that moral restraint *may* come through moral tastes. I am arguing that it *has to*, because the other alternative— prudential restraint derived from externally produced incentives—is incapable of dealing with golden opportunities and is therefore incapable of supporting the rational extension of genuine trust. With duty-based moral restraint being derived from moral tastes, the relevant cost is not triggered by externally produced consequences that arise from detection. The relevant cost is triggered by internal consequences that result from the act itself, in the form of feelings of guilt that are involuntarily experienced even if the act is undetected.

In his *Passions Within Reason*, Robert Frank (1988) made essentially this very same point over twenty years ago. In his words:

> The honest individual . . . values trustworthiness for its own sake. That he might receive a material payoff for such behavior is completely beyond his concern. And it is precisely because he has this attitude that he can be trusted in situations where his behavior cannot be monitored . . . even if the world were to end at midnight . . . the genuinely trustworthy person would not be motivated to cheat. (Frank, 1988, 68–69)

Russell Hardin, who has insisted that the extension of trust must be based on the rational expectation of trustworthiness, and who introduced the powerful idea of encapsulated interest as a basis for trust behavior, also acknowledges that trust-worthiness itself might also be normatively based. That is, *A* trusts *B* because *A* believes that *B* believes that behaving in an untrustworthy manner is immoral. In this case, *A* need not be motivated by his own morality to base his willingness to trust *B* on *B*'s morality. Ostrom and Walker (2003, p. 8) appear to concur with Hardin's recognition of this point, stating that: "Hardin argues that to account for trust, one must first account for trustworthiness. Trustworthiness can be seen as primarily based either on incentives or on normative attributes of the decision maker . . . Trustworthiness is normatively based if the trustee feels morally obli-gated to fulfill the trust." Yet virtually no progress has been made to develop a plausible theory regarding what form such moral tastes must take, and/or what kinds of moral beliefs might instantiate them.

To summarize, people who possess moral tastes instantiated by moral beliefs that comport with the moral foundation can be genuinely trusted. This is because moral tastes do not require the possibility of detection to produce a cost in the form of feelings of guilt for behaving opportunistically. Instead, in such cases the person involved can be rationally expected to feel guilty even if the trusting party knows that the trusted party knows he cannot be caught. This produces credible moral restraint even if golden opportunities are likely to arise. Such individuals can be trusted never to engage in first, second, or third-degree opportunism in all but the most exceptional of circumstances (and some people even then!).

GENERALIZED TRUST

As noted above, trustworthiness derived from interpersonal utility effects can be effective even for golden opportunities, and can therefore support genuine trust. But in Chapter 6 we found that interpersonal utility effects weaken with group size, and not just because we don't care enough about our fellow man. Interper-sonal utility effects become irrelevant because the harm to any individual becomes imperceptible. So unconditional trustworthiness derived from interpersonal utility effects cannot provide a basis for genuine trust in large group contexts. We will have to look elsewhere for a theory of unconditional trustworthiness if we are to support genuine trust in large groups.

Incentive-based trustworthiness is the first logical place to look for a possible basis for generalized trust. It might conceivably be applicable to large groups, because the mechanisms involved have no particular reason to weaken with larger group size. If people don't steal because they are closely monitored, for example, then the solution to the problem in large groups is simply to hire more monitors. If anything, there might be economies of scale to be enjoyed.

The problem is that even if incentives could produce trustworthy behavior in large group contexts, such trustworthiness would not be unconditional trustwor-thiness because it is derived from incentives that are produced by external mech-anisms. For incentives to work, sanctions must be triggered by something, which is by definition irrelevant for golden opportunities. So we are right back where we started: incentive-based trustworthiness cannot be a basis for the rational extension of genuine trust.

So, with theories of trustworthiness based on interpersonal utility effects, we can potentially enjoy genuine trust. But it is limited to small groups and therefore cannot support generalized trust. With incentive-based theories of trustworthiness, we can potentially enjoy generalized trust, but it is not genuine. *Is there any basis for trust that is consistent with rationality, and is both genuine and generalized in nature?* My claim is that moral beliefs that comport with the moral foundation can provide such a basis.

I have already explained how an ethic of duty-based moral restraint can produce unconditional trustworthiness, and therefore the rational extension of genuine trust, even in the absence of interpersonal utility effects. My claim is that duty-based moral restraint, instantiated by moral beliefs, also constitutes a plausible story for how a condition of generalized trust might arise. To be specific, all that is required is that moral beliefs that instantiate an ethic of duty-based moral restraint in individuals be held by a sufficiently high proportion of individuals in the population as to make the presumption of unconditional trustworthiness rational.

In this case, the trustworthiness involved is unconditional, so the trust it engenders is genuine and generalized. This is because principled moral restraint attaches feelings of guilt to negative moral acts themselves. Such feelings of guilt have no reason to weaken with group size or social distance, because the issue is not the harm done to others or how much we care about them. So, in addition to producing unconditional trustworthiness that is rational at the micro level, duty-based moral restraint can produce a norm of unconditional trustworthiness (and therefore a norm of extending trust) at the macro level, too. This is no small difference, for when a society is a high trust society, institutions that are themselves dependent on trust are viable, which leads to even lower transaction costs generally.

The key point is that duty-based moral restraint works through internalized incentives, via feelings of guilt that are tied to negative moral actions themselves, rather than to their effects. So an individual who possesses an ethic of duty-based moral restraint does not embezzle small amounts of money from his employer, but this is not because of the harm it might cause. He does not embezzle because doing so would make him feel guilty about being an embezzler. Although it is true that if a significant harm were caused, too, he might feel even guiltier, it is nevertheless the case that if he feels sufficiently guilty about the act of embezzlement itself, then no harm need result in order for him to refrain from embezzling. Generalized trust can therefore arise in any society if a sufficiently high proportion of its individuals possess moral beliefs that comport with an ethic of duty-based moral restraint so it is irrational to presume that others are not trustworthy.[16]

Finally, moral beliefs that *require* that people extend trust, unless there is specific evidence of untrustworthiness, were shown to be unsustainable (Uslaner 2002).

Duty-based moral restraint, however, permits individuals to refuse to extend trust. Since always being trustworthy—even with respect to someone who might not deserve such decent treatment—does not open one up to predation, it is not unsustainable in the way that a duty to extend trust is.

The Transaction Cost Economics (TCE) Critique

Although TCE scholars are acutely aware of the ubiquitous problem of opportunism, many are skeptical about the importance of genuine trust because they view institutions as sufficient to deal with it in most economic contexts.[17] The world's most prominent TCE scholar, Oliver Williamson, has even argued that the concept of trust is at best superfluous. In his own words:

> . . . . it is redundant at best and can be misleading to use the term 'trust' to describe commercial exchange for which cost-effective safeguards have been devised in support of more efficient exchange. Calculative trust is a contradiction in terms. [Williamson 1993, p. 463]

> I maintain that trust is irrelevant to commercial exchange and that reference to trust in this connection promotes confusion. [Oliver Williamson, 1993, p. 469][18]

This position is plausible with respect to many commercial transactions, because the closer a transaction is to a spot market exchange (suggested by the adjective *commercial*), the less opportunity there is for opportunism. Complex transactions such as those in large, modern firms obviously create many more opportunities for opportunism, but TCE scholars argue that such circumstances simply induce the creation of more advanced institutional mechanisms to combat it.

Although it is true that institutions solve many of the same problems that trust solves (e.g., see Yamagishi, Cook, Watabe 1998), this does not demonstrate that the ability to genuinely trust others is superfluous.[19] Just because something is not necessary does not mean it does not produce better outcomes. Could one not argue that guns are superfluous because spears have already demonstrated an ability to kill an enemy? Similarly, institutions can get the job done, and indeed did a good job getting the job done through most of human history, but that does not preclude the possibility that for many kinds of transactions, genuine trust made possible by unconditional trustworthiness does the job even better.

In Chapters 2–4, I explained why transactions within firms present a problem of local knowledge that is every bit as fundamental as the local knowledge problem Hayek argued exists across the whole of society. Recall that Hayek argued that market pricing creates value for societies by addressing this local knowledge problem. But as Coase (1937) pointed out, within firms, market pricing is not what directs resources. Wherever the localization of knowledge is a problem that market pricing cannot solve, relational contracts are often what fills the gap. The problem is that relational contracts can only do this to their fullest extent if those who possess local knowledge can be trusted not to engage in third-degree opportunism. Genuine trust is required for the fullest use of local knowledge within firms, because the golden opportunities that inevitably arise from the use of relational contracts are often beyond the reach of hardwired moral intuitions, strategic factors inherent in human relationships, and institutional mechanisms—because all of these approaches require an observable predicate event.

Recall that in Chapter 3, I also argued that external mechanisms can only address the problem of third-degree opportunism by eliminating golden opportunities through strict routines and procedures. But that necessarily means that local knowledge will be thrown away. This is analogous to the problem of throwing away local knowledge across the whole of society by replacing market pricing with central planning. Since the local knowledge problem intensifies with specialization, and specialization rises with production scale, it follows that the existence of unconditional trustworthiness that makes possible the full use of relational contracts averts the tradeoff between production scale and the efficient use of information throughout a firm's hierarchy.

Economists have paid little attention to the problem of local knowledge within firms. They therefore do not fully recognize the importance of relational contracts, or the directly related problem of their vulnerability to third-degree opportunism. In so doing, they dismiss the importance of firm owners being able to genuinely trust those who possess local knowledge with sufficient discretion to act on it.

Most economists presume that trustworthiness cannot be taken as a modeling prior, so for this reason much of the literature on relational contracts focuses on the need for them to self-enforcing through repeat play effects. Indeed, a classic paper on the subject by Baker, Gibbons, and Murphy (2002) argues that an important aspect of relational contracts is that they *cannot be dependent on third-party enforcement*, so such contracts *must be* self-enforcing. The unstated corollary is that such contracts can therefore only be fully employed with respect to decision makers who are of very low social distance from principals, but in that case we are back to trading away size for efficiency.

The problem is that the conventional approach to the study of relational contracts ignores the problem of third-degree opportunism that inevitably arises in the context of relational contracts. When such opportunities are "golden" this problem is by definition beyond the reach of externally produced incentives, including those that arise from repeat play effects. The conventional approach, therefore, seriously underestimates the importance of genuine trust that makes it possible to use relational contracts to their fullest extent. This is a serious omission, for nothing less than the *sine qua non* of a prosperous market economy—large yet *thoroughly* entrepreneurial firms—is critically dependent on the ability to fully employ relational contracts. I will have more to say about this issue in the next and last chapters.

Conclusion

Theories of trust based on an imperative to extend trust are unsustainable, so a plausible theory of *genuine* trust ultimately requires a plausible theory of unconditional trustworthiness. Interpersonal utility effects can produce genuine trustworthiness, and therefore the rational extension of genuine trust. But because of the empathy problem, this provides an insufficient basis for generalized trust. Incentive-based trustworthiness might explain generalized trust, because it is conceivable that an external mechanism could give rise to assurance in a large group setting. But because of their external nature, such incentives cannot deal with golden opportunities, so the trustworthiness involved is not unconditional and therefore the trust engendered is not genuine.

So theories based on incentives can potentially give us generalized trust, but not genuine trust, while theories based on interpersonal utility effects can potentially give us genuine trust, but not generalized trust. Not surprisingly, then, the existing literature has not been able to produce a theory of trust behavior that comports with the existence of a high trust society, because no existing approach is capable of producing trust that is both genuine and generalized. To enjoy having a high trust society, such trust must be rational, genuine and, ideally, also generalized. But this is only possible if extending trust is a rational response to a perceived norm of unconditional trustworthiness, such as would be made possible by moral beliefs that comport with the moral foundation.

But a theory that avoids the shortcomings of existing theories is not necessarily a correct theory. For this reason, theories must be subjected to empirical scrutiny. I have shown in this chapter that not only does a high trust society, based on shared moral beliefs that comport with the moral foundation, solve key theoretical problems with existing models—it also largely comports with existing empirical evidence, while existing theories of trust largely don't. In the concluding chapter, I will outline a number of sharp implications of the moral foundation for future empirical work regarding trust.

Robert Frank was right—a necessary condition for the existence of genuine trust is that the expected moral restraint upon which it is based must ultimately be derived from moral tastes. Moral restraint cannot involve rational calculation at the time a golden opportunity presents itself; it must be a manifestation of tastes that we already possess. Here I have extended Frank by addressing the question of what characteristics such moral tastes must have so as to *maximize* general prosperity. We must now turn to the question of how people come to have such tastes.

CHAPTER 10

Culture

If we learn anything from the history of economic development, it is that culture makes almost all the difference.—David Landes, 2000, p. 2

Introduction

In Chapter 9 I compared trust derived from moral beliefs that comport with the moral foundation to other theories of trust behavior. I explained why, with the exception of Robert Frank's commitment model, existing theories of trust simply do not address the problem of golden opportunities. Most scholars appear to be unaware of this problem, especially as it relates to third-degree opportunism in large groups such as large firms.

Frank's model can explain trust behavior even between individuals who do not particularly care about each other, which is a necessary condition for the existence of trust in the context of large groups and impersonal exchange. Most importantly, Frank's model demonstrates why genuine trust can only *rationally* exist if trustworthiness is derived from moral tastes. But while Frank correctly identified this necessary condition for genuine trust, such trust is not by nature generalized. In his model, trustworthiness is not presumed (indeed, he provides a very compelling explanation for why it can't be) so people must search for trustworthy partners. It is precisely for this reason that involuntary emotional displays are such an important part of trust behavior in his model.

For genuine trust to also be generalized, it must also be the case that a preponderance of individuals in society possess moral beliefs that comport with the moral foundation. So where do the required moral tastes come from, and how might they come to be adopted by the preponderance of individuals in a given society? I will now argue that the most plausible mechanism through which the moral foundation comes to be held by a sufficiently high proportion of the population to make it rational to presume that others are trustworthy is culture in the form of moral beliefs that are passed from generation to generation. As a result, a society's ability to enjoy the benefits of being a high trust society is strongly linked to its culture.[1] Significantly, reaching this conclusion does not involve endorsing any specific culture or any specific moral belief.

My argument begins by positing that the required moral tastes are either inherited directly through genes, derived from moral beliefs discovered through our own introspective moral theorizing, or acquired from others through moral beliefs that we learn from them. I will argue that the required moral tastes are not plausibly genetically inherited or introspectively discovered with sufficient consistency and concentration across the whole of society. This is because there are evolutionary dynamics at work that insure that too many people will be untrustworthy for a truly high trust society to emerge in these ways.

I will then argue that the most plausible mechanism by which a preponderance of individuals come to hold moral beliefs that comport with the moral foundation is that they are taught them as children by adults who hold such beliefs themselves. The younger children are when they are taught such beliefs, the more likely those beliefs will function as tastes that are antecedent to rational decision making. Moreover, the younger children are when they are taught such beliefs, the more likely they will produce a sufficiently consistent pattern of behavior to constitute a social norm.[2]

Genetically Inherited Moral Tastes

One explanation for where moral tastes might come from that comports with the moral foundation is that we genetically inherit them. This idea is attractive because it provides a very general explanation for moral behavior. It is also comforting to think that our morality is a fundamental part of our human nature.

Of more direct relevance here is that it can potentially provide a basis for explaining unconditional trustworthiness consistent with rationality, because moral tastes, in this view, are antecedent to rational decision making. Those who possess the relevant hardwired characteristics in sufficient measure are moral not so much by choice as by having a biological predisposition, which circumvents the prudence problem. As such, they are credibly and unconditionally trustworthy and therefore can be rationally extended genuine trust.

There has been an avalanche of scholarly work that explores the connection between moral behavior and evolutionarily grounded traits in the fields of evolutionary biology, evolutionary psychology, neuroscience, cognitive science, the emerging field of neuroeconomics, and even philosophy.[3] Many of the arguments advanced in these literatures are quite compelling.

Hardwiring determines the ability to create new neural pathways, and determines the limits of what ideas can do, so the study of such mechanisms is clearly an important part of the puzzle. The question here is not, therefore, whether there are important hardwired factors involved with moral thinking. Of course there are. Of relevance here is the precise nature of the role that inherited factors play in logically organizing moral tastes in the mind of any given individual and, to the extent that such tastes are shared, in establishing a social value system and social norms.

UNCONDITIONAL TRUSTWORTHINESS AT THE MICRO LEVEL

There is little doubt that at least *some* of the moral tastes we possess are inherited. These tastes likely go a long way toward explaining the existence of genuine trust in small groups across all societies throughout all of human history. But shortly I will argue that they are nevertheless inadequate for explaining genuine trust in the context of large groups. This is a point best appreciated by first understanding how hardwired factors can, and likely do, support genuine trust in small groups.

A hardwired predilection for reciprocity could provide a channel through which genes support trustworthy behavior. Vernon Smith has argued that a predilection for reciprocity explains much of the cooperative behavior that we observe in human societies. Ernst Fehr and others have developed models and conducted empirical research that shows the power of reciprocity to explain cooperative behavior. I have argued in Chapter 9, however, that reciprocity is by nature a matter of personal exchange, and therefore a matter of particularized, rather than generalized trust. Reciprocity is therefore unable to explain the emergence of generalized trust of any sort, let alone generalized trust that is also genuine in nature.

Another mechanism that might provide a channel through which genes produce trustworthiness is involuntary emotions. Jack Hirshleifer argued that our hardwired capacity for experiencing emotions evolved to serve as a commitment device. If others know that our emotions may compel us to retaliate when exploited, then they will be less likely to attempt to exploit us in the first place, because the threat of retaliation is credible even if it would appear to be irrational to retaliate. Emotions differ from tastes precisely because their involuntary nature overrides rational decision making. *Involuntary emotional responses* to opportunistic victimization raises the expected cost borne by opportunists who are considering taking advantage of us by exploiting our own rationality to their advantage, so our emotions solve what Thomas Schelling (1960) famously called the "pre-commitment problem."

Robert Frank argued that emotions act as a commitment device because we have no control over *involuntary emotional displays* that result from feeling guilty about lying, cheating, stealing, etc. It follows that if we possess sufficiently strong involuntary emotional responses (e.g., blushing when lying), others will be assured that if we were to behave opportunistically, we would inevitably reveal ourselves. Such individuals benefit from having a reputation for being unable to deceive, because they are sought by others as transaction partners. Involuntary emotional displays provide the basis for a theory of trust in which the key challenge is to identify people who possess the requisite emotional make-up. This varies across individuals, so it is effectively a micro-level story of rational trust. Frank therefore envisioned trust behavior as a search model in which people search for those individuals who have the highest likelihood of being trustworthy because they appear to have the strongest predilection for involuntary emotional displays.

These approaches comport with observed behavior in everyday life. All societies appear to be able to sustain genuine trust in the context of personal exchange and small groups. It is quite plausible that we have inherited many of the mechanisms required to produce a capability to sustain genuine trust, *even in the absence of strong interpersonal utility effects*. But this is based on trustworthiness that must be determined on a person-by-person basis. So even though the commitment model does not require interpersonal utility effects to support genuine trust, it still does not provide the basis for generalized trust.

UNCONDITIONAL TRUSTWORTHINESS
AT THE MACRO LEVEL

Having moral restraint grounded in tastes is a necessary condition for having trustworthiness that stands up to the temptation of golden opportunities, but it is not a sufficient condition for regarding a person as being unconditionally trustworthy. In Chapter 7 we learned that other conditions need to be met in order to conclude that an individual is unconditionally trustworthy. Among these are that his reluctance to behave opportunistically is not conditioned on external incentives (it involves moral and not merely prudential restraint), is not conditioned on group size (is not subject to the empathy problem), and is not affected by competing moral objectives (not subject to the greater good rationalization problem). Taken together, these conditions produce an ethic of duty-based moral restraint. In Chapter 8 we learned that another necessary condition for concluding that an individual is unconditionally trustworthy is that duty-based moral restraint is not eroded by duty-based moral advocacy.

There are at least three reasons why it is unlikely that the psychological mechanisms that evolved to support genuine trust in small group contexts are capable of supporting moral beliefs that comport with the moral foundation. The first is that duty-based moral restraint does not arise directly from the same psychological mechanisms from which our hardwired moral intuitions arise. Duty-based moral restraint is based on the abstract ideas of principled moral restraint and the lexical primacy of moral prohibitions. Although we inherit the ability to think abstractly, we do not inherit abstract ideas themselves. Indeed, one reason for the success of humans is that our ability to think abstractly allows us to manipulate ideas that are not hardwired, which makes behavior extraordinarily flexible.

Another reason to doubt that we biologically inherit an ethic of duty-based moral restraint is that duty-based moral restraint does not derive its value from supporting trust behavior in small group contexts. The problem is that the traits we have inherited largely evolved in a small group context. Benefits that arise at the macro level, therefore, have no reason to be accounted for in our genes, because there was no reason for natural selection to take account of them. As we know, our ancestors lived in very small groups.

Finally, as I alluded earlier, Frank's theory explains the existence of genuine trust, while at the same time explaining why there will always be many untrustworthy people (I shall elaborate the details of this argument later in this chapter). This implies that Frank's theory is quite self-consciously not a theory of generalized trust, and demonstrates why it is very unlikely that trustworthiness, derived *solely* from hardwired traits that effectuate the required involuntary emotional responses, will be able to produce generalized trust.

EXPLAINING DIFFERENCES IN MEASURED LEVELS OF TRUST ACROSS SOCIETIES

The general problem with theories of trust that view our trust behavior as largely hardwired is that they cannot explain differences in measured trust across societies. In my view, there is actually very little variation in small group trust across societies, but there is great variation in large group trust. Confusing matters even more is that in societies where large group trust does not exist, small group trust will, to compensate, be especially intense and even more visible, as people try to expand their range of transactions by bringing as many people as possible into their circle of trust. This they do by trying to convince us that interpersonal utility effects exist between them and us.

This comports with my claim above, which is that while it is plausible that small group and personalized trust is based rather directly on inherited factors, it is not plausible that large group trust is, or even can be. If we are all hardwired to be trustworthy irrespective of group size context, then people in all societies should always be trustworthy. And it would, in turn, be rational for everyone to presumptively extend trust, producing a condition of generalized trust. But they don't. So unless one argues that there are significant differences in genetic makeup as it relates to moral and emotional predilections, inherited moral tastes cannot explain differences in average levels of trust across societies. Something else must also be at work. My claim is that the something else is moral beliefs that are learned, and that ultimately govern how people *think about* morality.

Although Frank's theory can explain variations in trustworthiness *within* most populations, it does not explain variations in average trust across populations, because there are societies in which nearly everyone is trustworthy with respect to a wide range of transactions. Empirical studies of trust, such as those based on the *World Values Survey,* and casual observation make it clear that high trust societies do, in fact, exist.[4] In my view, this does not mean that Frank's commitment model is wrong; it simply means that the commitment model is a model of the most common form of trust behavior in the world, but most of the world is only able to sustain small group trust.

Although genetic variation is very low in humans, it is sufficiently different to produce substantial differences in objectively measurable characteristics (average height, hair texture, face shape, skin color, etc.). It follows that it is possible that there are also differences across groups in the functioning of psychological mechanisms that mediate moral behavior (e.g., strength of empathizing, strength of guilt response, etc.), as well as intuitive moral values. This is an intriguing possibility, but I seriously doubt that it is of much importance. Countries like the United States have demonstrated that when humans of very different genetic and ethnic backgrounds are exposed to a particular set of moral and ideological beliefs, many readily adopt those beliefs, change their behavior to comport with them, and begin conveying them to their children. In doing so, each subsequent generation becomes more American. This would not happen if differences in genes across societies is what explains most of the difference in trust behavior across societies. There is as yet no compelling evidence to suggest that the differences in trust behavior we observe across groups is a result of genetic differences across those groups. Quite the contrary, anecdotal evidence suggests the opposite, as is exemplified in America's melting pot.

Introspectively Discovered Moral Beliefs

If we do not genetically inherit moral tastes that support trust that is both genuine and generalized in nature because we cannot genetically inherit the moral beliefs that would be required to instantiate them, then perhaps the required moral tastes are instantiated by moral beliefs that many of us inevitably discover through our own introspection.

The possibility that the moral foundation is something most people discover for themselves is plausible, if we believe that it is a kind of self-evident truth to most people. What I mean by this is that even though the required ideas involved are abstract and therefore cannot be directly inherited, they are conclusions that are, for most people, inevitably reached by application of our hardwired moral intuitions. For example, virtually all humans conclude that tormenting babies for fun or murdering for sport is wrong, because such ideas are rather direct implications of hardwired moral intuitions (our hardwired sense of harm-based moral restraint would produce a great deal of guilt). This kind of argument is sometimes made by proponents of natural law theory. This phenomenon would, of course, most plausibly occur with respect to ideas that comport most closely with our hardwired moral intuitions. So the plausibility of people discovering for themselves an ethic of duty-based moral restraint, while rejecting an ethic of duty-based moral advocacy, is directly related to how close each is to the hardwired moral intuitions we all share because of our common evolutionary history.

But the three central ideas of the moral foundation—principled moral restraint, lexical primacy of moral prohibitions, and rejection of duty-based moral advocacy—are abstract ideas that cannot be inherited genetically and, moreover, largely conflict with the moral intuitions we *do* genetically inherit. For example, our hardwired moral intuitions can lead us to embrace greater good rationalizations for doing harm. But this directly contradicts abiding by the moral foundation.

In most cases, the creation of these abstract ideas cannot be fully traced to any particular person. More likely they evolved from generation to generation, with changes occasionally producing net benefits for individuals and/or the group as a whole, and thereby providing the foundation for subsequent evolution. Each new round of changes makes it possible to cooperate effectively in even larger groups than before, or makes it possible to more effectively cooperate in the same sized groups as before. Each round of changes produces mostly losers, but occasionally a round occurs where a change to existing ideas produces even greater net benefits, and so on.[5]

Of course, some people argue that their moral beliefs are of their own invention. This is certainly true in some cases, but in my view, most people who make such claims are likely to have been heavily influenced by what they learned from their environment without realizing it. We are all familiar with the idiom that there is nothing new under the sun, because every bit of music, writing, art, and so forth, possesses elements of what the creator acquired from his environment even if he does not remember when, where, or how it was acquired. I submit that the most plausible explanation for why people possess moral beliefs that comport with the moral foundation is that these ideas already existed, and they were then exposed to them.

In my view it is very unlikely that people who are genetically hardwired to have moral intuitions that are small group in nature will somehow introspectively discover a large group ethic that is so contrary to their own basic human nature, as well as to their own welfare. Rare is the moral philosopher who has done so. But it is impossible to rule out this possibility for all individuals. What would trust behavior look like in such a case? Recall that the moral foundation does not require that we extend trust; it only requires that we always behave in a trustworthy manner. Trust behavior that would be supported by such individuals would, therefore, require them to search for others with similar beliefs. Although it is conceivable that some individuals with similar beliefs can be found, it is quite another thing indeed to believe that enough people in society would discover such beliefs on their own as are needed to produce generalized trust. In the next section, I will discuss evolutionary dynamics that are inimical to this possibility. As such, trust behavior that might result from introspectively discovered moral beliefs can at best give rise to genuine trust at the micro level, and as such is personalized rather than generalized in nature.

Finally, the proposition that we might intuit the moral foundation for ourselves, and therefore be able to sustain trust at the macro level, doesn't fit the facts. The incentives involved are very general. The hardwired moral intuitions from which such reasoning would be derived are also general. If we assume people are, on average, equally able to appreciate the advantages of adopting the moral foundation and also equally inclined and able to do so, then—as is the case with natural law—there should be little variation in moral beliefs and little variation in average levels of trust across societies. But in reality there is a great deal of variation in both.

Acquired Moral Beliefs

If moral tastes that comport with the moral foundation are not genetically inherited, and are not self-evident truths that most people introspectively discover on their own, then they must be acquired from other people. But being exposed to the required moral beliefs is not enough to effectuate duty-based moral restraint. Individuals must also choose to abide by them. Why would someone make such a choice?

The most obvious reason why is that one sincerely believes the moral belief involved. The other possibility is that the required moral tastes are adopted because the individual foresees that such moral tastes will serve his long-run material interests. This is the implicit position of mainstream economists and many other social scientists. I will employ what should by now be a familiar argument to show that genuine trust is impossible if the required moral tastes are adopted merely as an act of enlightened self-interest; that is, merely as a matter of prudence.

ADOPTING THE REQUIRED MORAL TASTES FOR PRUDENTIAL REASONS

If Bob chooses to adopt specific moral tastes only because he expects higher payoffs in the future from doing so, then it would be irrational for him not to act on all golden opportunities. This is an inescapable conclusion, unless we believe that Bob will somehow forget his original reason for adopting such moral tastes in the first place. If the reason for adopting such moral tastes was to produce an implicit behavioral rule that leads to a higher payoff in the future, then that very logic will also compel Bob to conclude that a golden opportunity that harms no one is an obvious exception to *that* rule. Of course the greater the potential gain, the stronger would be Bob's incentive to reach this perfectly valid conclusion. Bob would, therefore, prove untrustworthy in precisely the circumstances in which trustworthiness matters most.

There is no escaping the fact that *why* one holds the required moral tastes matters as much as having the *right kind* of moral tastes. Although it is perfectly rational to choose, solely as an act of enlightened self-interest, to adopt moral tastes in period *t* to produce *what looks like* moral restraint in period *t+1*, such restraint is properly viewed as prudential restraint that functions like a behavioral rule of thumb, such as never eating between meals. How we come to have the required moral tastes also matters.

One could argue that a person might invest in moral tastes in the present to produce restraint in the future, for no other reason other than enlightened self-interest, but that over time, such a person might come to have his personality changed by the new pattern of behavior he has adopted. Consider the famous tipping example from Robert Frank (1988, p. 18–19):

> The decision to tip in the distant city is in part a decision about the kinds of character traits one wishes to cultivate. For while modern biologists have established that the capacity to develop various character traits is inherited, no one has successfully challenged the nineteenth-century view that indoctrination and practice are required for them to emerge. The direction of causality between character and behavior thus runs both ways. Character influences behavior, of course. But behavior also influences character. Despite our obvious capacities for self-deception and rationalization, few people can maintain a predisposition to behave honestly while at the same time frequently engaging in transparently opportunistic behavior.

In my view, this is a better story of how we strengthen moral conviction with regard to moral tastes that we already have (e.g., putting us in touch with our hardwired capacities for empathy, sympathy, and guilt) than it is a story of the decision to adopt a particular moral belief in the first place. This is an important distinction, because we have already seen that the underlying moral beliefs end up making all the difference.

Even a purely amoral rationalist, who gets used to not even considering acting on small opportunities as they come along, does not, because of this behavior, come to invent a new moral theory that produces utterly moral restraint. So while the purely amoral rationalist may not be so cynical as to be merely biding his time until a golden opportunity comes along, he will nevertheless discover instant logical clarity when a particularly tempting golden opportunity presents itself, since he will have a very powerful incentive to achieve such clarity. And this will be truer the larger the group over which the costs of opportunism are spread, regardless of how earnest he is about being reluctant to harm others—because the larger the group, the less likely he will actually harm anyone.

ADOPTING THE REQUIRED MORAL BELIEFS FOR MORAL REASONS

Consider now the possibility that a person is exposed to a moral belief and sincerely chooses to adopt it because he actually believes it. If that moral belief holds that undertaking negative moral actions is wrong, even if no one is harmed (principled moral restraint), and that negative moral actions cannot be justified by positive moral actions (lexical primacy of obedience of moral prohibitions), then in future periods the individual will experience involuntary emotions of guilt if he undertakes negative moral actions even if undetected.

So if an individual sincerely chooses to hold moral beliefs that comport with the moral foundation, this can plausibly produce unconditional trustworthiness and, hence, plausibly engender the extension of genuine trust to him. Moreover, if the beliefs are held with great conviction, then moral tastes will be very strong and will produce very strong emotions of guilt. If others know that this individual holds the required moral beliefs with strong moral conviction, then they know he will be unconditionally trustworthy with respect to all but the most exceptional of transactions.[6]

People can be exposed to new moral beliefs as adults and then choose to adopt those beliefs. Such a decision can be both rational and sincere, if such persons are genuinely persuaded of the validity of the moral belief. This accurately describes many religious conversions.[7] Now we turn to the possibility that people acquire their moral beliefs as children. We will see that the transmission of moral beliefs from adults to children is more likely to support a social norm of unconditional trustworthiness and, hence, more likely to support a high trust society.

The Case for Culture

The discussion above led to the conclusion that the required moral beliefs are not plausibly genetically inherited and are, for most people, unlikely to be introspectively discovered. Instead, if a person is to hold moral beliefs that comport with the moral foundation, such beliefs will most likely have to be learned from others. I shall now argue that culture is the most plausible mechanism through which moral beliefs that comport with the moral foundation come to be held by a preponderance of members of society.

Culture is the name for that which we inherit from prior generations, not through our genes but through learning.[8] It works, in part, through tastes we acquire when young and, for the most part, are stuck with as adults. Most people are largely oblivious to the fact that they do not completely control what they believe, because what they believe has much to do with what they were taught at a very young age, which then frames all subsequent learning. As such, culture provides a mechanism through which abstract ideas can be instantiated as tastes before the time of decision making. I will now argue that unlike the mechanisms already discussed, culture can produce a social norm of unconditional trustworthiness and, in so doing, can explain the existence of high trust societies.

If we think of moral behavior completely in terms of a one-period static model, then the decision to adopt moral beliefs that comport with the moral foundation is made by the same person who must abide by it. If such moral beliefs are sincerely chosen, then this presents no problem for those who depend on that individual's trustworthiness. But if such an ethic is chosen purely as a matter of prudence, because of higher expected payoffs, then restraint will disappear when the individual is confronted with golden opportunities.

But what if we consider something closer to reality, such as a two-period model in which parents and other adults of period t decide which moral beliefs to inculcate into the children of period t. In period $t + 1$, the children of period t will then be adults themselves, with a new generation of children of their own. In this case, the decision to inculcate moral beliefs is not generally made by the same person who will abide by them as an adult. Suppose C teaches B a specific moral belief at time t. If B sincerely adopts the belief at time t, then at time $t + 1$, from A's point of view, B's moral disposition is not something he chose for himself but is instead a taste that is antecedent to rational decision making. As such, it influences decision making at a pre-rational stage of the process.

Moral restraint derived from moral tastes acquired in this way is therefore not subject to the prudence problem and is, equivalently, in no way time inconsistent. Consequently, in period t there is no particular reason why adults cannot cultivate moral tastes in children that are expected to unleash, in period $t + 1$, involuntary emotions that support an ethic of unconditional trustworthiness when the children of period t become adults. In this way, any given generation of adults shapes the "givens" of rational choice for the next generation. This approach to culture comports with Landes (2000), Francois and Zabojnik (2005), Guiso, Sapienza, and Zingales (2006, 2008ab), and Bisin and Verdier (2011). This approach is also perfectly consistent with a familiar hallmark of culture, which is that adults attempt to inculcate beliefs as early in childhood as possible, because they understand that the younger a child is when first exposed to a belief, the truer it is that his adoption of that belief is more accurately viewed as being *absorbed* than *chosen*. This is especially true if the moral belief in question is the only one the child is exposed to, and is the only one that every other adult in that child's world appears to hold.[9]

By separating the decision to adopt a moral belief from the consequences of holding it, culture has a unique ability to solve the prudence problem. This is important because no one would rationally choose to hold moral beliefs that foreclose being able to act on golden opportunities unless some kind of moral belief compelled them to do so. Moral beliefs learned as young children, however, are generally taken by them as given in adulthood, even if the specific religious narrative that conveyed them has long since been abandoned. Rejecting the narrative is not the same thing as rejecting the moral values or the manner of thinking that results from how the narrative organized the logical relationship between such moral values.

The truer it is that we don't really choose to hold the moral beliefs that we hold, the more likely they will function like tastes. A person from a given country might love a dish that is a staple from his country although few people outside the country like it—it is a taste, but the individual did not genetically inherit it and did not really choose it, either. The truer it is that moral beliefs function as tastes, and are not merely philosophical ideas, the more likely it is that they will exert their influence on moral thinking at a *pre-rational* stage of analysis, because in the model of rational choice, tastes are antecedent to rational decision making.

We have ample anecdotal evidence that learned moral beliefs can produce tremendously strong tastes, because they clearly produce tremendously strong emotions. Suicide bombers to advance jihad, crusaders who risked death to "liberate" the holy land, people who chose to be burned at the stake rather than recant their faith, etc., are all people who clearly didn't make such choices based on moral beliefs they held out of mere prudence. They made such choices because of the strength of their conviction—the strength of their moral tastes. So it seems quite plausible that learned moral beliefs should be able to produce sufficiently strong emotions of guilt to discourage people from behaving opportunistically, even when there is no chance of being detected. It by no means stretches credulity to posit that if *A* believes that *B* was taught by his parents, pastors, and teachers, moral beliefs that comport with the moral foundation, and *A* has no evidence that *B* has ever behaved in an untrustworthy way in the past, then it is rational for *A* to be willing to trust *B* for all but the most exceptional of transactions.

We also have ample statistical evidence that culture (which obviously includes learned moral beliefs) plays an important role in sustaining trust and in the functioning of societies. Guiso, Sapienza, and Zingales (2003, 2004ab, 2006, 2008abc, 2010) and Tabellini (2007, 2008ab, 2010) considered the transmission of preferences and/or beliefs over time, and found that culture matters. Algan and Cahuc (2010) found that the "*inherited* trust of descendants of U.S. immigrants is significantly influenced by the country of origin and the timing of arrival of their forebears." (p. 2060, emphasis added) This strongly suggests that trust behavior is heavily affected by culture in the form of ideas passed from generation to generation. Luttmer and Singhal (2011) found that for immigrants, public policy preferences regarding income redistribution are strongly affected by country of birth. Grosjean (2011) found that even after accounting for spatial proximity and institutions in Europe, significant differences in social (generalized) trust can be detected in some cases even after 400 years, which strongly suggests that history and therefore culture matters.

Gorodnichenko and Roland (2010) found evidence that individualism significantly contributes to long-run growth. Gorodnichenko and Roland (2011) found that among a number of other cultural factors (identified by Hofstede, 2001) that might affect long-run growth, individualism was the most important. Given

Deepak Lal's (1998) argument that an ethic of individualism can be largely traced to the rise of Christianity, this finding suggests that religious beliefs may be driving the individualism result.

The extraordinary effort that many societies put toward transmitting moral beliefs from generation to generation suggests that culture isn't just about teaching something that might be of future value to someone, and it isn't merely tradition for tradition's sake. Such inculcation goes beyond a desire on the part of a teacher to expose the learner to particular beliefs—it also involves working to insure that those beliefs are accepted. This is likely because people in all societies understand that the more fully beliefs are inculcated, the more they will function as tastes by the time actual decision making occurs. This drives a wedge between the decision to teach a specific belief to B at time t, and decision making by B in time period $t+1$. This is obviously easier to accomplish the younger the learner is when first exposed to the relevant beliefs.

Moreover, the earlier an individual is exposed to a moral belief, the more likely it is that all subsequent learning will be shaped by the moral belief, and that it becomes a point of reference with respect to all future thinking. It is very hard for those who were exposed to a given moral belief early in life to understand how powerfully that belief affects all subsequent thinking, much as it is hard to describe the outside of a box if you are inside of it.[10] This is an utterly obvious point, for if it were not true, we would not see such vigorous efforts to inculcate moral beliefs at the earliest age, along with efforts to limit exposure to other beliefs, as well as the widespread use of operant conditioning to reinforce approved moral beliefs. Even though children will have access to competing moral beliefs as adults, religious leaders and parents are confident that the moral beliefs they have transmitted to the next generation will have so strongly shaped the way that generation thinks about the world around them that there is little risk of backsliding. And history shows they are largely right.

In short, my claim is that the majority of people in most societies are more or less stuck with the moral tastes that their parents, and their society as a whole, inculcated into them as children. As such, most people—but not all, certainly—are largely prisoners of tastes that they regard as theirs, but that were for the most part decided for them by others in the previous generation. It is true that the individual is free to not choose to continue to hold moral beliefs taught to him as a child, but why would he? What one chooses to believe or not believe is determined in large part by what one has already been exposed to, and if competing ideas that are too complex for a child to develop on his own are kept away until after the brain's psychological mechanisms that support moral behavior have firmed up, then the idea that one is completely free to choose what one believes becomes increasingly unlikely for any given individual as he or she ages.[11]

People choose how they behave, of course, but that does not mean that the tastes governing such choices are also simply a matter of choice. Although people are also free to choose to change their tastes, it is still the case that the tastes they have at the time they would make such a choice were largely given to them by others, and would affect *that* choice. This is an unpleasant thought, especially for individualistic economists. This is a hard thing for academics in general to accept, because many are academics precisely because they were children who expressed great incredulity about many bits of conventional wisdom.

Let me stress that I am not arguing that it is necessary that the individual in question be a child when the required moral beliefs are learned. It is only necessary that if moral restraint is needed in a given time period, the adoption of the requisite moral beliefs must be sincerely made at an earlier time period. My point here is simply that the younger a person is when exposed to a given moral belief, and the more guarded that person is from competing moral beliefs, the more likely such beliefs will function as moral tastes.

CONVICTION

The content of moral beliefs is primary to the strength of moral conviction with which they are held. This is because the strength of the guilt response is only relevant if a response is triggered in the first place, and this is determined by the content of moral beliefs. But the strength of moral conviction also matters. This is because the key to effectuating moral restraint is having *sufficiently strong* feelings of guilt to make the net payoff to opportunism negative for all but the most exceptional of golden opportunities. The level of guilt is directly related to how strongly one holds his moral beliefs.

An obvious question is whether it is realistic to suppose that the cultural transmission of moral beliefs is able to convey such moral beliefs with enough conviction to eliminate the commons dilemma associated with opportunism. Casual empiricism certainly suggests that when it comes to culturally instantiated moral beliefs, there is no shortage of moral conviction. People of nearly all faiths are often willing to endure horrible fates for themselves, and even their loved ones, rather than recant their faith. Human history is replete with examples of people doing just that.

Moreover, with moral beliefs that comport with the moral foundation, people are not being asked to move heaven and earth—they are only required to refrain from engaging in negative moral acts. At the same time, the pressure to undertake positive moral acts—which is substantial under many moral beliefs—is largely removed under the moral foundation. This is not a terribly high "moral conviction bar" for an individual to get over. This is yet another indication of a recurring theme in this book: what really matters is not moral earnestness, but how people think about morality. There is, therefore, no particular reason to doubt that it is possible for people to hold moral beliefs that comport with the moral foundation, with sufficient conviction, to make it rational for others to expect them to be trustworthy with respect to all but the most exceptional of transactions.

CONSISTENCY

Moral tastes are also most likely to be consistently held if the moral beliefs that instantiated them were consistently learned across individuals in society in the first place. Culture, of course, often involves a rather rigorous and systematic attempt to teach specific moral beliefs in a very specific and consistent way. The problem of consistency is related to, but nevertheless distinct from, the issue of moral conviction. We all know of examples of people who adopt a religion in adulthood and who are very committed to it. The problem of consistency is more a matter of sheer arithmetic.

When adults choose to hold a given moral belief, they are normally choosing among many possible alternatives. If there are n alternatives to choose from, then there is on average only a $1/n$th probability that any particular belief will be chosen. With children, however, adults normally try to limit exposure to competing moral beliefs. Since what we are taught as children frames subsequent learning, for most people the probability that any other specific moral belief will later be chosen over what they were taught as children is far less than $1/n$th. This means that the cultural transmission of moral beliefs, through adults indoctrinating children and limiting exposure to other moral beliefs, is far more likely to produce consistency from generation to generation than moral beliefs chosen by adults for themselves.[12]

In short, the younger and more exclusively people are taught moral beliefs, the more stable they will be from generation to generation, and therefore the more consistently they will be held across the entire society in any given generation. In many societies, adults work hard to teach children specific moral beliefs and to insure the lesson is learned well and reinforced by operant conditioning, yet the lessons learned don't produce a high trust society. My point here is simply that with respect to the moral foundation, the most plausible mechanism through which it might give rise to consistent moral behavior is for it to be derived from moral beliefs that were very consistently taught to children and reinforced in the first place.

Note that this description of how culture can transmit moral beliefs is consistent with the commonly held idea that moral behavior is fundamentally a matter of character rather than circumstance. It also comports with our greater willingness to forgive and forget opportunism in children than in adults. With adults, we may forgive, but we are unlikely to forget. With children, however, it is possible that their moral character is still a work in progress, because the ideas that produce duty-based moral restraint are abstract in nature, and are therefore more likely to be understood by older children than younger children.[13] A young child who lies and steals often grows up to be a respectable adult. This suggests that at some level, people understand that reliably moral behavior must be grounded in tastes, and therefore the older someone is, the harder it is to believe that he will change his moral tastes, so the harder it is to forget what he does.

EFFICIENT SEARCH

Evidence that *B* possesses moral beliefs that comport with the moral foundation also provides a more useful thing to look for than whether *B* possesses strong involuntary emotional responses. Discovering that an individual always blushes when he lies, for example, means we are inferring that someone can be trusted from observing what happens when he behaves in an untrustworthy way. How, then, can we ever identify someone who never behaves in an untrustworthy way in the first place? Aren't these precisely the people we really want to find? And what does one make of another *adult* person who never blushes? Is he someone who never lies, or is he someone who is an excellent liar? Finally, what if the person has moral beliefs that hold that being untrustworthy in some circumstances is not immoral so there is nothing to feel guilty or embarrassed about, and therefore no blushing? It would seem that a much more useful thing for *A* to look for in *B* is the absence of evidence of previous opportunistic behavior and the presence of evidence of having moral beliefs that comport with the moral foundation.

If people can identify others who possess moral beliefs that comport with the moral foundation, then they will prefer such individuals as transaction partners, especially if interpersonal utility effects are weak. The possession of moral beliefs that comport with the moral foundation can, therefore, produce a "green beard," a locution that describes ". . . an arbitrary, recognizable phenotypic signal linked to altruistic behavioral traits . . . [That] allows committed cooperators to seek each other out, and to safely open themselves to the dangers of defection in potentially profitable games with otherwise bad dominant structures." (Dawkins 1976)

The green beard takes the form of what people say and how they act. I think we have learned to associate certain clues with stalwart trustworthiness. I do not claim that gathering evidence to determine the nature of a person's moral beliefs is easy, but what is the alternative? How does one gather evidence about whether an individual actually does the right thing, even when there is no possibility of being observed? Moreover, I strongly suspect that moral beliefs that comport with the moral foundation are hard to mimic. Those whose moral restraint is not principled in nature generally do not appear to understand how obvious and disappointing this is to others whose morality is. They justify their actions, and even look for moral reassurance, in ways that reveal that they are unprincipled. They seem completely oblivious to how offensive and troubling their rationalizations are to those whose moral restraint is principled in nature.

Culture and a High Trust Society

I have argued that culture is the most plausible mechanism through which moral beliefs that comport with the moral foundation are adopted. But the arguments made thus far do not demonstrate that the genuine trust engendered by culture will also be generalized. The arguments made thus far about culture pertain to personalized trust, not generalized trust. The obvious question now is whether the genuine trust derived from the cultural transmission of moral beliefs can also be generalized, and thereby support trust behavior across the whole of society to produce a high trust society.

In Chapters 2 and 7–9 I explained why generalized trust is so important. Many institutions that are crucial for producing a low transaction cost environment are not viable in low trust societies, because they are vulnerable to opportunism. They include but are not limited to having governmental and community respect for private property rights, having a trustworthy civil court system, peaceful voting in democracies with acceptance of the outcome as fair, and voluntary income tax collection.[14] Such institutions require that the preponderance of people (but not all, by any means) in society be unconditionally trustworthy. The higher the proportion of unconditionally trustworthy people, the better such institutions function. We take many of these institutions for granted in high trust societies, so it is difficult to appreciate how trust-dependent they are. But they are conspicuously absent in low trust societies, because there is no demand for them. When they are transplanted into low trust societies they are often corrupted, sometimes even becoming tools for opportunism. By serving as a mechanism that can plausibly produce a high trust society, culture can support the emergence and efficient operation of highly trust-dependent institutions.

Even labor markets—a crucial part of any economy—function more efficiently in a high trust society by making it possible to presume others are trustworthy. In a society in which nearly all people possess moral beliefs that ultimately support unconditional trustworthiness, the absence of negative information will normally be sufficient to presume that an individual can be trusted in all but the most exceptional of circumstances. It is much less costly to verify that there is no clear evidence of someone having ever been arrested for theft, fraud, etc., than it is to affirmatively conclude that he can be trusted in all circumstances because trust has been earned over a period of time.

Regarding my oft-repeated qualification "for all but the most exceptional of circumstances," it is largely self-evident which transactions are likely to prove too tempting to leave to presumptive trust, even if all relevant actors are presumed to be unconditionally trustworthy. So the decision to extend trust is fundamentally changed from having to determine whether each and every individual involved is trustworthy (which is what one must do in a low trust society), to determining whether the transaction involved is truly exceptional (which is usually self-evident). Even in the most trustworthy society, banks have vaults. But this merely reflects the self-evident fact that very large sums of money (1) drive up the cost of being wrong, and (2) increase the likelihood that a normally trustworthy person will be too sorely tempted. This is much more efficient than having to determine whether each and every individual is trustworthy.

At first this appears to contradict the idea of duty-based moral restraint, but in reality it illustrates the plausibility of the moral foundation. Recall that the moral foundation was derived vis-à-vis a thought experiment, within which I took care to constrain the exercise to limit moral restraint to being effectuated through psychological mechanisms that people actually have. This means that moral restraint is ultimately derived from feelings of guilt. It follows, then, that it is possible for someone who has never been tempted to behave opportunistically in his entire adult life, because he possesses moral beliefs that comport with the moral foundation, to nevertheless act on an opportunity to obtain $100,000,000 without harming anyone and with no chance of detection. If the moral foundation could not account for such a possibility, it would stretch all credulity. So the fact that it can should be taken as an indication of its plausibility.

Finally, even firm culture is affected by being in a high trust society. In a low trust society, opportunism is ubiquitous, so mangers are preoccupied with monitoring. In a high trust society opportunism is far less frequent, so managers will spend less time monitoring and more time actually coordinating. In a low trust society a manger's motives will always be suspect, so he will be given very little discretion. In a high trust society, managers feel free to deviate from established routines and are even encouraged to do so. Managers in high trust societies are therefore more likely to act like creative entrepreneurs than rule-preoccupied bureaucrats, so the firm's decision making up and down its hierarchy is much more entrepreneurial in nature.[15]

THE ESS PROBLEM

If having a high trust society is so beneficial, then why are they so rare? The answer is that there is a fundamental obstacle to the emergence of generalized trust. This obstacle was first identified by Frank (1988). Although moral restraint is inherently a manifestation of individual behavior, generalized trust cannot percolate from the bottom up. This is because as the proportion of the population that possesses traits that makes individuals trustworthy rises, natural selection will increasingly favor dishonest traits. The reason is that as the proportion of the population that is trustworthy rises, individuals will be more likely to presume that others are trustworthy. This makes them easy victims, and thereby drives up the return to opportunism. This means that if moral restraint is derived solely from genetically inherited traits, it is inevitable that a substantial portion of the population won't inherit traits that support trustworthiness.

The logic of this argument is not limited to genetically inherited traits. If, for example, trustworthiness is solely derived from introspectively discovered moral beliefs or prudential restraint, as is implicitly assumed by neoclassical models, then evolutionary dynamics still insure that, as the proportion of the population that is trustworthy rises, the return to being trustworthy falls. So as a society's proportion of unconditionally trustworthy people rises to a level at which it becomes rational for people to begin to presumptively trust others, the returns to not being unconditionally trustworthy, so people are able to act on golden opportunities, begins to rise.

This I call the "ESS problem." ESS is an acronym for "evolutionarily stable strategy."[16] The basic problem is that the evolutionary benefit of having traits that support unconditional trustworthiness falls when the benefits of being opportunistic rise. As a result, any trait or factor that supports unconditional trustworthiness will become less likely to be passed on. Even if parents attempt to inculcate moral tastes into their children to effectuate moral rather than prudential restraint, such parents will start to spend less time doing so, and perhaps more time emphasizing the advantages of being clever. The most salient point about the ESS problem is that it virtually guarantees that if moral restraint is in any way a function of material payoffs, a society will not achieve a condition of generalized trust. This is because it is precisely at the point where it becomes rational to presume that others are trustworthy—the hallmark of a high trust society—that the return to opportunism begins to skyrocket.

But, given this argument, how can we explain the existence of high trust societies such as we find in Scandinavian countries (Guiso, Sapienza, and Zingales, 2006)? In such countries, something apparently must have solved the commons dilemma associated with opportunism and thereby overcame this obstacle to generalized trust. In existing high trust societies, something must have provided moral restraint even in the face of rising returns to opportunistic behavior, overcoming the rising return to opportunism, as the norm of presuming strangers to be trustworthy emerged. As is the case with social dilemmas generally, the individuals involved are powerless to bring about that "something" on their own (Binmore, 2005).

CULTURE SOLVES THE ESS PROBLEM

The obvious question, then, is whether the same evolutionary dynamics apply to moral beliefs that comport with the moral foundation if they are culturally transmitted. In my view, culture is the key to the development and efficient operation of a market economy in part because it provides the most plausible solution to the ESS problem.

When an individual adopts moral beliefs that comport with the moral foundation, he will now be trustworthy in contexts that he might not have been before. He might therefore benefit from being more reliably trustworthy, so it is easy to envision the spread of moral beliefs that comport with the moral foundation because they produce higher returns for him and others like him *than before*, at the micro level.

In Chapter 2 I alluded to the conclusion that if moral beliefs are held with such strong conviction that guilt costs are always expected to exceed the expected utility gain from behaving opportunistically, then the net return to behaving opportunistically will always be negative, and the commons dilemma associated with opportunism will disappear. In this case, the increasing returns to opportunism resulting from the emergence of a norm of extending trust, because one can rationally presume others are unconditionally trustworthy, can potentially prove to be irrelevant. Put another way, if moral beliefs are held with sufficient moral conviction, then moral restraint will be unaffected by rising returns to opportunistic behavior.

What does this have to do with the ESS problem? When the reason for holding moral beliefs that comport with the moral foundation has nothing to do with material payoffs, the effect of rising payoffs to opportunism will not matter at all if those moral beliefs are held with sufficiently strong conviction. As a result, moral beliefs that parents, pastors, and teachers teach children are much less likely to be abandoned just because a rising practice of presuming that others are trustworthy makes the returns to opportunism skyrocket.

So as the proportion of people in a society who possess moral beliefs that comport with the moral foundation rises, the rise in the expected material benefit of behaving opportunistically will not result in more opportunistic behavior on the part of those who abide by the moral foundation. For them such benefits will not overcome the guilt costs that they expect to experience from behaving opportunistically.[17] This is truer the greater the conviction with which such moral beliefs are held. It follows that having a sufficiently high proportion of the population possess moral beliefs that comport with the moral foundation, with sufficiently strong conviction, can overcome the ESS problem and thereby make it possible for unconditional trustworthiness to emerge as a social norm.

This is by no means a perfect mechanism. Even a person who possesses moral beliefs that comport with the moral foundation, and holds those beliefs with very strong conviction, might behave opportunistically. But it is one thing to do so, get away with it, and then merely enjoy the spoils. It is quite another to do so, get away with it, only to be racked with guilt later—guilt made all the worse because one's opportunistic success was tied directly to being extended genuine trust. Children often underestimate the power of guilt, but in most cases they learn it the hard way over time. With moral beliefs that comport with the moral foundation, "experiments" in opportunistic behavior are so consistently bad (even with respect to golden opportunities) that their subconscious mind stops wasting resources on treating opportunism as an open question. When, for example, was the last time you considered stealing a candy bar because a cashier ducked into the bathroom? I suspect you never even consider doing such things, because your subconscious mind does not regard them as topics worthy of consideration.[18]

There may also be self-enforcing convention effects that arise as a society closes in on enjoying a social norm of unconditional trustworthiness. Consider the "chump effect," which refers to the tendency to feel like a chump if you obey moral prohibitions while everyone else doesn't (Frank 1988). The chump effect is obviously a function of your beliefs about others' beliefs. If you are convinced that everyone around you also abides by the moral foundation, then you don't worry about being a chump. If others pull ahead of you, it must be from their being luckier, more talented, or working harder. You aren't happy about that, but you can live with it. The main point is that there is no way to rationalize behaving opportunistically, because you simply do not believe that they got ahead of you by behaving in an opportunistic way.

If, however, you are convinced that nearly everyone around you will lie, cheat, or steal as necessary to get ahead, then not doing so yourself seals your fate, and you will feel like a chump. In my view, this is one reason why culture is so important. A hallmark of culture is the systematic inculcation of very consistent moral beliefs into children, so they observe at an early age that everyone around them is being taught the same stories. As a result, even those who cheat will often agree that what they did was wrong. This undermines the power of "codes of silence" that exist because people implicitly agree not to snitch on each other. Culturally transmitted moral beliefs can, therefore, move unconditional trust-worthiness from being a mere social norm to a strong social convention, because if everyone, including the opportunists themselves, agrees that opportunism is inherently wrong, they are more likely to feel morally compelled to report such behavior to authorities, or at least tell others of it. This undermines codes of silence, and reduces the chump effect. One need not suffer in silence to avoid being impugned.

The main point is that as the expected material benefits of being opportunistic rise, due to a nascent norm of presuming that others are unconditionally trust-worthy, the *net benefit* of opportunistic behavior remains negative if guilt costs are sufficiently high. This means that if moral beliefs that comport with the moral foundation are inculcated consistently across the whole of society, with suffi-ciently strong conviction, there is no particular reason why the proportion of the adult population that is unconditionally trustworthy cannot grow to such a high level that it becomes rational to presume others in the society—even complete strangers—can be regarded as being unconditionally trustworthy over the set of all but the most exceptional of transactions. An unwillingness to extend trust becomes more of a matter of pessimistic eccentricity than an indication of reason-able prudence. And, knowing that others may infer that an untrusting person is engaging in psychological projection, even highly pessimistic people will feel indi-rect social pressure to extend genuine trust, which further contributes to a social norm of extending trust. This contributes even more to making genuine trust generalized in nature.

One could argue that even in high trust societies, the level of moral conviction associated with moral beliefs has fallen dramatically, so how could they continue to be high trust societies? Perhaps they in fact no longer are—there has indeed been a well-documented reduction in measured trust in the West over the last 50 years.[19] An important empirical question is how much of this reduction in measured trust is due to a reduction in conviction, versus a drift away from moral beliefs that at least roughly comport with the moral foundation.

Every human society is filled with people who have hardwired moral intuitions that support moral behavior in general, and trustworthiness in particular. Most people in all societies are also smart enough to understand the benefits of having a trustworthy reputation. Yet it is not the case that every society is a high trust society. As a purely empirical matter, then, trustworthiness derived from hardwired moral intuitions, introspectively discovered moral beliefs, or even the adoption by adults of moral beliefs that comport with the moral foundation, cannot explain why only a few societies are high trust ones, while most are not.

In my view, the culprit is the ESS problem associated with these foundations for trust. The evolutionary dynamics that give rise to the ESS problem ultimately result from the commons dilemma, associated with opportunism becoming more daunting as a society comes closer to being truly high trust in nature. But culture need not suffer from this problem when it involves moral beliefs that are held for reasons other than material payoffs. There is no reason why a specific moral belief cannot come to be held by a preponderance of people in a given society and, because it produces significant utility benefits at the individual level and material benefits at the societal level, there is no reason why it cannot also be sustainable at both the micro and macro levels. Indeed, it will likely confer advantages over low trust societies. In so doing, culture in the form of sincerely held moral beliefs may explain the large differences in measured trust across societies, something that existing theories of trust simply cannot do.

Conclusion

Hardwired moral intuitions and introspectively discovered moral beliefs, while no doubt able to produce genuine trust in small group contexts, are implausible mechanisms for supporting genuine trust in large group contexts, especially when transactions are also impersonal in nature so that the effects of mutual affection or repeat play are moot. As such, neither approach can explain genuine trust that is also generalized in nature, and therefore cannot explain the existence of high trust societies.

This was almost inevitable. High trust societies are rare across human societies over the course of human history. As such, the explanation for the existence of high levels of trust in just a few societies is not likely to come from a universal explanation for trust behavior. The traits we all share are small group traits, so the kind of trust behavior we all share is small group in nature, too. Highly general explanations for trust behavior are, therefore, inevitably going to be theories of small group trust, because the traits we all share evolved in a small group context. Ironically, this means that the more general a theory of trust is, the less likely it will prove to be a plausible theory of generalized trust.

The flexibility of culture in the form of learned moral beliefs also comports with the extreme variation in average levels of trust across societies. By acting as a mechanism that spreads consistent moral beliefs across the whole of a society, culture is consistent with existing evidence, in that the variance in moral/cultural beliefs is great enough to match the variance in levels of measured trust and measured economic performance across societies. Moreover, culture can provide an explanation for why levels of development differ so much, even among countries that have tried to adopt the most modern and sophisticated technologies and institutions of a market economy.

My claim is that it is plausible that a society can get lucky by becoming exposed to moral beliefs that comport with the moral foundation, and then transmitting these ideas culturally to future generations with sufficient levels of conviction and concentration to produce a high trust society. Differences in average levels of trust across societies can therefore be viewed as the result of some societies being fortunate enough to have stumbled upon moral beliefs that do a better job than those of other societies in helping it transcend the small group nature of its members.

Since trust increases payoffs at both the micro and macro levels, such beliefs can be sustainable as well, because low trust societies will not have the resources to conquer them. Because of economies of scale, small groups that compete directly with large groups cease to exist, so competition becomes increasingly a matter of ever larger groups competing with one another. How would they continue to evolve as a result of this competition? It cannot be through genes, of course, for they are largely common across human groups. It is implausible that it would happen through introspectively discovered moral beliefs because of their lack of consistency. The most likely mechanism would be culture in the form of moral beliefs that could be held consistently within groups, but that varies markedly from group to group. So culture can be viewed as an important margin of competition between groups, and even entire societies.

I realize that by arguing that culture matters, I am wading into dangerous waters. Economists in particular still tend to view culture as unimportant or as being affected by economic activity, rather than the other way around. Economists are also hostile to explanations based on tastes. But what if *the* explanation for a phenomenon just happens to be culture that manifests itself through tastes that are taken as given at the time of decision making? Are we obliged to reject such an explanation for the sake of paradigmatic elegance? Thankfully, social scientists—including some economists—have become increasingly willing to consider cultural explanations for the existence of such dramatic differences in general prosperity across societies.

While it is the exogenous nature of culture that concerns many social scientists when it comes to cultural explanations, this is precisely what makes it possible for moral restraint to hold up, even with respect to golden opportunities. If restraint is not derived from exogenous moral tastes, then it would be irrational for others to expect an individual not to act on golden opportunities. It is also the exogenous nature of culture that makes it possible to overcome the ESS problem at the macro level, because it is the fact that moral tastes are primary to rational decision making that insures behavior will not change in response to skyrocketing returns to opportunistic behavior, as the practice of presumptively extending trust becomes commonplace and institutional safeguards are relaxed.

Like most social scientists, economists have a strong preference for highly general explanations, for "universals." But it is also a mistake—indeed, it is intellectually dishonest—to constrain our search for explanations to those that are universal in nature. Improving our understanding of why there are large differences in success across societies is an intellectual endeavor of the highest importance. It is precisely culture's lack of universality that allows it to explain large differences across societies, despite our being genetically very similar and having access to all of the blueprints for all the institutions enjoyed by prosperous societies. The idea that the power of culture is its very non-universality is something that is completely obvious to everyone, except social scientists who are obsessed with universal explanations.

CHAPTER 11

Conclusion

My diagnosis of American society is informed by the notion that we are living during a period of erosion of the "social capital" that provides the basic framework for our culture, our economy, and our polity, a framework within which the "free society" in the classically liberal ideal perhaps came closest to realization in all of history.—James Buchanan, 2001, p. 187

Summary

So what did this book do, and why might it matter? As for what it did, it began by providing sharper arguments for why trust matters, and it connected trust behavior to moral beliefs. It then identified characteristics moral beliefs must have if they are to most fully support the development of a high trust society and, therefore, most fully support the development and operation of a market economy. It then explained why the most plausible means by which such moral beliefs will exist in sufficient concentration, consistency, and conviction to maximize general prosperity is if they are instantiated by culture.

I began in Chapter 2 by arguing that opportunism is *the* fundamental obstacle to the development and operation of a market economy, because it drives up transaction costs and thereby impedes the fullest realization of the gains from specialization. I explained that it is an especially daunting obstacle because it constitutes a commons dilemma. Employing concepts from contract theory, I categorized opportunism into three types, and explained why the third type, what I call third-degree opportunism, presents serious and largely unrecognized difficulties for the use of relational contracts.

In Chapter 3 I explained how size worsens the problem of opportunism by worsening the commons dilemma. Size also increases the localization of knowledge, which increases the need for relational contracts, while at the same time increasing the risk of third-degree opportunistic victimization from using them. This has important implications for undertaking economic activity in large group contexts such as large firms in an efficient, indeed thoroughly entrepreneurial, manner. To most fully use relational contracts to address the local knowledge problem, firm owners must be able to trust that decision makers will not engage in third-degree opportunism even when golden opportunities to do so present themselves. I then explained why prudential restraint is unable to fully support the use of relational contracts—only moral restraint can work.

In Chapter 4 I explained why differences in moral values across societies are unlikely to be able to explain differences in economic performance, because there is very little difference in moral values across societies with respect to behavior associated with economic activity. I then argued that in a market economy, transactions are voluntary and therefore inherently efficient, so exhortations to take positive moral actions are not needed and may be inefficient. What really matters are moral prohibitions against taking negative moral actions, because they combat opportunism and thereby help keep transaction costs low.

In Chapter 5 I provided an analysis of the relationship between the concepts of empathy, sympathy, and guilt. I then offered a simple theory for how guilt arising from sympathy, actuated by empathy due to harming others, produces a natural reluctance to behave opportunistically.

In Chapter 6 I argued that group size weakens our natural reluctance to harm others because it is subject to what I call *the empathy problem*. In other words, small group trust is not *scalable*. For this reason, large group trust cannot be created by simply extending the radius of small group trust. So for moral restraint to be operative even in large groups—to ultimately make a high trust and therefore prosperous society possible—it must also be principled in nature.

In Chapter 7 I argued that while moral tastes that comport with principled moral restraint solve the empathy problem, this is only a necessary condition for unconditional trustworthiness. Principled moral restraint works by attaching guilt to negative moral actions themselves, but one could feel even guiltier about failing to take positive moral actions. To solve this *greater good rationalization problem*, moral tastes have to also structure the value system in such a way as to make the obedience of moral prohibitions lexically primary to the obedience of moral exhortations. Taken together, such moral tastes produce an ethic of duty-based moral restraint.

In Chapter 8 I argued that for an ethic of duty-based moral restraint to be meaningful, it must not be undermined by an ethic of duty-based moral advocacy. So while negative moral actions must be governed by a nonconsequentialist theory of moral propriety, positive moral actions must be governed by a consequentialist theory of moral propriety. Nonconsequentialist moral restraint, coupled with consequentialist moral advocacy, is the moral foundation of economic behavior. If an individual possesses moral beliefs that comport with the moral foundation with sufficient conviction, then he is unconditionally trustworthy over a given set of transactions. The greater is that individual's level of moral conviction, the larger is the set of such transactions.

In Chapter 9 I compared trust behavior derived from moral beliefs that comport with the moral foundation to existing theories of trust. I found that whereas conventional theories of trust do not square well with existing empirical evidence on trust behavior at either the micro or macro levels, trust supported by moral beliefs that comport with the moral foundation does. I then discussed the implications this book has for the strongest arguments against the relevance of the concept of trust to the study of the development and operation of market economies. I then explained why, if a society is composed of a sufficiently high proportion of persons who abide by the moral foundation, it will enjoy the additional benefits of generalized trust. This makes it possible for its people to trust each other at the micro level while at the same time makes it possible for trust-dependent institutions to exist at the macro level.

In Chapter 10 I argued that moral beliefs that comport with the moral foundation are most plausibly instantiated in sufficient concentration, consistency, and conviction, across the whole of a society, if they are culturally transmitted. Of particular importance is culture's unique ability to separate the decision to have certain kinds of moral beliefs from the consequences of having them at the time of actually making moral decisions. This separation is also why culture uniquely overcomes a fundamental obstacle to the emergence of a truly high trust society—the ESS problem. So culture doesn't matter simply because moral beliefs matter and moral beliefs happen to be part of any society's culture. Culture matters instrumentally, too.

I would like to conclude this summary by reiterating that my goal was not to advance a new theory of morality. My goal was to determine the characteristics that moral beliefs must have if they are to best support the development and operation of a market economy and thereby maximize general prosperity. There is, therefore, nothing inherently more moral about the moral foundation of economic behavior. This exercise was from the beginning a self-conscious exercise in "what if" reasoning, a thought experiment proposed to stimulate new thinking about an old but very important topic.

As for why this exercise might matter, I will now discuss some implications for future theoretical and empirical work. I will close by offering some cautionary speculations.

Implications for the Culture versus Institutions Debate

There is no question that the study of institutions has done much to improve our understanding of how economies develop and operate. But because institutions must work through external incentives, they simply cannot effectuate restraint with respect to golden opportunities. Although this point is largely unrecognized, I contend that it is a serious one. This is because the maximization of general prosperity requires hyperspecialization, but this produces hyperlocalized knowledge and, hence, many golden opportunities. It follows that maximizing the set of transactions through which the gains from specialization can be effectuated requires some form of internalized restraint. Perhaps this can be achieved through moral beliefs, perhaps not, but it certainly cannot be achieved solely through institutions. Since shame also works through external incentives, this also constitutes a sharp argument in support of Lal's (1998) contention that guilt cultures are more likely to produce superior economic performance than shame cultures.

One could argue that the problem of golden opportunities is still not beyond the reach of institutions, because institutions can be used to eliminate the existence of golden opportunities in the first place. But as I explained in Chapters 3 and 9, attempting to eliminate the problem of golden opportunities through strict procedures and routines (through institutions) trades one problem for another, by robbing decision makers of the flexibility to respond optimally to changes in conditions. Such an approach therefore results in firm behavior that is bureaucratic rather than entrepreneurial in nature, and thereby exacerbates the natural tradeoff between firm size and entrepreneurial direction. The larger the firm, the greater is the problem of localization of knowledge due to specialization, so if the local knowledge problem is addressed by employing institutional mechanisms that limit discretion, then the larger a firm is, the less entrepreneurial it will be.

Since many of the institutions and institutional arrangements that are taken for granted in highly developed economies would not be viable, not be used to their fullest extent, or not function properly in a low trust society, it is incorrect to think of institutions as a substitute for trust. A society whose moral beliefs can only sustain a low trust society can neither create nor sustain highly trust-dependent institutions. Even if such institutions were to somehow be adopted, they would likely be corrupted. Conversely, high trust societies are able to make use of a much broader set of institutions and institutional arrangements than low trust societies, because many important institutions are trust-dependent themselves.

So why is there so much ambivalence toward the study of culture by those who focus on the study of institutions? Perhaps part of the reason is that institutions combat opportunism through prudential restraint in response to external incentives, so to argue that genuine trust is important is tantamount to arguing that incentives produced by institutions are not as important as previously believed, because genuine trust can only be derived from internalized mechanisms. Even those mainstream economists who largely ignore the role played by institutions still stress the role played by external incentives over internalized moral restraint.[1] For this reason, many social scientists, and especially economists, are eager to explain all phenomena as exercises in enlightened self-interest; that is, as nothing more than responses to incentives.

But the correct explanation for a phenomenon is not obliged to comport with an existing theory or paradigm, or a penchant for modeling elegance. There is no denying that social science would be more elegant if there was a

Descartes-like divide between tastes and incentives. But as Robert Frank first explained over 20 years ago, this was not to be. Some phenomena are just not well explained if we take tastes off the table. In my view, existing incentive-based theories of trustworthiness constitute a case of the theoretical tail wagging the dog, by *presuming* that trustworthiness *must be* an exercise in enlightened self-interest.

Another reason for ambivalence toward culture in general, and moral beliefs in particular, is that if culture matters, then this conflicts with the desire for an explanation that is highly universal in nature. This desire for universal explanations has produced great interest in theories of trust rooted in evolutionary psychology, cognitive science, and neuroeconomics. From this work we have learned much about the underpinnings of trust behavior. But if all there is to understanding trust is understanding universal factors like hardwiring, then why are there large differences in measured trust behavior across societies? One obvious answer is that there are large differences in institutions across societies. Since institutions powerfully shape the behavior we actually observe, variations in institutions across society are perhaps what explains differences in measured trust levels across societies.

But this begs the question of how *trust-dependent* institutions got off the ground in a low trust society in the first place. Or, if one argues that trust is produced by institutions, it begs the question of why low trust and therefore impoverished societies that exist today don't just adopt institutions that support high levels of trust. Why, indeed, has the practice of dropping market institutions into less developed countries failed repeatedly to produce general prosperity? Institutional economists have effectively circumvented this question by arguing that trust simply doesn't matter in the first place. But the arguments I have advanced here comport well with mounting evidence at the macro level that trust does, indeed, make a difference.[2]

But low trust societies can't just simply adopt institutions to produce a high trust society because the causation runs the other way. High trust societies have high trust institutions, of course, but not because such institutions produced trust.[3] On the contrary, it was a high level of trust that produced a demand for, and made possible the existence of, highly trust-dependent institutions. While it is certainly true that institutions affect observed trust behavior, a high trust society without trust-producing institutions does not destroy trust, and does not impede the emergence of trust-dependent institutions. Trust-producing institutions, however, do not inevitably produce a high trust society, because that requires trust that is both generalized and genuine, and I have shown that institutions simply cannot produce genuine trust.

I therefore submit that a society with weak institutions but that possesses moral beliefs that comport with the moral foundation will soon be on the path of rapid economic development because there will be ample incentive to devise and employ highly trust dependent institutions that support higher levels of prosperity and growth. This is especially true if such institutions do not have to be discovered because they can be copied from successful countries.

Those who argue that institutions obviate the need to study trust and culture essentially ignore or dismiss the importance of golden opportunities in general, and the problem of local knowledge in large firms in particular. Because of this, they do not fully recognize the fundamentally important role played by relational contracts, the vulnerability of such contracts to third-degree opportunism and, hence, the need for unconditional trustworthiness derived from internalized moral tastes. I have seen no evidence that scholars who reject the importance of trust and culture have also rejected the claim that relational contracts are crucial, or that they require unconditional trustworthiness to work to fullest effect. Indeed, I have seen no evidence that they have ever even considered these possibilities. Having no theory of third-degree opportunism, there was simply no reason to appreciate the need for unconditional trustworthiness to make possible the fullest use of relational contracts.

One reason those who argue that institutions obviate the need to study trust and culture may be that they are focusing on *what is* rather than *what might have been*. For example, perhaps they view the existence of an institution that combats opportunism in a low trust society as evidence that genuine trust is not needed because opportunism is, in fact, being combated. Such a conclusion may even be valid, if we limit our attention to the set of extant transactions. But the real problem is the set of transactions that never happen in the first place, because in the absence of unconditional trustworthiness undertaking them is not rational.

Showing that institutions can get the job done is not equivalent to showing that the job cannot be done better. Similarly, arguing that if genuine trust is truly important for economic behavior, we should see less sophisticated institutional mechanisms in high trust societies, is like arguing that as people earn more money we should find evidence of them borrowing less, or arguing that in low transaction cost societies we should see fewer lawyers. In reality, rich people want to buy larger houses and therefore borrow more, and in high trust societies, entirely new vistas of economic opportunity are opened up by low transaction costs, and therefore new forms of contracts, institutions, lawyers, etc., rush in fill institutional needs that are utterly moot in low trust societies.

So how does one answer the now oft-repeated query: Which matters most, culture or institutions? My answer is that they are so obviously interconnected that this is not even a fruitful question. Institutions and culture are, of course, both complements and substitutes for one another, even though institutional scholars have emphasized viewing them as substitutes. In my view, we have paid far too little attention to improving our understanding of how culture *complements* rather than substitutes for institutions.

Here is an example of the dynamic nature of complementary relationship between culture and institutions. A new moral belief is exogenously introduced that strengthens trust, making new kinds of institutions and a larger set of transactions viable. How far do economic actors push into this new and larger set of potential transactions? They initially push into areas where there are virtually no risks involved. But as long as things keep working out well they keep pushing further, little by little. This, in turn, creates demand for new support institutions—institutions that would have been irrelevant and perhaps even unfathomable before the arrival of the new moral belief. Those who possess certain kinds of moral beliefs will thrive more in the new *institutional* landscape, so the moral beliefs they hold and transmit to their children will become increasingly more important aspects of the *cultural* landscape. In this way, changes in culture can induce changes in institutions that then induce further changes in culture, and so on.

To summarize, as important as institutions are, a key implication of this book is that they can only go so far because of the problem of golden opportunities, which only worsens as economic activity is conducted in larger and more complex groups. A fruitful way to think of the relationship between culture and institutions is therefore this: to have the broadest set of institutions possible and for them to work to their fullest effect, a society must be a high trust society. This, in turn, is only possible if there is a cultural foundation in the form of a preponderance of people possessing moral beliefs that comport with the moral foundation. Viewed in this way, culture in the form of moral beliefs that comport with the moral foundation are not just complements of institutions, they are actually primary to them. Guido Tabellini, a pioneer in research on the effects of trust and culture on economic performance, echoes this sentiment:

> Well-functioning institutions are often observed in countries or regions where individual values are consistent with generalized morality, and under different identifying assumptions this suggests a *causal effect* from values to institutional outcomes. (Tabellini, 2008a, p. 255, emphasis added)

Implications for Future Work

THEORETICAL

From the discussion above, I hope it is clear that I believe that the dichotomy between culture and institutions is a false one. I suspect that many, perhaps most, social scientists already believe this and are therefore amenable to the proposition that culture and institutions obviously complement one another. As such, more fruitful questions than "Which matters?" or "Which matters most?" are "What is the nature of their relationship?" and "Do they coevolve and, if so, how?"

But it is one thing to think that culture matters. It is quite another to think that moral beliefs matter. It is quite yet another to think that moral beliefs play a particularly important role in the development and operation of a market economy, let alone to think that no single factor can do more to support the achievement of a condition of general prosperity and human flourishing than the moral beliefs of a society's people (I don't make the latter claim, but I suspect that future empirical work will support it).

Moreover, even if social scientists believe that culture matters, it does not necessarily follow that they can meaningfully account for it in their theories and models. Culture is not a well-defined concept, so it has proven too empirically intractable to have much scientific relevance (that is, for there to be falsifiable implications that can be derived from it that are objective enough to satisfy everyone). Although the locution "moral beliefs" is not terribly sharp, either, it is nevertheless sharper than "culture."

A theoretical implication of this book, then, is that it has sharpened the mechanism through which culture might affect economic behavior, as well as the development and operation of a market economy generally, by drawing the focus to moral beliefs *per se*. So what connects moral beliefs to economic behavior and the process of development? There are two closely related answers: the concepts of trust and social capital. Of course, neither trust nor social capital is terribly sharp, either, but they are still sharper than "moral beliefs" and they function as a bridge between morality and economic behavior. Moreover, trust can be sharply defined and measured, as is evidenced by a growing mountain of empirical work employing surveys and economic experiments.

Another theoretical implication of this book is that the concept of social capital can be sharpened, too, especially as it relates to trust behavior. There is much debate over the proper definition of the concept of social capital. I do not want to wade into that debate, but I would like to add the following theoretical possibility: individualized social capital that makes unconditional trustworthiness possible exists as specific neural pathways in the brain that are associated with specific ways of logically organizing moral values.[4] As such, this rather important form of social capital has a clear physical reality.

Ideas have the power to change culture, of course, but we have not fully appreciated how ideas can change the way the mind processes information, even the way we think, especially as it relates to economic behavior. In this book I have explored how ideas in the form of moral beliefs can affect how we think about morality, specifically by leading us to treat the obedience of moral prohibitions as lexically primary to the pursuit of moral exhortations. Just as technological change alters the nature of capital, so the amount of capital is no longer the whole story, moral beliefs can change the way people think about morality, so the amount of moral earnestness is no longer the whole story. With respect to the specific story proposed here, the key role played by the concept of social capital was that while it can change over time, it does not change at the moment of moral decision making. This solved the prudence problem by having restraint be derived from moral tastes that are not a function of the details of the moral decision at hand.

Evolutionary psychology and neuroeconomics have significantly deepened our knowledge of the mechanisms through which people think—including making economic and moral decisions. But the reach of this approach is by nature almost certainly limited to the analysis of small group behavior. This virtually guarantees that the ability of neuroeconomics to explain human accomplishment will be rather limited. Great societies become great by transcending the small group nature of those who comprise them. It is well understood that they employ institutions to great effect to do this. Economists contributed to our understanding of how humans achieve the sublime by having discovered, and then having deepened, our understanding of market institutions. As a result, it should surprise no one that market behavior, market institutions, and the functioning of a market economy as a whole, often does not comport with our hardwired intuitions. The point of this book is that an important means by which humans transcend their small group nature is culture in the form of moral beliefs that support trustworthiness, and thereby lower transaction costs in obvious and not so obvious ways.

Similarly, the moral foundation is rare because harm-based moral restraint is what we are born with, and is therefore what resonates most strongly with our conscience. The word "conscience" as used here is meant not to convey a ghost in the machine as envisioned by Descartes, but perhaps one as more accurately conveyed by Gilbert Ryle (1949) and Arthur Koestler (1967).[5] That ghost is relatively primitive, but nevertheless important and efficient in the context in which it evolved. But it is not up to the task of creating a large group society. The moral foundation is up to the task, but it is based on abstract ideas that must be taught and learned. Again, while the ability to create, understand, and adopt abstract ideas is hardwired, the ideas themselves are not. So whereas harm-based moral restraint is present in all normally functioning people, the moral foundation—if it is present in anyone at all—is only present in those persons who have been exposed to abstract moral beliefs that comport with it.

Finally, this book may have important theoretical implications for our understanding of relational contracts. Considering the role that unconditional trustworthiness might play in being able to use relational contracts to fullest effect, so as to effectuate entrepreneurial rather than bureaucratic decision making, is a new way of thinking about the role that relational contracts play in market economies. This contrasts sharply with current practice, which is to presume that unconditional trustworthiness is unfathomable, so an important element of relational contracts is that they be self-enforcing. Consider this quote from Baker, Gibbons, and Murphy (2002, p. 40), a seminal paper in the relational contract literature:

> . . . relational contracts cannot be enforced by a third party and so must be self-enforcing: the value of the future relationship must be sufficiently large that neither party wishes to renege.

While it is certainly true that third-party enforcement will not suffice, it does not follow that the contracts must therefore be self-enforcing. Another possibility is that relational contracts might be viable even if they are not inherently self-enforcing *if* decision makers can be genuinely trusted with the discretion they possess. But because the convention is to presume that such genuine trust is meaningless, a potentially critical factor governing the ability to use relational contracts in the first place is being overlooked.

EMPIRICAL

Being a product of a thought experiment, there is no guarantee that moral beliefs that comport with the moral foundation have ever been adopted by any human. Whether the moral foundation comports with moral beliefs that people already have, and therefore possibly explains differences in economic performance, is ultimately an empirical question. Fortunately, the analysis undertaken here has many interesting empirical implications regarding the interpretation of past work, and poses several new and interesting empirical questions for future work.

Regarding the interpretation of past work, much existing experimental evidence likely overestimates the presence of unconditional trustworthiness. Economic experiments are by nature conducted in a small group context, so small group psychological mechanisms are in play. In small group contexts, interpersonal utility effects and harm-based moral restraint will be operative even if the other party is anonymous. For this reason, such experiments can find evidence of trust behavior even in societies in which unconditionally trustworthy people are rare, because even in low trust societies there is still plenty of trust behavior in small group contexts—family, friends, and loci of repeated dealings that Fukuyama calls "circles of trust."

This possibility comports with the fact that experimental evidence from existing trust games finds that there is significantly more trust behavior than rational maximization can explain. At one level, this is encouraging since it suggests that we are naturally inclined to be trustworthy and to extend trust, because we do so even when rational calculation suggests that such behavior might not be prudent. But such comfort must be tempered by the fact that these games likely measure only small group trust, which should be abundant across all societies. Such trust, while important, is insufficient for fully supporting the development and operation of a market economy.

In other ways, however, existing experimental evidence may underestimate the presence of unconditional trustworthiness and genuine, generalized trust. This is because subjects, who might actually be unconditionally trustworthy, might appear to behave in an untrustworthy manner because they are given instructions that unintentionally frame the scenario as merely a game in the colloquial sense of the word. So in the case of the classic trust game first pro-posed by Kreps (1990), and employed in many variations by others since, returning anything between all or none of the money "invested" by the trusting party is viewed as being within the rules of the game as stipulated by the inves-tigator.

Perhaps what we are really observing is behavior in a game of strategy under an invented condition of conflicting interest, such as when we play someone else in chess—not rational trust made possible by the belief that the other party is always trustworthy in the real world. So when the trusted player does not return a fair split of the money, he might be behaving immorally, but he also might sim-ply be behaving in a manner analogous to a baseball player who "steals" second base. Such a decision tells us nothing about the person's morality or trustworthi-ness in real-world contexts.

There is fMRI trust game experiment evidence that shows specific parts of the brain being activated that are associated with strategic calculation when it comes to extending trust.[6] This suggests that trust behavior is therefore "calculative" in nature. But it is mistaken to infer from such evidence that trustworthiness is just a strategic exercise in manipulating incentives. This is because calculative or stra-tegic extension of trust is not inconsistent with trustworthiness that is based on moral tastes and is therefore completely nonstrategic in nature.

For these reasons, I contend that while most existing trust experiments tell us much about the most common form of human trust behavior (small group trust), they don't tell us much about the kind of trust behavior that I have argued matters most for most fully supporting the development and operation of a market economy. The kind of trust that matters most is not necessarily the trust that we observe the most. Indeed, quite the opposite is likely true; otherwise, most people in the world would live in high trust, highly prosperous societies. As such, it should be clear from the discussion above that existing empirical work is for the most part inadequate for evaluating the empirical relevance of the moral foundation.

Regarding future empirical work, how might the empirical relevance of the moral foundation be investigated? The first step is to determine how much of observed trustworthy-like behavior is the product of moral restraint rather than prudential restraint. One possible approach would be to conduct experiments in which the subject can choose to act opportunistically, and this act is then reported to a new playing partner in the next round with a certain probability. This report of prior action captures the idea that there is a certain chance of detection. A guar-antee of no report to future playing partners is effectively a case of a golden op-portunity. Restraint not being a function of probability of detection for a given subject would be indicative of that individual possessing moral rather than merely prudential restraint.

But recall that one can believe that something is generally morally wrong (and therefore possess moral rather than prudential restraint) but still do it. This is because *why* one believes something is morally wrong also matters. The next step would therefore be to conduct experiments that start with a sample of subjects who have already been determined to possess moral restraint, and then investigate whether their moral restraint is a function of the number of individuals over which the cost of opportunism is divided. If it is not, this would be indicative of principled and not merely harm-based restraint. This would address the possible overestimation of unconditional trustworthiness that is a shortcoming of existing experimental designs that unintentionally frame moral decision making in small group terms.

But also recall that one can possess an ethic of principled moral restraint while still being susceptible to greater good rationalization. The final step would therefore be to conduct experiments that start with a sample of those who have already been determined to possess moral restraint, and then investigate whether their moral restraint is a function of the size of a benefit made possible to others by an act of opportunism. There are, no doubt, many other possible experimental designs that could address these issues, waiting to be devised by experimental economists who are interested in the study of trust or morality.

These approaches provide sharper measures of unconditional trustworthiness and, hence, tell us about the viability of large group trust. Obvious secondary questions are these: Is there a significant difference across societies in the ratio of people whose trustworthiness is large group in nature to those for whom it is small group in nature? Does this ratio correlate with the existence of highly trust-dependent institutions and institutional arrangements? Do societies with the highest proportion of individuals who possess moral beliefs that comport with the moral foundation have the highest levels of measured unconditional trustworthiness? Does this proportion correlate with overall economic development and performance?

To answer these questions, I believe that surveys could be devised to determine whether a subject treats the obedience of moral prohibitions as lexically primary to the obedience of moral exhortations. At a micro level, such data could be compared to trust-game performance. At a macro level, such survey data could be generated across different countries, regions, etc., and compared to aggregate measures of trust and trustworthiness, as well as aggregate measures of economic performance.

The use of fMRI techniques could also be instructive. For example, are negative moral actions contemplated in different regions of the brain than positive moral actions?[7] If an fMRI showed that areas of activity in the brain responded differently to scenarios depending on whether they involve negative moral actions or positive moral actions, this would suggest that we do, in fact, have different ways of thinking about positive and negative moral actions. If so, what are the correlate functions of these respective regions? If negative moral actions are associated with areas that are active with respect to qualitative reasoning, while positive actions are associated with quantitative reasoning that would be interesting indeed. Do differences in these respective regions correlate with survey data that provides measures of lexical primacy? Do differences in these respective regions correlate with IQ, age, sex, age, religion, or nationality? Do people who live in post-Kantian societies show a more dramatic difference in areas of activity? And so forth.

Finally, because genuine trust is a matter of expecting moral restraint even in the face of golden opportunities, a sharp test of the presence of genuine trust is particularly difficult. Obviously, by definition we cannot observe whether one behaves in a trustworthy way in the context of a truly golden opportunity. But it is still possible to shed empirical light on the issue, by inferring the existence of unconditional trustworthiness from the existence of institutions and/or institutional practices that could only exist if it were rational to expect that golden opportunities will not be acted on. The most obvious example would be the widespread use of relational contracts that generously delegate decision-making authority to those who possess local knowledge in very large, complex, and dynamic firms.

Final Speculative Remarks

Hardwired moral intuitions that produce small group ways of thinking about the world likely have a self-fulfilling prophecy quality to them. If nearly everyone possesses moral beliefs that are very consistent with our hardwired moral intuitions, then they will not refrain from opportunism in contexts in which doing so is necessary if a society is to maximize general prosperity. So the small group way of thinking about moral decision making inevitably becomes correct, because it cannot sustain efficient cooperation in large groups. In the small groups that are viable, small group moral intuitions are, of course, sufficient.

The abstract moral beliefs that comport with the moral foundation, therefore, must almost certainly be introduced exogenously and then passed from generation to generation through moral instruction. Because abstract moral beliefs cannot be hardwired, they can vary substantially across societies and indeed do, so they can potentially explain persistent differences in economic performance across societies. Ironically, the hunt for universality that has inspired so many experimental economists, neuroeconomists, cognitive scientists, and evolutionary psychologists, robs their models of being able to do just that.

None of this means that improving our understanding of hardwired psychological mechanisms that support pro-social behavior is not important. Of course it is. But our universal hardwired moral intuitions are not enough—the content of our learned moral beliefs also matters, and likely proves decisive. This suggests that scholars who take solace in the fact that we have hardwired traits that support pro-social behavior may be mistaken.[8] Robustness derived from hardwired moral intuitions is compelling in the small group settings in which such intuitions evolved, but this has nothing to do with moral behavior derived from abstract ideas instantiated by moral beliefs that must be taught and learned. Such moral beliefs are matters of culture, not genes, and as such they are comparatively fragile.

THE RISE AND FALL OF SOCIETIES

There is a fundamental dilemma associated with the development of any human society: the good life requires cooperating in large groups, but we are indisputably a small group species. How do we overcome this dilemma? Just as we use our ability to think abstractly to solve engineering problems with math, we can use our ability to think abstractly to combat opportunism in large group settings with the right kinds of ideas. In my view, the rise and fall of civilizations over the course of human history does not reflect human frailty nearly as much as it reflects the tremendous power of ideas.

I suspect that new civilizations often emerge when a new idea comes along that makes effective cooperation possible on larger scales than before, thereby increasing prosperity and conferring a military advantage over competing societies. Such ideas are not hardwired, so they are highly adaptable. But because they are not hardwired, they are also not terribly robust—certainly not as robust as genes.

New ideas that increase the size of groups over which effective cooperation is possible, but that also conflict with hardwired intuitions, may be easy to sustain while things are improving rapidly (such improvement may indeed be seen as evidence of efficacy), but once a new steady-state is reached, it will likely prove difficult to sustain because people in that society will have become accustomed to the new, higher standard of living that was produced over many generations and will take it for granted. If, after arriving at this new standard of living, the idea that made it possible begins to weaken or is overtaken by another idea that is not equally capable of sustaining cooperation in large groups, the abandonment of the existing idea will not likely result in the immediate destruction of the accumulated institutions that coevolved with it, so the low transaction cost environment that has come to also be taken for granted will not disappear in dramatic fashion.

Moreover, even if no new idea comes along to undermine large group cooperation, the deck may be inherently stacked against any society being able to enjoy general prosperity *ad infinitum*. At any given point in time, genuine net welfare gains may be achieved at the margin by involuntary redistributive acts. Any such act does not immediately erode incentives or dismantle institutions, and therefore does not destroy the low transaction cost environment that has been built up over time. Think of a brick house assembled brick by brick over many years. While building it, we see the virtue of not selling any given brick for a candy bar, because our initial condition was bad and it is now steadily improving. But many years after it is completed our descendants begin to take it for granted and don't see the harm in removing just one brick so it can be sold to pay for something else. At the margin, this might produce a net increase in welfare. But if the removal of bricks is spread out enough over time, our descendants will find that they have returned to living out in the cold and they will count themselves as unlucky for not having what their distant ancestors had—never realizing that this "death by thousand cuts" is what they and their more immediate ancestors unwittingly chose to do to themselves.

An important lesson of this book is, therefore, that if ideas matter as much as I have argued they do, then highly prosperous societies are powerful but that power does not equal robustness. Such societies are, in fact, rather fragile by nature. Societies that enjoy general prosperity, in one way or another, derive their success from abstract ideas that make it possible to cooperate efficiently in large groups. But these ideas can be replaced by new ideas that are often just reincarnations of old, small group ideas, because such ideas obviously come naturally to us. In doing so, we can unintentionally destroy the foundation upon which our good life is built. Ignorance of the foundations upon which prosperous societies are made possible is therefore dangerous, especially in light of the fact that our hardwired intuitions can be counted on to chip away at such ideas, much as gravity never stops pulling on a Boeing 747 flying overhead. Never forget how ridiculous it is that such a thing can fly in the first place, and that staying in the air amounts to a continuous war against nature.

If having a high trust society is crucial for the maximization of general prosperity, and if such a high trust society requires moral beliefs that comport with the moral foundation, then it follows that a set of moral beliefs that comport at least reasonably well with the moral foundation may have been instrumental to making general prosperity possible in the prosperous societies of the world today. I do not make that claim here—it is an ultimately empirical claim, whose investigation is beyond the scope of this book. But given the potential costs involved if it is true, the possible erosion of the moral foundation warrants concern.

Those of us who live in the West have taken our way of life for granted for a very long time. Our inability to imagine the costs associated with nearly everyone acting as an opportunist, whenever it is prudent for them to do so, may be producing a dangerous insouciance. There is already a great deal of compelling evidence that our high trust society is being eroded "brick by brick." Putnam (2000) has documented a decline in trust even in high trust societies like the United States. Uslaner (2002) has also documented a precipitous decline in trust across many societies. As discussed in Chapter 2, there is also evidence that cheating in schools is becoming epidemic in the United States. When even well-known scientists cannot be trusted to maintain the integrity of their most trust-dependent institution—the blind referee process—perhaps it is time to start paying attention.[9]

In any case, as trustworthiness falls because a willingness to behave opportunistically rises, this will induce us to increasingly use formal institutions to hold such opportunism in check. This will make our organizations more bureaucratic and therefore less entrepreneurial over time, but the process will likely proceed too slowly to be perceived by any given generation. Intermediate goals that can be easily verified will replace the standard of maximizing the ultimate goal, because of the increasing inability to delegate decision making via relational contracts. This will lead to what Herbert Simon referred to as satisficing behavior, which is more consistent with having a culture of bureaucratic mediocrity than one of excellence, where good enough is good enough.

Whether moral beliefs in the West comport or have ever comported with the moral foundation, there is anecdotal evidence that the reduction of trust is already reducing the entrepreneurial nature of societies in the West. A common complaint about modern corporations is that success within them is more a matter of political skill than performance. This is a hallmark of bureaucracy, not entrepreneurial firms. Eventually, and perhaps too late, we may discover that we just are simply no longer a very innovative society.

A METHODOLOGICAL LAMENT

I am disturbed by the unwillingness of many social scientists to accept the proposition that the content of moral beliefs matters. Moral beliefs are not merely ethereal ruminations beyond the purview of serious scientific inquiry. But among social scientists, and among economists particularly, there seems to be a Cartesian mind-body dualism at work that holds that moral beliefs are not scientific enough to be taken seriously. This is nonsense. The content of moral beliefs resides in specific neural pathways that are clearly physical in nature. These pathways produce specific patterns of emotional conviction over commonly held moral values, and specific ways of logically organizing these moral values to one another. This, in turn, produces consistent patterns of behavior. What is unscientific about that?

As for the power of abstract ideas to affect human behavior, just exactly how much proof does one need? Throughout human history people have endured imprisonment, torture, death, committed suicide, prosecuted war, committed murder, and allowed the slaughter of their own children because of their moral beliefs. How much more proof does any scientist need of the power of beliefs, especially moral beliefs, to produce unyielding constraints or uncompromising imperatives that are no less real because they are internalized? Why is it so hard for social scientists in general, and economists in particular, to accept this rather obvious fact of life?

PARTING IRONIES

We humans want to flourish, and we do not like seeing other humans suffer, so we want to live in societies that enjoy a condition of general prosperity. Maximizing general prosperity requires cooperating efficiently in large groups. But we are, at our core, a small group species. We are, therefore, maladapted to achieve what we really want.

Economists naturally think in terms of incentives, so they naturally frame the issue of trust in terms of incentives. But if morality is indeed fully explained as an exercise in enlightened self-interest, then the fullest realization of the market economies that economists endeavor to explain could not exist. This is because as any society closes in on being a high trust society, the gains to opportunistic behavior skyrocket if opportunism is only combated by prudential restraint. This means that many of the institutions we take for granted in highly developed market economies could not exist if morality is nothing more than what most economists view it to be.

Another irony is what might be called the consequentialist paradox. In Chapter 8 I argued that it was mistaken to view the moral foundation as unsupportive of positive moral action, because societies that abide by the moral foundation will have the most resources to put toward positive moral actions. How much positive moral action has the government of Angola effectuated over the last 25 years? To point out that this is not a fair observation because Angola is poor is, of course, to miss the point entirely.

Yet another irony is that it is from the smallest unit of social analysis (the brains of individuals) that the greatest level of general prosperity is realized in the context of the largest unit of social analysis (society as a whole). It would be coy to fail to acknowledge that prevailing moral beliefs in the West appear to comport more closely to the moral foundation than prevailing moral beliefs elsewhere. It is also the case that the rise of the ethic of individualism began in the West, and continues to be strongest in the West. Perhaps this was and is more than a coincidence.

But the greatest and most surprising irony of all is this: *moral beliefs that stress the doing of good make it hard for us to trust each other*. This is truer the more earnest we are about doing good and the larger the group in consideration.

A FINAL, TROUBLING SPECULATION

If it is indeed true that the development and operation of a market economy is best supported by moral beliefs that comport with the moral foundation, then it would follow that societies that wish to become (or stay) prosperous would do well to undertake efforts to insure that moral beliefs that comport with the moral foundation are inculcated into children as early and as consistently as possible. Yet in most countries in the West today, nothing could be farther from the truth.

No one knows how close prevailing moral beliefs in the West are to adequately comporting with the moral foundation. But closer is almost certainly better than farther. Overwhelming evidence of increasing levels of cheating and falling levels of trust should be viewed as possibly indicative of prevailing moral beliefs drifting farther away from the moral foundation, and should therefore be viewed with alarm.

The rise of cheating and the decline of trust should not surprise anyone familiar with character and morals education curricula now present in most K–12 schools in the West. Such curricula indulge our hardwired moral intuitions by encouraging consequentialist moral restraint and sometimes coupling it with duty-based moral advocacy. So in an effort to strengthen moral behavior, we may be systematically promoting modes of moral reasoning that sharply undermine the moral foundation. The result could very well be fewer resources with which to undertake positive moral action and a greater ability to rationalize bad behavior, perhaps even horror, in the future.

NOTES

Chapter 1

1. For an excellent discussion of the wide range of benefits—moral and otherwise—of supporting a condition of general prosperity and rapid economic growth, see Benjamin M. Friedman's *The Moral Consequences of Economic Growth* (2005).

2. Note that this is in stark contrast to the modern "do the right thing" approach to moral instruction. The "do the right thing" approach to moral instruction is predicated on the notion that what is most needed to improve society is to exhort people to be more moral. But this means that if economic performance is affected by morality, then the "do the right thing" approach to morality implies that low economic performance is due to people in such societies not being sufficiently moral.

3. This contrasts with the natural approach to the study of morality, which is to view it as largely a matter of moral earnestness. Consider, for example, Daniel Friedman's excellent book *Morals and Markets* (2008). He views the problems with Russia's kleptocracy and Japan's asset market bubbles as illustrations of the problem of being at the extremes of too little morality and too much morality. As a historical matter, this may be all there is to understanding those examples. But this book explains why, if the goal is maximizing general prosperity, an issue that is far more important than having the right level of morality is having the right kind of morality—specifically the right kind of moral beliefs.

4. This does not mean that moral values play no role at all in supporting the development and operation of a market economy. For a fascinating discussion of how the rise of moral values associated with the bourgeoisie likely supported the rise of capitalism, see Deirdre McCloskey's *The Bourgeois Virtues* (2006).

5. See Stephen Covey's *The Speed of Trust* (2008) and Ann Bernasek's *The Economics of Integrity* (2010) for many examples of how genuine trust maximizes the set of viable transactions and the ease with which they are undertaken.

6. The approach taken in this book is therefore consistent with Timur Kuran's (2009a, 2009b) argument that since it is obvious that both culture and institutions play crucial roles in supporting improved economic performance, the real challenge for understanding the rise of civilization is investigating the nature of the complementarities involved (including but not limited to how culture supports institutions and vice versa). In this book I explain precisely how culture in the form of moral beliefs makes possible a specific form of trust that, in turn, makes possible important institutions and institutional arrangements.

7. The extensive managerial trust literature, which focuses on the role that trust plays within firms, takes the TCE critique quite seriously. Much of this literature is reviewed in the *Handbook of Trust Research*, edited by Reinhard Bachmann and Akbar Zaheer (Edward Elgar: Northampton, MA, 2006).

8. Third-degree opportunism is defined and discussed more fully in Chapter 2.

9. Although the exercise I undertake in this book applies to any kind of economic activity, I focus on transactions that occur within firms because firms are so central to the functioning of market economies. If one is asked to visualize "capitalism" or "a free market economy" one of the first images that pops in one's mind is that of a large firm. This is for good reason—firms are indeed the "engines of growth" (Baumol 2002). Development history is therefore largely the study of the rise of firms of greater size and complexity, as well as the rise of institutions that made their evolution possible.

10. See Williamson (1993) and Guinanne (2005).

11. Paul Seabright (2004) provides an excellent natural history account of how humans effectuated ever greater gains from specialization by devising formal and informal institutions that complemented their existing psychological dispositions to facilitate cooperation in ever larger groups.

12. Lee and Persson (2011) also present a model that casts doubt on the idea that generalized (large group) trust is just an extension of the radius of personalized (small group) trust.

13. See especially Marc Hauser's *Moral Minds* (2006) and Michael Shermer's *The Mind of the Market* (2008).

14. This restatement of Kant was taken from Herbert Gintis' review of *Natural Ethical Facts* by William D. Casebeer (2003).

15. Robin Dunbar (1992, 1993) has become famous for what is now known as "Dunbar's number," which is the claim that human brains well support groups of no larger than about 150 individuals. Dunbar's number was popularized by Gladwell (2000).

16. See, for example, Rawls (1971), Scheff (1990), Williams (1993), Margalit (1996), Elster (1999), and Davis (2000). For an excellent review, see Zimmerling (2003).

17. For an excellent review, see: Guiso, Sapienza, and Zingales, "Does Culture Affect Economic Outcomes?" *Journal of Economic Perspectives*, 20(2), Spring 2006, 23–48. They note that (pp. 26) "Classical economists were comfortable in using cultural explanations for economic phenomena". They point out that more recently "Iannaccone (1988) and Coleman (1990) begin to interpret religious and social norms as the result of a group-level optimization. This approach spawned a large literature that treats many aspects of culture as endogenous. . . . In this intellectually coherent body of work, it was very difficult to find any space for an independent role of culture." Note that the word *independent* is synonymous with the word *exogenous* in this context. They continue (p. 27): "In the decades immediately after World War II, the work of Gramsci and Polanyi was enormously influential in political science and sociology (see the excellent survey by DiMaggio, 1994), but fell on deaf ears among economists. . . . Not only did economics lose interest in its relation with culture, but as economics became more self-confident in its own capabilities, it often sought to explain culture as a mere outcome of economic forces." The authors pointed out the irony in that this movement was strongest among those in the Chicago School, and yet it exemplified the same hostility to cultural explanations as Marx.

18. According to David Landes (2000, p. 2):

> Yet culture, in the sense of the inner values and attitudes that guide a population, frightens scholars. It has a sulfuric odor of race and inheritance, an air of immutability. . . . Besides, criticisms of culture cut close to the ego and injure identity and self-esteem. Coming from outsiders, such animadversions, however tactful and indirect, stink of condescension.

> An increasing number of social scientists and even economists have begun looking seriously at culture. For a recent review see Guiso, Sapienza, and Zingales (2006). There is also a rapidly growing body of literature devoted to the study of social capital and trust, which strongly suggests a greater willingness to take culture seriously.

19. Indeed, perhaps one reason for the intense interest in the concept of social capital is that it deals with issues that have historically fallen under the heading of culture but in

a way that appears less idiosyncratic and therefore less likely to offend. Dasgupta (2003) has pointed out that it is difficult to talk about social capital without talking about culture.

20. Fred Hirsch (1976) famously argued that capitalism erodes the very moral foundation upon which it is based, so it is inherently unstable (Hirshmann 1982).

21. The arguments developed in this book will explain why entreaties for people to be more willing to trust each other (e.g., Eric Uslaner's *The Moral Foundations of Trust*, 2002) or to care more about each other (e.g., J.D. Trout's *The Empathy Gap*, 2009) cannot solve the problem of opportunism where doing so matters most. We will also find that our hardwired mechanisms, which appear to have so much promise for providing a universal theory of morality and/or trust, are almost certainly destined to fail.

Chapter 2

1. Smith observed that a talented pin maker could make upwards of twenty pins per day working by himself. However, a pin-making firm that employed ten workers who effectuated gains from specialization through the division of labor could make "upwards of forty-eight thousand pins a day." This implies an increase in productivity of nearly 24,000% per worker! Moreover, one would expect even greater gains with respect to more complicated forms of production.

2. Cosmides and Tooby (1992) have argued that humans have evolved "mental modules" that make them especially adept at detecting cheating and free-riding. This suggests that opportunism has been a fundamentally important problem over much of the course of human evolution.

3. This argument comports with the work of Parente and Prescott (2002), who make a similar argument about technology. Less developed countries need not develop their own new technologies—they can simply buy it. The puzzle, therefore, is not why they can't develop it, but why they won't buy it.

4. Hernando de Soto (1989, 2000) has made much of the need for proper recording of property and so forth to unleash capital in LDCs. But the problem isn't the lack of institutional mechanisms that formalize property ownership. The problem is that in such societies, ownership means nothing, and pieces of paper don't change that. If a government possesses the ability and inclination to seize property or debase it through arbitrary and capricious taxation, what value is a piece of paper entitling one to be the victim of such activities?

5. Margaret Levi (1999, p. 6) expresses this idea thusly:

   As Williamson reminds us, the premise of transaction costs analysis (indeed of all economic analysis) is opportunistic behavior. This means the baseline behavior is distrust, not trust. Modeling distrust will help reveal how much of a problem it is and when the creation of trust is the remedy.

6. Note that this has nothing to do with trusting *A*'s judgment or competence. Here we are only concerned with the moral dimension of trust.

7. Some readers might be offended by such a consequentialist approach to moral behavior (recall that consequentialist theories of morality hold that moral propriety is based on the ultimate outcome of moral action). Please hold your fire. Later, I will explicitly account for the possibility that moral behavior might be principled in nature, and this will turn out to be very important indeed.

8. If the only sanction is making the victim whole, then as long as the opportunist is undetected some of the time, it pays to continue to engage in a high level of opportunistic exploitation.

9. Indeed, for most people even the contemplation of such acts makes them feel guilty and therefore is psychically costly. This will turn out to be important in Chapter 5.

10. Why not account for the cost of feeling guilty as a constraint? Guilt is not a finite, scarce resource, and as such is not analogous to a consumer's budget; there is no endowment of guilt to be drawn upon. In a fuller model that considers non-golden opportunities, the cost of retaliation enters the model as a constraint.

11. Robert Frank (2008, p. 48, in Paul Zak's *Moral Markets*) offers an example of how guilt costs can be converted into monetary equivalent measures.

12. How opportunistic people are observed to be is not the same thing as how opportunistic they would be, in the absence of external mechanisms to discourage such behavior. That the widespread looting in the aftermath of hurricane Katrina took so many by surprise is evidence of this point. Toshio Yamagishi's work on Japanese trustworthiness also seems to bear this out. Institutional safeguards that work well with respect to well-defined and routine activities can create the impression that people are less opportunistic than they really are. Exceptional events, like a hurricane, dispel the myth.

13. One might object that a 20-fold increase is unrealistic. A quick comparison of the per capita GDP of high trust societies to low trust societies will show that this is far from unrealistic (see, for example, Knack and Keefer, 1997; Knack and Zak, 2001).

14. Frank (1988, p. 19) puts it thusly: "They [Opportunists] reason, with seemingly impeccable logic, that their own behavior will not much affect what others do. Because the state of the world is thus largely independent of how they themselves behave, they conclude that it is best to take what they can and assume others will do likewise. As more and more people adopt this perspective, it becomes increasingly difficult for even basically honest persons not to do so."

15. See the Appendix at the end of this chapter for a brief presentation of the commons dilemma game in matrix form, and a discussion of how it applies to opportunistic behavior.

16. This suggests that the fundamental problem is that we don't care enough about each other. If we cared more about each other, things would improve because we would feel guiltier about those we harm through our opportunistic behavior. In Chapter 6 we will see why caring more about each other is not enough to overcome the commons dilemma associated with opportunistic behavior where doing so matters most.

17. In a society in which there is no concept of property whatsoever, and so taking some of what B just made without permission is deemed as okay, a trust is not violated; therefore, this would not be an example of opportunism. In many animal populations this occurs, and because we suspect that no trust is violated, we normally don't think of such appropriative behavior as opportunism or in any way treacherous; we just think of it as animals acting as they do.

18. Note that Ronald Coase (2006) and others have expressed doubts about the relevance of the examples used in that paper, and therefore have called into question the general principle being illustrated.

19. This is precisely what we see in many countries that are, or were only recently, less developed (e.g., China), where gift giving is an important part of relationship building, which comes before formal dealing. See Matt Ridley (1996) for an interesting discussion of gift giving for this and other reasons.

20. The concept of relational contracts is normally traced back to Macaulay (1963) and Macneil (1978). According to Baker, Gibbons, and Murphy (2002, p. 40):

    Relational contracts within and between firms [therefore] help circumvent difficulties in formal contracting . . . A relational contract thus allows the parties to utilize their detailed knowledge of their specific situation and to adapt to new information as it becomes available.

21. Note that Williamson (1975) did not actually use the locution "relational contract," because it was introduced by McNeil (1978) three years later. Williamson (1985) later expanded his treatment of relational contracts to consider transaction relations outside of firms.

22. While it is natural to think of third-degree opportunism and relational contracts in the context of firms, relational contracts—and therefore the problem of third-degree opportunism—exist more widely. Baker, Gibbons and Murphy (2002, pp. 39–40) note that:

Business dealings are also riddled with relational contracts. Supply chains often involve long-run, hand-in-glove supplier relationships through which the parties reach accommodations when unforeseen or uncontracted events occur.

23. In addition, to the extent that some kinds of production are more susceptible to opportunism than others, the existence of widespread opportunism introduces an inefficiency through another distortion: resources will flow from production that is highly susceptible to opportunism to those less susceptible, even if there is a comparative advantage to production of the first type.

24. This closely follows the presentation provided by Izquierdo, Gotts, and Polhill (2004).

Chapter 3

1. *Nature*, May 18, 2006.

2. Hayek (1976, 1979) had much to say about the implications of the distinction between small and large groups for the emergence of a market society and freedom. I will discuss Hayek in much greater detail later.

3. In Dunbar's (1993) own words:

   . . . there is a cognitive limit to the number of individuals with whom any one person can maintain stable relationships, that this limit is a direct function of relative neocortex size, and that this in turn limits group size.

4. Throughputs are inputs to a production process other than labor or capital. When baking cakes, for example, labor (the baker) uses capital (mixers, bowls, an oven) to transform throughputs (ingredients) into the final product—the cake.

5. This is from Book I, Chapter I of *The Wealth of Nations*. I am indebted to Donald Boudreaux for pointing out that Smith had made this argument, and for the quote.

6. This does not mean that a very small country cannot have a market society. Small countries, such as those in central Europe, overcome this problem by belonging to a larger market society. If the smaller countries of central Europe were completely isolated from all other countries, they would not be successful market societies.

7. This is also known as the 1/nth problem, first raised by Kandel and Lazear (1992). Adams (2002) raises a possible objection to this problem, arguing that if individuals are complements, the resulting increasing-returns effect could solve the free-riding problem. Costa (2005), however, conducted experiments that demonstrated that whether individuals functioned as substitutes or complements, an increase in n increased free-riding and, incredibly, this result was stronger when individuals are complements.

8. Recall that the Folk Theorem essentially tells us that there is always a way to preserve cooperation, if the difference in payoffs between the cooperative and uncooperative outcomes is sufficiently large, and/or the number of future periods is infinite or the terminus not well defined, and/or the individuals involved have a sufficiently low discount rate.

9. I am making an implicit assumption to the effect that the variance in total output due to random factors does not fall with increasing n. If these random factors are independent, it is easy to show that variance actually rises with n. Obviously, if the variance of the random component of output fell as fast, or even faster, than the relative size of the reduction to output from opportunistic action, then any individual would remain as obvious as if n were small. Variance would have to fall with n for my argument to fail, but this would require a strong negative correlation. I am not claiming that variance rises with n, I am only implicitly assuming that it does not fall.

10. This is why if a dozen *free* market economists found themselves shipwrecked, they would, without hypocrisy or contradiction, immediately engage in central planning.

11. This can be relatively gentle, such as choosing a less risky investment project over the one that the decision maker believes is the best one from the principal's point of view.

12. *Institutions*, broadly construed, includes those elements of social capital that combat opportunism. There is no bright line between institutions and social capital. For example, Avner Grief's (1993) pioneering work on the role of the ghenzi in providing a basis for trade among Maghribi traders is normally viewed as a contribution to our understanding of how institutions emerge to solve problems of opportunism even in the absence of government force, but social capital theorists could just as easily claim this to be an excellent example of an effective social network.

13. This interpretation comports with North and Thomas' (1973) *The Rise of the Western World.*

14. An important feature of the modern theory of institutions is that in addition to addressing the problem of opportunism, institutions address the problem of bounded rationality. But the assumption of bounded rationality does not mean people are irrational; it only means that there are constraints on their ability to make the most rational choices as judged by an external evaluator who possesses perfect information and unlimited cognitive abilities.

15. Obviously, one can say this of social capital as well, if by social capital one means social networks that exist to produce incentives for providing assurance one will not be cheated, thereby reducing the risk of transaction behavior. In what follows, social capital that works through incentives derived from the environment will be subsumed into the word *institutions.*

16. Robert Frank (1988) was the first to stress the difference between prudential versus moral restraint. This distinction was central to his commitment model of trust and it plays an important role in what follows.

17. Although some who study social capital envision moral imperatives for trustworthiness (Uslaner 2002), the theory of social capital need only assume a rational response to incentives (Coleman 1990; Hardin 2002; Levi 1998). Therefore neither institutional theory nor social capital theory requires morality.

18. Note that sharpening the performance measure only substitutes one problem for another— what we want, ideally, are decisions to be made in a way that always comports with maximizing profit for the firm as a whole, not decisions that maximize some instrumental variable that provides a sharper measure of performance, so as to avoid confounding factors that increase risk exposure.

19. Having an entrepreneur at the top is better than not having one, but how entrepreneurial a firm is, is also dramatically affected by entrepreneurial decision making throughout the firm. The truer it is that decision makers throughout the firm possess the discretion required to act on local knowledge so as to pursue the owner's interests, the more entrepreneurial each and every decision is and, hence, the more entrepreneurial the firm is.

20. Frederique Six (2005, p. 1) characterizes the close connection between trust and relational contracts nicely: "Trust . . . encourages information sharing, enriches relationships, increases openness and mutual acceptance and enhances conflict resolution and integrative problem solving. The presence of trust, it has been argued, reduces the need for detailed contractual and monitoring devices and is thus important in governance. And taking it one step further, in complex environments, detailed contracting and monitoring are often undesirable since they may constrain the scope and motivation for quality and for innovation based on individual variety and initiative."

Chapter 4

1. In short, I am endeavoring to be consistent with the "naturalistic" approach to social science. For examples of this approach, see the work of Robert Frank, Ernst Fehr, and Herbert Gintis. For a general discussion of this approach, see Binmore (2005).

2. Note that Deepak Lal (1998) and others have distinguished between cultures of guilt and cultures of shame. Guilt differs from shame, because whereas shame is derived from feelings of embarrassment and humiliation that result from being discovered, feelings of guilt will be experienced even if there is no chance of discovery.

3. One could argue that an important moral value for the realization of prosperity is the belief that it is good for one to maximize material possessions. Those who are hostile to market economics appear to believe that this is a value of central importance to a capitalist system, and therefore capitalism engenders the inculcation of this value. I do not believe that a desire for material goods or status requires the cultivation of any particular moral values, because for rather obvious reasons, our hardwiring is sufficient to produce a preoccupation with such objectives.

4. Henceforth, we will dispense with the modifiers "social" and "moral" and stipulate that references to "the value system" mean "the social moral value system" as defined above.

5. Lawrence Kohlberg (1981) has documented that the rationale given for moral judgments also varies substantially with age.

6. Those familiar with Adam Smith's *The Theory of Moral Sentiments* (1759) will recognize that the dichotomy proposed here is very similar to Smith's distinction between justice and beneficence.

7. According to Hayek (1985):

   We need . . . an evolutionary theory of morals . . . and [its] essential feature will be that morals are not a creation of reason, but a second tradition independent from the tradition of reason, which helps us adapt to problems which exceed by far the limits of our capacity for rational perception. [This quote appeared in a speech given at Oesterreichisches College, Wien, 1985. This quote was taken from Zak (2008)].

8. An excellent review of Smith's *The Theory of Moral Sentiments* can be found in Otteson (2002). Smith's central argument is that it is a part of our basic human nature to desire that our beliefs be in harmony with those around us; that we seek sympathy of moral sentiments (sympathy, as Smith uses the term, is more closely related to the idea of harmony than empathy or feeling sorry for someone else). As a result, when our actions induce disapprobation, we are inclined to adjust our behavior, and even our beliefs, because, apparently, our behavior and/or beliefs are not in harmony with those around us. Conversely, when our actions induce approbation, we become even more confident that our behavior in a given circumstance and our beliefs are appropriate.

9. A moral value that calls for an action that reduces the welfare of those around the actor is unlikely to evolve into a *social* moral value. Consider the practice of "ratting out" others, which has never been regarded as much of a virtue, even though in principle it should be. I suspect that "ratting out" others has never become a virtue because if A frequently "rats out" those around him, it is likely that he is doing so as an exercise in opportunism. This means that he is likely an opportunist, so even if we don't fear being "ratted out" because we follow all the rules, he might make us a victim of some other form of opportunism.

10. I thank Oliver Williamson for pointing out that if this distinction is merely a matter of positive or negative language, it will prove to be trite. This distinction, to be meaningful, must therefore be rooted in the effect on the welfare of others.

11. Not providing help in such a circumstance normally reveals a desire to see the struggling person harmed. Persons with such preferences frighten us for good reason. This is consistent with the fact that while we generally expect someone to extend a pole from the edge of a pool to save a drowning man, we don't expect someone to jump into a river to do so, especially if he/she is not a good swimmer. It is also consistent with feeling acrimony toward those who can share something with us at zero cost, but refuse to do so, even though doing so would appear to be a dominant strategy unless pleasure was taken in seeing us harmed. This is how "not sharing" can produce hostility. In Chapter 7 we will see how this can facilitate the rationalization of opportunism.

12. What follows is worked out more fully in Rose (2002).

13. One could object that the distinction between cooperative and exchange type transactions is a distinction without a difference. It is true that many cooperative transactions can be reinterpreted as exchanges, but the concepts of cooperation and exchange are not equivalent. Why this is true cannot be adequately discussed here, but the arguments that follow are not affected by the outcome of that argument.

14. It does not follow that if there is a market failure to be rectified, then moral exhortations will be an efficient means of solving such problems. There are well-known mechanisms of collective action that will likely provide a more efficient solution.

15. Thinking of ethics in terms of constraints is also central to James Buchanan's framework. Buchanan (1994, p. 63) states:

> We may start from the premise that individual behavior is morally-ethically constrained. We do not behave opportunistically in each and every encounter; we do not act in accordance with some "as-if" cost-benefit reckoning, as might be made against the formal legal structure of rewards and penalties. Many of us do not steal, even if we should be certain that there is no possibility of discovery, apprehension, and punishment.

16. The exception, discussed earlier regarding positive moral actions for which failure to act is equivalent to disobeying a moral prohibition, is an exception that proves the rule, because such exceptions were based on the fact that there was no cost for undertaking the positive moral act. So it follows that the universal quality derived from zero cost is retained, even for negative moral actions that began as positive moral actions.

Chapter 5

1. Gneezy (2005) presented experimental evidence suggesting that, contrary to traditional economic theory, people consider the harm their actions may impose on others. The basic idea is that people are averse to experiencing feelings of guilt (see also Charness and Dufwenberg, 2006).

2. Frans de Waal, who has studied chimpanzee behavior and found ample evidence of empathy among chimpanzees, makes a similar argument about the importance of moral sentiments among humans. According to de Waal (1996, p. 87):

> Despite Immanuel Kant's opinion that kindness out of duty has greater moral worth than kindness out of temperament, if push comes to shove, sentiments win out. This is what the parable of the Good Samaritan is all about.

3. What follows can be regarded as a fleshing-out of the "harm principle" put forth by John Stuart Mill (1859) as a basis for limiting the ability of government to intervene in private affairs. This principle was later immortalized in Oliver Wendell Holmes' famous quote "The right to swing my fist ends where the other man's nose begins."

4. As Frank (1988, p. 153) puts it:

> . . . while specific moral norms are enormously varied and complex, they are supported by a limited number of highly uniform emotional capacities. . . . The desire to avoid unpleasant affective states, in Kagan's scheme, is the principal motivating force behind moral behavior. People will try to avoid actions, motives, and qualities that make them feel afraid, sorry for those less privileged, anxious, bored, fatigued, or confused. The specific actions or circumstances that trigger these emotions will depend heavily on cultural context. But the motivating emotions are always and everywhere the same.

His reference to Kagan is Jerome Kagan (1984).

5. Adam Smith (1982 [1759], p. 9) put it well:

> As we have no immediate experience of what other men feel, we can form no idea of the manner in which they are affected, but by conceiving what we ourselves would feel in a like situation.

6. This was taken from an interview conducted by Peter Tyson (2005) for NOVA Science NOW.

7. The idea of sympathy is closely related to an idea of keen interest to social scientists ever since the publication of Trivers (1971) and Axelrod (1984)—the idea of reciprocal altruism. Biologists sometimes explain altruism through kin selection, as governed by Hamilton's theory of relatedness, which shows that it pays to protect those who are related to us.

8. See "Emotions as Guarantors" by Jack Hirshleifer (1987), *Passions Within Reasons*, by Robert Frank (1988), and "If Homo Economicus Could Choose his Utility Function, Would He Want One With a Conscience?" also by Robert Frank (1987). Behavioral economists have adopted most of these ideas. The central model in *Passions Within Reason* is the commitment model, which Frank contrasts with the self-interest model.

9. According to Fessler and Haley (2003, p. 16):

   Although guilt can be elicited by a variety of events (including simple norm violations), the central elicitor is the infliction of harm on another, whether intentional or unintentional (Hoffman 1982; Keltner and Buswell 1996).

10. For an example of an exception, see Gneezy (2005). He found evidence that ". . . people not only care about their own gain from lying; they also are sensitive to the harm that lying may cause the other side. The average person prefers not to lie, when doing so only increases her payoff a little but reduces the other's payoff a great deal." (p. 385)

11. As but one example of a very good book written on empathy alone, see Frans de Waal's *Good Natured*, 1996.

12. According to Frank (1988, p. 128) even Charles Darwin

   . . . sketched a preliminary account of how conscience and other moral sentiments might have sprung from a general sense of sympathy. He argued that sympathy, in turn, was useful because it made a person better able to function in groups.

13. According to Frans de Waal (1996, p. 89):

   For primates, as for humans, to most effectively help others, one needs to understand their needs and feelings. To gauge the depth of animal empathy and social intelligence, studies focus on response to distress, self-awareness, the transmission of information, and the manipulation of relationships.

14. Intentionality is a concept from cognitive psychology that is gaining currency with social scientists generally. For example, see Douglass North's *Understanding the Process of Change* (2005).

15. Many animals appear to care about others of their species, especially their offspring. Cats appear to be able to empathize with their owners but are not very sympathetic, while dogs appear to be empathetic and sympathetic.

16. The assertion that $\theta_0 > 0$ is consistent with Gordon Tullock's oft-quoted quip that nearly everyone has a nickel's worth of concern for his fellow man. This quip was made, presumably, to emphasize that minor acts of kindness are easily explained in terms of their low cost.

17. Note that I am not arguing that every single individual has $\theta_0 > 0$. I am only pointing out the obvious—most of us take a small amount of pleasure in the well-being of our fellow man, even strangers; this made good evolutionary sense, because it helps keep us out of trouble.

18. The subscript of B reflects the fact that not everyone would have the same guilt response with respect to a given act, taken at the expense of given person, in a given circumstance.

Chapter 6

1. In the next chapter I will explain why misguided attempts to solve the empathy problem in these two ways also worsens another problem—that of greater good rationalization.

2. One could argue that as a philosophical matter, it is the *total* harm that makes the difference. I do not contend that such an argument is wrongheaded, but I believe that we are not likely to be hardwired to think of harm in this way. With the exception of a rare philosopher, such a conclusion would have to be derived from an abstract moral belief that one is taught.

3. That this might be a conjecture of fundamental importance is evidenced by the fact that the distinction between consequentialist and nonconsequentialist theories of morality is of fundamental importance in modern moral philosophy. We will explore this point more fully in the next two chapters.

4. Although I didn't know it at the time I developed the model below, some of the basic ideas involved had already been addressed long ago in a fascinating paper by James Buchanan (Buchanan 1965).

5. Mathematically, as $n \to \infty$, $\Delta U_i(x, n) \to 0$ and therefore $g(x)\theta_i E[\Delta U_i(x, n)] \to 0$.

6. Now it may be true that if everyone did x_1 all the time, it would produce measurable harm, but you are not proposing that. Your doing x_1 in this instance does not constitute everyone doing x_1 all the time, or even everyone always doing x_1 in this instance.

7. Hunt (2007) argues in *Inventing Human Rights: A History* that novels had a dramatic effect on human rights. Her argument illustrates the power of empathy. By reading stories of harm done to others, we identify with them and are compelled to feel as though the event directly involved us. The more engaging is the story and the more realistic are the characters, the more strongly our sense of empathy is aroused. Echoing this sentiment, Richard Rorty (1989) explained in *Contingency, Irony, and Solidarity* that "books. . .helps us become less cruel."

8. One might object that the exponent of 2 is unrealistically high, but that is mistaken. The increase in output actually compares well with Adam Smith's example of the pin factory (recall that in his example, productivity per worker increased by nearly 24,000%). Such an increase in productivity would require an exponent larger than 4. If Adam Smith was right about the importance of organizing economic activity in large groups, it pays handsomely to address anything that limits the size of groups within which production occurs.

9. If, instead, I believe that people who earn or have lots of money do so because they either work very hard and/or have made large investments in their own human capital, then stealing from them is not taking something that just as easily could have been mine to begin with; it amounts to stealing the most precious thing any human has—his time.

10. It is not surprising that we might have this reaction. Through most of our evolutionary history, an unwillingness on the part of A to promote B's welfare, when doing so costs A nothing, was likely interpreted by B as a signal of hostility. Given the potential unforeseen benefits of reciprocity, B knows that A's dominant strategy is to always promote B's welfare in such cases.

11. Another contributing factor to there being a weak response to counterfactual losses is that we generally don't know with certainty what the alternative gains would be, so we must estimate them. Since that estimate is a subjective one made by the person who possesses the relevant local knowledge, it is easy to see how someone can convince himself that while the *potential* counterfactual cost is high, the *expected* counterfactual cost is less so, because we don't know for certain.

12. Ken Binmore (2005) has rightly stressed the inadequacies of moral theories based on what he calls "philosophical skyhooks," which are nothing more than bald assertions without scientific basis. He advocates a naturalistic approach, which requires analyzing moral behavior vis-à-vis the psychological mechanisms humans actually have, not those that moral philosophers tell us we should have.

13. In more detailed terms as used in the Appendix, suppose that n is so large that harm-based moral restraint is zero, producing a "tragedy of the commons" type of outcome. If we add sufficiently strong principled moral restraint, then the dilemma is eliminated completely for any n, no matter how large. This is because with sufficiently strong principled moral restraint, g^p is pushed so high that the net payoff for *DEFECT* will be too low for *DEFECT* to be a dominant strategy (indeed, *DEFECT* can even become negative regardless of n). This means it is never rational to choose *DEFECT*, regardless of what anyone else does and regardless of n, so the commons dilemma simply disappears because a necessary condition for the commons dilemma to exist is that *COOPERATE* < *DEFECT*.

14. See Barro and McCleary (2002, 2003) for a discussion of how belief in heaven and hell can affect economic growth. See McCleary and Barro (2006) for a recent and broad review of this growing literature.

15. Religious beliefs in primitive, small group societies are largely preoccupied with explaining the physical world and with currying favor with the gods for better treatment. Comparatively speaking, the religions of modern large group societies are very preoccupied with matters of right and wrong.

16. This closely follows the presentation provided by Izquierdo, Gotts, and Polhill (2004).

Chapter 7

1. An example of such "black and white" thinking as it relates to morality is honor codes such as exist at the U.S. military academies, where the remedy is expulsion, while there is no such thing as a violation for failing to help anyone for anything. I thank James Buchanan for pointing this out.

2. Note that the word *unconditional* has two senses. It means that trustworthiness has nothing to do with how circumstances affect the likelihood of detection or the punishment if detected. In addition, it means that trustworthiness has nothing to do with how circumstances affect who is harmed or benefited, or by how much. So it is also unaffected by group size *or* the social distance between affected parties. It most certainly does not mean that there are never any exceptions. In Chapter 8 we will see that duty-based moral restraint provides a straightforward basis for identifying genuine exceptions.

3. According to a poll conducted by *Common Sense Media*, cheating is up dramatically but

   What's surprising, however, is not just the alarming number of students who say they cheat, but also the number of students who think it's OK to do so. . . . Only about half of students polled admit that cell phone use during tests is a serious cheating offense, and just 16 percent say calling or texting friends to warn them of a pop quiz is cheating; instead, they believe they're simply helping a friend. [eSCHOOL NEWS, 18 June 2009]

4. The idea that people limit their most vulnerable interactions to "circles of trust" is discussed in Frank Fukuyama's (1995) book *Trust*.

5. Guiso, Sapienza, and Zingales (2006, p. 35) put it thusly: "When contracts are incomplete, many deals are made just by shaking hands, which means relying on trust. An entrepreneur who works in an unstructured environment is more exposed to these types of deals. Hence, trustworthy individuals will have a comparative advantage in becoming entrepreneurs."

6. A more rigorous definition of lexicographic preferences is offered by Mas-Colell, Whinston, and Green (1995, p. 46):

   Define $x \geq y$ if either "$x_1 > y_1$" or "$x_1 = y_1$ and $x_2 > y_2$." This is known as the *lexicographic preference relation*. The name derives from the way a dictionary is organized; that is, commodity 1 has the highest priority in determining the preference ordering, just as the first letter of a word does in the ordering of a dictionary. When the level of the first commodity in the two commodity bundles is the same, the amount of the second commodity in the two bundles determines the consumer's preferences.

7. There are, of course, exceptions. We will discuss exceptions later in Chapter 8.

8. Michael Shermer (2008), in the chapter of his book *The Mind of the Market* titled "Don't Be Evil," alludes to the imperative (the word *Don't* is unequivocal) to not undertake negative moral actions, over the importance of taking positive ones.

9. See Simon (1957) for a discussion of the efficiency properties of rules of thumb.

10. Note that what appear to be exceptions to this are generally those acts of omission that are *de facto* acts of commission. This is discussed further in the next chapter.

11. The concept of non-tuism comes from Philip Wicksteed (1910). Some take it to mean the absence of interpersonal utility effects, but in my view this is an over-reading of Wicksteed. I share Peter Klein's view that what Wicksteed had in mind was a kind of agreement to set aside interpersonal utility comparisons—to act as if we are unconcerned with the welfare of each other, even though we almost certainly are to at least a small degree. The benefit of doing so is that it focuses transactions on their economic merit, which produces the highest level of general prosperity in the long run.

12. A fine example from as early as 480 BC is King Leonidas's Spartans at the battle of Thermopylae. Leonidas and the Spartans he commanded knew they faced certain death by choosing to block the progress of Persia's Xerxes the Great.

13. Charles Goodnight (1836–1929) is one of the most famous ranchers of the American West. With Oliver Loving, he founded the Goodnight-Loving trail.

14. It should be noted, however, that a few scholars already recognize the importance of internalized restraint. See Stringham (2011) for a review.

15. The consumption of most goods is rival in nature, meaning that if I eat a hamburger you cannot eat that same hamburger. Non-rival refers to the property that one person's consumption of a good does not impede another person's. An example would be listening to a radio program.

16. Indeed, any hardwired capacity we have is almost certainly ultimately consequentialist in nature, because in evolution all that ultimately matters is actual payoffs. Nature only cares about outcomes.

Chapter 8

1. What about charitable behavior directed toward transaction partners in order to increase future business? Such actions are irrelevant in this context. They produce economic value in their own right, and would be pursued for purely prudential reasons even by a completely immoral person.

2. This, in a nutshell, explains the popularity of "rights talk," which creates moral obligations by arguing that certain positive moral actions must be undertaken as a matter of duty because the beneficiaries have a right to the benefits of such actions.

3. This is not a small point. In a society that is impoverished because too few people abide by the moral foundation, even those individuals who want to abide by the moral foundation might, out of desperation, feel compelled to undertake negative moral actions.

4. The Hebrew word *Tzedakah* refers to actions such as giving to the poor, but it is not the same as the concept of *charity* in English. *Tzedakah* is derived from *Tzadei-Dalet-Qof*, which is generally interpreted to mean justice not in terms of process, but justice in terms of the final outcome (by virtue of being fair). Whereas charity in English is often viewed as being a product of benevolence, in Judaism charitable acts such as giving to the poor are viewed as acts of effectuating a just or righteous outcome.

5. Adam Smith, *The Theory of Moral Sentiments*, Section II, Chapter 1, (Liberty Fund) p. 79: "This virtue is justice: the violation of justice is injury: it does real and positive hurt to some particular persons, from motives which are naturally disapproved of. It is, therefore, the proper object of resentment, and of punishment, which is the natural consequence of resentment. As mankind go along with, and approve of the violence employed to avenge the hurt which is done by injustice, so they much more go along with, and approve of, that which is employed to prevent and beat off the injury, and to restrain the offender from hurting his neighbours [sic]."

6. Smith's friend and mentor, David Hume, was even less strident than Smith on this point. Hume also wrote about justice, but whereas Smith viewed justice as more important than the "other virtues," Hume gave no indication of such a priority. This suggests that Hume understood the importance of distinguishing between positive and negative moral actions, while Smith recognized the additional benefit of justice being recognized as being more important. But in the writing of neither is there any indication whatsoever of lexical primacy, or that justice should be viewed as a matter of duty.

7. Recall that in Chapter 4, I argued that whereas exhortations to take positive moral actions were necessarily matters of degree, and therefore quantitative in nature (analogous to Kant's definition of imperfect duties), prohibitions against taking negative moral actions were well defined, and therefore qualitative in nature (you either lied or you didn't, analogous to the perfect duty to *not lie*).

8. I largely agree with Ken Binmore (2005) that this was nothing more than an assertion hung from a philosophical skyhook. Kant simply does not provide a compelling argument for why morality is ultimately derived from duty.

9. Jack Hirshleifer (1995) introduced to economics the distinction between scramble and interference competition found in biology (Nicholson 1954). Scramble refers to competition that does not involve undermining a competitor's performance or success as part of the

process (e.g., a zebra and a gazelle eating grass). Interference competition refers to competition in which undermining a competitor's performance or success is part of the process (e.g., a lion killing a hyena).

10. Gunnthorsdottir and Rapoport (2006) provide experimental evidence that competition between groups solves public good games.

11. One might ask by what moral theory is that choice justified? I suspect what is going on is quite simple: we can more easily empathize with people who are alive today than with those who are, as yet, only hypothetical.

12. This comports with Michael Shermer's conclusion in *The Mind of the Market* (2008). He argues that what really matters in the conduct of business is the "Don't be evil" standard for behavior.

13. Note the significance of the locution *ad hoc*. It comports with the distinction between act versus rule approaches to evaluating moral behavior. But it is rules that overcome social dilemmas generally, including the commons dilemma associated with opportunism. A clear rule is a necessary but not sufficient condition for solving coordination failure games. Rule-following societies, therefore, enjoy higher levels of prosperity because they possess a rule-following culture that affords better coordination.

14. Note that under the moral foundation, exceptions cannot be based on the strength of conviction derived from the desirability of a positive moral action, because this robs prohibitions of their lexical primacy.

15. Rose (2000) develops a theory of the firm and of profit seeking by firms that illustrates the efficiency gains resulting from a governance structure that recognizes the single objective of profit maximization. In short, when the welfare of the workers in the firm is viewed as a constraints to be obeyed, rather than as objectives to be pursued, there is more output to be split among all inputs and firm owners in the long run.

16. A key factor in sorting out intent is the cost of acting. If there were significant costs to extending an oar, no one would complain about inaction. No one expects a poor swimmer to jump into a fast-moving river to save a drowning man. The same would be true if he was miles away, or he had to pay his life savings for the right to pick up the oar. It is only when there is little or no cost involved that we can validly infer that inaction indicates a preference for having harm come to the drowning individual. It is for this reason that everyone expects you to at least extend an oar to a drowning man if one is handy.

Chapter 9

1. Generalized trust is increasingly being referred to as *social trust* (Guth, Levati, and Ploner 2008). See Rothstein and Uslaner (2005) for a discussion of generalized (social) trust and particularized trust.

2. For those interested in an exhaustive review of the trust literature, see Hardin (2002), James (2002), Guinanne (2005), Six (2005), Bachman and Zaheer (2006), Algan and Calhuc (2010), Guiso, Sapienza, and Zingales (2010), and Tabellini (2010).

3. *Handbook of Trust Research*, edited by Reinhard Bachmann and Akbar Zaheer (Edward Elgar: Northampton, MA, 2006). "Trust, transaction cost economics, and mechanisms." Philip Bromiley and Jared Harris, p. 124.

4. Levi (1999) has noted that "There is a growing recognition among economists, political scientists, and political economists that something more than formal incentives or credible commitments are necessary to produce better models of internal relationships within the firm (see, e.g., Arrow 1974; Kreps 1990; and Miller 1992)."

5. As Guiso, Sapienza, and Zingales (2006, p. 33) put it, "Suppose that we observe (as it is indeed the case) that Swedes trust others more. Is this trust culturally driven or is it the rational prior driven by the different level of trustworthiness prevailing in the country?" Their earlier work (Guiso, Sapienza, and Zingales, 2004b) suggests it is the latter, because the willingness of Swedes to trust varies across countries, and is positively related to shared religions and negatively related to a history of wars.

6. Joan Mansbridge (1999, p. 290) defines altruistic trust as trust in which ". . . one trusts the other more than is warranted by the available evidence, as a gift, for the good of both the other and the community." Mansbridge (2001) also argued that altruistic trust, when coupled with an ethic of trustworthiness, can indeed produce a society that is markedly more productive than other societies.

7. The question is "Generally speaking, would you say that most people can be trusted or that you can't be too careful in dealing with people?"

8. Ben-Ner and Putterman (2001) discuss the separation of the concept of trustworthiness from trust. Seabright (2004, p. 27) argues that a disposition for reciprocity that is not tempered by rational calculation provides unsustainable support for cooperation. Breuer and McDermott (2008) present a model and empirical evidence that supports the idea that trustworthiness is indeed primary to a willingness to extend trust.

9. Binmore (2005) shares my concern (and Williamson's) that game theory rooted trustworthiness is not really trust or trustworthiness at all, but merely a matter of incentives.

10. Manski (2000) gives a brief review of the origins of the term. Most view it as originating with Coleman (1988) or Putnam (1993). Durlauf (1999) credits Loury (1977), while Glaeser, Laibson, Scheinkman, Soutter (2000) credit Jane Jacobs (1961). Ostrom and Ahn (2003) say the idea can be traced as far back as Tocqueville (1945[1840]).

11. Note that presumptive trust can nevertheless be conditioned on the kind of transaction involved. In other words, if a given transaction involves a very high value, and little likelihood of an opportunist being caught, it might not be rational to extend trust even if one is in a high trust society with a social convention of presumptive trust. Even the Swedes have bank vaults. But the key is that the decision to extend trust in a high trust society that enjoys presumptive trust is not conditioned on the individual involved (unless there is negative information to suggest such presumption is unwarranted) but, rather, on the transaction. This is much more efficient, for it is much easier to identify highly tempting situations than it is to verify that each and every person involved is trustworthy.

12. Recall that the question is, "Generally speaking, would you say that most people can be trusted or that you can't be too careful in dealing with people?"

13. There is an abundance of experimental economics literature that shows that people are quite willing to trust others, even strangers, in one-shot games (Camerer and Thaler 1995). An obvious question is whether the willingness to trust varies across groups and societies. Ensminger (2003) finds that there are substantial variations, and this points to the need for theories of trust that are capable of explaining this cross-sectional variation. But even in the lowest trust societies that Ensminger encountered, there was still far too much trustworthiness to be consistent with the predictions of the "trust as prudence" model.

14. See McCabe and Smith (2003) for a review and interesting discussion.

15. The exogenous nature of moral tastes is the key to producing unconditional trustworthiness and therefore making it rational to extend genuine trust. This point was first made by Robert Frank but was largely ignored, because it constituted methodological heresy for those in the best position to understand its salience. This issue is discussed in greater detail in the next chapter.

16. This turns out to be very difficult for a society to achieve for very fundamental evolutionary reasons. In the next chapter I will address how this difficulty may be overcome.

17. For a critique of the TCE critique, see Bromiley and Harris (2006).

18. For a more extensive treatment of Oliver Williamson's views on trust, see his *Organization Theory: From Chester Barnard to the Present and Beyond* (1995, pp. 241–242).

19. Ernst Fehr (2008, p. iii) puts the issue nicely: "Despite its proposed importance . . . It is still not clear whether trust is just an epiphenomenon of good institutions or whether it plays an independent causal role capable of shaping important aggregate economic outcomes."

Chapter 10

1. The strong connection between trust and culture is increasingly being recognized. As Guiso, Sapienza, and Zingales (2006, p. 29) put it:

   The opening through which culture entered the economic discourse was the concept of trust. Following the political scientists like Banfield, Putnam and Fukuyama, economists such as Knack and Keefer (1997) and La Porta, Lopez de Silanes, Shleifer and Vishny (1997) started to study the economic payoff of trust.

   Banfield (1958) is generally recognized as the first to explain the lack of social, political, and economic development in "backward" countries as being the result of culture. Harrison and Huntington (2000) provide an excellent overview.

2. Francis Fukuyama's definition of culture captures the spirit of this thought nicely. In his book *Trust* (1995, p. 34), he defines culture as "inherited ethical habit." Later in the same book (p. 41), he states:

   As the word *culture* itself suggests, the more highly developed ethical rules by which people live are nurtured through repetition, tradition, and example. These rules may reflect a deeper adaptive rationality; they may serve economically rational ends; and in the case of a few individuals they may be the product of rational consent. But they are transmitted from one generation to another as arational social habits. These habits in turn guarantee that human beings never behave as purely selfish utility maximizers postulated by economists.

3. This literature is too vast to adequately review here. Some recent highlights are *The Moral Animal* by Robert Wright (1994); *Good Natured* by Frans de Waal (1996); *Altruistically Inclined* by Alexander J. Field (2001); *Hardwired Behavior* by Laurence R. Tancredi (2005); *Primates and Philosophers* by Frans de Waal, Stephen Macedo, and Josiah Ober (2006); *Moral Minds* by Marc Hauser (2006); *The Evolution of Morality* by Richard Joyce (2007); *The Mind of the Market* by Michael Shermer (2008); *Moral Markets* edited by Paul Zak (2008); and *Neuroeconomics* edited by Paul W. Glimcher et al. (2009).

4. How, for example, can one explain such high levels of trust in Scandinavia, where people think nothing of leaving their newborns unattended outside of shops?

5. Note that this account does not foreclose a metaphysical explanation for the creation of the required moral beliefs. The required moral beliefs could have been given to man by God, but this would not change the most important point, which is that individuals are not introspectively discovering such beliefs for themselves, across most of society, and repeatedly generation after generation.

6. See Tan and Vogel (2008) for evidence that knowledge of a transaction partner's religiosity, which should proxy moral conviction, does increase others' willingness to extend trust.

7. History also tells us that new religions often spread like wildfire among adults in a society. This spread occurs through adults deciding to abide by new beliefs, not children simply adopting what they are taught by their parents.

8. This is very consistent with the definition offered by Guiso, Sapienza, and Zingales (2006, p. 23), who define culture as ". . . those customary beliefs and values that ethnic, religious, and social groups transmit fairly unchanged from generation to generation." For a thorough review of the relevant technical literature on the subject of cultural transmission and socialization, see Bisin and Verdier (2011).

9. Francois and Zabojnik (2005) put it well: "The usual focus on incentive structures in motivating behaviour plays no role here. Instead, we emphasise more deep-seated modes of behaviour and *consider trustworthy agents being socialised to act as they do*." (p. 51, emphasis added)

10. As Guiso, Sapienza, and Zingales (2006, p. 25) point out:

    Emigrants from southern, low trust regions of Italy, for instance, tend to carry with them their mistrust to their new locations (Guiso, Sapienza and Zingales, 2004a). Similarly, people who are raised religiously exhibit some common beliefs and preferences, even if they reject religion as adults (Guiso, Sapienza, and Zingales, 2003).

11. In *Trust* (1995, pp. 35–36), Fukuyama notes:

     He [Aristotle] goes on to explain that "our moral dispositions are formed as a result of the corresponding activities. . . . It is therefore not of small moment whether we are trained from childhood in one set of habits or another; on the contrary it is of very great, or rather of supreme importance."

12. Guiso, Sapienza, and Zingales (2006, p. 25) write:

     . . . parents have a natural tendency to teach their children what they have learned from their own parents, without a full reassessment of the current optimality of those beliefs (Bisin and Verdier, 2000; Fernandez, Fogli and Olivetti, 2004).

13. A reasonable objection to this point is that one hallmark of the moral behavior of young children is the thoughtless application of rules (Kohlberg 1981). In my view this is a small point, because such restraint is arguably better viewed as prudential rather than moral in nature. Indeed, when adults behave this way (insist on a particular rule being obeyed even when it is absurd to do so), others normally dismiss such behavior as having far less to do with morality than with a childish obsession with obeying rules.

14. For a broader discussion of the role that culture plays in the evolution of institutions see Richerson and Henrich (2009).

15. See Stephen Covey's *The Speed of Trust* (2008) and Anna Bernasek's *The Economics of Integrity* (2010) for examples.

16. An evolutionarily stable strategy was a concept first introduced by Maynard Smith (1982). The basic idea is that some strategies are unlikely to persist, because they are easily invaded by others. On the other hand, some are able to withstand being overturned in this way, and are therefore stable through time.

17. This is a very hard proposition for economists to accept, because rational choice theory appears to imply that everyone has "his price." But this is not necessarily the case. There is abundant evidence of even very poor people who do not act on golden opportunities. So while it is certainly true that some have "a price," it is not true that everyone does (at least not with respect to things they might actually experience in their lives).

18. This comports with an important point made by Vernon Smith (2008, p. 322):

     Cartesian constructivism applies reason to individual action and for the design of rules for institutions that are to yield socially optimal outcomes, and constitutes the standard socioeconomic science model. But most of our operating knowledge and ability to decide and perform is nondeliberative [sic]. Because such processing capacities are scarce, our brains conserve attention and conceptual and symbolic thought resources, and proceed to delegate most decision making to autonomic processes (including the emotions) that do not require conscious attention.

19. See any number of studies, especially Putnam (2000) and Uslaner (2002).

Chapter 11

1. See Stringham (2011) for an excellent discussion of this issue.
2. See recent evidence reported by Dearmon and Grier (2009).
3. This is not an overstatement. Recently Schwab and Ostrom (2008, p. 222) stated:

     . . . exchange of goods and services does not occur between strangers in the absence of trust-enhancing institutions. By tracing the interaction of trust, reputation, and reciprocity through the evolution of a simple institution to a complex one, we argued that the problem of imperfect information makes it difficult for exchange partners to rely on each others' reputations, and that one reason institutions evolve is to make reputation management less costly, more stable, and more effective.

4. See Glaeser, Laibson, and Sacerdote (2002) for a discussion of the theoretical advantages of thinking about social capital in terms of what they call "individual social capital."

5. Arthur Koestler, in his book *Ghost in the Machine*, argues that what appears to be "the mind" is really an artifact of the conscious outer layers of the brain, looking inward to the less conscious, less refined, inner layers of the brain. I think Koestler was basically right.

6. fMRI is an acronym for *functional MRI*. See King-Casas et al. (2005), Camerer and Fehr (2006), and Miller (2005).

7. Regarding positive moral action, using fMRI imaging, Tankersley, Stowe and Heuttel (2007) found that altruism appears to involve very specific regions of the brain.

8. Fukuyama (1999) states that "Strong biological tendencies urge human beings toward cooperation, limiting the extent to which social capital can dissipate. Further, people are capable of cooperative behavior spontaneously, as game theory illustrates." See also de Waal (1996), Field (2001), Hauser (2006), and Shermer (2008).

9. I am referring to the hacked emails from the University of East Anglia's Climatic Research Unit in 2009. Even top level scientists were manipulating the article referee process—which is the institutional cornerstone of scientific integrity—to insure that a very disingenuous means of presenting data would not be discovered.

REFERENCES

Abreu, D. (1998). On the Theory of Infinitely Repeated Games with Discounting. *Econometrica* 56(2), 383–396.

Adams, C. (2002 October). Does Size Really Matter? Empirical evidence on group incentives. Federal Trade Commission Bureau of Economics Working paper No. 252.

Akerlof, George. (1970). The Market for Lemons. *Quarterly Journal of Economics*, 84, 488–500.

Alchian, A. A. and Demsetz, H. (1972). Production, Information Costs, and Economic Organization. *American Economic Review*, 62, 777–795.

Algan, Yann and Cahuc, Pierre. (2010). Inherited Trust and Growth. *American Economic Review*, 100(5), 2060–2092.

Anderson, Elizabeth. (1993). *Value in Ethics and Economics*. Cambridge, MA: Harvard University Press.

Aron, Debra J. (1998). Ability, Moral Hazard, Firm Size, and Diversification. *Rand Journal of Economics*, 19, 72–87.

Arrow, Kenneth. (1972).Gifts and Exchanges. *Philosophy and Public Affairs*, 1, 343–362.

Arrow, Kenneth. (1974).*The Limits of Organizations*. New York: W. W. Norton.

Arrow, Kenneth. (1973). Some Ordinalist-Utilitarian Notes on Rawls' Theory of Justice. *Journal of Philosophy* 70(9), 245–263.

Axelrod, Robert. (1984). *The Evolution of Cooperation*. New York: Basic Books.

Bachman, Reinhard and Zaheer, Akbar, eds. (2006). *Handbook of Trust Research*. Northampton, MA: Edward Elgar.

Bain, Joseph. (1956). *Barriers to New Competition*. New York: John Wiley & Sons.

Baker, G.; Gibbons, Robert; Murphy, K. J. (2002). Relational Contracts and the Theory of the Firm. *Quarterly Journal of Economics*, 117(1) 39–84.

Banfield, Edward C. (1958). *The Moral Basis of a Backward Society*. New York: Free Press.

Banerjee, Sanjay; Bowie, Norman E. and Carla Pavone. (2006). An Ethical Analysis of the Trust Relationship. In Reinhard Bachman and Akbar Zaheer, eds. *Handbook of Trust Research*, p. 303. Northampton, MA: Edward Elgar.

Barnett, Randy. (1998). *The Structure of Liberty*. Oxford: Clarendon Press.

Baron, Jonathan. (1998). Trust: Beliefs and Morality. Chapter 15 in Avner Ben-ner and Louis Putterman, eds. *Economics, Values, and Organization*. Cambridge, UK: Cambridge University Press.

Barrera, Albino. (1999). The Evolution of Social Ethics: Using Economic History to Understand Economic Ethics. *Journal of Religious Ethics*, 27(2), 285–306.

Baumol, William J. (2002). *The Free-Market Innovation Machine: Analyzing the Growth Miracle of Capitalism*. Princeton and Oxford: Princeton University Press.

Ben-ner, Avner and Louis Putterman, eds. (1998). *Economics, Values, and Organization*. Cambridge, UK: Cambridge University Press.

Berg, Joyce; Dickhaut, John; Kevin McCabe. (1995). Trust, Reciprocity, and Social History. *Games and Economic Behavior*, 10, 122–142.

Bergstrom, Theodore C. (2002). Evolution of Social Behavior: Individual and Group Selection, *Journal of Economic Perspectives*, 16(2), 67–88.

Bernasek, Anna. (2010). *The Economics of Integrity: From Dairy Farmers to Toyota, How Wealth is Built on Trust and What That Means for Our Future*. New York: Harper Collins.

Bethell, Tom. (1998). *The Noblest Triumph: Property and Prosperity Through the Ages*. New York: St. Martin's Press.

Binmore, Kenneth. (2005). *Natural Justice*. New York: Oxford University Press.

Bisin, Alberto and Thierry Verdier. (2000). Beyond the Melting Pot: Cultural Transmission, Marriage, and the Evolution of Ethnic and Religious Traits. *Quarterly Journal of Economics*, 115(3), 955–988.

Bisin, A., and Verdier, T. (2011). The Economics of Cultural Transmission and Socialization. In Jess Benhabib, Alberto Bisin, and Matthew O. Jackson, eds. *The Handbook of Social Economics*. Amsterdam: North-Holland.

Blaug, Mark. (1992). *The Methodology of Economics: Or How Economists Explain*, 2nd ed. Cambridge, UK: Cambridge University Press.

Boland, Lawrence. (1982). *The Foundations of Economic Method*. New York: Allen & Unwin.

Bourdieu, Pierre. (1986). Forms of Capital, In John G. Richardson, ed. *Handbook of Theory and Research for Sociology Education*, pp. 241–260. Wesport, CT: Greenwood Press.

Bowen, J. Ray and Rose, David C. (1998). On the Absence of Privately Owned, Publicly Traded Corporations in China: The Kirby Puzzle. *The Journal of Asian Studies*, Volume 57(2), 442–452.

Braguinsky, Serguey and Rose, David C. (2009). Competition, Cooperation, and the Neighboring Farmer Effect. *Journal of Economic Behavior and Organization*, 72(1), 361–376.

Breuer, Janice Boucher and John McDermott. (2008). Trustworthiness and Economic Performance. December 2008, Working Paper, University of South Carolina.

Bromiley, Philip and Harris, Jared. (2006). Trust, transaction cost economics, and mechanisms. In Reinhard Bachmann and Akbar Zaheer, eds. *Handbook of Trust Research*, pp. 124–143. Northampton, MA: Edward Elgar.

Buchanan, James M. (1965). Ethical Rules, Expected Values, and Large Numbers. *Ethics*, 76, 1–13.

Buchanan, James M. (1994). *Ethics and Economic Progress*. Norman, OK: University of Oklahoma Press.

Buchanan, James M. (2001). *Moral Science and Moral Order*. Indianapolis: Liberty Fund.

Buchanan, James M. and Yoon, Yong, J., eds. (1994). *The Return of Increasing Returns*. Ann Arbor: University of Michigan Press.

Butler, Jeff, Paola Giuliano and Luigi Guiso. (2009). The Right Amount of Trust. National Bureau of Economic Research, Working Paper 15344.

Camerer, Colin and Thaler, Richard H. (1995). Anomalies: Ultimatums, Dictators and Manners, *Journal of Economic Perspectives*, 9, 109–220.

Camerer, Colin F. and Fehr, Ernst. (2006).When does economic man dominate social behavior? *Science*, 311(5757), 47–52.

Casebeer, William D. (2003). *Natural Ethical Facts*. Cambridge, MA: MIT Press.

Carter, Michael R. and Marco Castillo. (2003). The Economics Impacts of Trust and Altruism: An Experimental Approach to Social Capital in South Africa. University of Wisconsin Working Paper, February 2003.

Chandler, Alfred D., Jr. (1977). *The Visible Hand*. Cambridge, MA and London: The Belknap Press of Harvard University Press.

Charness, Gary and Dufwenberg, Martin. (2006). Promises and Partnership. *Econometrica*, 74, November, 1579–1601.

Chassang, Sylvain. (2010). Building Routines: Learning, Cooperation, and the Dynamics of Incomplete Relational Contracts. *American Economic Review*, 100(1), 448–465.

Coase, Ronald. (1937). The Nature of the Firm. *Economica*, 4, 386–405.

Coase, Ronald. (2006). The Conduct of Economics: The Example of Fisher Body and General Motors. *Journal of Economics & Management Strategy*, 15(2), 255–278.

Coleman, James S. (1988). Social Capital in the Creation of Human Capital. *The American Journal of Sociology*, 94, Supplement: Organizations and Institutions: Sociological and Economic Approaches to the Analysis of Social Structure, pp. S95–S120.

Coleman, James S. (1990). *Foundations of Social Theory*. Cambridge, MA: Harvard University Press.

Commons, John R. (1924). *Legal Foundations of Capitalism*. New York: Macmillan.

Commons, John R. (1934). *Institutional Economics*. Madison, WI: University of Wisconsin Press.

Costa, Francisco J. M. (2005 December). An Experimental Analysis of Moral Hazard in Team. *Munich Personal Archive RePEc*, Working Paper No. 2958.

Cowen, Tyler. (1993). The Scope and Limit of Preference Sovereignty. *Economics and Philosophy*, Vol. 9(2), 253–269.

Cosmides, Leda and Tooby, John. (1992). Cognitive Adaptations for Social Exchange In Jerome H. Barkow, Leda Cosmides, and John Tooby, eds. *The Adapted Mind*, pp. 163–228. New York: Oxford University Press.

Covey, Stephen M. R. (2008). *The Speed of Trust: The One Thing that Changes Everything*. New York: The Free Press.

Cox, James C. (2002). Trust, Reciprocity, and Other-Regarding Preferences: Groups vs. Individuals and Males vs. Females. In Rami Zwick and Amnon Rapoport, eds., *Advances in Experimental Business Research*. New York: Kluwer Academic Publishers.

Cox, James C. (2004). How to Identify Trust and Reciprocity. *Games and Economic Behavior*, 46(2), 260–281.

Cox, James C. (2003). Trust and Reciprocity: Implications of Game Triads and Social Contexts. University of Arizona Working Paper.

Dasgupta, Partha. (2003). Social Capital and Economic Performance: Analytics. In Elinor Ostrom and T. K. Ahn, eds. *Critical Studies in Economic Institutions: Foundations of Social Capital*, pp. 309–339. Cheltenham, UK: Edward Elgar.

Dasgupta, Partha. (1988). Trust as a Commodity. In Diego Gambetta, ed. *Trust: Making and Breaking Cooperative Relations*, pp. 49–72. New York and Oxford: Basil Blackwell.

Davis, Richard. (2003). Honor, Shame, and the Roots of Community. First Charles Lecture 2000, Earlham College, September 27. Available at: www.earlham.edu/~rel/dick-davis/davis-chas1.html.

Dawes, Robyn M. and Thaler, Richard H. (1988). Cooperation. *Journal of Economic Perspectives*, 2(3), 187–197. [Quoted in *Economics, Ethics, and Public Policy* by Charles K. Wilber]

Dawkins, Richard. (1976). *The Selfish Gene*. New York: Oxford University Press.

Delhey, J. and Newton, K. (2003). Who trusts? The Origins of Social Trust in Seven Societies. *European Societies*, 5(2), 93–137.

de Soto, Hernando. (1989). *The Other Path: The Invisible Revolution in the Third World*. New York: Harper & Row.

de Soto, Hernando. (2000). *The Mystery of Capital: Why Capitalism Triumphs in the West and Fails Everywhere Else*. New York: Basic Books.

de Waal, Frans. (1996). *Good Natured: The Origins of Right and Wrong in Humans and Other Animals*. Cambridge, MA: Harvard University Press.

de Waal, Frans. (2006). *Primates and Philosophers: How Morality Evolved*. Princeton: Princeton University Press.

Dearmon, Jacob and Grier, Kevin. (2009). Trust and Development. *Journal of Economic Behavior and Organization*. 71(2), 210–220.

Diamond, Jared. (1997). *Guns, Germs, and Steel: The Fates of Human Societies*. New York: W. W. Norton.

DiMaggio, Paul. (1994). Culture and Economy. In Neil Smelser and Richard Swedberg, eds. *The Handbook of Economic Sociology*, pp. 27–57. Princeton: Princeton University Press.

Dunbar, R. I. M. (1992). Neocortex Size as a Constraint on Group Size in Primates. *Journal of Human Evolution*, 22, 469–493.

Dunbar, R. I. M. (1993). Coevolution of Neocortical Size, Group Size and Language in Humans. *Behavioral and Brain Sciences* 16(4), 681–735.

Durlauf, Stephen and Fafchamps, Marcel. (2004). Social Capital. Working paper.

Durlauf, Stephen. (1999). The Case 'Against' Social Capital. *Focus*, 20, 1–5.

Durlauf, Steven N. (2002). Symposium on Social Capital: Introduction. *Economic Journal*, 112, F417–F418.

Dworkin, Ronald. (1977). *Taking Rights Seriously*. Cambridge, MA: Harvard University Press.

Dyer, J. H. and Chu, W. (2003). The Role of Trustworthiness in Reducing Transaction Costs and Improving Performance: Empirical Evidence from the United States, Japan, and Korea. *Organization Science*, 14(1), 57–68.

Elster, Jon. (1998). Emotions and Economic Theory. *Journal of Economic Literature*, 36(1), 47–74.

Elster, Jon. (1990). Selfishness and Altruism. In Jane J. Mansbridge (ed.), *Beyond Self-Interest*, pp. 44–52. Chicago: University of Chicago Press.

Elster, Jon. (1999). *Alchemies of the Mind. Rationality and the Emotions*. Cambridge: Cambridge University Press.

Ensminger, Jean E. (2004). Market Integration and Fairness: Evidence from Ultimatum, Dictator, and Public Goods Experiments in East Africa. In Henrich, Boyd, Bowles, Camerer, Fehr, and Gintis (Eds.), *Foundations of Human Sociality: Economic Experiments and Ethnographic Evidence from Fifteen Small-Scale Societies*, pp. 356–381). New York: Oxford University Press.

Evensky, Jerry. (1993). Ethics and the Invisible Hand, *Journal of Economic Perspectives*, 7,(2), 197–205.

Evensky, Jerry. (2005). Adam Smith's Theory of Moral Sentiments: On morals and why they matter to a liberal society of free people and free markets. *Journal of Economic Perspectives*, 19(3), 109–130.

Fehr, Ernst and Gachter, Simon. (1998). Reciprocity and Economics: The Economic Implications of Homo Reciprocans. *European Economic Review*, 42, 845–859.

Fehr, Ernst. (2008). On the Economics and Biology of Trust. University of Zurich and the Institute for the Study of Labor, Discussion Paper 3895.

Fehr, Ernst; Fishbacher, Urs; von Rosenbladt, Bernhard; Schupp, Juergen; Wagner, Gert. (2003). A Nation-Wide Laboratory Examining Trust and Trustworthiness by Integrating Behavioral Experiments into Representative Surveys. *CESifo* Working Paper 866.

Fehr, Ernst; Fishbacher, Urs; Gachter, Simon. (2002). Strong Reciprocity, Human Cooperation and the Enforcement of Social Norms. *Human Nature*, 13(1), 1–25.

Fernandez, Raquel; Fogli, Alessandra; Olivetti, Claudia. (2004). Mothers and Sons: Preference Formation and Female Labor Force Dynamics. *Quarterly Journal of Economics*. 119(4), 1249–1299.

Fessler, Daniel M. T. and Haley, Kevin J. (2003). The Strategy of Affect: Emotions in Human Cooperation. In Peter Hammerstein ed. *Genetic and Cultural Evolution of Cooperation*, pp. 7–36. Cambridgde, MA: MIT Press.

Field, Alexander J. (2001). *Altruistically Inclined: The Behavioral Sciences, Evolutionary Theory, and the Origins of Reciprocity*. Ann Arbor: University of Michigan Press.

Francois, Patrik, and Zabojnik, Jan. (2005). Trust, Social Capital, and Economic Development. *Journal of European Economic Association*, 3(1), 51–94.

Frank, Robert H. I. (1987). f Homo Economicus Could Choose His Own Utility Function, Would He Want One with a Conscience? *American Economic Review*, 77(4), 593–604.

Frank, Robert H. (1988). *Passions Within Reason: The Strategic Role of the Emotions*. New York: W. W. Norton.

Frank, Robert H. (2004). *What Price the Moral High Ground? Ethical Dilemmas in Competitive Environments*. Princeton: Princeton University Press.

Frank, Robert H. (2008). The Status of Moral Emotions in Consequentialist Moral Reasoning. In Paul J. Zak, ed. *Moral Markets: The Critical Role of Values in the Economy*. Princeton: Princeton University Press.

Friedman, Benjamin M. (2005). *The Moral Consequences of Economic Growth*. New York: Vintage Books.

Friedman, Daniel. (2008). *Morals and Markets*. New York: Palgrave Macmillan.

Fudenberg, Drew and Maskin, Eric. (1986). The Folk Theorem in Repeated Games with Discounting or with Incomplete Information. *Econometrica*, 54(3), 533–554.

Fukuyama, Francis. (1995). *Trust: The Social Virtues and the Creation of Prosperity*. New York: The Free Press.

Fukuyama, Francis. (1999). *The Great Disruption: Human Nature and the Reconstitution of Social Order*. New York: The Free Press.

Gachter, Simon (2002). Ernst Fehr. Altruistic Punishment in Humans. *Nature*, 415, 137–140.

Gambetta, D. (1988) *Trust: Making and Breaking Cooperative Relations*. Oxford: Basil Blackwell.

Gauthier, David. (1986). *Morals by Agreement*. New York: Oxford University Press.

Gert, Bernard. (2004). *Common Morality: Deciding What to Do*. New York: Oxford University Press.

Gibbons, Robert. (2001). Trust in Social Structures: Hobbes and Coase Meet Repeated Games. In Karen Cook, ed. *Trust in Society*, pp. 332–353. New York: Russell Sage Foundation.

Gladwell, Malcolm. *The Tipping Point—How Little Things Make a Big Difference*. New York: Little, Brown and Company.

Glaeser, Edward; Laibson, David; Scheinkman, Jose A.; Soutter, Christine L. (2000). Measuring Trust. *Quarterly Journal of Economics*, 115(3), 811–846.

Glaeser, Edward; Laibson, David; Sacerdote, Bruce. (2002). An Economic Approach to Social Capital. *Economic Journal*, 112(483), 437–458.

Glimcher, Paul W.; Camerer, Colin F.; Fehr, Ernst; Poldrack, Russell A. (2009). *Neuroeconomics: Decision Making and the Brain*. Place: Academic Press.

Gneezy, Uri. (2005). Deception: The Role of Consequences. *American Economic Review*, 95(1), 384–394.

Goergen, Marc. (2008).Corporate Stakeholders and Trust. ECGI Working Paper Series in Finance, Paper Number 213/2008.

Gorodnichenko, Yuriy and Roland, Gerard. (2010). Culture, Institutions and Long Run Growth. NBER Working Paper 16368. Cambridge, MA.

Gorodnichenko, Yurily and Roland, Gerard. (2011). Which Dimensions of Culture Matter for Long Run Growth? *American Economic Review*, 101(3), 492–498.

Greenfeld, Liah. (2002). *The Spirit of Capitalism*. Cambridge, MA: Harvard University Press.

Greif, Avner. (1993). Contract Enforceability and Economic Institutions in Early Trade: The Maghribi Traders' Coalition. *American Economic Review*, 83(3), 525–548.

Grosjean, Pauline. (2011). The Weight of History on European Cultural Integration: a Gravity Approach. *American Economic Review*, 101(3), 504–508.

Grossman, Herschel I. (2003). Choosing Between Peace and War. NBER Working Paper 10180, National Bureau of Economic Research, Inc.

Guinanne, Timothy. (2005). Trust: A Concept Too Many. Yale University Working Paper, February 2005.

Guiso, Luigi; Sapienza, Paolo; Zingales, Luigi. (2003). People's Opium? Religion and Economic Attitudes. *Journal of Monetary Economics*, 50(1), 225–282.

Guiso, Luigi; Sapienza, Paola; Zingales, Luigi. (2004a). Does local financial development matter?. *Quarterly Journal of Economics*. 119(3), 929–969.

Guiso, Luigi; Sapienza, Paola; Zingales, Luigi. (2004b) The Role of Social Capital in Financial Development. *American Economic Review*, 94(3), 526–556.

Guiso, Luigi; Sapienza, Paola; Zingales, Luigi. (2006). Does culture affect economic outcomes? *Journal of Economic Perspectives*, 20(2), 23–48.

Guiso, Sapienza, and Zingales, Luigi. (2008a). Social capital as good culture, *Journal of the European Economic Association*, 6(2–3), 295–320.

Guiso, Sapienza and Zingales, Luigi. (2008b). Long Term Persistence. NBER Working Paper 14278.

Guiso, Luigi; Sapienza, Paola; Zingales, Luigi. (2008c). Trusting the Stock Market, *Journal of Finance*, 63(6), 2557–2600.

Guiso, Luigi; Sapienza, Paola; Zingales, Luigi. (2009). Cultural Biases in Economic Exchange? *Quarterly Journal of Economics*, 124(3), 1095–1131.

Guiso, Luigi; Sapienza, Paola; Zingales, Luigi. (2010). Civic Capital as the Missing Link. In Benhabib, Jess; Bisin, Alberto; Jackson, Matthew O., eds. *The Social Economics Handbook*. Amsterdam: North-Holland.

Gunnthorsdottir, A.; Rapoport, A. (2006). Embedding Social Dilemmas in Intergroup Competition Reduces Free-riding, *Organizational Behavior and Human Decision Processes*, 101(2), 184–199.

Guth, Werner and Tietz, Richard. (1985). Strategic Power versus Distributive Justice: An Experimental Analysis of Ultimatum Bargaining. In H. Brandstatter and E. Kirchler, eds. *Economic Psychology: Proceedings of the* 10th *IAREP Annual Colloquium*, Linz, Austria.

Guth, Werner; Levati, Vittoria; Ploner, Matteo. (2008). Social identity and trust–An experimental investigation. *Journal of Socio-Economics*, 37, 1293–1308

Hardin, Garrett. (1968). The Tragedy of the Commons. *Science*,. 162(3859), 1243–1248.

Hardin, Russell. (1993). The Street Level Epistemology of Trust. *Politics & Society*, 21(4), 505–529.

Hardin, Russell. (1995). Trustworthiness, *Ethics*, 107(1), 26–42.

Hardin, Russell. (2002). *Trust and Trustworthiness*. New York: Russell Sage Foundation.

Harrison, Lawrence E. (1985). *Underdevelopment is a State of Mind*. Lanham, MD: University Press of America.

Harrison, Lawrence E. and Huntington, Samuel P., eds. (2000). *Culture Matters: How Values Shape Human Progress*. New York: Basic Books.

Harsanyi, John. (1975). Can the Maximin Principle Serve as a Basis for Morality? A Critique of John Rawls' Theory. *American Political Science Review* 69(2) 594–606.

Hart, Oliver. (1995). *Firms, Contracts, and Financial Structure*. New York: Oxford University Press.

Hart, Oliver and Moore, John. (1990). Property Rights and the Nature of the Firm. *Journal of Political Economy*, 98, 1119–1158.

Hauser, Marc. (2006). *Moral Minds: How Nature Designed our Universal Sense of Right and Wrong*. New York: HarperCollins.

Hausman, Daniel M. and McPherson, Michael S. (1996). *Economic Analysis and Moral Philosophy*. Cambridge: Cambridge University Press.

Hayek, Friedrich A. (1945). The Use of Knowledge in Society. *American Economic Review*, 35(4), 519–530.

Hayek, Friedrich A. (1973). *Law, Legislation and Liberty (Vol. 1): Rules and Order*. Chicago, IL: The University of Chicago Press.

Hayek, Friedrich A. (1976). *Law, Legislation and Liberty (Vol. 2): The Mirage of Social Justice*. Chicago: University of Chicago Press.

Hayek, Friedrich A. (1979). *Law Legislation and Liberty (Vol. 3): The Political Order of a Free People*. Chicago, IL: University of Chicago Press.

Hayek, Friedrich A. (1988). *The Fatal Conceit: Errors of Socialism*. Chicago, IL: University of Chicago Press.

Henrich, Joseph; Boyd, Robert; Bowles, Samuel; Camerer, Colin; Fehr, Ernst; Gintis, Herbert; McElreach, Richard. (2001). In Search of Homo Economicus: Behavioral Experiments in 15 Small-Scale Societies, *American Economic Review*, 91(2), 73–78.

Henrich, Joseph; Boyd, Robert; Bowles, Samuel; Camerer, Colin; Fehr, Ernst; Gintis, Herbert, eds. (2004). *Foundations of Human Sociality: Economic Experiments and Ethnographic Evidence from Fifteen Small-Scale Societies*. New York: Oxford University Press.

Helpmann, Elhanan and Krugman, Paul R. (1985). *Market Structure and Foreign Trade: Increasing Returns, Imperfect Competition, and the International Economy*. Cambridge, MA: MIT Press.

Herrnstein, Richard J. (1976). *The Matching Law*. New York: Russell Sage Foundation.

Hirsch, Fred. (1976). *Social Limits to Growth*. Cambridge MA and London: Harvard University Press.

Hirshleifer, Jack. (1978). Natural Economy versus Political Economy. *Journal of Social Biological Structures*, 1, 319–337.

Hirshleifer, Jack. (1982). Evolutionary Models in Economics and Law: Cooperation versus Conflict Strategies. *Research in Law and Economics*, 4, 1–60.

Hirshleifer, Jack. (1987). On the emotions as guarantors of threats and promises. In Dupre, J. A., ed. *The Latest on the Best*, pp. 307–326. Cambridge, MA: MIT Press.

Hirshleifer, Jack. (1995). Anarchy and its Breakdown. *Journal of Political Economy*, 103(1), 26–52.

Hirshleifer, Jack. (1988). The Analytics of Continuing Conflict, *Synthese*, 76,(2), 201–233.

Hirshleifer, Jack. T (2001). *The Dark Side of the Force: Economic Foundations of Conflict Theory*. Cambridge, UK: Cambridge University Press.

Hirshmann, Albert O. (1982). Rival Interpretations of Market Society: Civilizing, Destructive, or Feeble? *Journal of Economic Literature*, 20(4), 1463–1484.

Hoffman, M. L. (1982). Affect and Moral Development, *New Directions in Child Development*, 16, 83–103.

Hofstede, Geert. (2001). *Culture's Consequences: Comparing Values, Behaviors, and Organizations Across Nations*. (2nd edition). Thousand Oaks, CA: Sage Publications.

Holmstrom, Bengt. (1982). Moral Hazard in Teams. *Bell Journal of Economics*, 13, 324–340.

Hosmer, L. T. (1994). *Moral Leadership in Business*. Homewood, IL: Irwin.

Hume, David. (1888). *A Treatise on Human Nature*. Oxford: Clarendon.

Hunt, Lynn Avery. (2007). *Inventing Human Rights: A History*. New York: W. W. Norton.

Iannaccone, L. (1988). A Formal Model of Church and Sects. *American Journal of Sociology*, 94(Supplement), 241–268.

Ichino, Andrea and Maggi, Giovanni. (2000). Work Environment and Individual Background: Explaining Regional Shirking Differentials in a Large Italian Firm. *Quarterly Journal of Economics*, 115(3), 1057–1090.

Izquierdo, Luis R.; Gotts, Nicholas M.; Pohill, Gary J. (2004) Case-Based Reasoning, Social Dilemmas, and a New Equilibrium Concept. *Journal of Artificial Societies and Social Simulation*, 7(3), Available at: http://jasss.soc.surrey.ac.uk/7/3/1.html.

Jacobs, Jane. (1961). *The Death and Life of Great American Cities*. New York: Random House.

James Jr., Harvey S. (2002). The Trust Paradox: A Survey of Economic Inquiries into the Nature of Trust and Trustworthiness. *Journal of Economic Behavior and Organization*, 47, 291–307.

Jensen, Michael. (1983). Organization Theory and Methodology. *Accounting Review*, 50, 319–339.

Jones, T. M. (1995). Instrumental Stakeholder Theory: A Synthesis of Ethics and Economics. *Academy of Management Review*, 20, 404–437.

Joyce, Richard. (2007). *The Evolution of Morality*. Cambridge, MA: MIT Press.

Kagan, Jerome. (1984). *The Nature of the Child*. New York: Basic Books.

Kahneman, Daniel; Knetsch, Jack L.; Thaler, Richard H. (1986). Fairness and the Assumptions of Economics. *Journal of Business*, 59(4), S285–S300.

Kandel E. R., Schwartz J. H., Jessell T. M. (2000). *Principles of Neural Science*, 4th ed. New York: McGraw-Hill.

Kandel, Eugene; Lazear, Edward. (1992). Peer Pressure and Partnerships. *Journal of Political Economy*, 100, 801–817.

Kandori, M. (1992). Social Norms and Community Enforcement. *Review of Economic Studies*, 59, 63–80.

Katz, Leo. (1996). *Ill-Gotten Gains: Evasion, Blackmail, Fraud, and Kindred Puzzles in the Law*. Chicago: University of Chicago Press.

Keltner, D. and Buswell, B. N. (1996). Evidence of the Distinctiveness of Embarrassment, Shame, and Guilt: A study of recalled antecedents and facial expressions of emotion. *Cognitive Emotion*, 10, 155–171.

King-Casas, Brooks; Tomlin, Damon; Anen, Cedric; Camerer, Colin F.; Quartz, Stephen R.; Montague, P. Read. (2005). Getting to Know You: Reputation and Trust in a Two-Person Economic Exchange, *Science*, 308(5718), 78–83.

Klein, Benjamin; Crawford, Robert G.; Alchian, Armen. (1978). Vertical Integration, Appropriable Rents, and the Competitive Contracting Process. *Journal of Law and Economics*, 21, 297–326.

Klein, B. and Leffler, K. B. (1981). The Role of Market Forces in Assuring Contractual Performance. *Journal of Political Economy*, 89, 615–641.

Knack, Stephen and Keefer, Philip. (1997). Does Social Capital Have an Economic Payoff? A Cross-Country Investigation. *Quarterly Journal of Economics*, 112(4), 1251–1288.

Knight, Frank H. (1921). *Risk, Uncertainty, and Profit*. Boston, MA: Houghton Mifflin Co.

Koestler, Arthur. (1990 [1967]). *The Ghost in the Machine*. Penguin.

Kohlberg, Lawrence. (1981). *Essays on Moral Development. Volume 1: The Philosophy of Moral Development*. San Francisco, CA: Harper & Row.

Korsgaard, M.; Schwiger, D.; Sapienza, H. (1995). Building Commitment, Attachment, and Trust in Strategic Decision-Making Teams: The Role of Procedural Justice. *Academy of Management Journal*, 38(1), 60–84.

Kreps, David M. (1990). Corporate Culture and Economic Theory, In James E. Alt and Kenneth A. Shepsle, eds. *Perspectives on Positive Political Economy*, pp. 90–143. Cambridge: Cambridge University Press.

Kreps, David M.; Milgrom, Paul; Roberts, John; Wilson, Robert. (1982). Rational Cooperation in the Finitely Repeated Prisoners' Dilemma. *Journal of Economic Theory*, 27, 245-252.

Kropotkin, Peter. (1972 [1902]). *Mutual Aid*. New York: New York University Press.

Krugman, Paul. (1995). Increasing Returns, Imperfect Competition and the Positive Theory of International Trade. In G. Grossman and K. Rogoff, eds. *Handbook of International Economics, Volume 3*. North Holland, Amsterdam.

Kuran, Timur. (2009). Preface: The Economic Impact of Culture, Religion and the Law. *Journal of Economic Behavior and Organization* 71, 589-592.

Kuran, Timur. (2009). Explaining the Economic Trajectories of Civilizations: The Systemic Approach. *Journal of Economic Behavior and Organization* 71, 593-605.

Lal, Deepak. (1998). *Unintended Consequences: The Impact of Factor Endowments, Culture, and Politics on Long-Run Economic Performance*, Cambridge, MA: MIT Press.

La Porta, Rafael; Lopez de Silanes, Florencio; Shleifer, Andrei; Vishny, Robert. (1997). Trust in Large Organizations. *American Economic Review*, 87(2), 333-338.

Landa, Janet Tai. (1994). *Trust, Ethnicity, and Identity: Beyond the New Institutional Economics of Trading Networks, Contract Law, and Gift-Exchange*. Economics, Cognition, and Society Series. Ann Arbor: University of Michigan Press.

Landes, David S. (1998). *The Wealth and Poverty of Nations: Why Some are so Rich and some are so Poor*. New York: W. W. Norton.

Landes, David. (2000). Culture Makes Almost All the Difference. In L.E. Harrison and S.P. Huntington, eds. *Culture Matters: How Values Shape Human Progess*, pp. 2–13. New York: Basic Books.

Lee, Harper. (1960). *To Kill a Mockingbird*. New York: Popular Library Press.

Lee, Samuel and Persson, Petra. (2011). Circles of Trust. SSRN Working Paper 1736200.

Levi, Margaret. (1998). A State of Trust. In Margaret Levi and Valerie Braithwaite, eds. *Trust and Governance*, pp. 77–101. New York: Russell Sage.

Levi, Margaret. (1999). When Good Defenses Make Good Neighbors: A Transaction Cost Approach to Trust and Distrust. New York: Russell Sage Foundation Working Paper 140.

Loury, Glenn. (1977). A Dynamic Theory of Racial Income Differences. In P. A. Wallace and A. Le Mund, eds. *Women, Minorities, and Employment Discrimination*, pp. 153–186. Lexington, MA: Lexington Books.

Luttmer, Erzo F. P. and Singhal, Monica. (2011). Culture, Context, and the Taste for Redistribution. *American Economic Journal: Economic Policy*, 3, 157–179.

Mill, John Stuart. (1859). *On Liberty*. London: Oxford University Press.

Macaulay, S. (1963). Non-contractual Relations in Business. *American Sociological Review*, 28, 55–70.

Macleod, Bentley. (2007). Can Contract Theory Explain Social Preferences? *American Economic Review*, 97(2), 187–192.

Macneil, I. R. (1978). Contracts: Adjustments of long-term economic relations under classical, neoclassical, and relational contract law. *Northwestern University Law Review*, 72, 854–906.

Mandeville, Bernard. (1988). *The Fable of the Bees or Private Vices, Publick Benefits, Volume 1*. Indianapolis: Liberty Fund.

Mansbridge, Jane. (1999). Altruistic Trust. In Mark Warren, ed. *Democracy and Trust*, pp. 290–309. New York: Cambridge University Press.

Mansbridge, Jane. (2001). A 'Moral Core' Solution to the Prisoner's Dilemma. In Joan W. Scott and Debra Keates, eds. *Schools of Thought: Twenty-five Years of Interpretative Social Science*, pp. 330–347. Princeton: Princeton University Press.

Manski, Charles F. (2000). Economic Analysis of Social Interactions. *Journal of Economic Perspectives*, 14(3), 115–136.

Margalit, Avishai. (1996). *The Decent Society*. Cambridge, MA: Harvard University Press.

Mayer, R. C.; David, J. H.; Schoorman, F. D. (1995). An Integrative Model of Organizational Trust. *Academy of Management Review*, 20(3), 709–734.

Mas-Colell, Andreu; Whinston, Michael D.; Green, Jerry R. (1995). *Microeconomic Theory*. New York and Oxford: Oxford University Press.

McCabe, K. A.; Rassenti, S. J.; and Smith, V. L. (1996). Game Theory and Reciprocity in Some Extensive Form Experimental Games. *Proceedings of the National Academy of Sciences USA*, 93(13), 421–428.

McCabe, Kevin A. and Smith, Vernon L. (2003). Strategic Analysis in Games: What Information Do Players Use? In Elinor Ostrom and James Walker, eds. *Trust and Reciprocity: Interdisciplinary Lessons From Experimental Research*, pp. 275–301. New York: Russell Sage Foundation.

McAllister, D. J. (1995). Affect- and cognition-based trust as foundations for interpersonal cooperation in organizations. *Academy of Management Journal* 38(1), 24–59.

McMurtry, Larry. (1985). *Lonesome Dove: A Novel*. New York: Simon & Shuster.

McCloskey, Deirdre. (2006). *The Bourgeois Virtues: Ethics for an Age of Commerce*. Chicago: University of Chicago Press.

Milgram, S. (1963). Behavioral Studies of Obedience. *Journal of Abnormal and Social Psychology*, 67, 371–378.

Miller, Greg. (2005). Economic Game Shows How the Brain Builds Trust. *Science*, 308 (5718),36.

Miller, Gary. (1992). *Managerial Dilemmas: the Political Economy of Hierarchy*. New York: Cambridge University Press.

Misztal, B. A. (1996). *Trust in Modern Societies: The search for the bases of social order*. Cambridge, MA: Polity Press.

Mokyr, Joel. (1990). *The Lever of Riches: Technological Creativity and Economic Progress*. New York and London: Oxford University Press.

Neilson, W. S. (1999). The Economics of Favors. *Journal of Economic Behavior and Organization*, 39, 387–397.

Nicholson, A. J. (1954). An Outline of the Dynamics of Animal Populations. *Australian Journal of Zoology*, 2, 9–65.

North, Douglass C. and Thomas, Robert P. (1973). *The Rise of the Western World: A New Economic History*. Cambridge, UK: Cambridge University Press.

North, Douglass C. (1981). *Structure and Change in Economic History*. New York: W. W. Norton.

North, Douglass C. (1991). *Institutions, Institutional Change, and Economic Performance*. Cambridge, UK: Cambridge University Press.

North, Douglass C. (1994). Economic Performance Through Time. *American Economic Review*, 84(3), 359–368.

North, Douglass C. (2005). *Understanding the Process of Change*. Princeton, NJ: Princeton University Press.

Nozick, Robert. (1974). *Anarchy, State, and Utopia*. New York: Basic Books.

Nunn, Nathan and Wantchekon, Leonard. (2009). The Slave Trade and the Origins of Mistrust in Africa, National Bureau of Economic Research, Working paper No. 14783.

Ofek, Haim. (2001). *Second Nature: Economic Origins of Human Evolution*. Cambridge, UK: Cambridge University Press.

Olson, Mancur. (1965). *Logic of Collective Action*. Cambridge, MA: Harvard University Press.

Ostrom, Elinor. (2003). Toward a Behavioral Theory Linking Trust, Reciprocity, and Reputation. In Elinor Ostrom and James Walker, eds. *Trust and Reciprocity: Interdisciplinary Lessons From Experimental Research*. New York: Russell Sage Foundation.

Ostrom, Elinor and T. K. Ahn, eds. (2003). *Critical Studies in Economic Institutions: Foundations of Social Capital*. Cheltenham, UK: Edward Elgar Publishing Ltd.

Ostrom, Elinor and Walker, James, eds. (2003). *Trust and Reciprocity: Interdisciplinary Lessons from Experimental Research*, pp. 19–79. New York: Russell Sage Foundation.

Otteson, James R. (2002). *Adam Smith's Marketplace of Life*. Cambridge, UK: Cambridge University Press.

Parente, Stephen L. and Prescott, Edward C. (1994). *Barriers to Riches*. Cambridge, MA: MIT Press.

Persico, Joseph. (1994). *Nuremberg: Infamy on Trial*. New York: Viking Adult.

Piderit. (1993). *The Ethical Foundations of Economics*. Washington, DC: Georgetown University Press.

Portes, Alejandro. (1998). Social Capital: Its Origins and Applications in Modern Sociology. *Annual Review of Sociology*, 24, 1–24.

Povinelli, Daniel J. and Bering, Jesse M. (2002). The Mentality of Apes Revisited. *Current Directions in Psychological Science*, 11(4), 115–119.

Putnam, Robert D. (1993). The prosperous community: Social capital and public affairs. *The American Prospect*, 13, 35–42.

Putnam, Robert D.; Leonardi, Robert; Nanetti, Raffaella Y. (1993). *Making Democracy Work: Civic Traditions in Modern Italy*. Princeton, NJ: Princeton University Press.

Putnam, Robert D. (1995). Bowling Alone: America's Declining Social Capital. *Journal of Democracy*, 6, 65–78.

Putnam, Robert D. (2000). *Bowling Alone: The Collapse and Revival of American Community*. New York: Simon & Shuster.

Rawls, John. (1971). *A Theory of Justice*. Cambridge, MA: Harvard University Press.

Read, Leonard. (1958). *I Pencil: My Family Tree as Told to Leonard E. Read*. A pamphlet published at Irvington-on-Hudson, NY: The Foundation for Economic Freedom, Inc.

Richerson, Peter and Boyd, Robert. (2005). *Not By Genes Alone: How Culture Transformed Human Evolution*. Chicago: University of Chicago Press.

Richerson, Peter and Henrich, Joseph. (2009). *Tribal Social Instincts and the Cultural Evolution of Institutions to Solve Collective Action Problems*. Workshop for Political Theory and Policy Analysis, Indiana University Bloomington.

Ridley, Matt. (1996). *The Origins of Virtue: Human Instincts and the Evolution of Cooperation*. New York: Penguin Books.

Ring, P. S. and Van de Ven, A. H. (1992). Structuring cooperative relationships between organizations. *Strategic Management Journal*, 13, 483–498.

Rorty, Richard. (1989). *Contingency, Irony, and Solidarity*. Cambridge, UK: Cambridge University Press.

Rose, David C. (1992). Bankruptcy Risk, Firm-Specific Managerial Human Capital and Diversification. *Review of Industrial Organization*, 7(1), 65–73.

Rose, David C. (1997). Do Firms Diversify Because Managers Shirk? A Reinterpretation of the Principal-Agent Model of Diversification. *Review of Industrial Organization, Volume* 12(3), 389–398.

Rose, David C. (2000). Teams, Firms, and the Evolution of Profit Seeking Behavior. *Journal of Bioeconomics*, 2(1), 25–39.

Rose, David C. (2002). Marginal Productivity Analysis in Teams. *Journal of Economic Behavior and Organization*, 48, 355–363.

Rosenthal, Sandra B. and Bucholz, Rogene A. (1999). *Rethinking Business Ethics: A Pragmatic Approach*. Ruffin Series in Business Ethics. New York: Oxford University Press.

Rothstein, B. and Uslaner, E. (2005). All for all: equality, corruption, and social trust. *World Politics*, 58, 41–72.

Rousseau, D. M. S.; Sitkin, R. Burt; Camerer, C. (1998). Not So Different After All: A cross-discipline view of trust. *Academy of Management Review*, 23(3), 393–404.

Rubin, Paul H. (2002). *Darwinian Politics: The Evolutionary Origin of Freedom*. New Brunswick, NJ: Rutgers University Press.

Ryle, Gilbert. (1949). *The Concept of the Mind*. Chicago: University of Chicago Press.

Sako, M. (1998). Does trust improve business performance? In C. Lane and R. Bachmann, eds. *Trust Within and Between Organizations*, pp. 88–117. Oxford: Oxford University Press.

Sapienza, Paola; Toldra, Anna; Zingales, Luigi. (2007). Understanding Trust. CEPR discussion paper no. Dp6462. Available at: http://papers.ssrn.com/sol3/papers.cfm?abstract_id=1138575

Sen, Amartya. (1987). *On Ethics and Economics*. Oxford, UK: Basil Blackwell.

Seabright, Paul. (2004). *The Company of Strangers: A Natural History of Economic Life*. Princeton, N.J.: Princeton University Press.

Scheff, T. J. (1990). *Microsociology*. Chicago, IL: Chicago University Press.

Schelling, Thomas. (1960). *The Strategy of Conflict*. Cambridge, MA: Harvard University Press.

Schwab, David and Ostrom, Elinor. (2008). The Vital Role of Norms and Rules in Maintaining Open Public and Private Economies. In Paul J. Zak, ed. *Moral Markets: The Critical Role of Values in the Economy*. Princeton and Oxford: Princeton University Press.

Scherer, F. M. (1970). *Industrial Market Structure and Economic Performance*. Chicago: Rand McNally & Co.

Shermer, Michael. (2008). *The Mind of the Market: Compassionate Apes, Competitive Humans, and Other Tales from Evolutionary Economics.* New York: Times Books, Henry Holt and Company.

Shleifer, Andrei. (2004). Does competition destroy ethical behavior? *American Economic Review,* 94(2), 414–418.

Simon, H. (1957). *Administrative Behavior* (2nd edition). New York: Macmillan.

Singer, Tania and Fehr, Ernst. (2005). The Neuroeconomics of Mind Reading and Empathy. *American Economic Review,* 95(2), 340–345.

Singer, Tania; Seymour, Ben; O'Doherty, John P.; Kaube, Holger; Dolan, Ray J.; Frith, Christopher D. (2004). Empathy for Pain Involves the Affective but not Sensory Components of Pain. *Science,* 303(5661), 1157–1162.

Six, Frederic. (2005). *The Trouble with Trust: The Dynamics of Interpersonal Trust Building.* Northampton, MA: Edward Elgar.

Skyrms, Brian. (1996). *Evolution of the Social Contract.* Cambridge, UK: Cambridge University Press.

Smith, Adam. (1982 [1759]). *The Theory of Moral Sentiments.* D. D. Raphael and A. L. Macfie, eds. Indianapolis: Liberty Fund Press.

Smith, Adam. (1981 [1776]). *An Inquiry into the Nature and Causes of the Wealth of Nations.* R. H. Campbell and A. S. Skinner, eds. Indianapolis: Liberty Fund Press.

Smith, Maynard. (1982). *Evolution and the Theory of Games.* Cambridge, UK: Cambridge University Press.

Smith, Vernon L. (1998). The Two Faces of Adam Smith. *Southern Economic Journal,* 65(1), 1–19.

Smith, Vernon L. (2008). *Rationality in Economics: Constructivist and Ecological Forms.* New York: Cambridge University Press.

Smith, K.; Carroll, S.; Ashford, S. (1995). Intra- and Interorganizational Cooperation: Towards a Research Agenda. *Academy of Management Journal,* 38(1), 7–23.

Sobel, Joel. (2002). Can we trust social capital? *Journal of Economic Literature,* 40(1), March, 139–154.

Solow, Robert M. (1995). Trust: The Social Virtues and the Creation of Prosperity (Book Review). *New Republic,* 213, 36–40.

Somanathan, E. and Rubin, Paul H. (2004). The Evolution of Honesty. *Journal of Economic Behavior and Organization,* 54(1), 1–17.

Solow, Robert M. (1956). A Contribution to the Theory of Economic Growth, *Quarterly Journal of Economics,* February 1956, 65–94.

Solow, Robert M. (1957). Technical Change and the Aggregate Production Function, *Review of Economics and Statistics,* 39, 312–320.

Spanolo, Giancarlo. (1999). Social Relations and Cooperation in Organizations. *Journal of Economic Behavior and Organization,* 38(1), 1–25.

Steinbeck, John. (1961). *The Winter of Our Discontent.* New York: Viking Press.

Stringham, Edward Peter. (2011). Embracing Morals in Economics: The Role of Internal Moral Constraints in a Market Economy. *Journal of Economic Behavior and Organization,* forthcoming.

Tabellini, Guido. (2010). Culture and Institutions: Economic Development in the Regions of Europe. *Journal of the European Economic Association,* 8(4): 677–716.

Tabellini, Guido. (2008a). Institutions and Culture: Presidential Address European Economic Association. *Journal of European Economic Association,* 6(2–3): 255–294.

Tabellini, Guido. (2008b). The Scope of Cooperation: Values and Incentives. *Quarterly Journal of Economics,* 123(3): 905–950.

Tabellini, Guido. (2007). Morality and Economic Performance. *Economist's View,* December 22. http://economistsview.typepad.com/

Tan, Jonathan H. W. and Vogel, Claudia. (2008). Religion and Trust: An Experimental Study. *Journal of Economic Psychology,* 29, 832–848.

Tancredi, Laurence R. (2005).*Hardwired Behavior: What Neuroscience Reveals about Morality.* Cambridge: Cambridge University Press.

Tankersley, D., Stowe, C. J., Heuttel, S. A. (2007). Altruism is associated with an increased neural response to agency. *Nature Neuroscience,* 10(2), 150–151.

Teece, David. (1992). Competition, cooperation, and innovation: organizational arrangements for regimes of rapid technological progress. *Journal of Economic Behavior and Organization*, 18, 1–25.

Thiroux, Jacques. (1995). *Ethics: Theory and Practice*. (5th ed.) Englewood Cliffs, NJ: Prentice Hall.

Tocqueville, Alexis de. (1990). [1835]. *Democracy in America. Vol. I*. New York: Vintage.

Trivers, Robert L. (1971). The Evolution of Reciprocal Altruism. *Quarterly Review of Biology*, 46, 35–57.

Trout, J. D. (2009). *The Empathy Gap: Building Bridges to the Good Life and the Good Society*. New York: Viking.

Tullberg, Jan. (2008). Trust–The Importance of Trustfulness and Trustworthiness. *Journal of Socio-Economics*, 37, 2059–2071.

Turchin, Peter. (2006). War and Peace and War: The Rise and Fall of Empires. New York: Plume (Penguin Group Ltd.).

Tyler, Tom R. and Huo, Yuen J. (2002) *Trust in the Law: Encouraging Public Cooperation with the Police and Courts*. New York: Russell Sage Foundation.

Tyson, Peter. (2005). Monkey Do, Monkey See. *NOVA Science NOW*, 1 January 2005. http://www.pbs.org/wgbh/nova/body/glaser-monkey.html

Twain, Mark. (2001 [1884]). *The Adventures of Huckleberry Finn*. Berkeley, CA: University of California Press.

Uslaner, Eric M. (2002). *The Moral Foundations of Trust*. Cambridge, UK: Cambridge University Press.

Uslaner, Eric. (2008). The Foundations of Trust: Macro and Micro. *Cambridge Journal of Economics*, 32(2), 289–294.

Vandberg, Victor. (1992). Rationality, Morality, and Exit. *American Political Science Review*, 86, 418.

Vandberg, Viktor J. (1994). *Rules and Choice in Economics*. London: Routledge.

Weber, Max. (1958) [1904]. *The Protestant Ethic and the Spirit of Capitalism*. New York: Scribner's.

Wicksteed, Philip H. (1910). *The Common Sense of Political Economy*. New York: Macmillan and Co.

Wilber, Charles K. (1998). Ethics and Morality. In *Encyclopedia of Political Economy*, pp. 323–326. London: Routledge.

Wilber, Charles K. (1998). Economics and Ethics. In John B. Davis, D. Wade Hands and Uskali Maki, eds. *The Elgar Handbook to Economic Methodology*, pp. 138–142. Northampton, MA: Edward Elgar Publishing.

Wilber, Charles K. and Hoksbergen, Roland . (1986). Ethical Values and Economic Theory: A Survey, *Religious Studies Review*, 12(314), 205–214.

Williams, Bernard. (1993). *Shame and Necessity*. Berkeley: University of California Press.

Williamson, Oliver E. (1975). *Markets and Hierarchies: Analysis and Antitrust Implications*. New York: The Free Press.

Williamson, Oliver E. (1979). Transaction Cost Economics: The Governance of Contractual Relations. *Journal of Law and Economics*, 22, 233–261.

Williamson, Oliver E. (1985). *The Economic Institutions of Capitalism*. New York: The Free Press.

Williamson, Oliver E. (1993). Calculativeness, Trust, and Economic Organization. *Journal of Law & Economics*, 36(1), 453–486.

Williamson, Oliver E., ed. (1995). *Organization Theory: From Chester Barnard to the Present and Beyond*. New York and Oxford: Oxford University Press.

Wilson, James Q. (1993). *The Moral Sense*. New York: The Free Press.

Witt, Ulrich. (1986). Evolution and stability of cooperation without enforceable contracts. *Kyklos*, 39, 245–266.

Wright, Robert. (1994). *The Moral Animal: The New Science of Evolutionary Psychology*. New York: Pantheon Books.

Yamagishi, Toshio. (1986). The Provision of a Sanctioning System as a Public Good, *Journal of Personality and Social Psychology*, 51, 110–116.

Yamagishi, Toshio. (1999). *From assurance based society to trust based society: Where is the Japanese system heading?* (In Japanese) Tokyo: Chuo Koron Shinsha.

Yamagishi, Toshio. (2000). *Trust*. Boulder, CO: Westview Press Inc.

Yamagishi, Toshio and Midori Yamagishi. (1994). Trust and Commitment in the United States and Japan. *Motivation and Emotion*, 18(2), 129–166.

Yamagishi, Toshio; Cook, K; Watabe, M. (1998). Uncertainty, Trust, and Commitment Formation in the United States and Japan. *American Journal of Sociology*, 104, 165–194.

Younkins, Edward W. (2002). *Capitalism and Commerce: Conceptual Foundations of Free Enterprise.* Oxford: Lexington Books.

Zaheer, A.; McEvily, B.; Perrone, V. (1998). Does Trust Matter? Exploring the Effects of Interorganizational and Interpersonal Trust on Performance. *Organization Sciences*, 9(2), 141–159.

Zak, Paul J. (2008). *Moral Markets: The Critical Role of Values in the Economy.* Princeton and Oxford: Princeton University Press.

Zak, Paul J.; Knack, Stephen. (2001). Trust and Growth. *Economic Journal*, 111(470), 295–321.

Zimmerling, R. (2003). 'Guilt Cultures' vs 'Shame Cultures': Political Implications? Paper given at the International Conference on Reassessing Democracy, June 20–21, 2003, IU Bremen.

INDEX

Adams, C., 227n7
The Adventures of Huckleberry Finn (Twain),
  81, 100
agriculture, 49
Algan, Yann, 5, 191
altruistic/moralistic trust, 160–61, 236n6
amoral rationalist, 188
Anderson, Elizabeth, 121–22
animals, 32, 90, 226n17, 231n13, 231n15,
  234n9
Aristotle, 238n11
Arrow, Kenneth, 146, 158
Axelrod, Robert, 164, 230n7

Bachman, Reinhard, 223n7
Baker, G., 178, 212, 226n20,
  226n22
Banerjee, S., 5
Banfield, Edward C., 4, 237n1
Baron, Jonathan, 160
behavior. *See also* economic behavior;
  moral behavior; trust behavior
  character and, 188
behavior standards, moral prohibitions
  and, 77–78, 230n16
beliefs. *See also* moral beliefs
  harmony of, 229n8
benevolence, 150–51, 235n11
  charity, 136–37, 234n4
  kindness, 230n2, 231nn16–17
Ben-Ner, Avner, 236n8
Bernasek, Ann, 223n5
Binmore, Ken, 29, 84, 86, 132, 234n8,
  236n9
Bisin, Alberto, 190

bounded rationality, 228n14
Bourdieu, Pierre, 164, 236n10
Bowie, N. E., 5
brain
  empathy and, 83, 87
  empirical evidence about, 214–16,
    239n6
  positive moral action and, 215,
    239n7
  social capital and, 211
Breuer, Janice Boucher, 236n8
Buchanan, J. M., 41, 114, 146–47, 204,
  230n15, 232n4
bureaucracy, entrepreneurialism
  compared to, 53, 57, 60, 106, 197,
  212, 217–19
Butler, J., 14

Cahuc, Pierre, 5, 191
capital. *See also* social capital
  physical, 33
capitalism, 225n20, 229n3
Carter, Michael R., 172
Castillo, Marco, 172
Chandler, Alfred, 42
charity, 136–37, 234n4
cheating
  by scientists, 218, 239n9
  by students, 116, 220–21, 233n3
Chicago School, 224n17
children
  consistency for, 194, 238nn12–13
  early reinforcement for, 190, 192
  habit of mind for, 125, 199, 238n18
  involuntary emotions and, 190

CPSIA information can be obtained at www.ICGtesting.com
Printed in the USA
LVOW10s0900181213

365661LV00001B/1/P